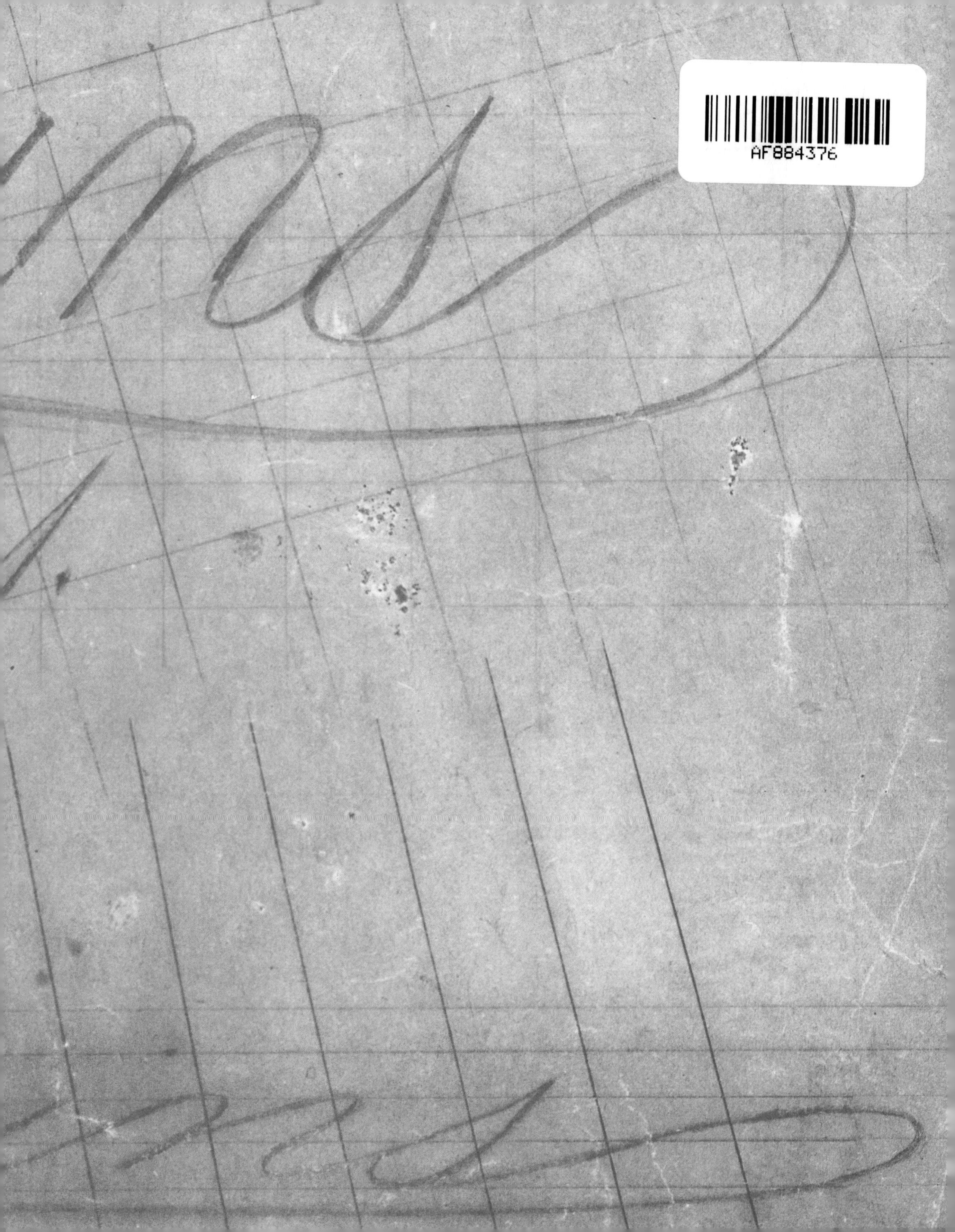

SIGNS OF THE ARTIST

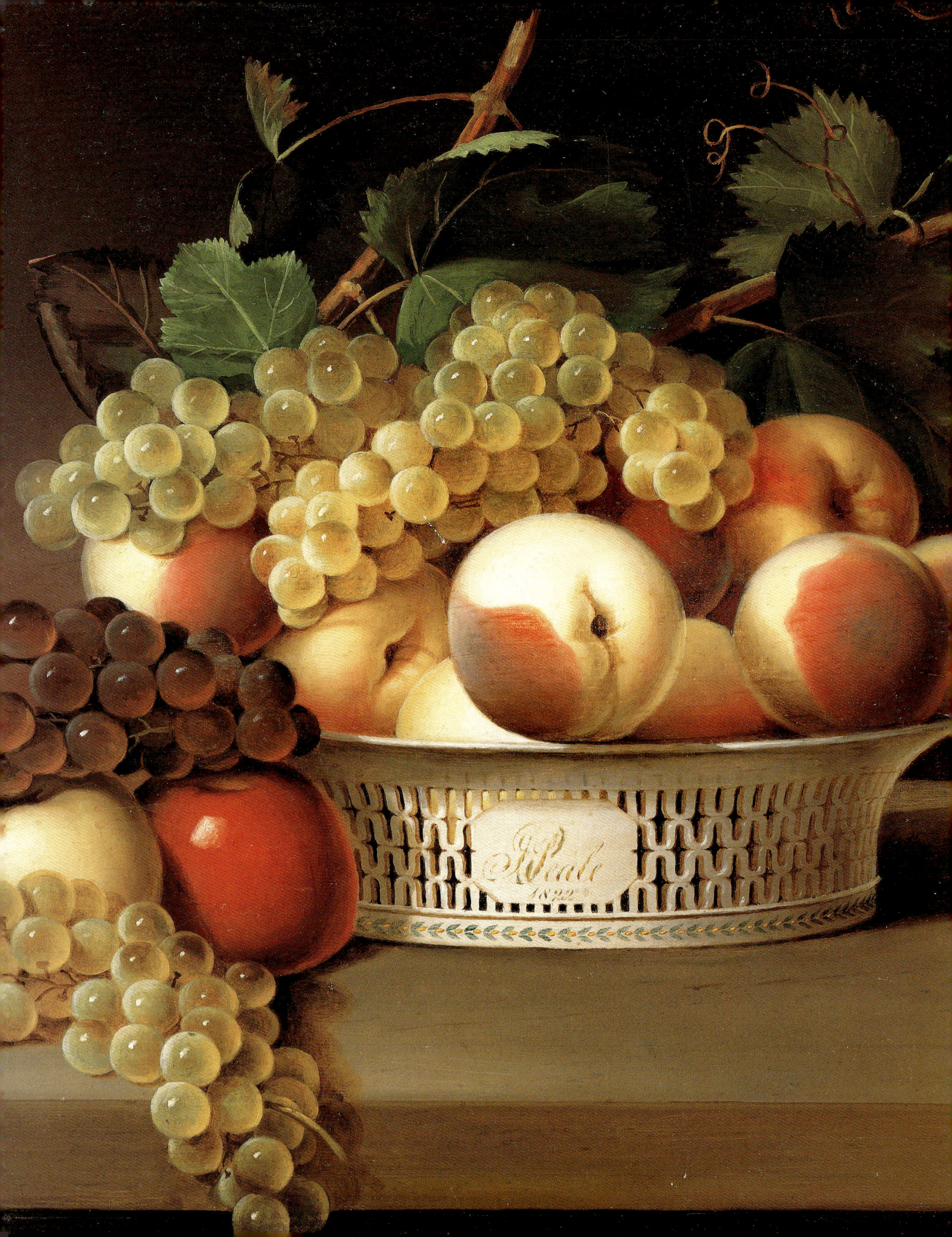
J. Peale
1822

SIGNS OF THE ARTIST

Signatures and Self-Expression in American Paintings

JOHN WILMERDING

YALE UNIVERSITY PRESS | *New Haven and London*

The frontispiece and chapter-opening art are details of the following figures: frontispiece, fig. 40; preface, fig. 100; Chapter 1, fig. 1; Chapter 2, fig. 52; Chapter 3, fig. 76; Chapter 4, fig. 93; and Chapter 5, fig. 143.

Designed by Susan Marsh
Set in Monotype and Berthold Walbaum by Duke & Company
Printed in Singapore by CS Graphics

Library of Congress Cataloging-in-Publication Data

Wilmerding, John.
Signs of the artist : signatures and self-expression in American paintings / John Wilmerding.
p. cm.
Includes bibliographical references and index.
ISBN 0-300-09779-4 (hardcover : alk. paper)
1. Painters—United States—Autographs. 2. Signatures (Writing). I. Title.
ND205.W523 2003
759.13'02'78—dc21

2002155890

A catalogue record for this book is available from the British Library.

The paper in this book meets the guidelines for permanence and durability of the Committee on Production Guidelines for Book Longevity of the Council on Library Resources.

10 9 8 7 6 5 4 3 2 1

To the next generation:

STODDY, AUSTIN, AND FRICK

SOMES AND HAYES

AND ELECTRA

CONTENTS

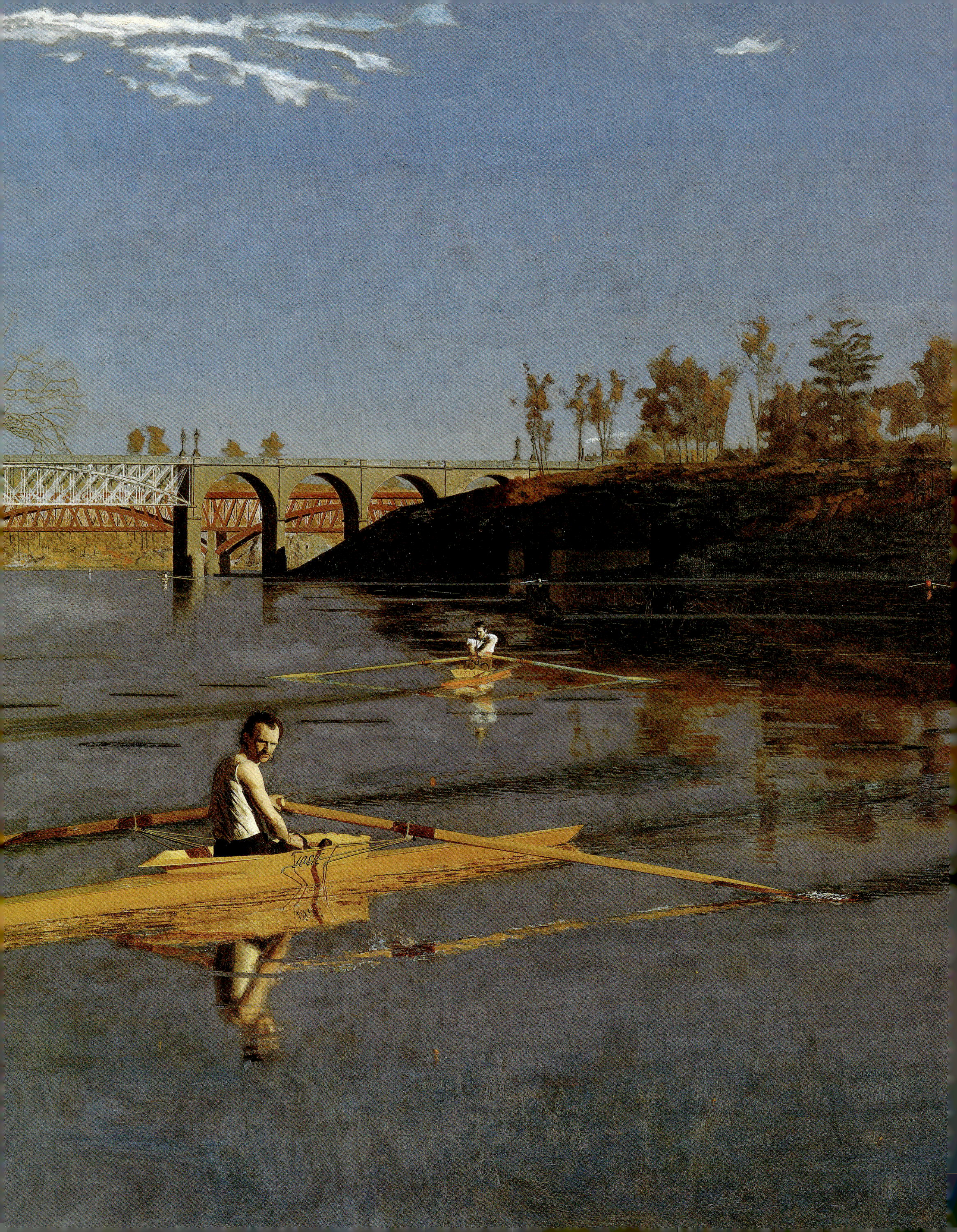

PREFACE

OUR SIGNATURES ARE UNIQUE. Our written names, even more than our handwriting generally, carry something of our individual personality. We assign the signatures on the Declaration of Independence almost as much importance as the document itself, and because of its size and prominence, John Hancock's has become possibly the most famous signature in American history — so much so that his name has become identified with the very act of writing one's name, as in the common phrase "Put your John Hancock here." In Washington, D.C., presidential signings of important legislation have become high-visibility affairs, with the president often employing dozens of pens to complete his signature and pass out as tokens of the occasion. With our signatures, we activate passports and credit cards, validate driving licenses, authorize wills, and write checks to pay our bills. And if we do not read or write, we put an "X" to ratify a document. In the year 2000, Congress approved a measure to make so-called electronic signatures as binding as those in ink. The advent of online contracts and such "e-signatures" represents a millennial shift: the mystique and legality of a signed name go back as far as handwriting itself.

For an artist a signature can acquire even more significance. On a work of art it confirms originality to a dealer or purchaser, even when an unsigned work has all the stylistic and technical characteristics of that artist's hand. A buyer instinctively feels more confident if a signature is present, and its absence can often affect the market value considerably. Thus, forged signatures are as problematic and challenging in the art world as forged works. Most Americanists are well aware of the history of the confusion between the paintings of William Michael Harnett and those of John F. Peto. While the work of the former is well documented, the latter's passed into a period of obscurity during the first half of the twentieth century. Peto exhibited and sold little during his lifetime; his was a largely withdrawn existence on the New Jersey shore, away from Philadelphia and New York, the major centers of artistic and commercial activity. Although the two artists' respective styles are today easily distinguished, this was not always so. Because their training and subjects were similar, and because they were close associates for a time, when Peto's paintings were rediscovered beginning in the 1940s, they were at first thought to be by the markedly higher-valued Harnett and marketed as his. When they bore an unfamiliar and troublesome signature by Peto, they went off to restorers for cleaning and returned with Harnett's name overpainted to assure their value and sale.

An artist's signature, however, is more than just an index of authenticity. In recent years it has also become big business, as two examples blatantly attest. By the mid-1960s, Andy Warhol was marking his canvases and prints with a stamped signature—a practice consistent with the deliberately mechanical and impersonal processes of the Factory. Since his death, and with the establishment of the Warhol Museum and the Andy Warhol Foundation, an expanding business operation has been marketing Warhol reproductions and other merchandise, such as neckties and coffee mugs, that carry the stamped signature, presumably certifying them as authentic Warhol-inspired objects. In a similar sales effort, the so-called Eakins Shop accompanying the 2001–2 Thomas Eakins retrospective at the Philadelphia Museum of Art offered on its shelves a baseball cap bearing the artist's distinctively calligraphed signature as an emblem. The form of his name had taken on a life of its own.

This book is not so much about the quirkiness of individual signatures or monograms per se, though sometimes the size or other variations of such inscriptions are clues to artistic egos. Nor is the focus on signatures placed conventionally *on* the physical picture surface as such (usually along an edge or near the corner of a canvas), but rather on those *in* the pictorial space depicted by the artist on paper, panel, or canvas. The artist's name or initials may appear as if painted on a wall or carved into a floorboard, on an object within an interior or "outdoors" in a landscape. The placement of these signatures is obviously intentional, meant to do more than just identify authorship or affirm authenticity. They both represent and stand in for the artist, situating the maker within the subject of the picture. Sometimes these gestures demonstrate mere cleverness or technical finesse, but in many instances they suggest, consciously or subliminally, associations with the setting or situation depicted. In other words, these inscriptions are often fragments of autobiography, concentrated glimpses of self-portraiture, or, more properly, self-representation. Our aim is to look closely at these tantalizing traces, for they appear at telling moments in the work of American artists from the colonial period to the present; not in all works nor even in all the works of any one artist, but often enough to enhance or cast light on the larger meaning of the work as a whole — and the nature of the artist as well.

The scholarship on this subject is sporadic and less than comprehensive. In the European field there is pertinent writing on Dutch still-life and Venetian Renaissance painting, and in American art several colleagues have written insightfully about both a number of artists who have projected themselves into their work and the personal meaning with which their signatures are charged. Most notably among these authors are Robin Frank on Charles Demuth; Doreen Bolger on William M. Harnett; Henry Adams, Nicolai Cikovsky, Barbara Dayer Gallati and Jules Prown on Winslow Homer; and Lillian Miller on Charles Willson Peale. This project hopes to place their good work into a broader context, providing a systematic exploration of an aspect of American art that is not only frequently great fun, but, more often than not, serious fun.

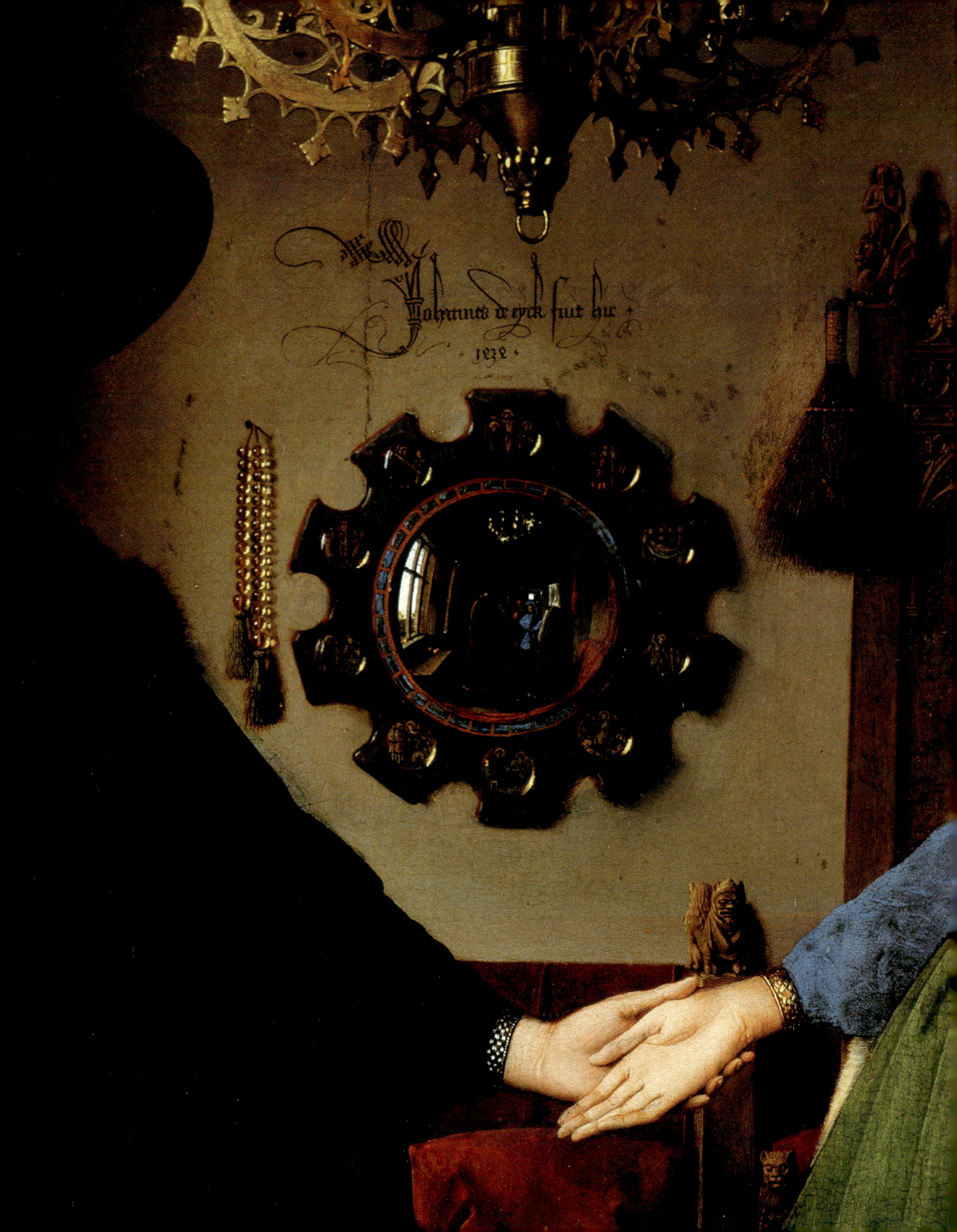
Johannes de eyck fuit hic
1434

CHAPTER 1 European Precedents

SIGNATURES ARE FOREMOST a mark of individual identity. The idea of single artistic personalities emerges toward the end of the Middle Ages and the beginning of Renaissance humanism in Europe, as the collaborative artistic production of the monastic workshop gradually gave way to notions of individual artistic ambition and accomplishment. The invention of single-point perspective and revival of classical systems of proportion led to greater clarity in fixing the human figure's place in the world. A new interest in realism was manifest in the specific characterization of portraiture and the accurate recording of nature. The rise of private patronage was but one factor supporting the flourishing of individual careers and the concept of artistic self-consciousness. The anonymous artisan now became a singular creative professional who wished to leave an identifiable sign of authorship.

One of the earliest and best-known examples of a prominent recording of artistic presence in a work is Jan van Eyck's *Arnolfini Marriage* of 1434 (fig. 1), where the signature is literally central in the image. This Northern Renaissance wedding portrait shows us Giovanni Arnolfini with his wife, Giovanna Cenami, presumably taking their vows and facing the witnesses standing before them in the viewer's space. We see that space clearly displayed in the convex mirror situated between them on the wall behind. The complexity of this reflected space extends to include the window view at the left, giving us a glimpse of an orange tree in the garden outside and oranges on the sill and table just below the window. In addition, there are twelve scenes depicting Christ's Passion within the surrounding mirror frame, arranged like hours on a clock face, with the Crucifixion placed at the top.

Just above the mirror is the elaborate calligraphy of the artist's signature — "Johannes de Eyck fuit hic, 1434" ("Jan van Eyck was here, 1434")

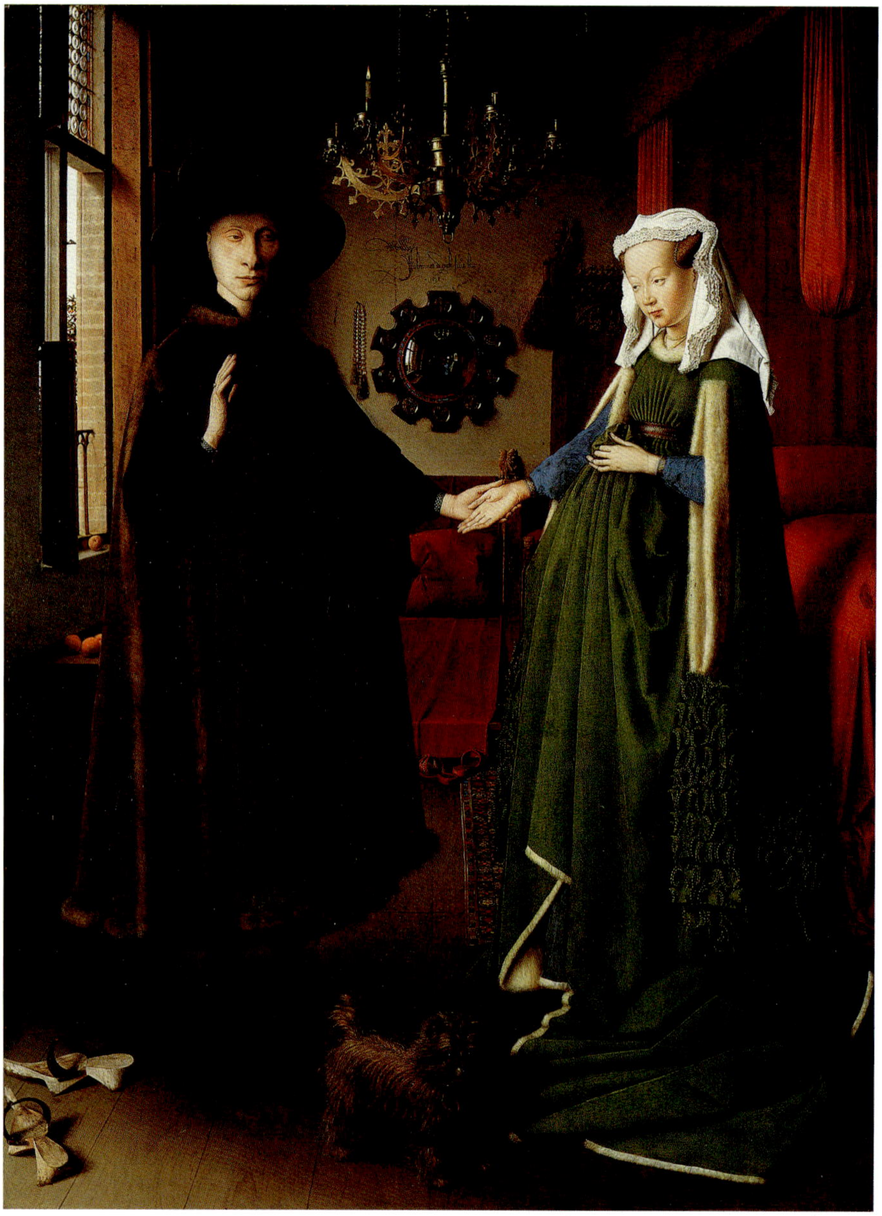

Fig. 1. Jan van Eyck, *The Portrait of Giovanni Arnolfini and His Wife Giovanna Cenami ("The Arnolfini Marriage")*, 1434. Oil on wood, 32 ¼ x 23 ⅜ in. (82 x 59.5 cm). The National Gallery, London

—with which he locates himself at the focal point of our vision in the middle of these intersecting fictive spaces. From this we presume that he was in the Arnolfini house and possibly even witness to their marriage; he was certainly

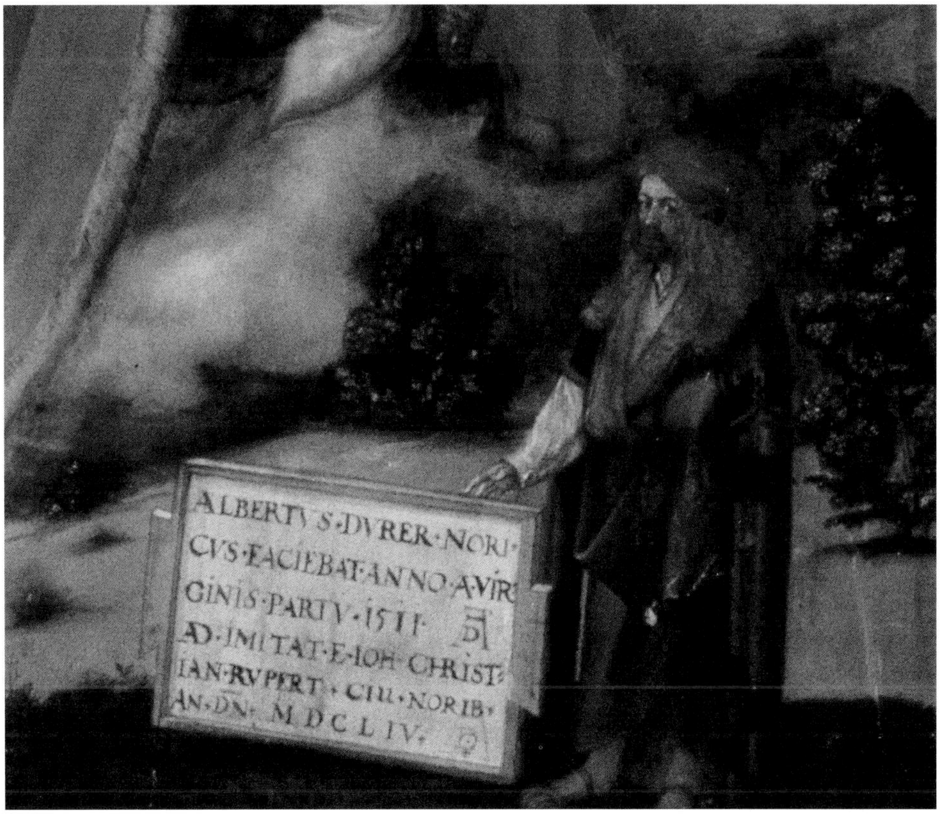

Fig. 2. Albrecht Dürer, *Adoration of the Holy Trinity, with Dürer's Self-Portrait at the Bottom Right* (detail), Allerheiligenbild, 1511. Oil on poplar wood, 53 ⅛ x 48 ⅝ in. (135 x 123.4 cm). Kunsthistorisches Museum, Gemäldegalerie, Vienna

present on the canvas. But in the thinking of one historian, the direct juxtaposition of van Eyck's name with the Crucifixion vignette below may also be meant to suggest that, just as Christ lives on after his death, so too the artist lives on to engage viewers in the future.[1] Not least, the energetic script (echoed in the shimmering tracery of the chandelier immediately above), together with the assertive presence of its maker, aligns the painter's creative power with God's.

Almost a century later, at the height of the Renaissance in the north, Albrecht Dürer frequently placed his familiar AD monogram on a small plaque or shield within the landscape or architectural spaces depicted in his woodcuts and engravings. In two particularly unusual examples, the paintings *The Martyrdom of Ten Thousand Christians*, 1508 (Kunsthistorisches Museum, Vienna) and *Adoration of the Holy Trinity*, 1511 (fig. 2), he inserted his self-portrait alongside his signature into the middle of these subjects. The first shows him walking with a colleague believed to be the poet Conrad Celtis, and holding a banner with his name and an inscription, near the center of the composition of massacred figures. In the second he stands at the lower corner presenting an inscription with his name and monogram, as if it were in miniature a painting within the painting.[2] In both paintings, the self-portrait and the signature are not only juxtaposed, they are fused, if not interchangeable, with one another. In this way, Dürer becomes an imaginative participant in his work, his image one of authorship as well as inventiveness.

The self-portrait within a picture was an occasional conceit appearing in Italian Renaissance paintings as well. Perugino is not believed to have painted any conventional self-portrait, but in 1496 he did include a trompe l'oeil painting of himself hung illusionistically on an architectural pilaster, itself part of a much larger fresco (fig. 3).[3] Beneath the image hangs a similarly framed tablet inscribed with a statement that he was the painter. Centered between depictions of ancient heroes, his artistic presence calls just as much attention to himself. Later, there is the famed example of Michelangelo including his flayed mask and upper torso staring out in his Sistine Chapel fresco of *The Last Judgment*, 1537–41. Perhaps equally well known is the graphic image of suffering contained in the early baroque painting by Caravaggio, *David with the Head of Goliath*, 1606 (fig. 4), in which the features of the decapitated Goliath have been accepted, even during Caravaggio's lifetime, as those of the artist himself.[4] Art historians have readily associated this dramatic vision of violence with the lurid events of

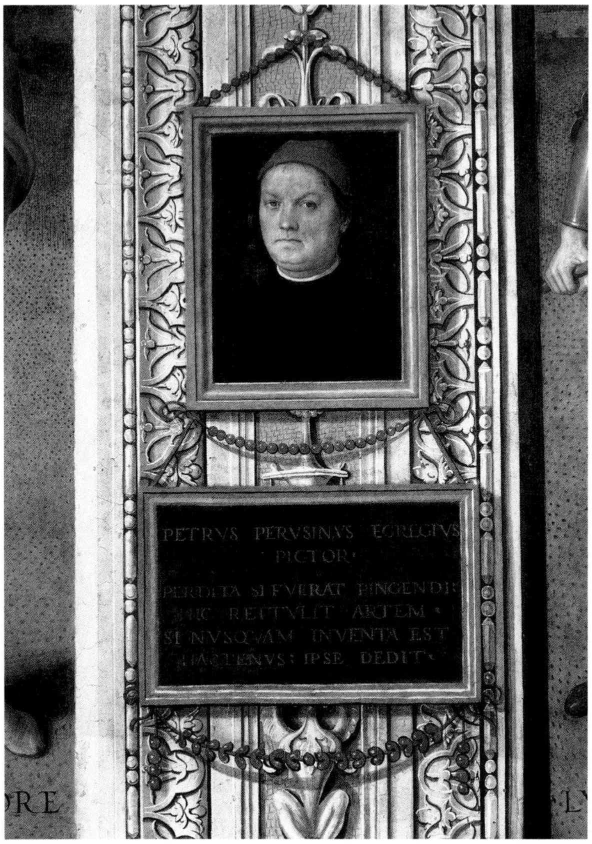

Fig. 3. Perugino, *Self-Portrait*, 1496. Fresco. Collegio del Cambio, Palazzo dei Priori (Comunale), Perugia, Italy

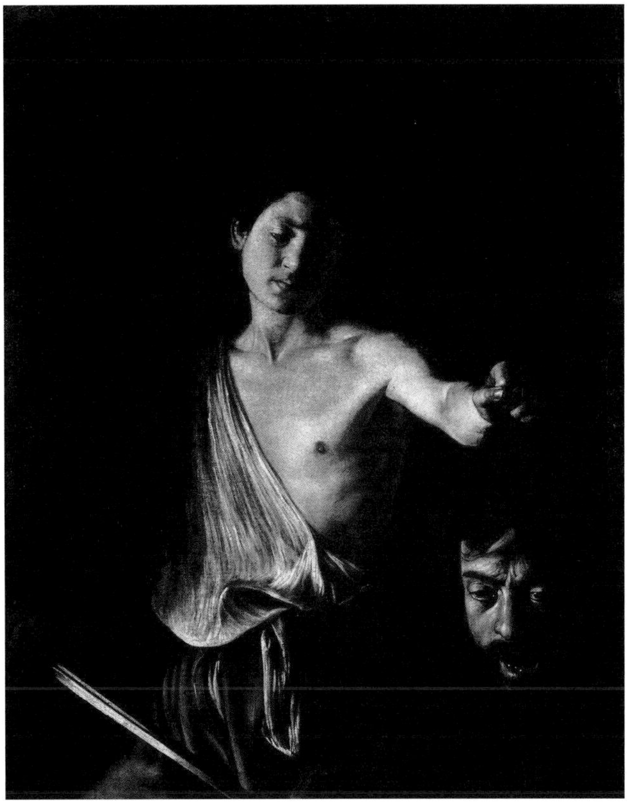

Fig. 4. Michelangelo Merisi da Caravaggio, *David with the Head of Goliath*, 1606. Oil on canvas, 49 ¼ x 39 ¾ in. (125 x 101 cm). Galleria Borghese, Rome / Bridgeman Art Library

Caravaggio's intense career and biography. In any event, these embedded self-images provide a model revived in much wittier fashion in later nineteenth-century American art by John Haberle (see fig. 78), whose tintype self-portrait would serve as his signature.

One of the most interesting figures at the intersection of north and south is Jacopo de' Barbari, who also introduces us to the extensive practice by Venetian artists in the Renaissance of placing themselves within their works, usually by means of imaginatively and often prominently located inscriptions. While the gesture was most commonplace up to the early Renaissance in portraiture and figurative paintings, still-life subjects soon provided an even more natural genre for authorial playfulness. Believed to be one of the earliest illusionist arrangements of objects is Jacopo's *Still Life with Partridge, Iron Gloves, and Crossbow Arrows*, 1504 (fig. 5). A Venetian painter, he was known to be working in Saxony and then the Netherlands early in the fifteenth century, and clearly brought with him the Italian mastery of spatial illusionism. Here, Jacopo deftly places against a plain textured wall the juxtaposed forms and tactile surfaces of animal and metal. Below

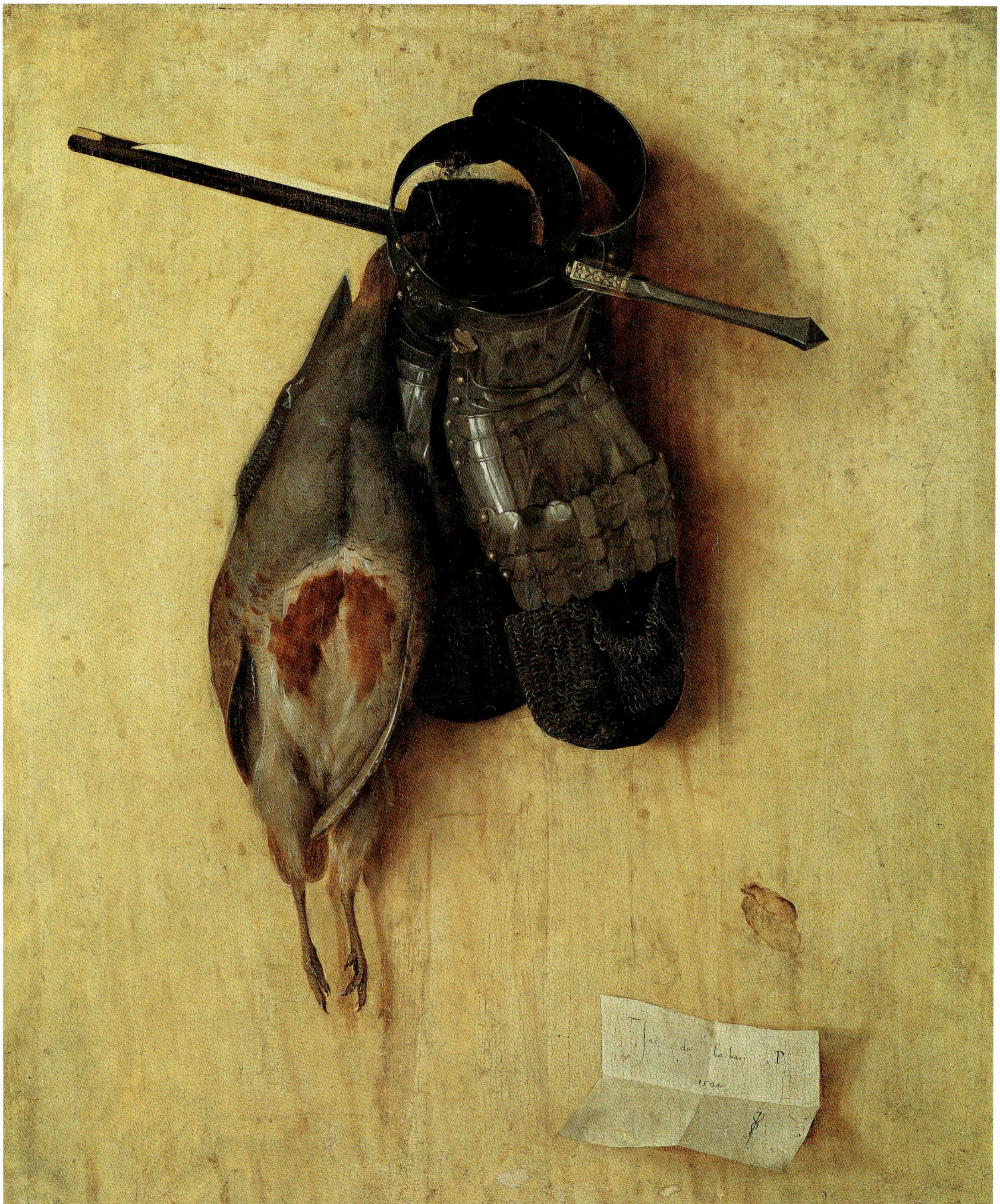

Fig. 5. Jacopo de' Barbari, *Still Life with Partridge, Iron Gloves, and Crossbow Arrows*, 1504. Limewood, 20 ½ x 16 ¾ in. (52 x 42.5 cm). Alte Pinakothek, Munich

he adds his signature and date on a small creased slip of paper, further calling attention to the artifice of trompe l'oeil painting.[5] A still life is already an artificial composition of objects brought together for their shapes, textures, and associations, and the act of painting them, especially life-size, lends another level of aesthetic cleverness. The signed *cartellino* identifies not only the maker but also his craft, a device we shall see Americans employing, from Charles Willson Peale to William M. Harnett (see figs. 35 and 86).

Jacopo was to have an influence on the inclusion of similar trompe l'oeil elements in subsequent Northern painting, such as the packets of letters clipped to the wall in the upper background of *Portrait of a Merchant*, ca. 1530 (National Gallery of Art, Washington, D.C.), by Jan Gossaert, called Mabuse. But he was also a product of a rich tradition in Venice, particularly prevalent from the mid-fifteenth to mid-sixteenth centuries, and well documented by Louisa C. Matthew in a survey of highlights from Jacopo and Giovanni Bellini, Andrea Mantegna, Carlo Crivelli, and Vittore Carpaccio to Lorenzo Lotto and Titian.[6] She provides several pertinent general observations about the inventive signing practices of this group. First, signatures could serve variously as indicators of one's self-conscious status as creator, an effort to establish a reputation, a demonstration of skill and imagination, an exercise of religious devotion, or the aspiration to virtuous memory and immortality. She also points out that signing was encouraged in maritime Venice for art shipped by sea in the active export business.[7]

A second important generalization relates to the reemergence of classicism generally in the Renaissance. With this came an enthusiasm for Roman numerals and lettering (now replacing the medieval taste for Gothic scripts), words or phrases from classical texts, and ancient inscriptions rendered as if they were fictively engraved into piers or lintels of classical architecture. Matthew further speculates that such designs may also be related to the flourishing book-printing industry in Venice and its pioneering introduction of the title page in book production at this time.[8] Venetian artists tended to favor two general types of inscription: the so-called *cartellino* — a piece of paper or letter, often creased, bent, or folded to heighten its illusionism within the picture space — and the architectural engraving. In part, these derive from the precedents in earlier painting of unfolding scrolls, often placed across the sky in landscape compositions or along pedestals supporting religious or mythological figures. Traditionally, these scrolls would be associated with utterances by Old Testament prophets.[9] In Venetian Renaissance hands

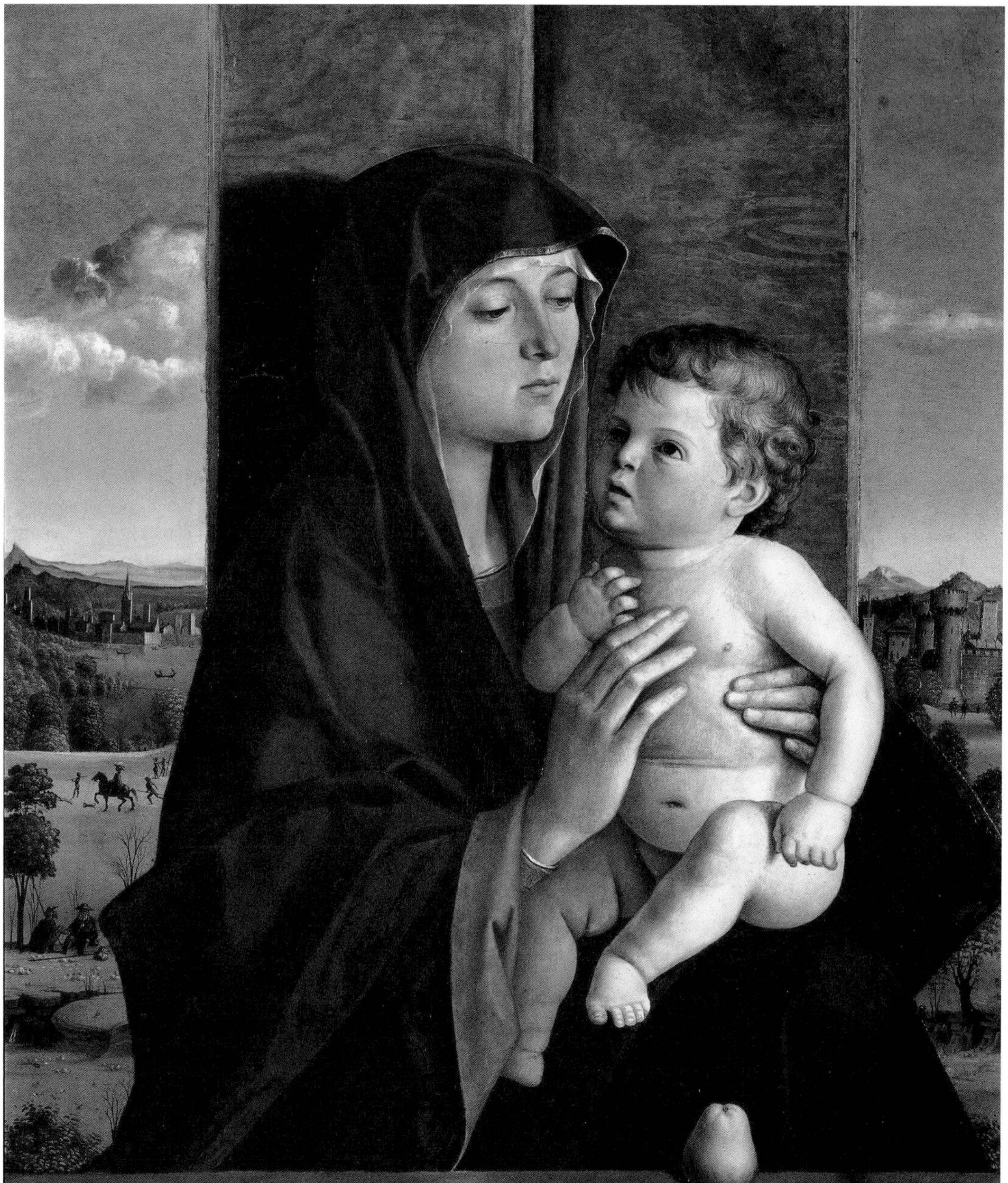

Fig. 6. Giovanni Bellini, *Madonna and Child (Madonna of the Pear)*, 1460s. Distemper on wood, 18 ½ x 13 ⅜ in. (47 x 34 cm). Accademia Carrara, Bergamo, Italy

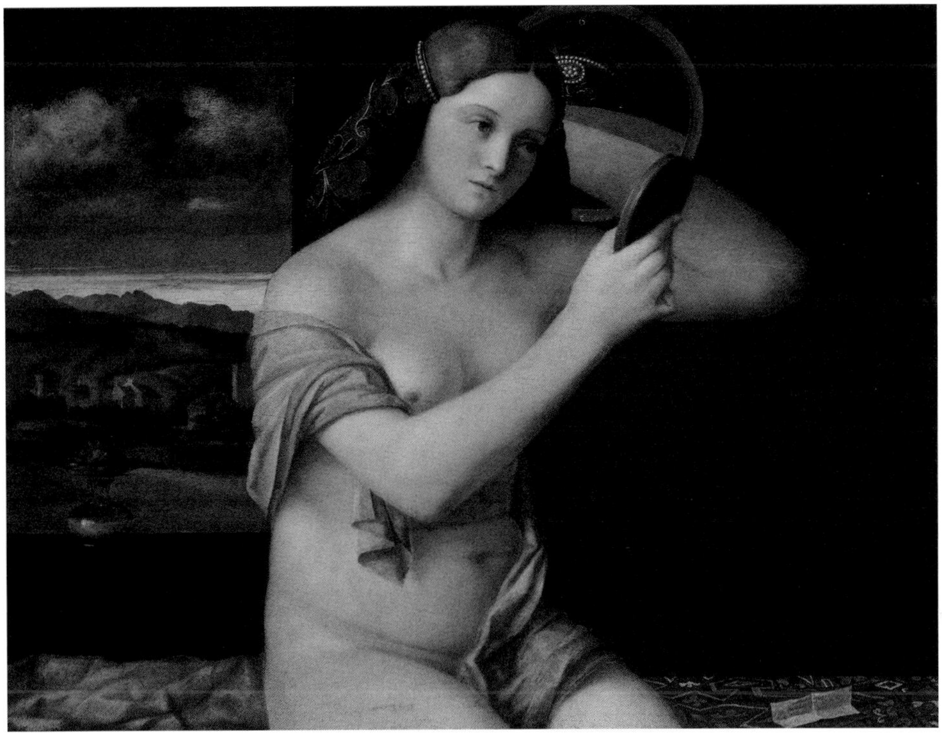

Fig. 7. Giovanni Bellini, *Young Woman at Her Toilet,* 1515. Oil on poplar wood, 24 ⅜ x 31 ⅛ in. (62 x 79 cm). Kunsthistorisches Museum, Gemäldegalerie, Vienna

they became imaginative devices for signing as well as enhancing the meaning of the painted subject.

A few important examples in each category are worth mentioning. Perhaps most straightforward is Jacopo Bellini's *Madonna and Child,* 1440s (Museo Tadini, Lovere), where the artist's signature appears on a small strip of paper attached to the center of the ledge supporting the Christ Child. Its lower right-hand corner is slightly turned outward, casting the barest shadow and sense of depth. A generation later, his son Giovanni placed in a similar position his Latinate inscription IOANNES BELLINVS P on a sharply creased slip with its upper right corner folded over, in his *Madonna and Child (Madonna of the Pear),* 1460s (fig. 6). A more informal but suggestive placement occurs in a late work, *Young Woman at Her Toilet,* 1515 (fig. 7), in which the signature is on a folded letter casually set down beside the woman. We must wonder about this intimate proximity between the artist and his subject and what kind of narrative may be hinted at here.[10] With very different subjects we shall see American painters like William Harnett and John F.

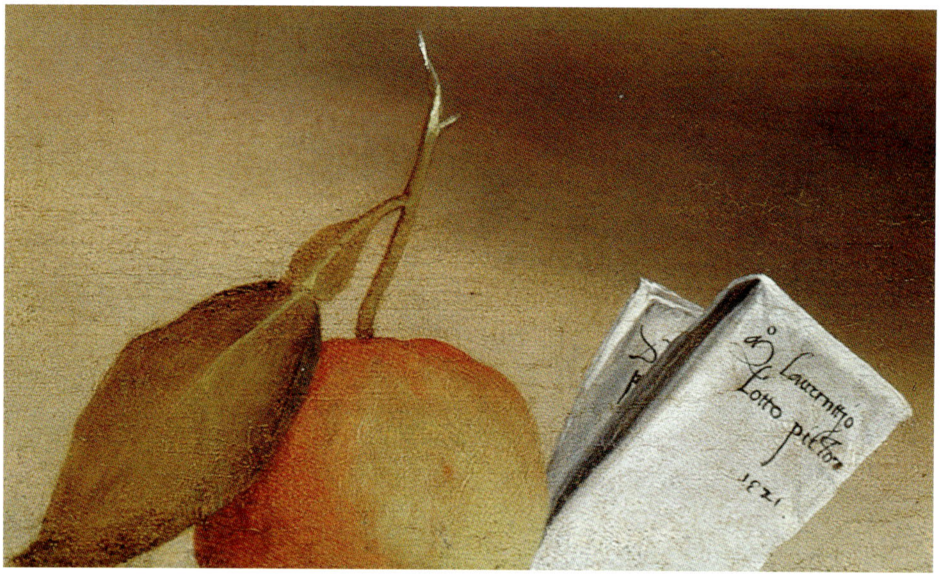

Fig. 8. Lorenzo Lotto, *Christ's Farewell to His Mother* (detail), 1521. Oil on canvas, 49 5/8 x 39 in. (126 x 99 cm). Staatliche Museen zu Berlin, Preußischer Kulturbesitz, Gemäldegalerie

Peto making similar provocative juxtapositions of their names with subject elements in their trompe l'oeil still-life compositions at the end of the nineteenth century (see figs. 86 and 91).

Titian may also have intended to indicate a personal connection with his subject in *Portrait of Jacopo Strada*, 1567–68 (Kunsthistorisches Museum, Vienna), when he inscribed his name as if in an address on the letter centered before the sitter. This possibly signals a business or social relationship with an individual known as a connoisseur and art collector, here expressed by the books above him, the sculpture in his hand, and the coins on the table. By contrast, Lorenzo Lotto shows that differences in subject matter were no inhibition to such gestures, by setting the folded letter with his signature illusionistically between his painting, *Christ's Farewell to His Mother*, 1521 (fig. 8), and its fictive frame.[11] On the one hand, this virtuoso detail calls attention to the juncture between the spaces of the picture and the viewer (and by implication to the maker's cleverness), and on the other it prominently serves as an act of devotion in the religious narrative. Peto and Haberle would enjoy a comparable visual playfulness, as they depicted printed cards and photographs, even nails and matches, wedged between the canvas and frame.

Among the more dramatic representations of an architectural inscription is Mantegna's *Saint Sebastian*, ca. 1459 (Kunsthistorisches Museum, Vienna), where the words "work of Andrea" written in Greek are engraved vertically down the marble pier to which the saint is bound. Louisa Matthew calls the prominent display of ancient language here "self-consciously inventive and learned."[12] (With capital Latin lettering Carlo Crivelli likewise engraved his name in the marble platform of his *Madonna and Child*, 1482 [Pinacoteca, Vatican Museums], as did Cima in his version of the same theme.) Just as bold was Titian's 1522 treatment of *Saint Sebastian* (fig. 9), which occupied the right-hand panel of an altarpiece. In fictive block letters TICIANUS FACIEBAT/ M.D. XXII is engraved across the base of the fallen marble column on which Sebastian's right foot stands. The musculature and torsion of the figure, historians have noted, recall the precedents of Michelangelo's and ancient sculpture.[13] Titian was surely calling attention to his learned knowledge by visually linking his name with the pose and glance of the figure above. For just as our eyes are drawn like the arrow to the powerful torso, so do we focus on the strong clear inscription below. Such self-conscious

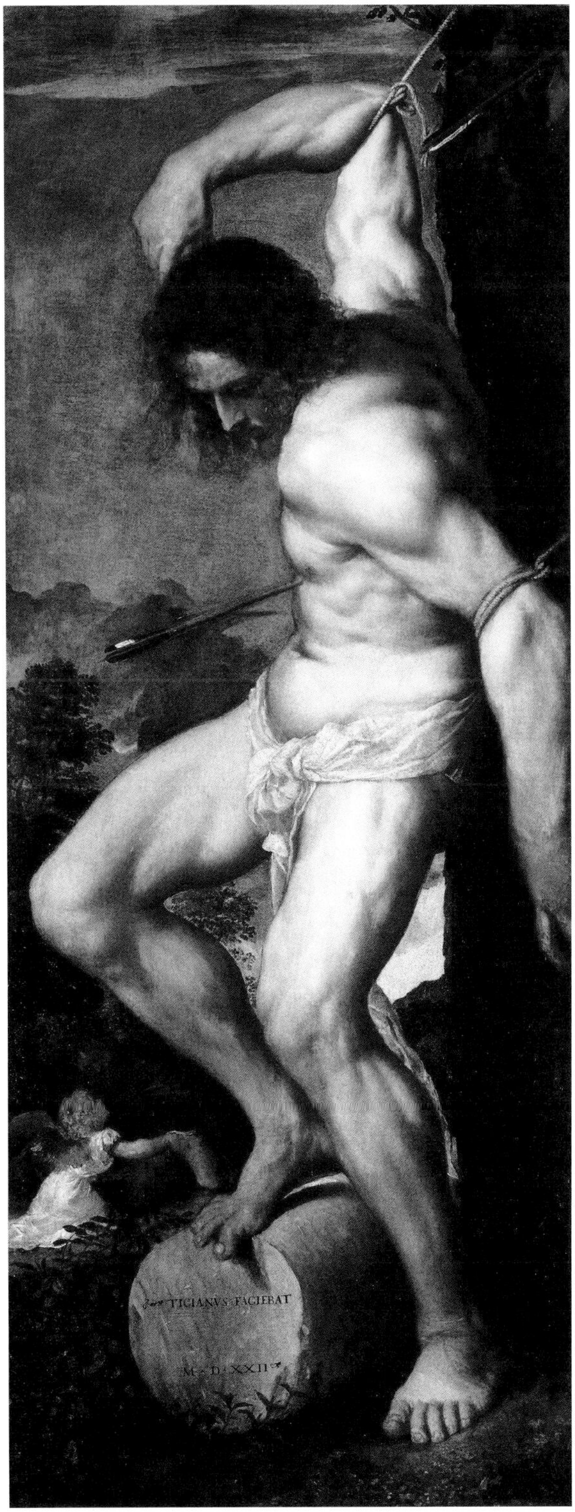

Fig. 9. Titian, *Saint Sebastian*, 1522. Oil on panel, 66 7/8 x 25 5/8 in. (170 x 65 cm). SS. Nazaro e Celso, Brescia, Italy

signatures by Titian were rare but obviously intentional in their conceptual impact. One late work reveals another original placement of his signature that forecasts the expanding variety of possibilities over subsequent centuries. He signed his name in red in *Tarquin and Lucretia*, 1568–71 (Fitzwilliam Museum, Cambridge, United Kingdom), inside one of Lucretia's slippers, which has fallen by the bed's nearby scene of violence.[14] As a reinforcement of the picture's meaning, this vivid manner of signing leads us well beyond the conventions of Renaissance Venice to other places and times.

As might be expected, when we move into the seventeenth century, both still life and self-portraiture continue to be major subject types for consciously expressive signatures. While Holland with its strong still-life and genre traditions would provide rich terrain for such conceits, noteworthy examples are also to be found in Spain and France. By the late sixteenth century, Italian still lifes were being imported to Spain, and the spread of humanism encouraged scientific research, a passion for flowers, and the collecting of curios. Such factors may have stimulated Juan Sánchez Cotán to turn in the 1590s from religious subjects to painting a series of so-called *bodegones*, highly austere and carefully designed fruit and vegetable still lifes (fig. 10).[15] He painted a dozen or more, several being variations of similar compositions, before entering a Carthusian monastery in 1603. His limited number of motifs and their dispersal in almost mathematical configurations, especially parabolic curves, reveal intense intellectual calculation. He generally favored shallow rectangular stone niches, normally used for storing vegetables, but the impenetrable black background is also suggestive of a window opening, and the surrounding frame on three sides further alludes to a picture format.

In just a couple of cases Cotán signed and dated these paintings, placing his signature at the center of the stone sill, literally within his subject, since some of the vegetables illusionistically project forward into the viewer's space. This placement identifies the artist with his artifice and his central presence inside this small universe of related geometries. We know that similar works in the Cotán manner were among the first to be exhibited in Philadelphia at the beginning of the nineteenth century, and would provide a clear influence on the early still lifes of Raphaelle Peale, whose signature frequently appears on the table edge in close proximity to reductive fruit arrangements similar to the one above. Peale never framed his pictures quite like this, but his calculation and illusionism reflect the same spirit of magical intensity and authorial oversight.

By definition, self-portraiture was an occasion for self-referencing on

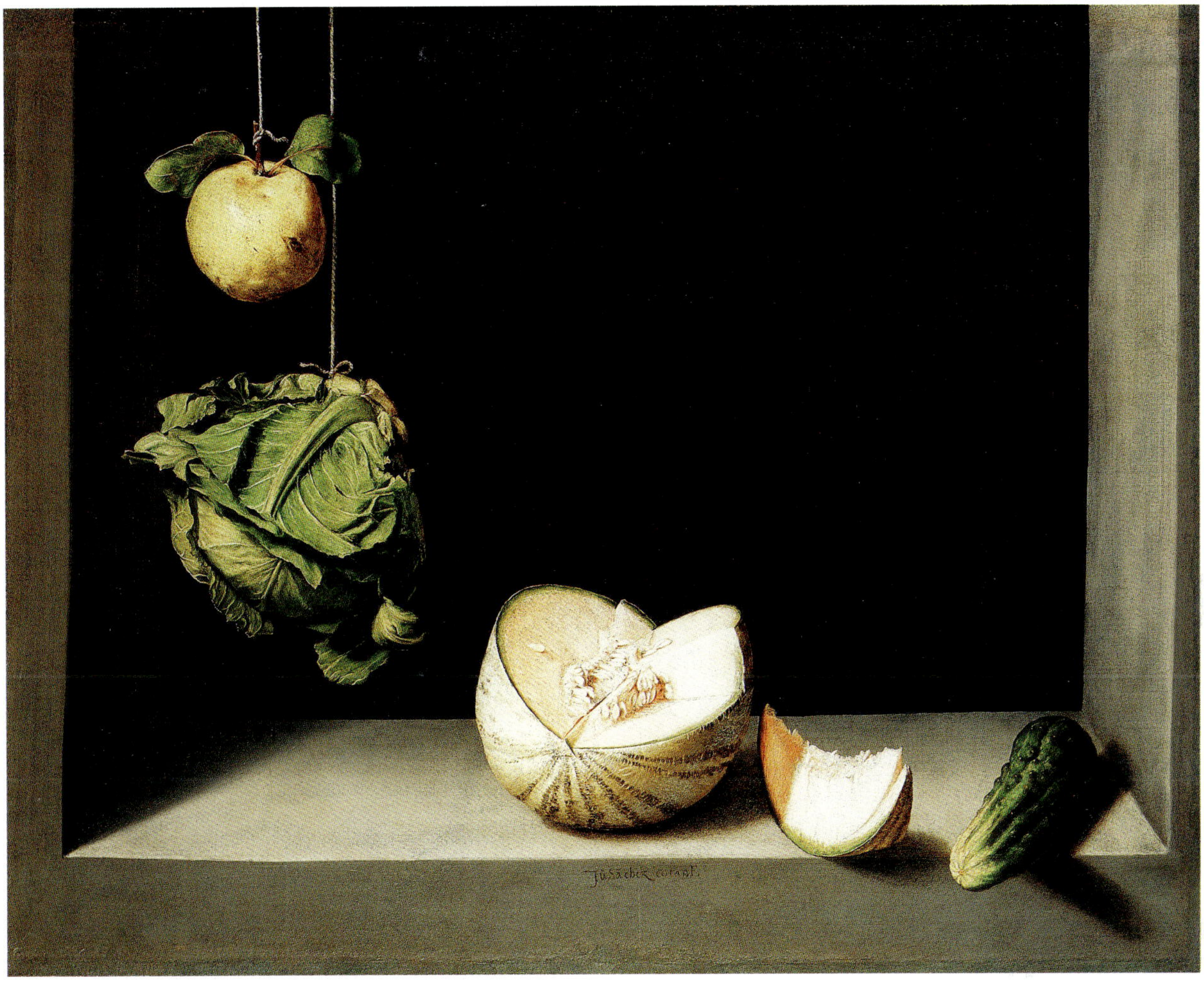

Fig. 10. Juan Sánchez Cotán, *Quince, Cabbage, Melon and Cucumber*, ca. 1602. Oil on canvas, 27 ⅛ x 33 ¼ in. (69 x 84.5 cm). San Diego Museum of Art, Gift of Anne R. and Amy Putnam / Bridgeman Art Library

more than one level, for not only could one depict one's image, but the painter could call attention to the process of making art, to complexities of visual engagement with the viewer, and to the profession as a trade. We can see these elements at play in Bartolomé Esteban Murillo's *Self-Portrait*, ca. 1670 (fig. 11), in which his image is painted within an oval frame set into the picture space. Nearby are drawing tools, a palette and brushes, and a signature inscribed on a piece of paper curling over the table edge in the foreground. Further complicating the sequence of fictive spaces are Murillo's hand reaching through the oval frame to grasp its outside surface, and the artist's glance,

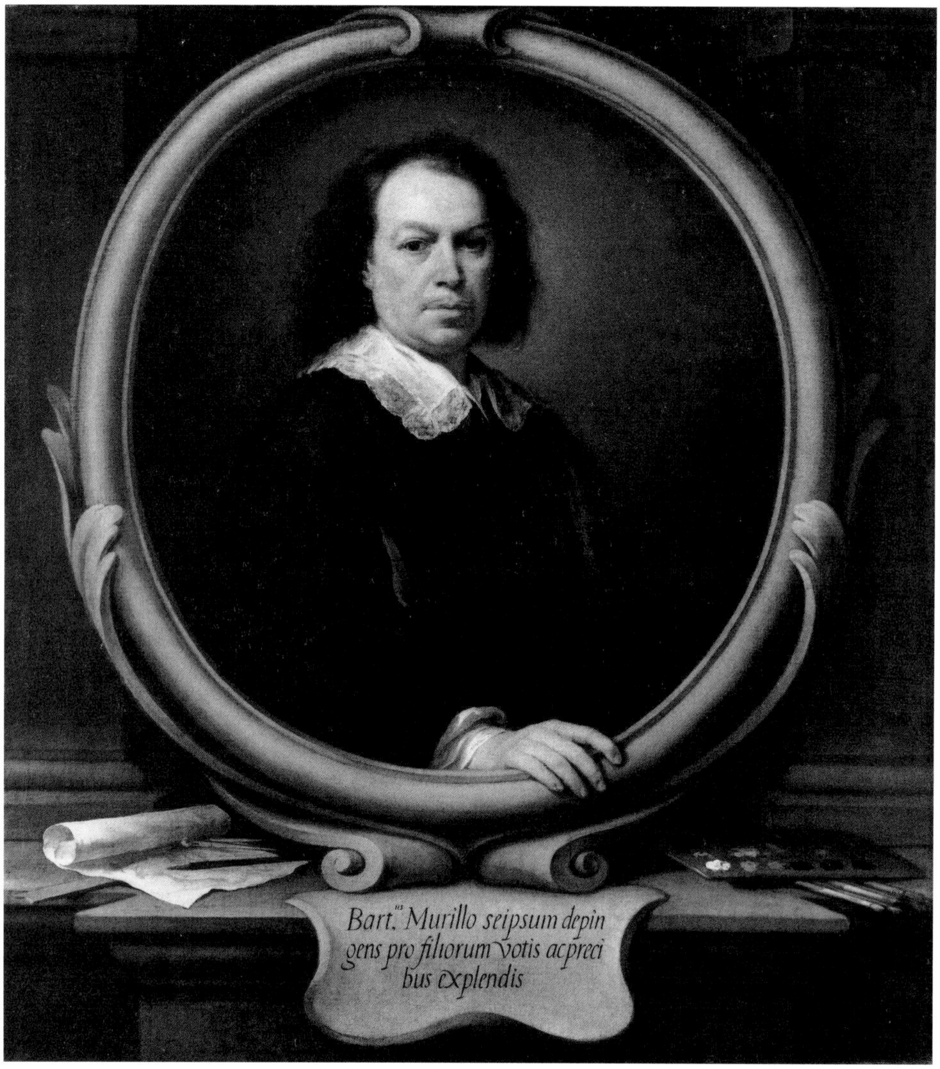

Fig. 11. Bartolomé Esteban Murillo, *Self-Portrait*, ca. 1670. Oil on canvas, 48 x 42 ⅛ in. (122 x 107 cm). The National Gallery, London

which looks out first from the figure's space and secondly across the painted studio space into the realm of the viewer.

Its corresponding achievement is Nicholas Poussin's celebrated *Self-Portrait*, 1650 (fig. 12). As historians have pointed out, Poussin intended to paint his portrait as if by someone else, not a self-portrait, for his patron.[16] Indeed, he is dressed not as a working painter but as a learned humanist, holding a folio rather than brushes or palette. He paints his image neither on a canvas nor within a frame, but standing free in front of several framed

Fig. 12. Nicholas Poussin, *Self-Portrait*, 1650. Oil on canvas, 38 ⅝ x 29 ⅛ in. (98 x 74 cm). Musée du Louvre, Paris

paintings overlapping one another against the back wall of the studio. The figure is separate from art yet juxtaposed to it. All the painted works and frames are parallel to the real canvas, while Poussin's gaze, turn of his shoulders, and the angle of the folio in his hand all project perpendicularly to this plane, connecting the studio's production via the artist to the patron and observer. Poussin's signature in Roman lettering reads quite assertively at the visual center of all this. Stylistically, of course, the inscription, along with the entire planar stability of the picture, exemplifies Poussin's embrace of the classical baroque, but its situation halfway between his head and hand also establishes the role both played in its production. Moreover, its large presence sits alone on the blank surface as if it too were a framed work of art.

When we turn to Dutch painting of the seventeenth century, with its tastes for materialist, scientific, bourgeois culture, not surprisingly we find a rich array of realistic, and often illusionistic, depictions of nature, portraiture, and above all still life. In the words of one historian: "Many painters called attention to their craft by including the tools of their trade in their paintings such as palettes, brushes, and other objects commonly found in artists' studios such as books, sculptures, and globes. Some painters . . . showed themselves in their still lifes as reflections in mirrors or vessels, as painted portraits, or through letters or awards. Whether witnessed in such self-portraits and autobiographical objects, amazing visual tricks, or the flaunting of artistic ability, still-life painters were among the most self-conscious of artists."[17]

That self-consciousness would be evident time and again in deftly positioned signatures. We may take account of several popular subject types, the first of which might be called the studio still life. Here the artist's space is filled with objects or curios, almost a cabinet of curiosities, sometimes a mixture of items arranged or awaiting selection for painting, sometimes a display of collections of sculpture, paintings, prints. Because these are images of art in the making, its appreciation, or perception, it was often natural for artists to insert their mark or presence into the scene. For example, Hendrick Hondius commented on the subject of his copper engraving *Vanitas,* 1626 (Bibliothèque du Seminaire, Fribourg), with inscriptions set into the top and bottom framing edges of the print. In addition, the image of Hercules on an engraved plaque within the composition bears his monogram, a nice visual pun on the double Hs. Similarly, a painting by Willem Van Haecht, *The Cabinet of Cornelis Van der Geest,* 1628 (Rubens's house, Antwerp), includes a whole array of contemporary fellow artists and works by them, collectors and patrons, a figure believed to be Van Haecht himself, along with a small canvas of his and a drawing of Apelles, alluding to the legendary ancient Greek painter.[18] Clearly, these interior signatures and self-references testify to the artist's engagement with his production and its place within his larger professional and social world.

Complementing these internal scenes was the occasional landscape with an imaginatively embedded signature, represented vividly by Jan Porcellis's *Tempest,* 1629 (fig. 13). Through a painted window frame we see ships caught in the raging seas of a turbulent storm. On the lower sill is a sheet inscribed

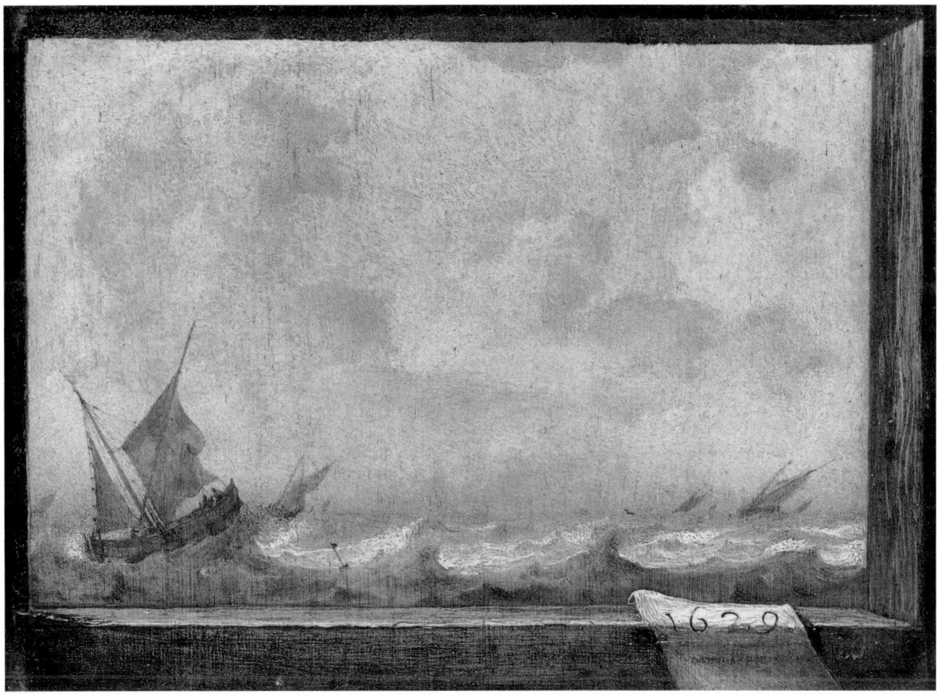

Fig. 13. Jan Porcellis, *Tempest*, 1629. Oil on canvas, 7 ¼ x 9 ½ in. (18.5 x 24 cm). Bayerische Staatsgemäldesammlungen, Munich

with the date and Porcellis's name, folded over its edge but ambiguously attached to the frame. Like Cotán's stone niches, the frame is visible only on a couple of sides, and suggests both canvas and a window view within it. The artist toys with what we are looking at and where our space ends and the picture's begins. At that juncture he paints his signature almost as a contrasting work of art to his painted scene above. The result is a subtle conflation of observation and invention.

We have already seen several examples in Italian painting of the self-portrait serving as signature. One of the more complicated in Dutch seventeenth-century painting is the *Self-Portrait*, 1646, by Joannes Gumpp (fig. 14), which gives us three different versions of the artist. The painter himself has his back to us, and his face is visible only in the repeated images at either side, one in the mirror to the left and one being painted on the canvas to the right. Just as each representation is different in its reality and truthfulness, so each image resides within a different geometric shape, that is, an octagon, rectangle, and circle.[19] The signature here is equally transformed: Gumpp's name appears on the small *cartellino* at the upper right in

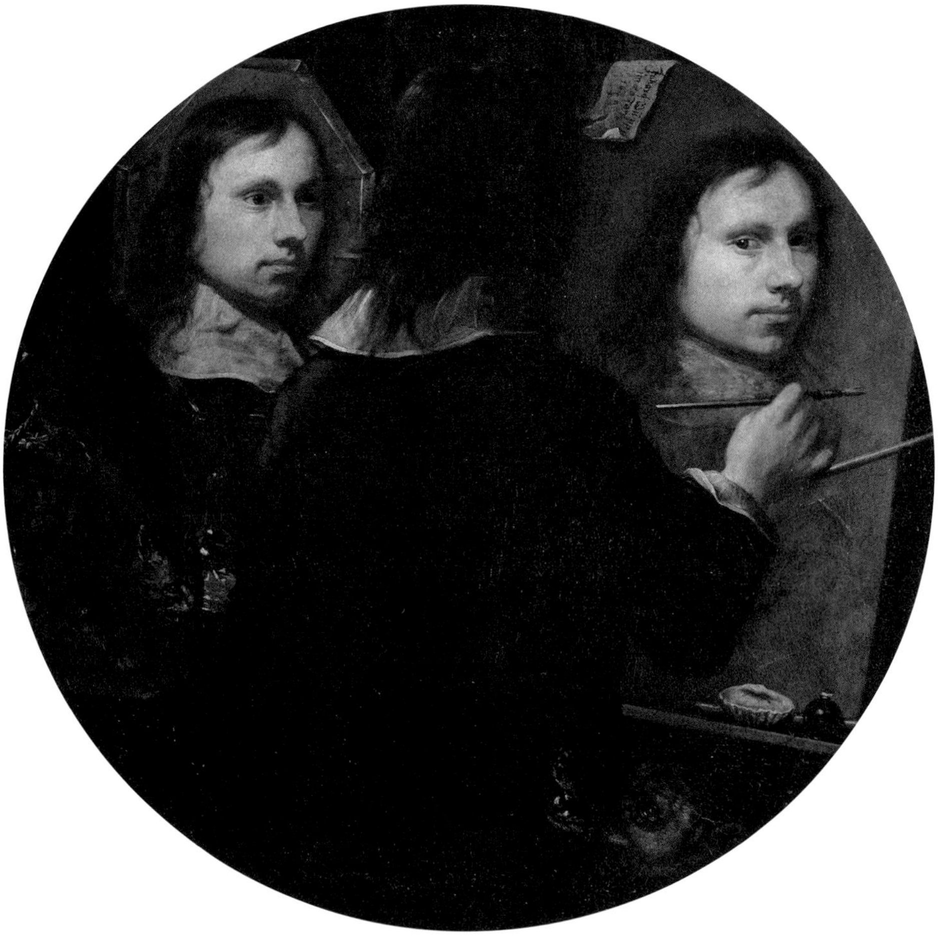

Fig. 14. Joannes Gumpp, *Self-Portrait,* 1646. Oil on canvas, 34 ⅞ x 35 in. (88.5 x 89 cm). Galleria degli Uffizi, Florence

the guise of a title for the interior painting. Five years later, David Bailly reworked this convention with his *Self-Portrait with an Allegorical Still Life,* 1651 (Stedelijk Museum De Lakenthal, Leiden), in which the artist portrays himself standing next to an elaborate tabletop still life. Included are two smaller painted self-portraits and the folded slip of paper with his signature.

Still life as an independent subject was a pervasive favorite among Dutch painters, and signatures were introduced into a wide range of themes from botanical and food to religious and vanitas. Among the earliest painters to concentrate on bouquets of flowers was Ambrosius Bosschaert, who favored setting his vases of blossoms in the middle of deep, arched window frames looking out to distant landscapes. Often he would sign these with a monogram

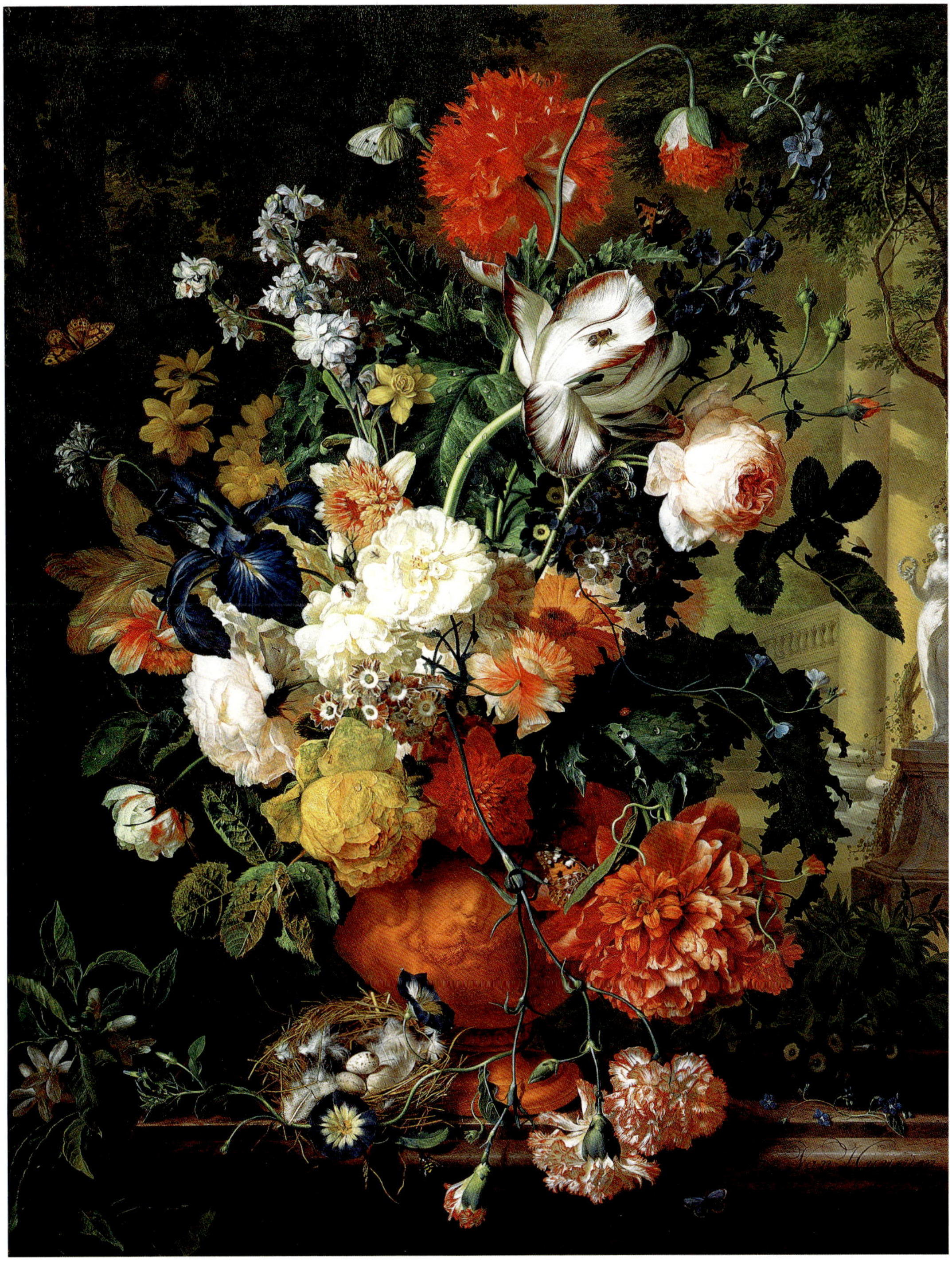

Fig. 15. Jan van Huysum, *Vase of Flowers on a Garden Ledge*, ca. 1730. Oil on panel, 31 ½ x 24 in. (80 x 61 cm). French & Company, New York

placed on the painted sill.[20] More than a century later, at the height of the tulip craze and the scientific interest in variegated blooms, Jan van Huysum represents the culmination of this tradition with his lush yet microscopically painted *Vase of Flowers on a Garden Ledge*, ca. 1730 (fig. 15). In a lovely parody of the bending stems and winding tendrils, he painted his signature over the rounded table edge in an elaborate wiry calligraphy. Both the use of the side of the table and a signature rendered as if it were a shoot growing out of the foliage would take on a new life in similar flower arrangements by Severin Roesen (see fig. 73) in mid-nineteenth-century America.

Other compositions involving books acquired secular as well as religious connotations. Gerrit Dou was an early master of trompe l'oeil gatherings (aside from his well-known genre subjects). One in particular is suggestive both for its objects and signature placement. *Money Bag and a Book on a Shelf*, 1647 (fig. 16), may have had a pendant depicting an hourglass, inkpot, and paper on a shelf, the same in size and date.[21] Together, scholars have argued, they present an allegory of the library, that is, a caution not to lose time in one's study or writing along with the rewards of scholarly endeavors. Of course, the hourglass has also traditionally stood as an emblem of vanitas and time's mortal passage. Only the Los Angeles panel bears Dou's monogram and the date, placed on the book's end, perhaps the most dramatic and strongly lit element to project beyond the shelf frame into our space. In this way he links the virtues of scholarly and artistic cleverness. Its simple

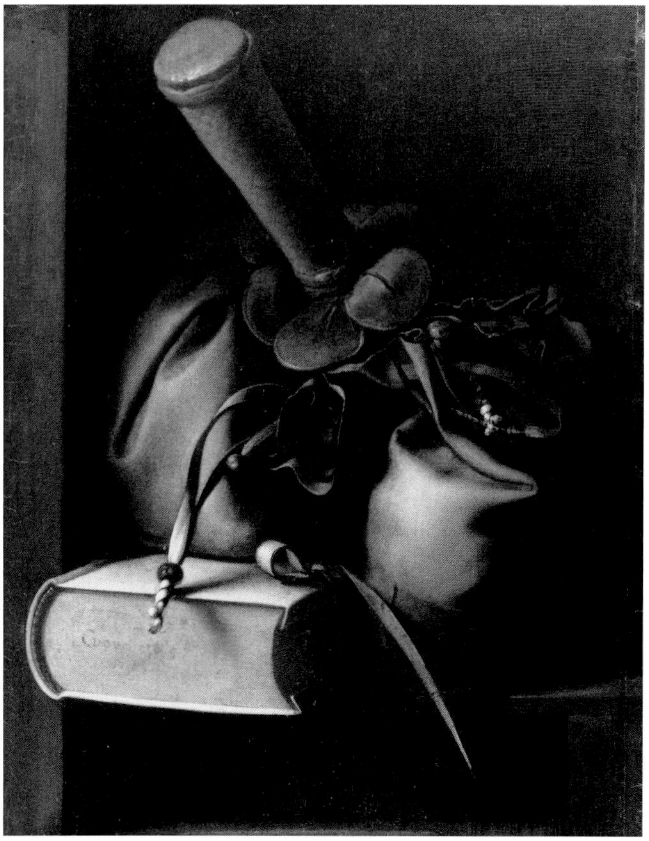

Fig. 16. Gerrit Dou, *Money Bag and a Book on a Shelf*, 1647. Wood, 9 x 6⅜ in. (22.9 x 16.3 cm). The Armand Hammer Collection, Fisher Gallery, University of Southern California, Los Angeles

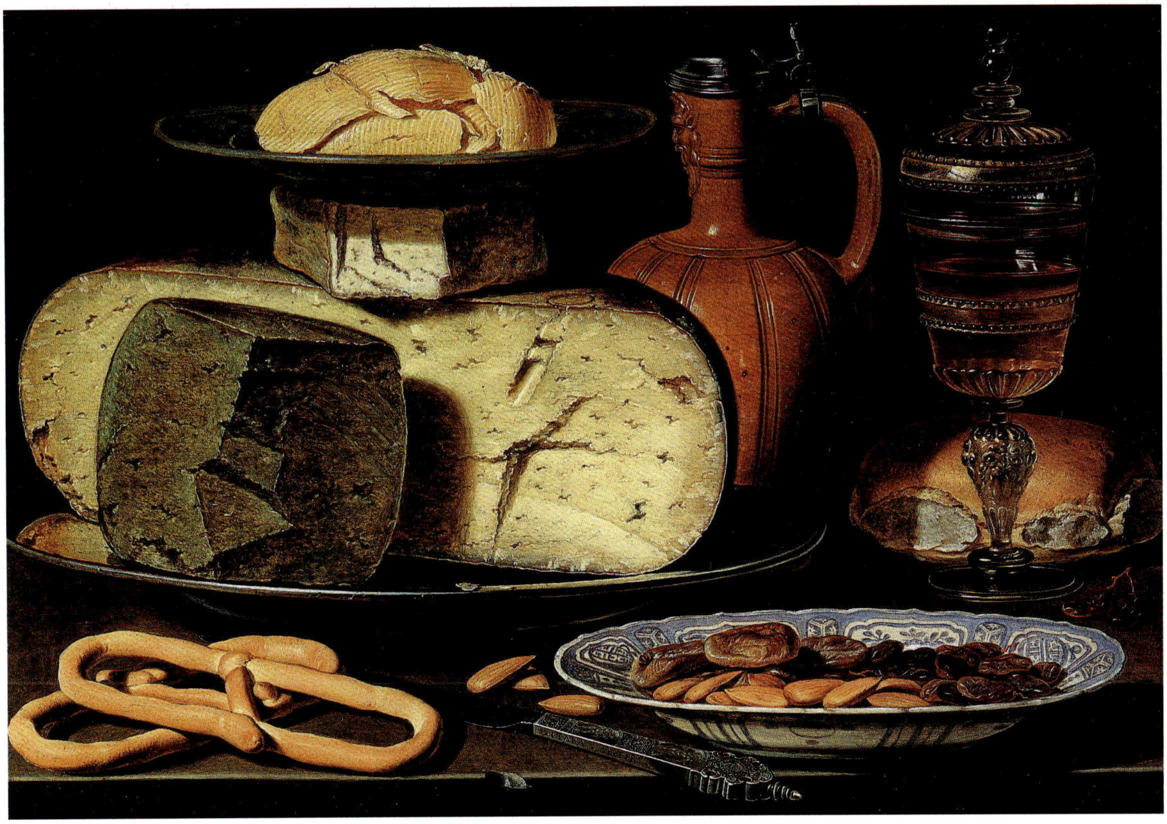

Fig. 17. Clara Peeters, *Cheeses with Almonds and Pretzels,* ca. 1612–15. Oil on panel, 13 ½ x 19 ¼ in. (34.3 x 48.9 cm). Private collection, United States

geometries stand in stark contrast to the baroque density of Maria van Oosterwijck's *Religious Still Life* of two decades later (Kunsthistorisches Museum, Vienna), with its globe, butterfly, biblical texts, skull, and hourglass constituting an elaborate allegory of piety and faith. Like the Dou, it too is signed and dated on a slip of paper projecting out of a book at the table's front edge.

Finally, the Dutch painted displays of food with special relish.[22] Numerous books on foods, the marketplace, and domesticity in Dutch life attest to the centrality of this subject, but we are here primarily interested in those expressive gestures of artistic intervention across this category of subject matter. One of the more ingenious signatures in a food still life of the early seventeenth century is Clara Peeters's in *Cheeses with Almonds and Pretzels,* ca. 1612–15 (fig. 17), thought to invoke a variety of possible associations, from abundance and profligacy to faith and moderation.[23] Within this rich complexity Peeters has introduced her mark in two ways, first, where her name appears inscribed along the side of the knife handle protruding in the foreground. This was commonly a wedding gift, and probably belonged to the artist herself. Second, she painted a small, reflected portrait of herself on the gleaming pewter lid of the brown pitcher in the center background. In both details she demonstrates her technical and conceptual agility.

Given the efforts at meticulous detailing and illusionism of form, texture, and space, it should be unsurprising to see Dutch painters repeatedly inscribing their names within these compositions. One common practice employed by such artists as Willem Kalf, Jan Davidsz. de Heem, Hubert van Ravesteyn, and Adriaen Coorte was to sign one's name in strong block lettering across the side of a tabletop.[24] Coorte's *Gooseberries on a Table*, 1701 (fig. 18), is a striking example. Like another tabletop he painted a few years before of five brightly lit seashells, this presents the stark geometries of the berries and vine pushed up to the sharp illuminated edge of the table, and set in relief against impenetrable blackness behind. Here, Coorte's large, clear inscription matches the spirit of his fruit arrangement, even to the bold swirling line that loops between and around his name and date in emulation of the leafy shoots above. This particular convention would carry through the eighteenth century with Jean-Baptiste-Siméon Chardin and into American food still lifes by artists from Raphaelle Peale to John F. Francis, Roesen, Harnett, and Peto.

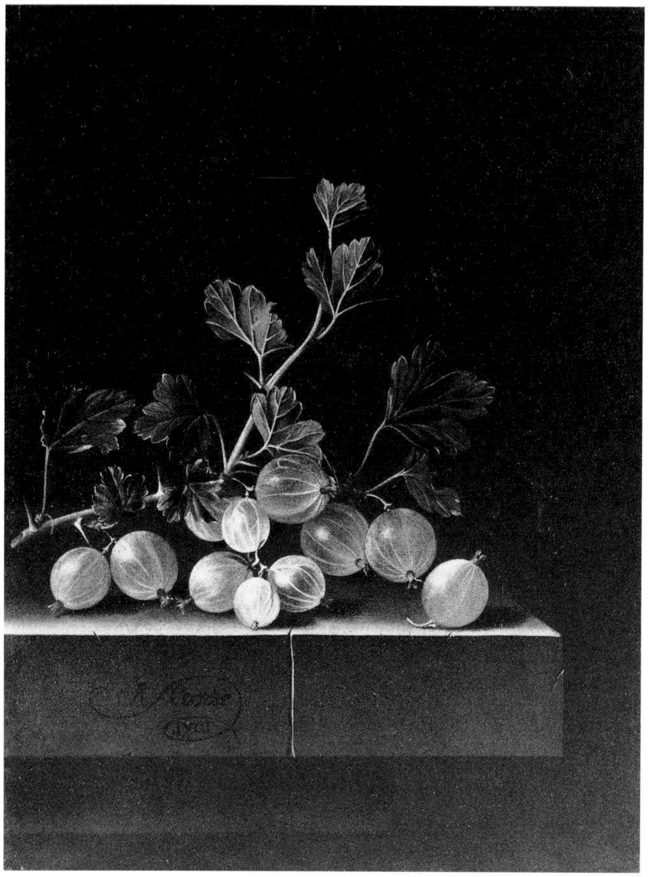

Fig. 18. Adriaen Coorte, *Gooseberries on a Table*, 1701. Oil on paper mounted on wood, 11 ¾ x 9 in. (29.7 x 22.8 cm). The Cleveland Museum of Art, 2002. Leonard C. Hanna, Jr. Fund

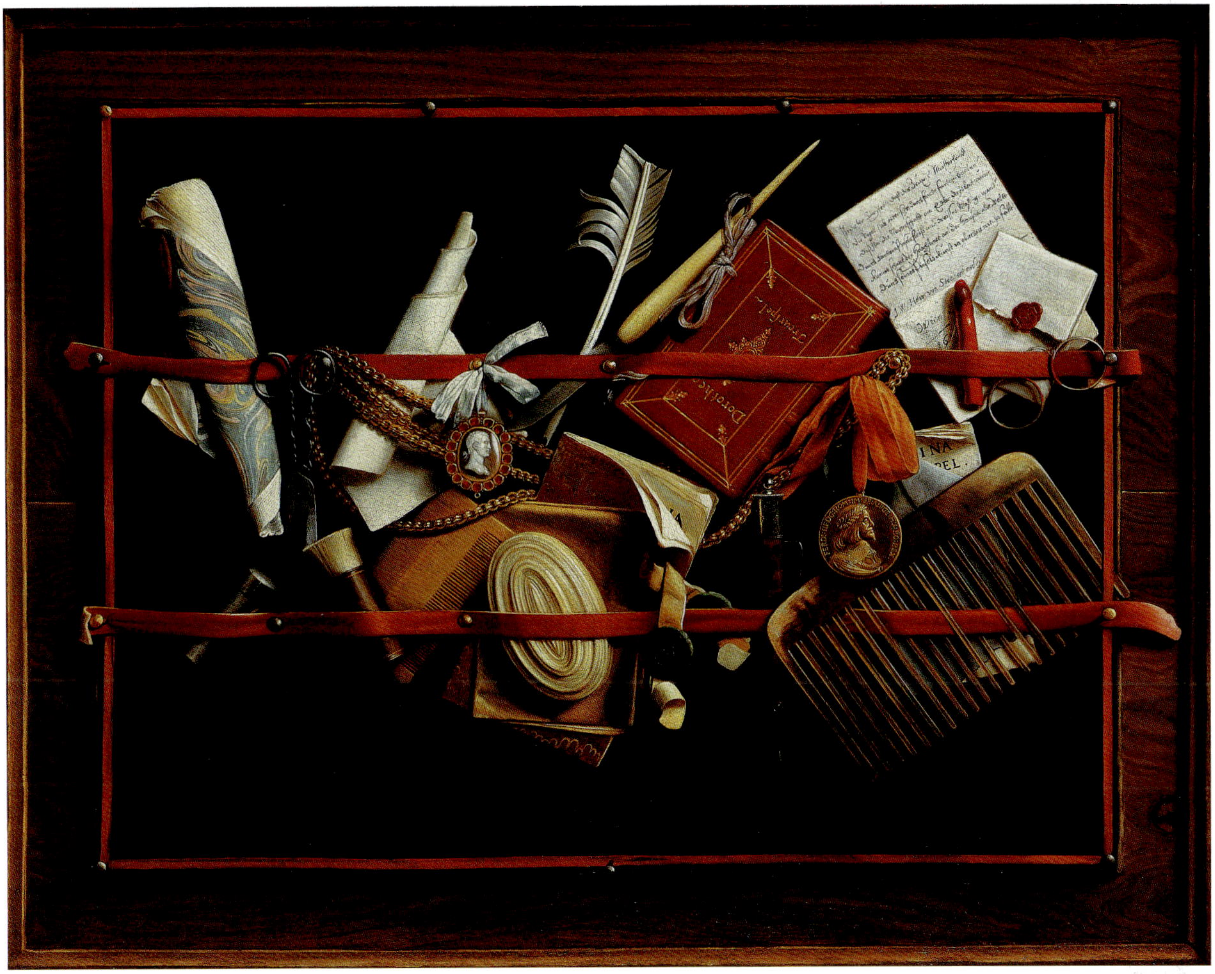

Fig. 19. Samuel van Hoogstraten, *Letter Board*, ca. 1666–78. Oil on canvas, 24¾ x 31⅛ in. (63 x 79 cm). Staatliche Kunsthalle, Karlsruhe, Germany

Special mention needs to be made of some of the other prominent trompe l'oeil artists of the seventeenth century. Samuel van Hoogstraten was a versatile figure who was the son of an artist and a pupil of Rembrandt; he was an author as well as a painter of portraits and history subjects. He became best known, however, for his illusionistic perspective boxes and other virtuoso deception pieces. These included painted corners of interiors sometimes hung within actual rooms in a play of spatial realities. He also specialized in objects arranged on flat surfaces such as fictive doors or wall panels, another format reinterpreted by Peto, Harnett, and Haberle. Within these assemblages, van Hoogstraten enjoyed inserting a variety of self-referential items, both serving as surrogate signatures and tying the artist to his playful visual counterfeits. Typical is his *Letter Board*, ca. 1666–78 (fig. 19).[25] Hanging from the upper cross tape is an imperial medallion on a gold chain, presented to the painter by Ferdinand III as a sign of esteem for his work. Nearby are books written by van Hoogstraten, one of which bears a seal with his initials, and spectacles, which he used but which also signal the subtle acts of seeing and perception conjured up here.

Wallerant Vaillant's letter racks also served as obvious precedents for Harnett and Peto in the later nineteenth century. After training in Antwerp, working as a court painter, and achieving notable success as a portraitist, Vaillant was one of the earliest to exploit the visual trickery of the rack format. Not surprisingly, his *Wooden Board with Letters and Writing Implements*, 1658 (Staatliche Kunstsammlungen, Dresden), indulges in the formal play of multiple rectangles — a variety of folded and creased letters displayed within the several crossing tapes — and the tantalizing illusionism of shallow space. Vaillant marks his date on the board in illusory chalk and his name on one of the letters. Meanwhile, his contemporary, Cornelius Norbertus Gijsbrechts, was producing equally provocative deceptions around the related themes of seeing, art making, and levels of reality. He entered the Antwerp Guild around 1659, about the time of his first paintings, and a decade later became a court painter to the Danish kings. Some of his letter rack pictures were even more complicated than Vaillant's in their visual deceits; for example, *Letter Rack with a Curtain*, 1668 (Statens Museum for Kunst, Copenhagen), displays a rod running across the top of the composition, and a curtain half pulled over the dense accumulation of overlapping letters pinned to the board. More daring still was his *Easel* from the same period, also in Copenhagen, with a painted canvas on it, along with letters, palette, brushes, and the back of another canvas, together blurring the fictive and the real in a perceptual tour de force.[26] The wording on the letter naturally informs us that Gijsbrechts was the image-maker.

One of Gijsbrechts's illusions, *An Open Cupboard Door*, 1665 (Fresno Metropolitan Museum, California), especially looks forward to Peto (see fig. 91), in the door protruding slightly forward from the wall and picture plane. Here all the elements are painted, but elsewhere the artist pushes his illusion a step further by having the door actually open on real hinges. Once again, he asserts his creative ingenuity by signing the print at center with his initials. Also in the 1660s, Gijsbrechts executed a series of vanitas assemblages, which usually combine a fictive tabletop picture, showing a skull,

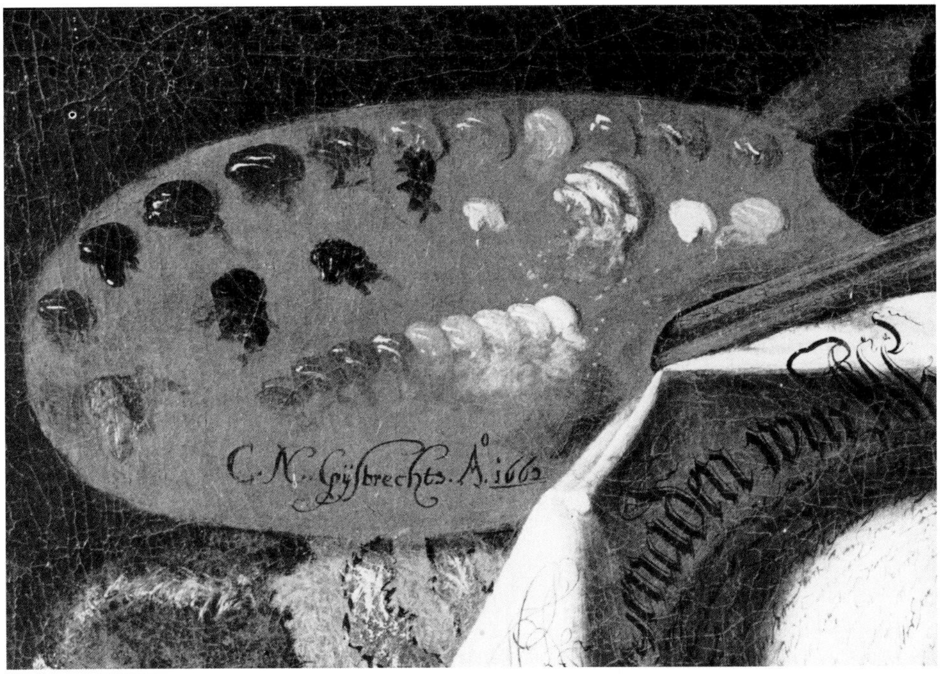

Fig. 20. Cornelius Norbertus Gijsbrechts, *Vanitas* (detail), 1662. Oil on canvas, 57 7/8 x 45 5/8 in. (147 x 116 cm). Bayerische Staatsgemäldesammlungen, Munich

hourglass, and candle, attached to a canvas stretcher in turn mounted on painted wall boards. Attached to the boards would be a medley of prints and letter scraps, while below in some versions a shallow shelf might hold painting or writing implements.[27] His Munich *Vanitas* (fig. 20) in particular has a palette with brushes on which the artist has recorded his name and the year, 1662. Placed just below his paint daubs, the calligraphy represents a contrasting action of the hand, while the palette's presence serves to mediate between the maker and his creation.

When we turn to the towering masters of the Dutch seventeenth century, Rembrandt and Vermeer, each located himself within a surprising variety of picture subjects. To continue for a moment with the trompe l'oeil tradition, we should note that in Rembrandt's *Holy Family*, 1646 (fig. 21), the signature is on a piece of furniture within the fictive space holding the figures, but situated just at the juncture where a curtain has been pulled aside to reveal not only the painted interior scene but also an illusionistic frame. We are looking at both a painting within a painting and a canvas that becomes a stage. But twenty years before this, Rembrandt strongly signed one of his earliest paintings, *Tobit and Anna with the Kid* (fig. 22), at the

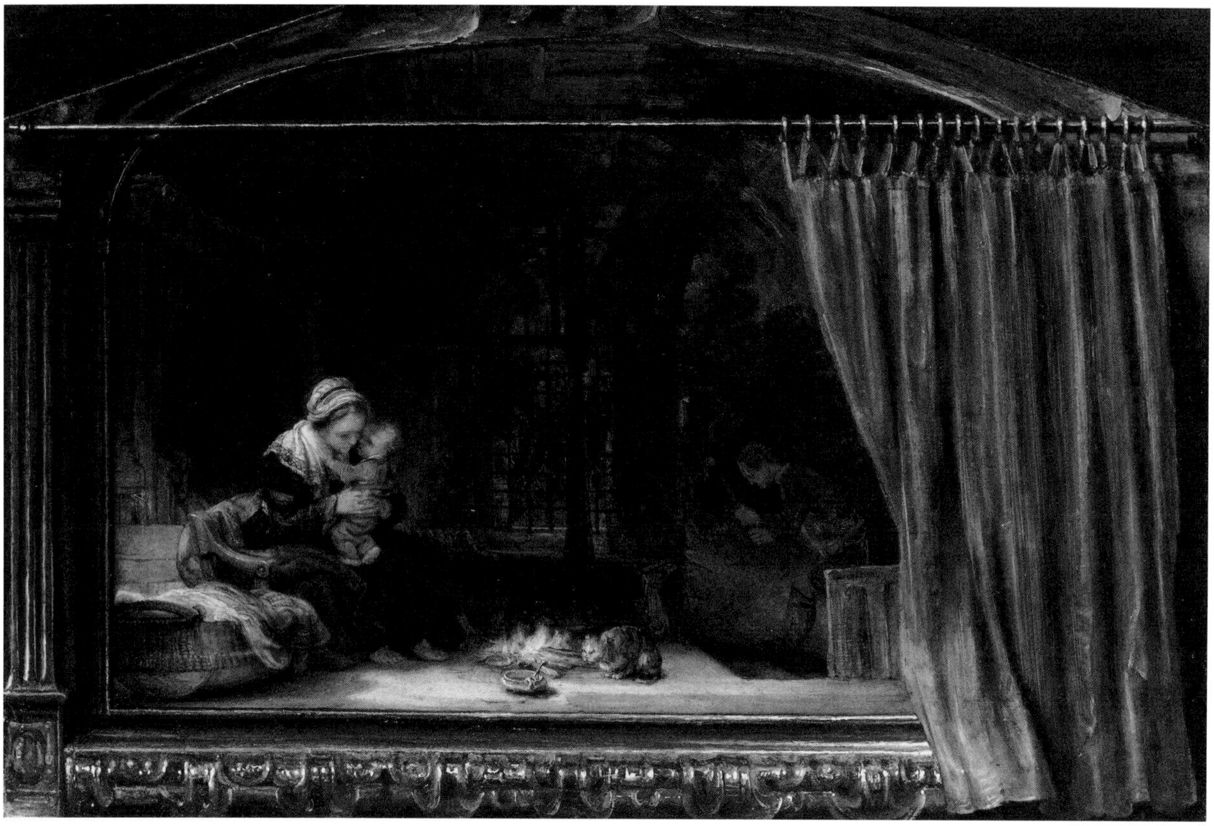

Fig. 21. Rembrandt van Rijn, *The Holy Family*, 1646. Oil on wood, 18 ¼ x 27 ⅛ in. (46.5 x 68.8 cm). Staatliche Museen, Kassel, Germany

lower left corner of the scene. If we look closely, we can see that the initials and date are painted not just on the canvas surface, but as if on the surface of the stone receding on the floor plane itself. This was a biblical story about literal as well as inner blindness and finding one's faith, subjects of revelation that would often preoccupy Rembrandt thereafter. Given his commitment to probing the depths of the human condition, both physical and spiritual, it is no wonder he often immersed himself so intimately in his subjects.

As is well documented, Rembrandt grew up and studied in Leiden, then apprenticed in Amsterdam, the two cities where he rose to prominence as a portraitist and subsequently as a religious and history painter. Occasionally, he signed portraits in central empty areas of the canvas, for example, in *Bust of an Old Man in a Fur Cap (Rembrandt's Father)*, 1630 (Tiroler Landesmuseum Ferdinandeu, Innsbruck), and *Portrait of an Eighty-Three-Year-Old Woman*, 1634 (National Gallery, London). His initials or name appear as if

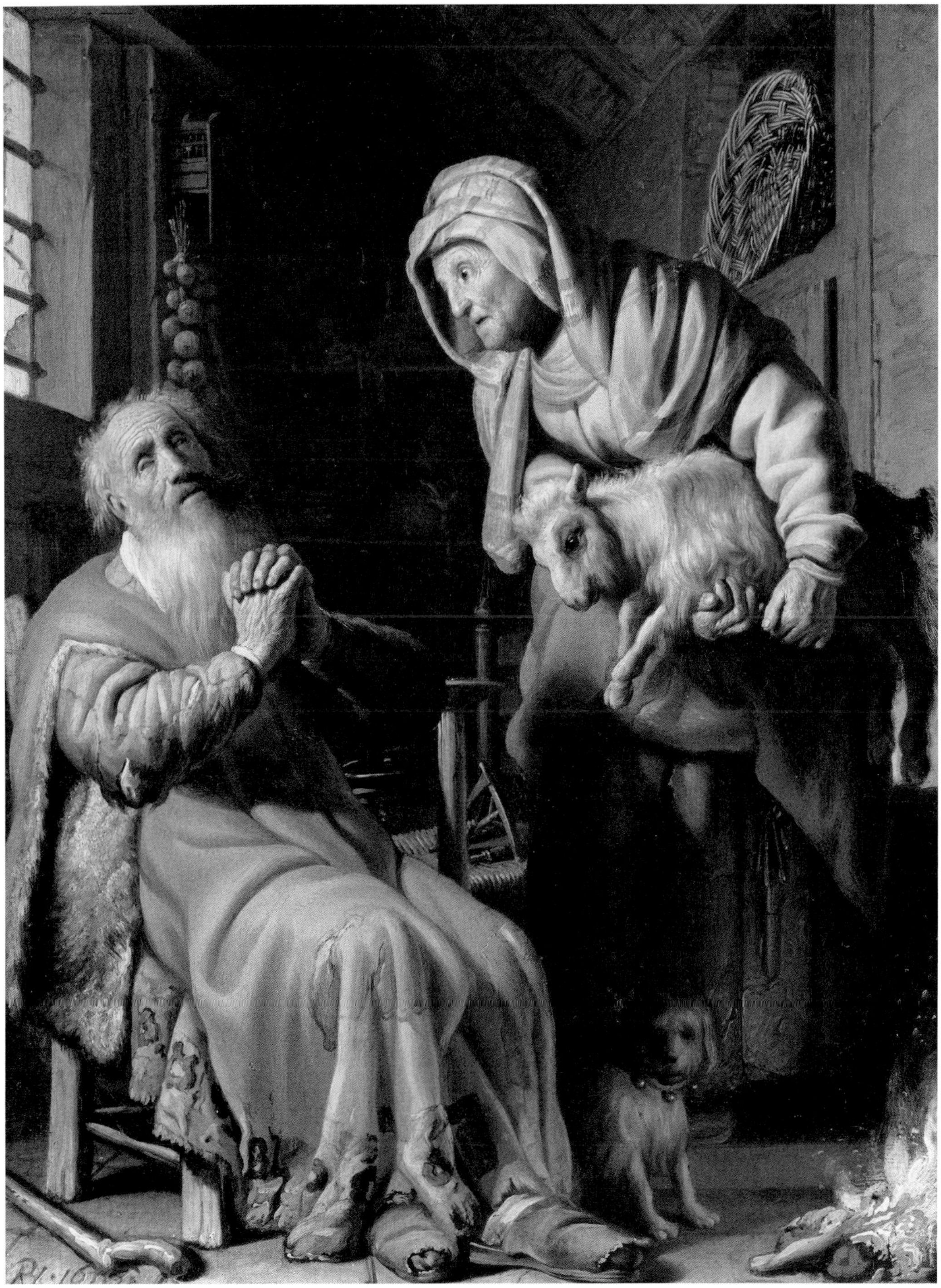

Fig. 22. Rembrandt van Rijn, *Tobit and Anna with the Kid*, 1626. Oil on panel, 9 ½ x 7 ⅛ in. (24 x 18 cm). Rijksmuseum-Stichting, Amsterdam

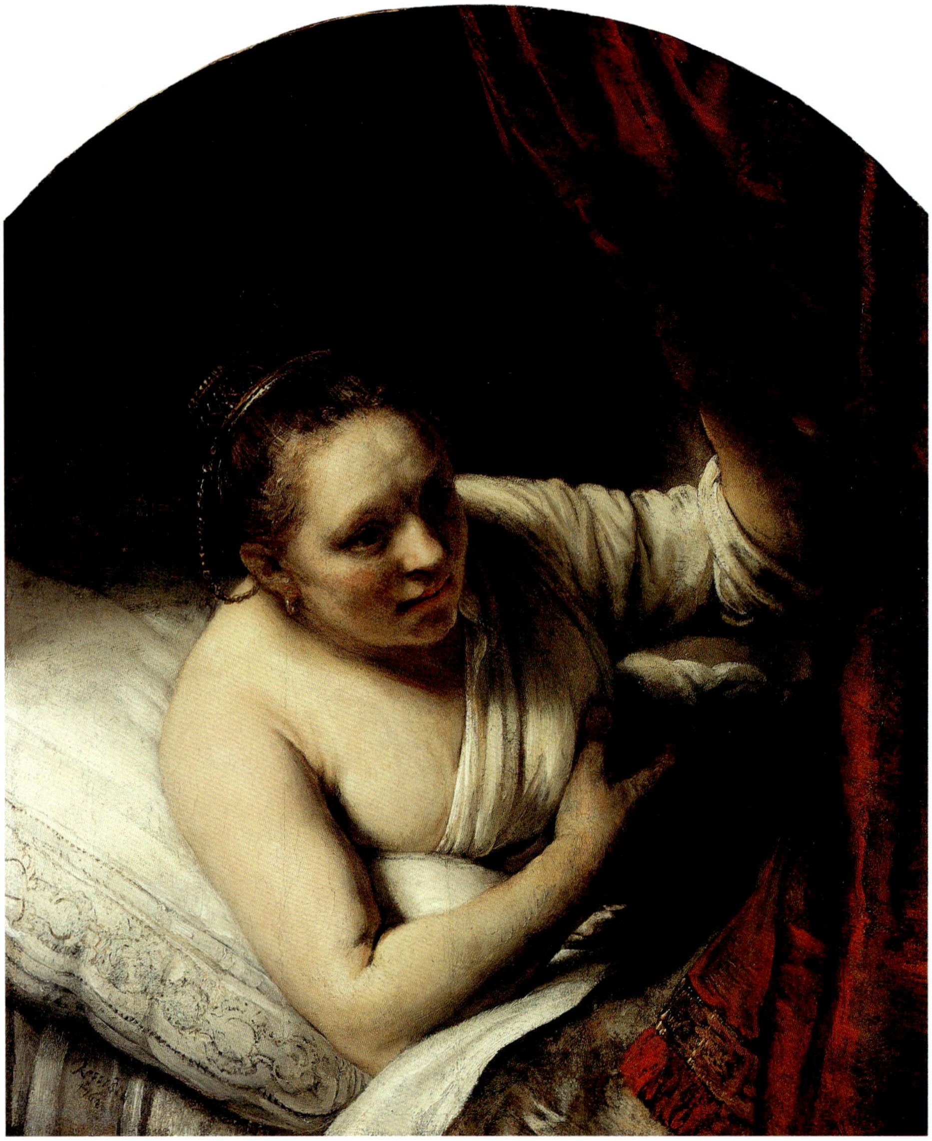

Fig. 23. Rembrandt van Rijn, *A Young Woman in Bed,* 1645. Oil on canvas, 31 ⅞ x 26 ¾ in. (81.1 x 67.8 cm). National Gallery of Scotland, Edinburgh

written on a blank wall immediately to the side of the figure, perhaps, we might speculate, as an expression of the artist's deep sympathy and identification with the sitter. A more obviously direct connection is evident in *Self-Portrait at the Age of 34,* 1640 (National Gallery, London). Rembrandt rests his right arm and hand on a balustrade crossing the bottom of the picture, and on this panel spells out his name and the date.[28] By the same token,

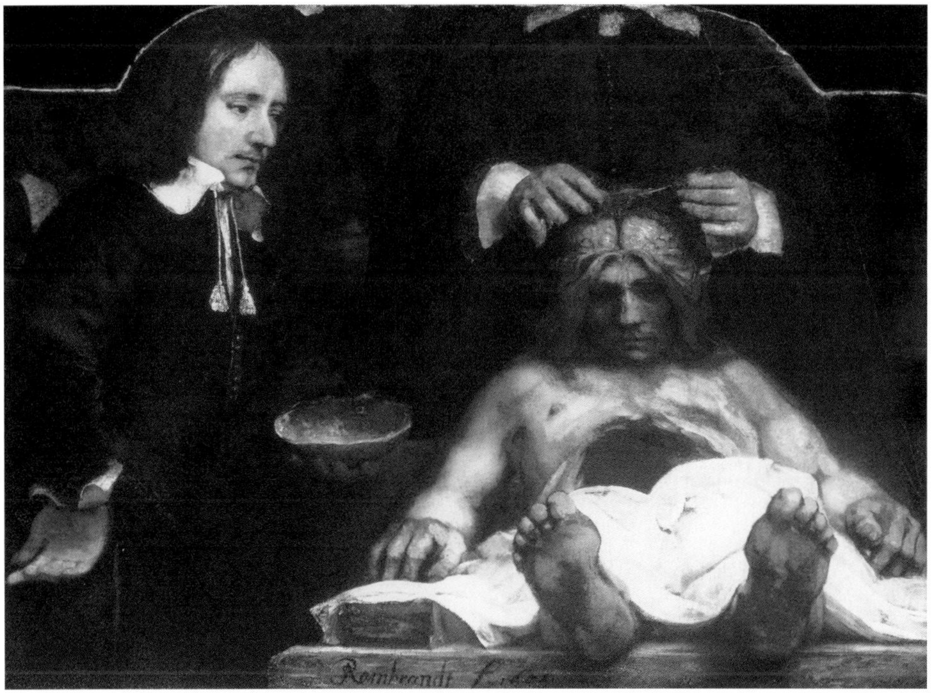

Fig. 24. Rembrandt van Rijn, *The Anatomy Lesson of Dr. Joan Deyman*, 1656. Oil on canvas, 39⅜ x 52¾ in. (100 x 134 cm). Amsterdams Historisch Museum

it would be logical for Rembrandt to make himself an intimate presence through his signature in *A Young Woman in Bed*, 1645 (fig. 23), believed by many Rembrandt scholars to be an image of his common-law wife, Hendricke Stoffels, his companion in his mature years after the death of his first wife, Saskia. The painting has also been associated with the pose in *Danaë* (Hermitage, Saint Petersburg) from the same period, and because of the intensity of her glance, with the themes of Hagar waiting for Abraham, or Sara waiting for her husband, Tobias, on their wedding night.[29] Whether we take this as a genre, portrait, or biblical subject, we surely feel the artist's close presence, signaled in his name nearby on the bedsheets.

A few other major works bear signatures noteworthy for their unusual placement, among them *The Anatomy Lesson of Dr. Joan Deyman*, 1656 (fig. 24). Not only does Rembrandt write his name at the bottom center of his canvas, it is on the end of the operating platform adjacent to the corpse's feet. Even more significantly, our eyes read his name at the convergence of two strong visual lines: the foreshortened outstretched arm of the body and the downward glance of Dr. Deyman. Intuitively, Rembrandt appears to link

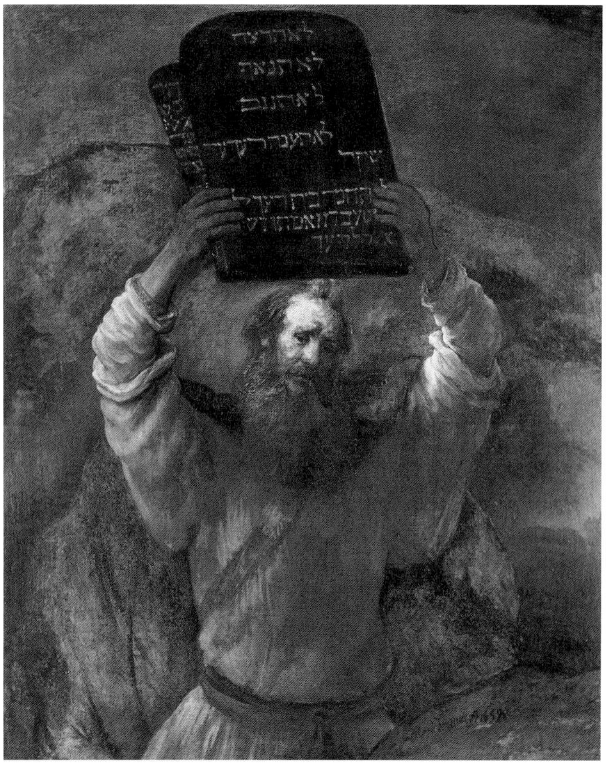

Fig. 25. Rembrandt van Rijn, *Moses Smashing the Tablets of the Law,* 1659. Oil on canvas, 66⅝ x 53¾ in. (168.5 x 136.5 cm). Gemäldegalerie, Berlin / Bridgeman Art Library

his own professionalism as an artist with the scientific calling of the physician, a device that the American Thomas Eakins will employ two centuries later. By contrast, his signature across the rock in the lower foreground of *Moses Smashing the Tablets of the Law,* 1659 (fig. 25), plays a slightly different role, as more of a complementary inscription to the Ten Commandments written on the tablets Moses holds over his head.[30] Though both are set on contrasting stones, the laws are engraved while the signature remains painted, a subtle play on the different forms of authorship.

Johannes Vermeer also signed some of his most important and intriguing pictures. We know his remarkable career is limited to some three dozen paintings, of which perhaps half are signed. (In one or two instances the inscriptions are unreliable and probably from a later date.) Like most of his paintings, Vermeer's lettering is orderly and clear, the blocklike forms and balanced lines as architectural as his painted interiors. Usually, he fused his initials together in a ligature, in some instances placing them conventionally in a corner of the canvas, while in others their location is eye-catching and proximate to a significant element of the composition. His inscriptions usually sit on a wall, reinforcing the flatness of the plane, always parallel to the picture surface, but for the most part set well back into it. Although he undertook occasional religious and allegorical subjects, what we indelibly remember him for are the hushed scenes of everyday life — with the exception of the two Delft city views — giving us single or paired (rarely three) figures engaged in thought, conversation, or creative activity. In these paintings light is at once a physical and metaphysical presence, on the one hand modeling

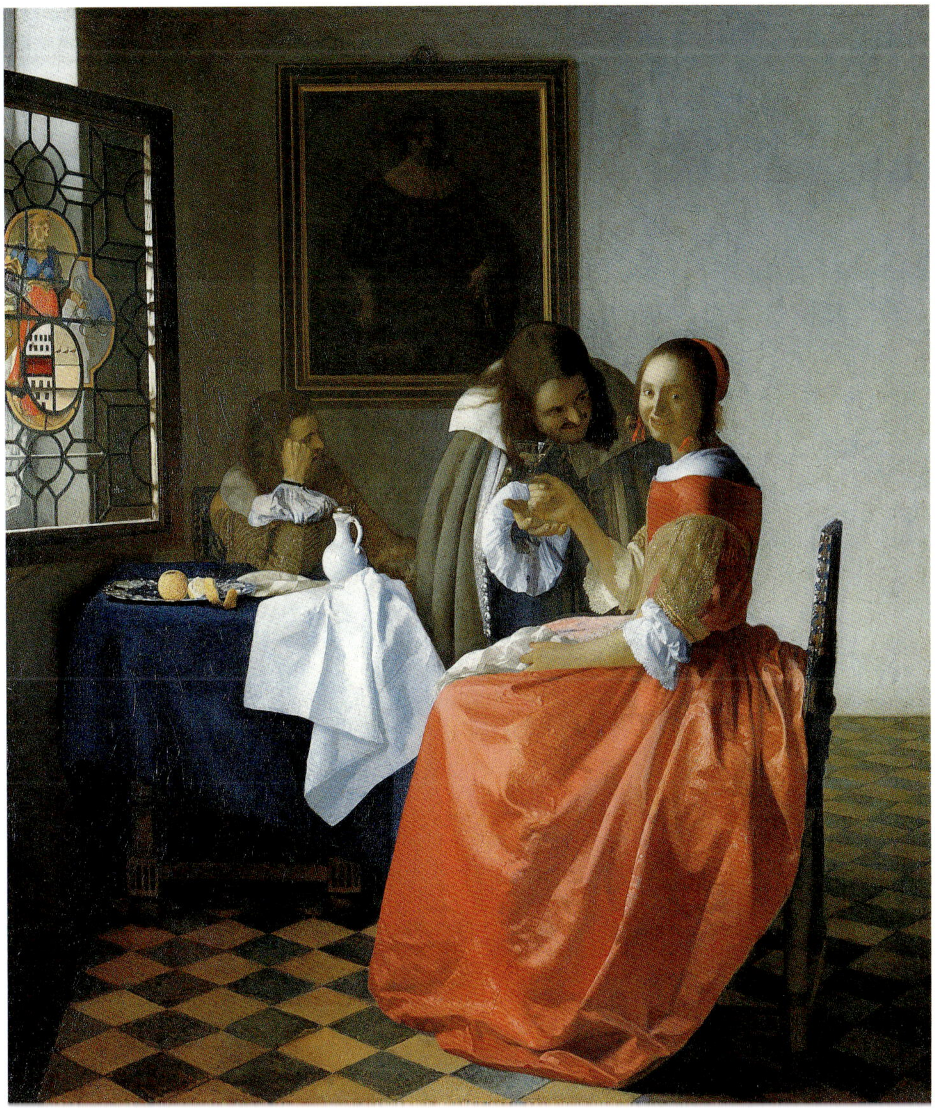

Fig. 26. Johannes Vermeer, *Interior with Two Gentlemen and a Girl with a Wine Glass,* 1662. Oil on canvas, 30 ¾ x 26 ⅜ in. (78 x 67 cm). Herzog Anton Ulrich-Museum, Kunstmuseum des Landes Niedersachsen, Braunschweig, Germany

forms and figures and fixing them in space; at the same time it caresses the sides of faces and the tops of hands in a revelation of emotional or psychological privacy.

So, what are we to make of Vermeer's visible markings of self, which are as calculated as his impeccably wrought perspectives, his geometries of plane and volume, his concentrations of glance and gesture? To cite a few of

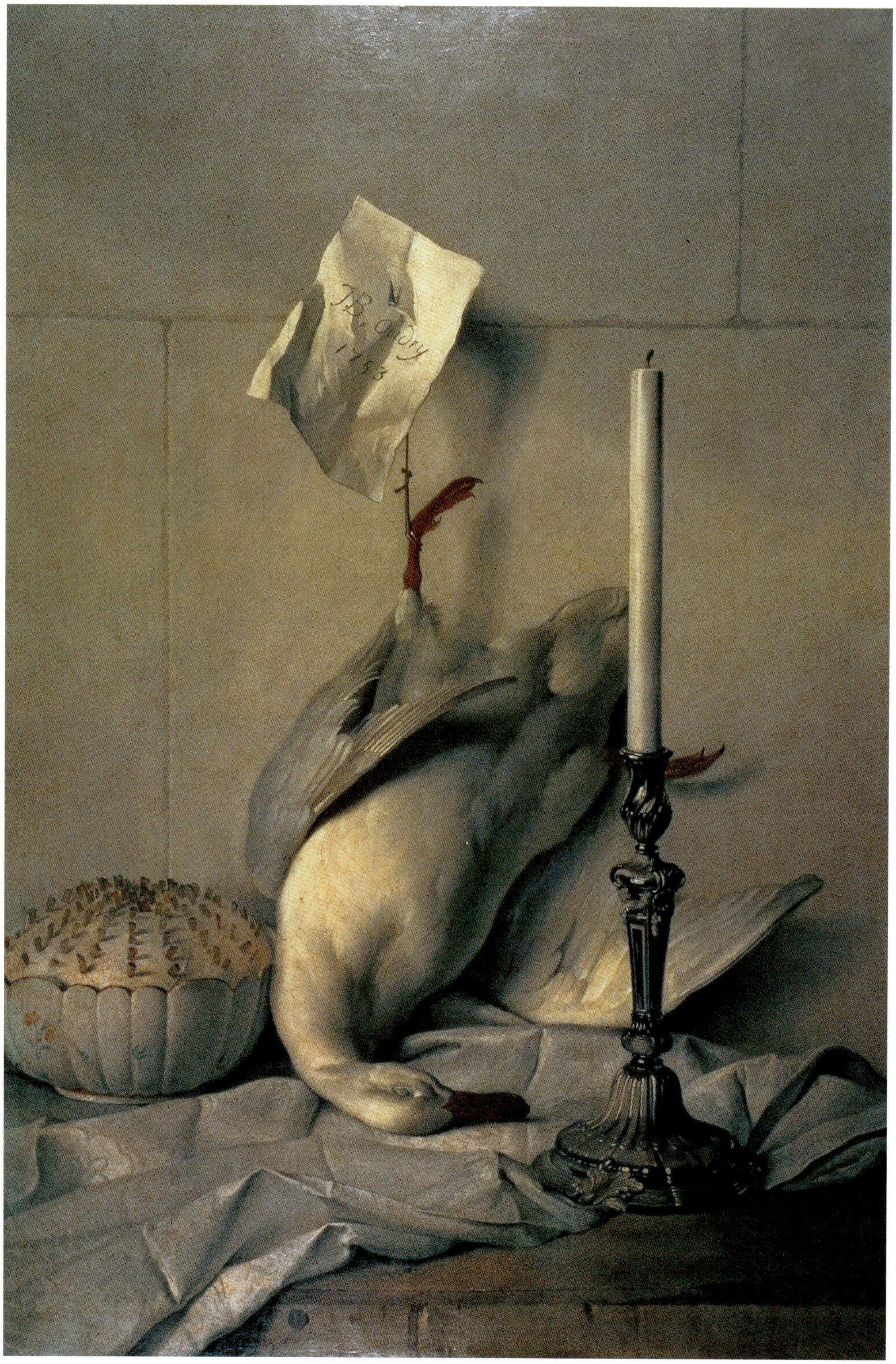
J.B. Oudry
1753

Opposite:
Fig. 29. Jean-Baptiste Oudry, *The White Duck,* 1753. Oil on canvas, dimensions unknown. Private collection / Bridgeman Art Library

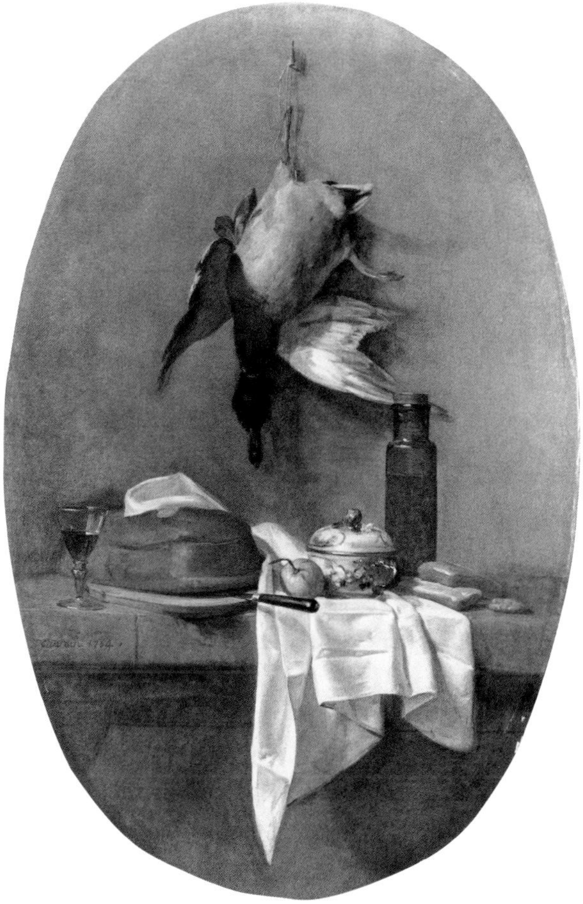

Fig. 30. Jean-Baptiste-Siméon Chardin, *Rafraichissements (Duck Hanging by One Leg, Pâté, Bowl and Jar of Olives),* 1764. Oil on canvas, 59 ¼ x 37 ½ in. (150.5 x 95.3 cm). Museum of Fine Arts, Springfield, Mass. James Gray Collection

taking us from the astronomer's eyes to his outstretched hand touching the globe, itself illuminated on the far side by light coming through the window from the world beyond.

Holland's artistic legacy passed through differing transformations into English, French, and American art of the eighteenth century. But it was in the work of Chardin especially that we see a number of the Dutch conventions for signing pictures continue. Some of his contemporaries, like Jean-Baptiste Oudry, also toyed with cleverly positioned inscriptions; Oudry's *White Duck,* 1753 (fig. 29), springs to mind. An austere symphony of whites, it presents the stillness and coldness of death. On the hook from which the bird hangs, floating in its own space, is the traditional white scrap of paper bearing Oudry's name and the year. Once again, the artifice of still life is the occasion for its maker's appearance in his own illusion, a celebration of his mental and technical abilities. It makes a useful comparison to Chardin's many

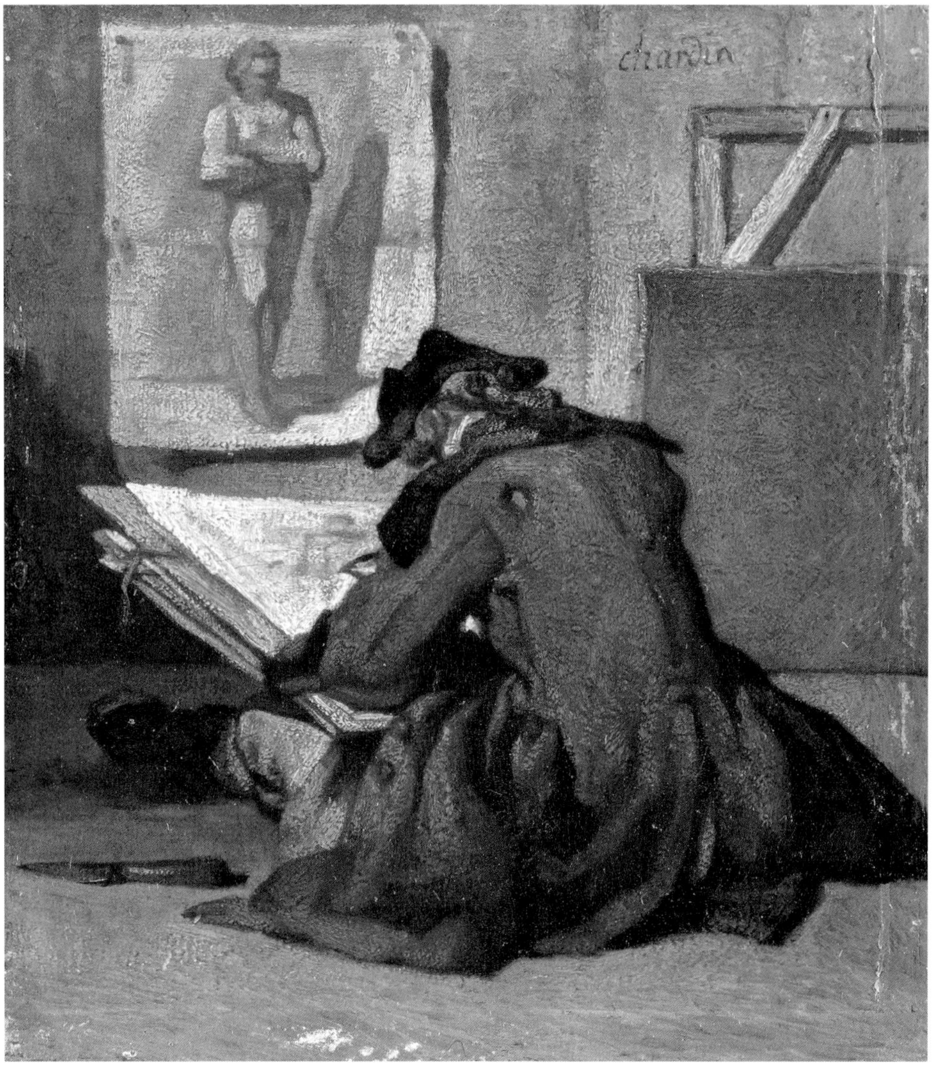

Fig. 31. Jean-Baptiste-Siméon Chardin, *Young Student Drawing*, ca. 1734. Oil on panel, 7 ⅝ x 6 ⅞ in. (19.5 x 17.5 cm). Nationalmuseum, Stockholm / Bridgeman Art Library

versions of dead game still lifes (fig. 30), where the palette is usually much more somber, the touch more textured, and the lighting more ambiguous and internalized. In these works, as in so many of his other tabletop arrangements, he paints his signature and date as if engraved in the stone ledge holding the dead game or food.[32] As we have seen, this location was not new to Chardin, and he serves as an intermediary for American painters like Raphaelle Peale and Harnett, who continue the gesture in the next century.

A prolific painter of still lifes, Chardin went against the grain of the French rococo with his grave and introspective air, his solidly constructed compositions, and psychological seriousness. Born at the very end of the seventeenth century, he lived through much of the eighteenth. After an early apprenticeship, he was accepted into the Académie de Saint-Luc, and began exhibiting his pictures in the late 1720s. During the following decade he started concentrating on kitchen still lifes and his first figure paintings. Some of these, like the still lifes, have suggestively placed signatures: he signed his name in *Young Student Drawing*, ca. 1734 (fig. 31), on the back wall of the studio adjacent to a pinned-up sketch and a couple of leaning canvases. By so doing, he identifies himself with the actions of making art in this image of intense mental and physical concentration. Few if any of the full-length figure scenes have such interior inscriptions, perhaps because they are more elaborate genre narratives. Rather, the series of *Soap Bubbles*, or *Young Man Blowing Bubbles*, ca. 1732–34 (versions in Los Angeles, Paris, and Washington, D.C.), have Chardin's name on the side of the stone ledge. But here the action is minimal, and the figures are seen close-up, so that the forms have the distillation of a monumental still life. Chardin aligns himself with the delicate conjurings of his subject, an artificer of innocent yet serious imaginings.

We are now ready to cross the Atlantic to consider how this range of models is continued and modified in the American tradition. Like its words, America's visual language would take shape through both inheritance and invention. The relationship of American artists to their works would show an awareness of European precedents along with an effort to leave their own marks in distinctive and fresh ways.

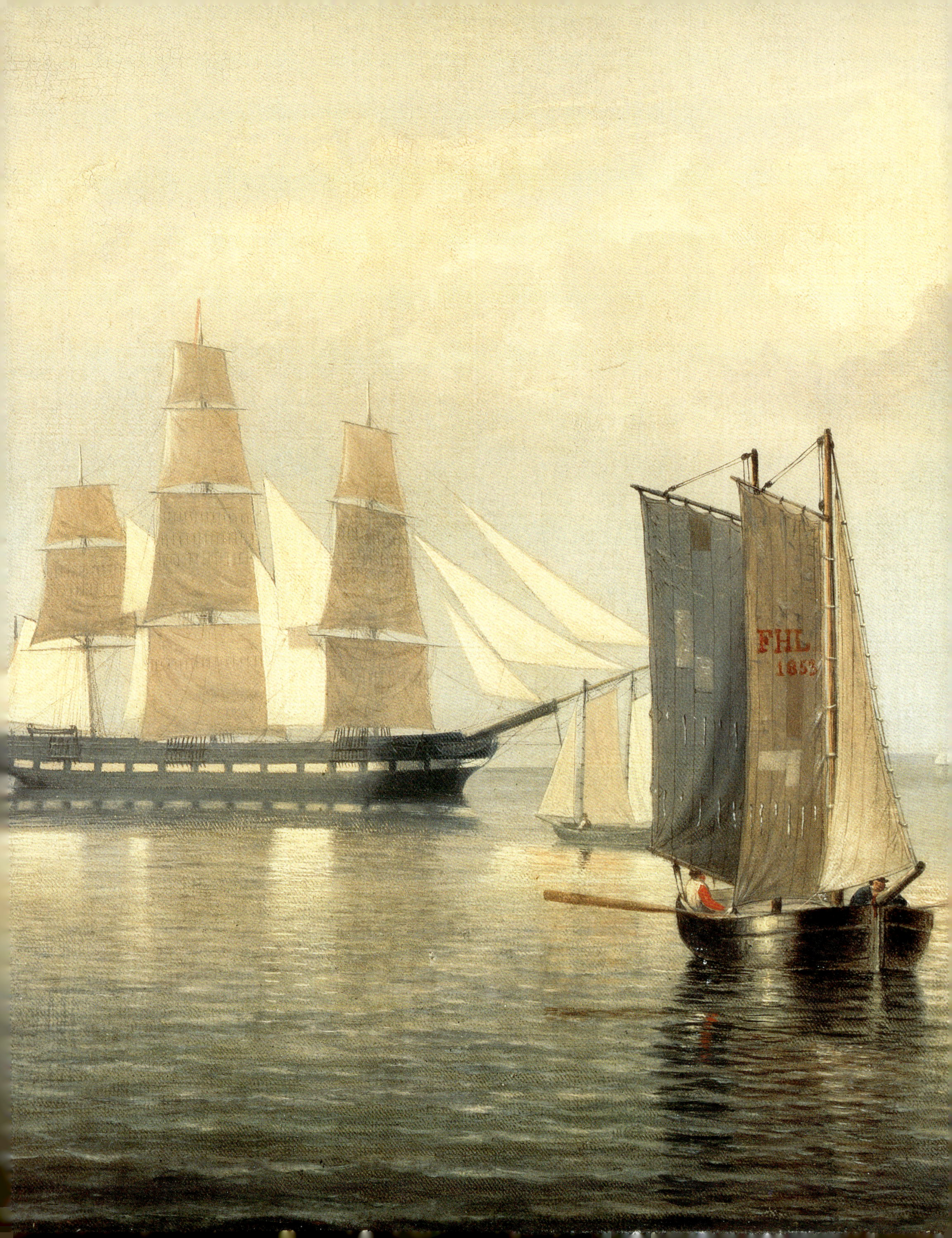
FHL

CHAPTER 2 American History, Still Life, and Landscape

ACKNOWLEDGED TO BE one of the first great masterpieces of American art, *Watson and the Shark* by John Singleton Copley, 1778 (figs. 32 and 33), was actually painted in London. Well known in at least three versions (Washington, D.C., Boston, Detroit, and possibly New York), it was Copley's first important history painting after he fled Boston with his family for London in 1774, at the height of the tensions on the eve of the Revolutionary War. By that time he was one of America's most accomplished painters, surpassing all his predecessors and contemporaries in Boston in technical ability and imagination. He also succeeded in confidently painting portraits for his politically polarized Whig and Tory clients. In London, as an expatriate painter, he would in effect be beginning a second career. But as Copley's exact contemporary from Philadelphia, the Quaker Benjamin West, reminded him, portraiture would not be enough to secure him an international reputation. West had left the British Colonies for London and the Continent as a youth, and by the time of the Revolution was well established in London — West was a founding member of the Royal Academy and a favorite of the court. He urged Copley to come abroad to experience the Grand Tour and engage in the high artistic callings of history, mythology, and religious painting.

At West's suggestion, Copley sent to an exhibition in London one of his best Boston portraits, the affectionate painting of his stepbrother Henry Pelham known as *Boy with a Squirrel*, 1765 (Museum of Fine Arts, Boston). In a famous exchange of correspondence West reported back that the London critics found Copley's work too "liney" by the painterly standards of the English rococo. Instead of the qualities that had made his depictions so appealing to American patrons — the solid realism of form, meticulous rendering of textures and details, and hard gleaming areas of color — his new public

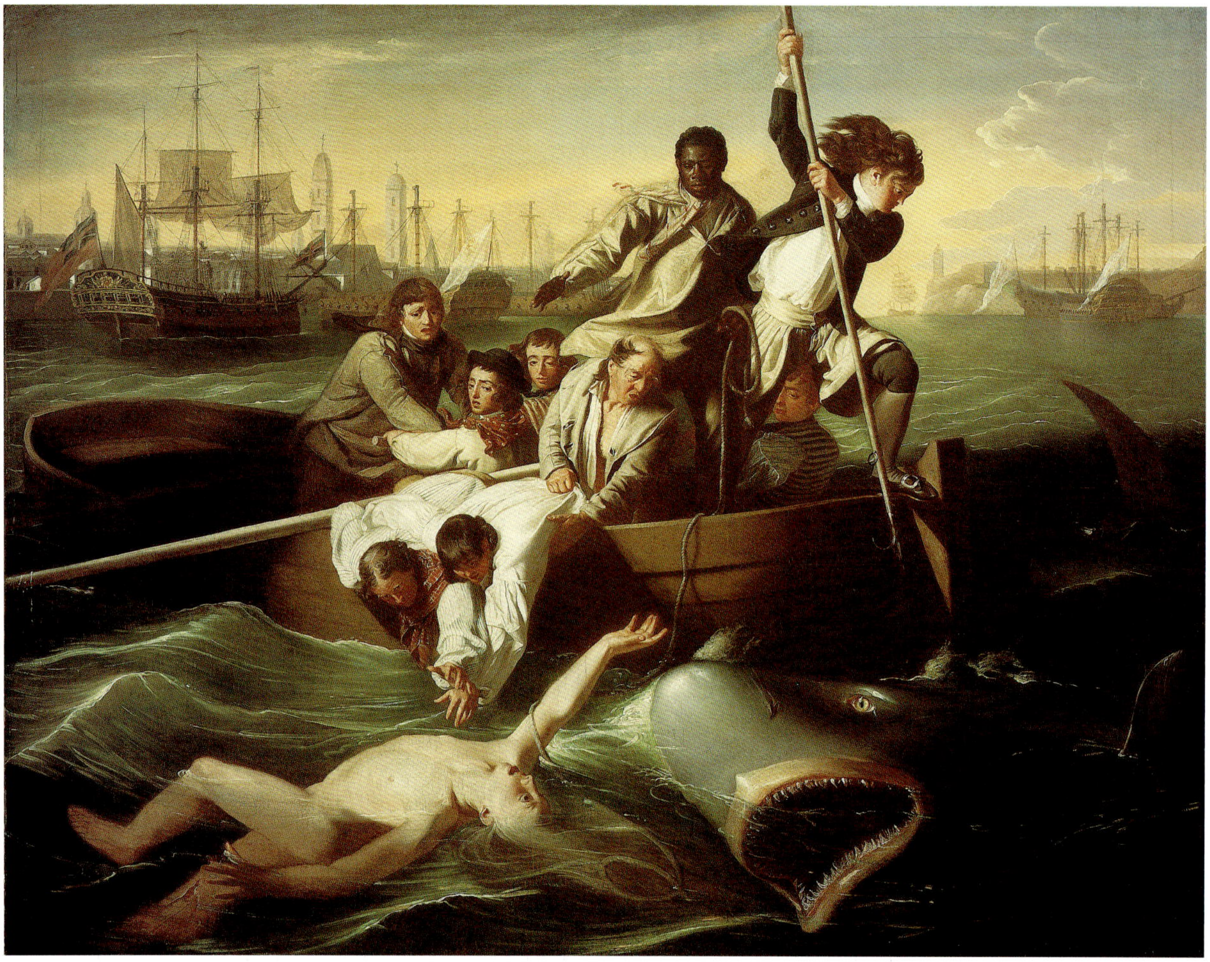

Fig. 32. John Singleton Copley, *Watson and the Shark*, 1778. Oil on canvas, 70 ⅜ x 72 ¼ in. (178.8 x 183.5 cm). Museum of Fine Arts, Boston. Gift of Mrs. George von Lengerke Meyer

called for looser brushwork and more nuanced effects of light and atmosphere. His first two ambitious efforts in England were also his first large-scale multi-figure compositions, *The Copley Family*, 1776–77 (National Gallery of Art, Washington, D.C.) and *Watson*. Both were self-portraits of a sort, the first a literal one of himself among his recently reunited family, depicting his optimistic emotional life; the second a more coded picture of the artist's turbulent political life at this moment.

The subject is well documented in the literature on Copley. The event depicted is a dramatic rescue from a shark attack on young Brook Watson in

Havana Harbor in 1749. Born in England, Watson was brought up in Boston by a merchant whose ships did business in the West Indies. After the attack, he settled in Canada, before moving to London and a prominent mercantile career supplying provisions to the British colonial army. He probably met Copley through acquaintances they shared with Sir Joshua Reynolds, and likely commissioned the shark picture, recalling for the artist the essential details of the gory incident, in which he lost the lower portion of his right leg.[1] Much recent critical literature has focused on the single black figure at the apex of the group of rescuers, a possible emblem of the triangular slave trade between England, Africa, and the Americas. Modernist views have noted the mirrored gestures of the outstretched arm of this figure and Watson's directly below, and their further visual linkage by the rope descending at the center from one to the other.[2] Is it too easy to associate both figures as marginalized, both victims? Copley is less than explicit about his political message, because this figure is also in the position of a calm divinity overseeing the salvation of a mortal from the threshold of hell.

Certainly, Copley intended to present his scene as an elevated moral experience, however charged the racial or national elements of this New World drama might be. We know he borrowed from several Renaissance and antique sources in painting and sculpture for his figural poses. Among the better-known are Raphael's *Transfiguration* in the Sistine Chapel, likely seen by Copley on his 1774–75 visit to Italy, for the overall composition; prints after Raphael's *The Miraculous Draft of the Fishes* and Rubens's *Jonah Thrown into the Sea* for the figures reaching into the water; possibly Rubens's various Lion Hunt compositions, with which Copley would also have been familiar through engravings, for the standing harpoon bearer; and *The Gladiator*, an antique marble in the Villa Borghese, for the outstretched form of Watson himself.[3] Finally, Copley was more immediately stimulated by the Revolutionary example of his associate Benjamin West, whose *Death of General Wolfe*, 1770 (National Gallery of Canada, Ottawa), was the first painting to present a modern history subject in contemporary dress. West's painting possessed all the high moral seriousness and classical and religious allusions of traditional history or mythology painting but with a daring new relevance. Copley strove for a similar effect.

Where in all this complex and provocative mix do we find the artist himself? Now it is time to observe his signature, discreetly yet prominently situated on the inside sternboard of the boat: "JSCopley.P.1778 — " (see fig. 33).[4] Not only is this a place where his name might be readily visible, but it

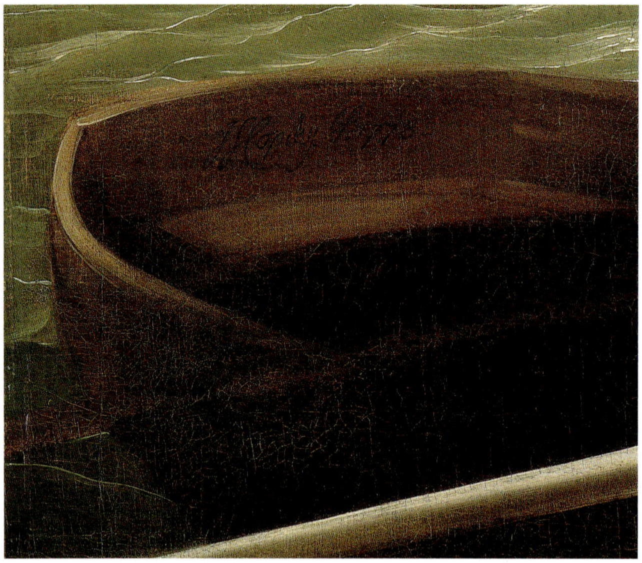

Fig. 33. John Singleton Copley, *Watson and the Shark* (detail of fig. 32), 1778

clearly locates the painter at the center of his work. Normally, the stern of a vessel is where the captain stands or sits, but here it is empty, except, by implication, by Copley, who oversees, as it were, both the making of his painting and the New World subject matter it depicts that would have been of natural interest to him. He is in the middle of a stylistic transition from his linear American art to the painterly English tradition, and from rendering individual portraits to what we might describe here as group portraiture in action. Different individuals explicitly modeled for each of these figures, while the whole addresses the larger social and political world of trade and race that Copley had entered with his move to London. Let us not forget that although he was now painting in London his subject lay on the American side of the Atlantic. His name *in* rather than *on* this great canvas suggestively reveals many of the tensions of his Anglo-American identity — or identities — at this time.

Following in West's footsteps, the Maryland-born Charles Willson Peale also responded to the lure of London. After some early training at home and a visit to Copley's studio in Boston, Peale went abroad in 1766 to work for two years in West's studio. But unlike both West and Copley, he made the important decision to return home, where he served for a time in Washington's army during the Revolution and pursued his artistic career in federal America. As such, his is the first body of original art by a figure of the colonial generation committed to a vision of the young nation. Throughout his versatile and successful professional life, Peale would identify with the callings of contemporary art and science. Not only did he paint his self-portrait on many occasions during his career — as if by examining himself he could know the world — but he also sired several generations of remarkably accomplished and inventive artists. Although a painter of occasional landscapes and of portraits for a variety of patrons, Peale arguably did his best work

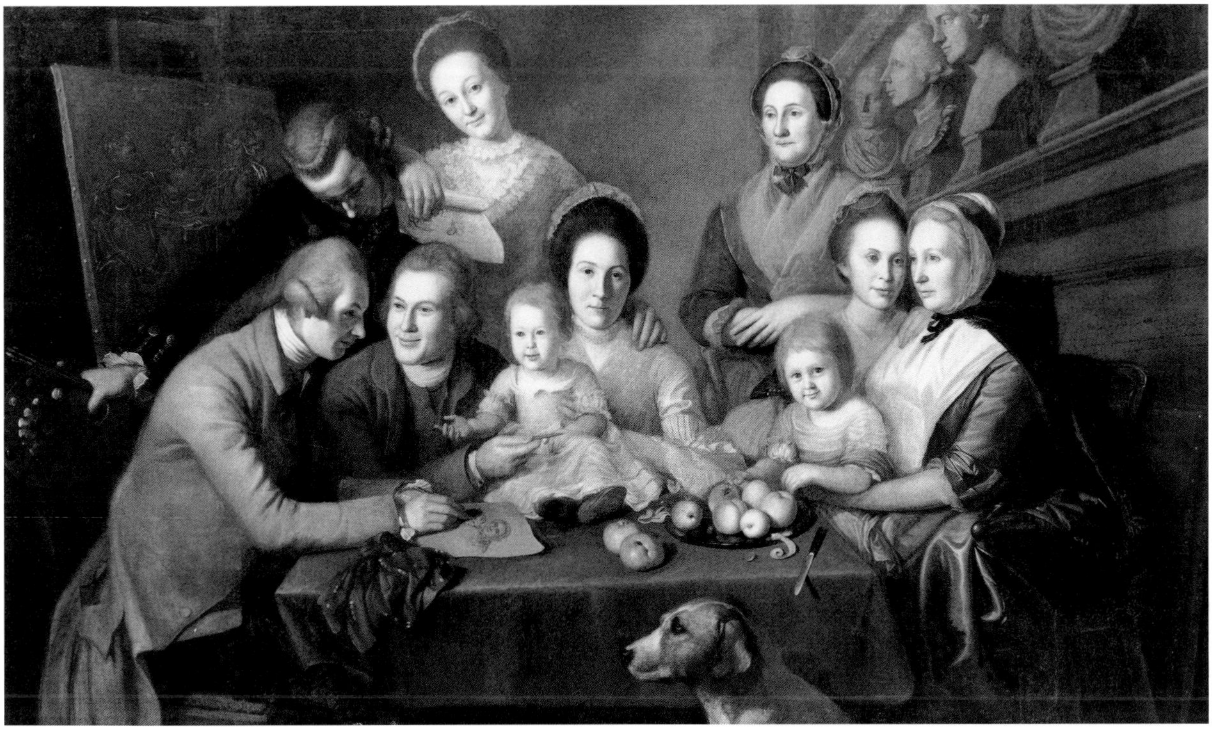

Fig. 34. Charles Willson Peale, *The Peale Family*, 1770–73/1809. Oil on canvas, 56 ½ x 89 ½ in. (143.5 x 227.3 cm). Collection of the New-York Historical Society

when he repeatedly returned to his family, often represented as painters or scientists, for his central subject matter.

His earliest ambitious group composition was just that: *The Peale Family*, 1770–73/1809 (fig. 34). At first observation it seems a quite conventional portrait, following the family gatherings painted by John Smibert, Robert Feke, West, and Copley in preceding years, which Peale could well have known. Yet it soon becomes evident that this is more than several individuals posing for their group likeness. From their glances we realize there are interactions among them, and from the details around them we can see that they are immersed in the collecting and making of art. Centered around Peale's wife and youngest daughter at the time, various members of his family from different generations pay attention either to the unseen artist at the viewer's vantage point or to Peale's brother engaged in drawing their mother opposite under the artist's supervision. As time went by, Peale included other relatives, culminating with the addition of the family dog, Argus, front and center.

More than portraiture, Peale's painting pays tribute to the various subjects and media of art: sculpted busts at the upper right, a canvas of the three Graces in the upper left background, the drawing and the still life on the table, and the genre element of the dog. Casual as the disposition of the peaches seems to be, their rounded forms are echoed by the ovoid heads above. In other words, almost all the subjects that Peale and his family of artists would paint in his lifetime and that his family would go on to paint after him are present here with the figures themselves. Peale "signed" this clever transformation of a family portrait in at least four subtle ways. The most obvious is the inscription he placed at the lower right edge of the canvas: "C.W. Peale painted these portraits of his family / in 1773. / Wishing to finish every work he had undertaken / — completed this picture in 1809!" He is present in the role of painter who holds his working palette and brushes at the left, but more emblematically, he leaves his name in the pictograph of the peach *peel* lower right; the projecting table knife by its side is also a stand-in for the painter's palette knife. Finally, the ongoing act of working on this self-imagery over four decades turns it into a family history, a visual autobiography.

Such conceptual wit likewise marked two of Peale's other major images, the first of which, *The Staircase Group*, 1795 (fig. 35), is perhaps his most engaging and technically magical canvas. Not just a work of masterful realism, its life-sized format, intentionally mounted in an actual doorframe with an attached lower step, makes this the first important work of trompe l'oeil in American art. Peale gives us two of his artist sons, Raphaelle in the center foreground and Titian at the upper left, turning as they ascend a household staircase. Given the immediacy and informality of their poses and glances outward, we have the feeling that Peale wanted to capture them as if he had just called out to them from before his easel in the studio. Titian's tight, spiral posture pivots around the left edge of the staircase, while Raphaelle's motion upward to the left mirrors the spatial volume itself while twisting fully around to engage both his father's eyes and ours.

In the American tradition a full-length portrait so casual and direct in its effect was utterly new. Like *The Peale Family* before it, this blends careful likenesses and formal harmony. Balancing the several crossing diagonals, for example, of stairs, legs, brushes, and maul stick are the repeating rhythms of ovals in the two heads, the wallpaper, Raphaelle's brass buttons, and his palette and paint daubs. In these calculated designs, in the seamless flow between painted and real space, and in the self-conscious presence of the artist/father, Peale crafted perhaps his most original image of self and family. He

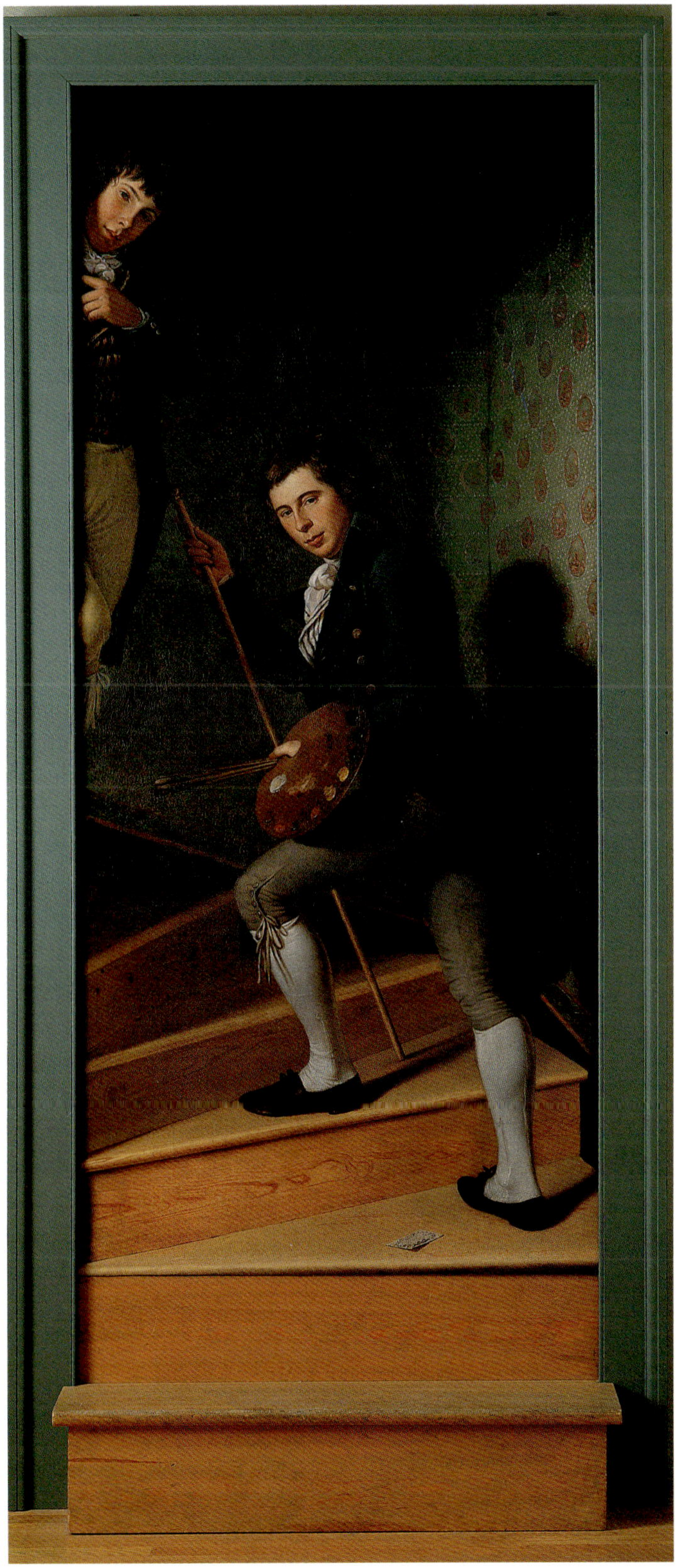

Fig. 35.
Charles Willson Peale,
The Staircase Group (Portrait of Raphaelle Peale and Titian Ramsey Peale), 1795. Oil on canvas, 89 x 39 ½ in. (226.1 x 100.3 cm). Philadelphia Museum of Art. George W. Elkins Collection

is present, of course, as the implied painter, the one looking into his boys' eyes, and inferentially on the bottom step, in the key detail that is either his calling card or a printed ticket to his museum. Either way, this latter-day *cartellino* (compare figs. 6 and 30) signals that Peale both made this work and made himself a part of it.

If *The Staircase Group* is an expression of Peale's artistic enterprise, then *The Exhumation of the Mastodon*, 1806 (fig. 36), is the corollary for his scientific life. Technically perhaps not as beguiling as the earlier painting, it is equally original in its modification of traditional typologies. It is in part a landscape painting, the setting for the genre activities in the foreground. But it is easy to recognize that this, too, is an extensive group portrait, with Peale and his family at the center of the action. The project that the artist directs here also turns this into a history painting that is personal as well as public and national in its narratives. The event is thoroughly documented in the Peale literature: the artist had read in the newspapers about a discovery of some mastodon bones in an upstate New York farmer's field. In the summer of 1801 he left Philadelphia for New York, where he boarded a boat to travel up the Hudson. En route he made numerous watercolor sketches of the passing landscape, a subject that would soon dominate the attention of the next generation of American painters. Peale's mission had the support of Thomas Jefferson, the recently inaugurated president of the United States and head of the American Philosophical Society.

On his arrival at the farm near West Point, Peale contrived the excavation machinery and oversaw the clearing of the bones from the muddy pit. During the following months he managed to assemble nearly two complete skeletons with the assistance of his sons, installing one skeleton in his new museum in Philadelphia and sending the other on tour in Europe as a display of American natural history and antiquity. The large painting, upon which he began work soon after, was also a contrivance, in that it blended actuality with imagination. Only his son Rembrandt accompanied him to the site, yet the picture depicts eleven of his children by his side or nearby. Confirming this as a pictorial autobiography is the presence of both his present wife and one earlier deceased.[5] Peale stands gesturing by the edge of the pit, in the pose of the Apollo Belvedere, reminding us of the elevated tradition of the antique. His outstretched arm also ties together the family gathering and the communal effort under way before them. Further, Peale's self-portrait triangulates with two other prominent figures: the farm's owner, John Masten, climbing up the ladder in the foreground and returning Peale's glance, and

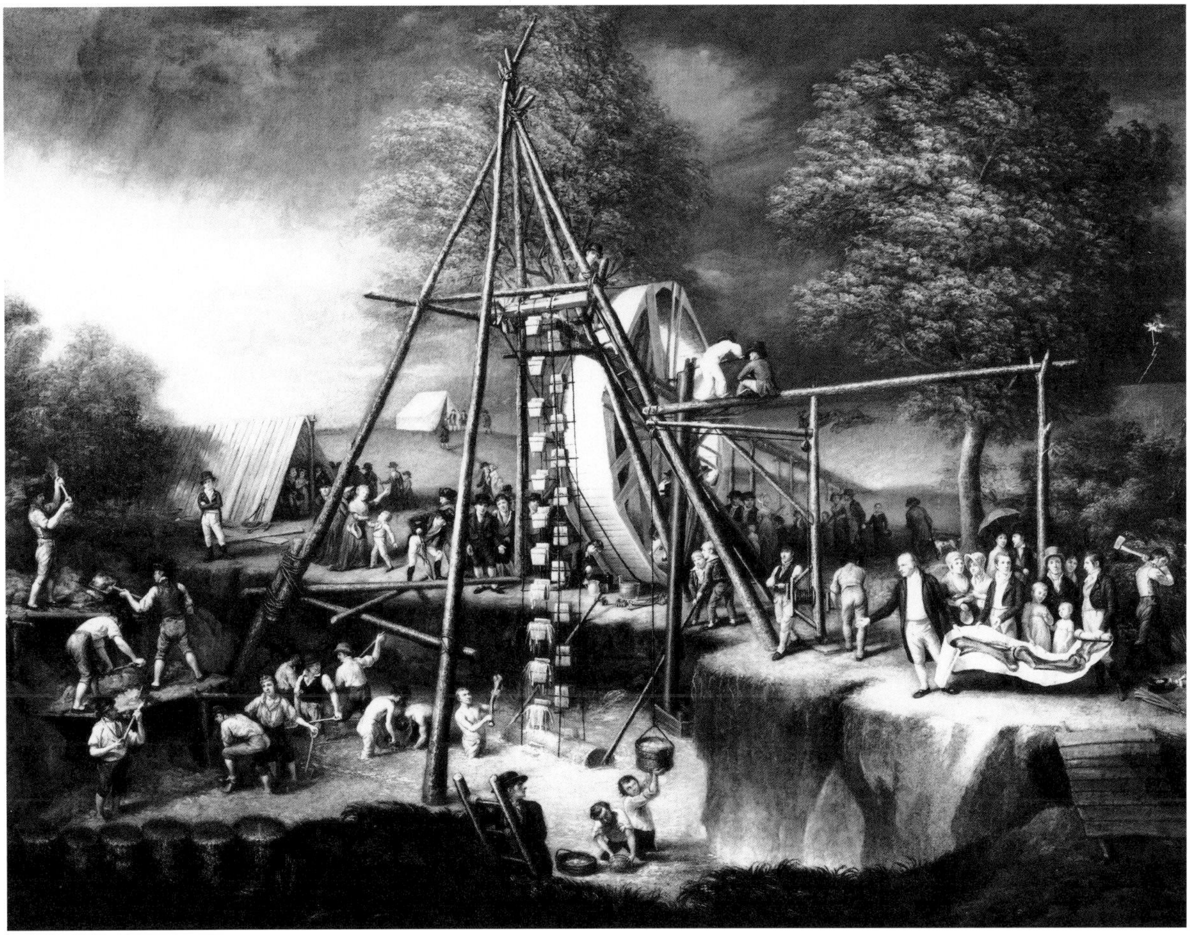

Fig. 36. Charles Willson Peale, *The Exhumation of the Mastodon,* 1806. Oil on canvas, 50 x 62 ½ in. (127 x 158.8 cm). The Maryland Historical Society, Baltimore, Md.

Alexander Wilson, the artist's neighbor in Baltimore and founder of American ornithology, who surveys the scene from the left background.

Ironically, we see almost nothing of the mastodon, only a fragment held up by a man in the center of the pit, and the leg bones depicted in the unscrolled drawing at the right. But here precisely is where Peale presents himself — in his full-length self-portrait, grasping the sheet of paper, which unfurls like the earlier peel from a peach, in short, a pictographic signature referring equally to his labors as an artist and scientist. Peale passed this visual pun on to his son Raphaelle, who became prominent in still-life painting over the coming decade or so, and who repeatedly exploited the device as his own visual signature.

Raphaelle was born on the eve of the Revolution, the eldest surviving son of Charles Willson Peale and his first wife. He grew up in his father's artistic shadow, and like others in the family attempted a variety of subjects before concentrating on still lifes. In his maturity, his paintings demonstrated an imaginativeness and technical finesse that outstripped his father's, even though his father considered Raphaelle a personal and professional disappointment. Recent historians have speculated on the conflict between the two as a possible explanation for Raphaelle's highly introspective, even hermetic, art, seemingly private and distant in its silence. His unhappy marriage, unreliability, and evident alcoholism constituted a life of disorder that may well have found compensation in the tranquil clarity and orderliness of his compositions.

Raphaelle also devoted himself to a subject matter theretofore deemed the least significant in the European hierarchy of artistic subjects, which had traditionally placed history, religion, and mythology above the more lowly categories of portraiture, landscape, genre, and still life. Some have argued that this realignment by Raphaelle was both a personal declaration of artistic independence and, in its humbleness and ordinariness, a democratizing of art.[6] Certainly, the elegant balances in his arrangements, the isolation of the parts while linking them together through harmonious internal rhythms, beautifully embody the political and social spirit of federal America. We may never fully decipher Raphaelle's psychological association with his still-life subjects, but from his numerous signatures, written and pictured, we can find someone deeply immersed in work that teases us with its possible associations and meanings.

The fact that Raphaelle placed himself so often within his compositions indicates how much he prized his technical prowess and conjuring powers of near illusionism. He is believed to have painted approximately one hundred and fifty still lifes — of which some fifty survive — in a concentrated period of a couple of decades. Among known examples, nearly two thirds are signed in the Dutch manner, that is, along the side edge of the table supporting the fruits arranged above. We know that Cotán's work was exhibited in Philadelphia in 1818 (see fig. 10), at a time when Peale was also showing his pictures at the Pennsylvania Academy, but Peale must also have seen imported Dutch pictures, whether originals, copies, or translations through prints. His inscriptions are usually quite specific about the subject, date, location, and maker, for example: "Apples & Fox Grapes by Raphaelle Peale / Phila. Sept. 7 1815."[7] They suggest how closely he tied himself to his art.

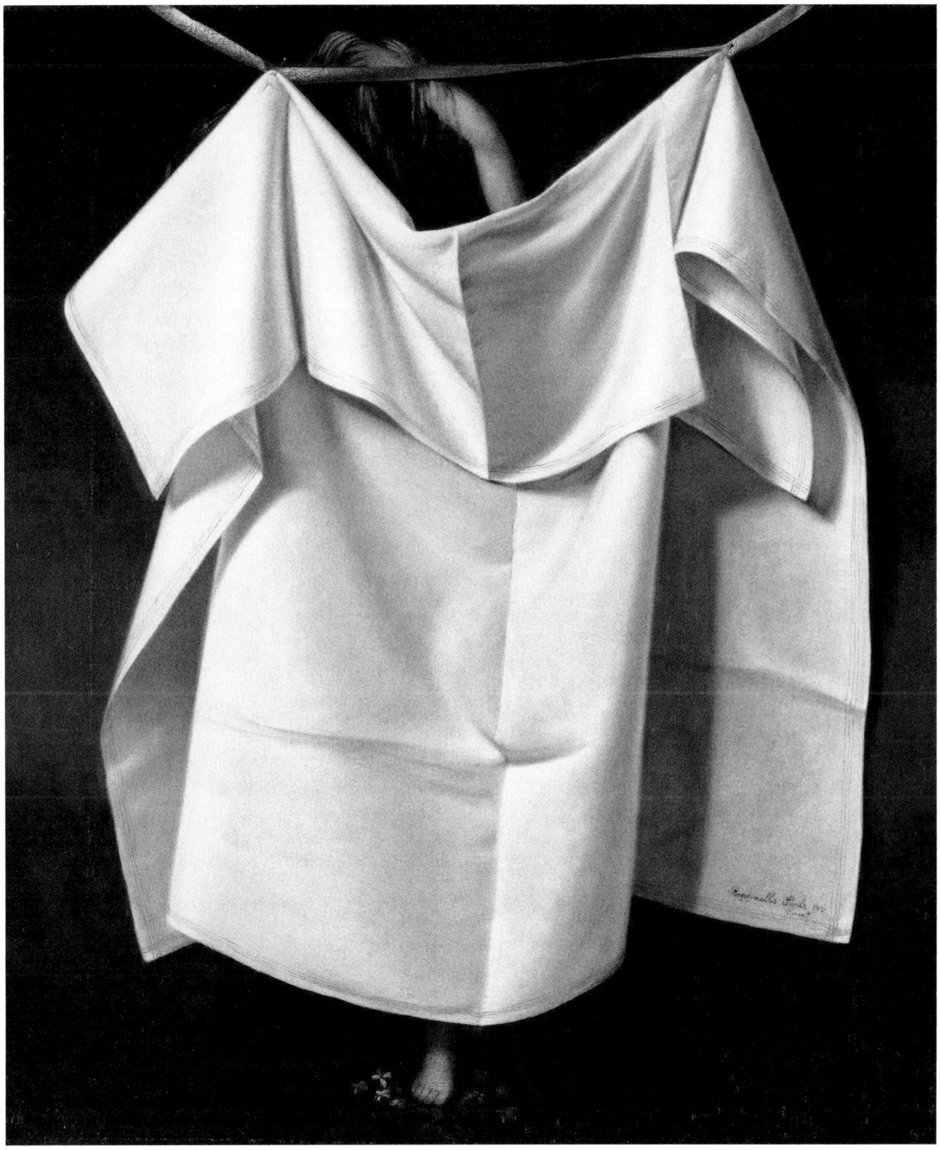

Fig. 37. Raphaelle Peale, *Venus Rising from the Sea—A Deception (After the Bath)*, ca. 1822. Oil on canvas, 29 ¼ x 24 ⅛ in. (74.3 x 61.3 cm). The Nelson-Atkins Museum of Art, Kansas City, Mo. Purchase

On one level, it is quite possible that the specific fruits and vegetables, as well as the dating, relate, as Jules Prown has argued, to the Peale family gardens: the image depicted would coincide with whatever ripe produce had been brought to the family table. For his part, Nicolai Cikovsky links Raphaelle's precision, on the one hand to his wish for independent control over his subject, and on the other to modern science, and its processes of empirical observation. Alexander Nemerov in turn emphasizes the context of Philadelphia as a leading center at the time of medicine, physiology, and natural science. In fact, all of these interpretations are plausible, and help us to see these still lifes as subjects intimately bound up with Peale's personal experience, rather than detached formal exercises.

Although Peale most often signed on the table edge, there is the singular example of *Venus Rising from the Sea — A Deception,* ca. 1822 (fig. 37), in which Peale has signed his name along the lower right border of the hanging cloth concealing the nude Venus. No doubt this gesture is in part an authorial reminder of his illusionist accomplishment, as signaled by the title. Nominally, the painting depicts what has been identified as an engraving (or a painting after a print) of Venus derived from a work by James Barry. We may speculate about how this tantalizing yet suppressed image of the goddess of love, partially covered by the unfolded cloth, might have taunted Peale's wife and hinted at the difficulties in their marriage. What is sure is that it deals just as much with the tricks of art as with the deceptions of love. In effect, Peale signs his name here to two canvases at once.

Following his father's precedent, Raphaelle elaborately signed his name in a handful of pictures with the pictograph of a curling fruit peel. At least two display oranges and one a peach; the peels in all of them are more exaggerated and attenuated than the one in Charles Willson's *Peale Family* (see fig. 34). Although ultimately the inspiration goes back to Dutch still lifes like those of Willem Claez. Heda, Raphaelle's seem intentionally prominent and centered. Indeed, they scroll out in thick curlicues not unlike the calligraphy of a handwritten signature. *Still Life with Orange and Book,* ca. 1815 (private collection), is quite simple: a reductive juxtaposition of an orange resting atop a book, embodiments perhaps of the worlds of nature and art, of learning through observation and reading, both worlds familiar to Peale.

Still Life with Oranges, ca. 1818 (fig. 38), gives us both forms of Peale's signatures. Across the table edge — which is visually coincident with the canvas plane itself — he wrote, "Painted for the Collection of John A. Alston Esqr. / The Patron of living American Artists Raphaelle Peale Phila." Paralleling this in form and meaning is his orange peel above.[8] Together, they appear to celebrate the happy collaboration of artistic patronage. A third variation, *Peaches,* ca. 1817 (fig. 39), introduces another element with possibly suggestive personal associations: the pearl-handled knife that appears in at least four paintings. In *Lemons and Sugar,* ca. 1822 (Reading Public Museum and

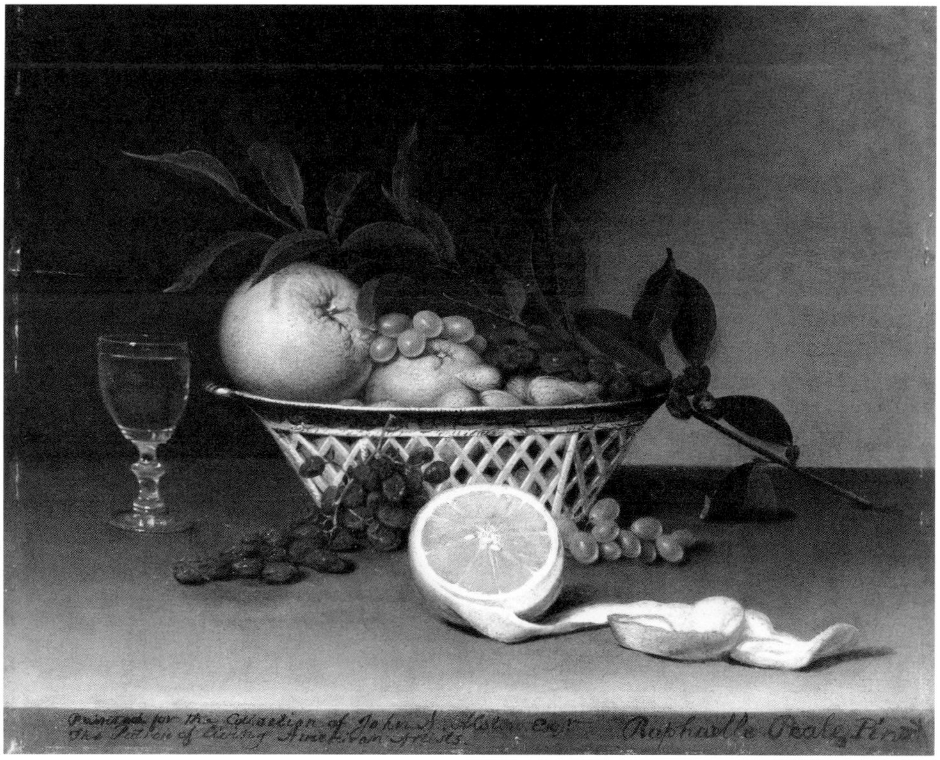

Fig. 38. Raphaelle Peale, *Still Life with Oranges*, ca. 1818. Oil on wood panel, 18 ⅝ x 22 ⅞ in. (47.4 x 58.3 cm). Toledo Museum of Art, Toledo, Ohio. Purchased with funds from the Florence Scott Libbey bequest in memory of her father, Maurice A. Scott

Art Gallery, Reading, Pennsylvania), it extends from the side of an open basket down to the table surface. The knife lies partially covered in *Fruit Piece with Peaches Covered by a Handkerchief*, ca. 1819 (private collection); it also lies partly beneath the opened slice of melon in *Still Life with Watermelon*, 1822 (Berry-Hill Galleries, New York). But in *Peaches* it provocatively sticks out from the center of the peeled peach. Here, too, it is a tool with multiple identities, commonly a part of the preparation and consumption of food, but also akin to the palette knife often used by painters. A third function aligns it with the realm of anatomy and dissection, a flourishing modern science in Peale's Philadelphia, as Nemerov shows. Given Raphaelle's contentious relations with his father and his wife, however, we might further be prompted to wonder about these aggressive displays of flayed skins and knife plunged into soft flesh.[9] Whatever the extent of Peale's expressions of self in his art, he clearly signed his name in a variety of literal and subliminal ways.

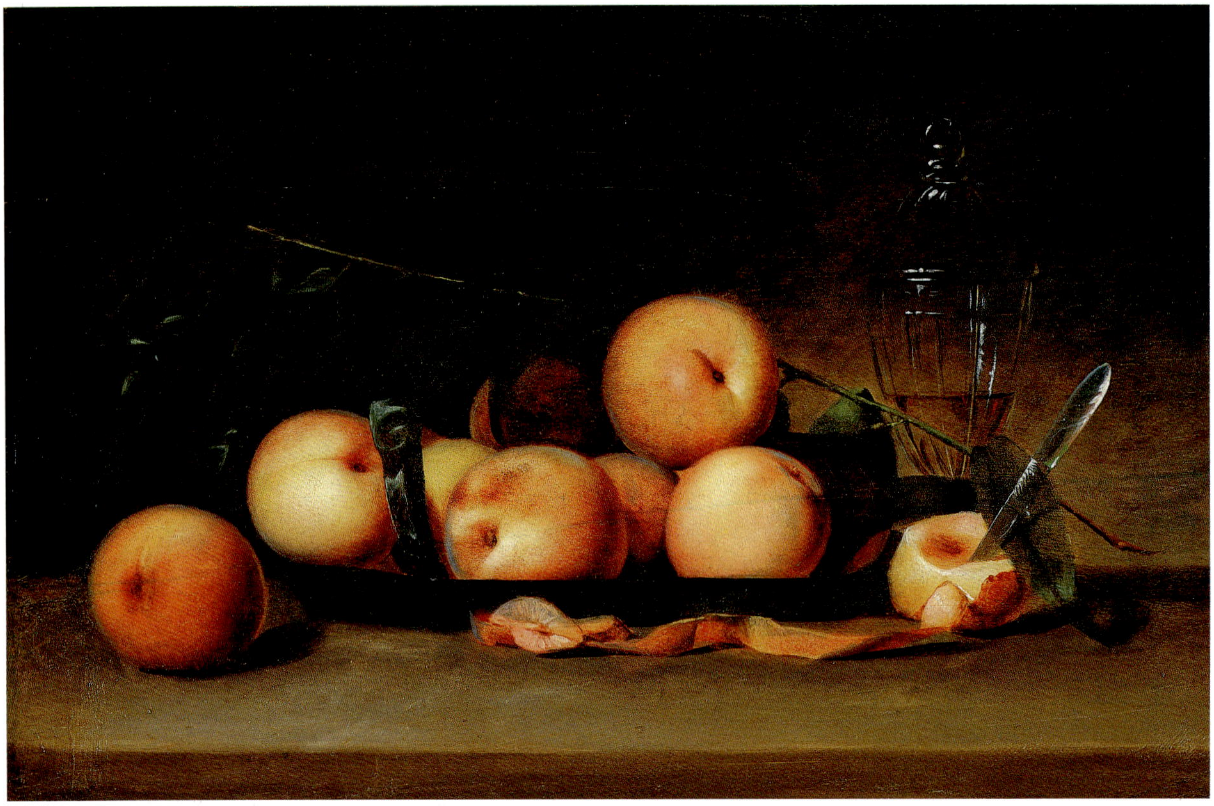

Fig. 39. Raphaelle Peale, *Peaches*, ca. 1817. Oil on wood panel, 13 ⅛ x 19 ¾ in. (33.3 x 50.2 cm). Courtesy of the Richard York Gallery, New York

These symbolic as well as actual signatures tell us about both authorship and autobiography.

By the 1820s another member of the family, James Peale, who was Charles Willson's brother and Raphaelle's uncle, had also taken up still-life painting, inspired and instructed by his relatives. At his best, his paintings approach the quality of his nephew's, though they tend to be more densely packed and finicky in detail. He followed their practice of signing some works on the side of his tables, but also enjoyed using the device of playing on the family name with coiled fruit peels in the foreground. One of his most beautifully executed works, *Fruit in a Chinese Export Basket*, 1822 (fig. 40), finds his signature unusually placed on the center panel of the porcelain basket. Like its Dutch predecessors, the swirling calligraphy of the inscription — "JPeale/1822" — subtly complements the sinuous rhythms of the surrounding fruit and vine stems. Unlike the charged mystery and

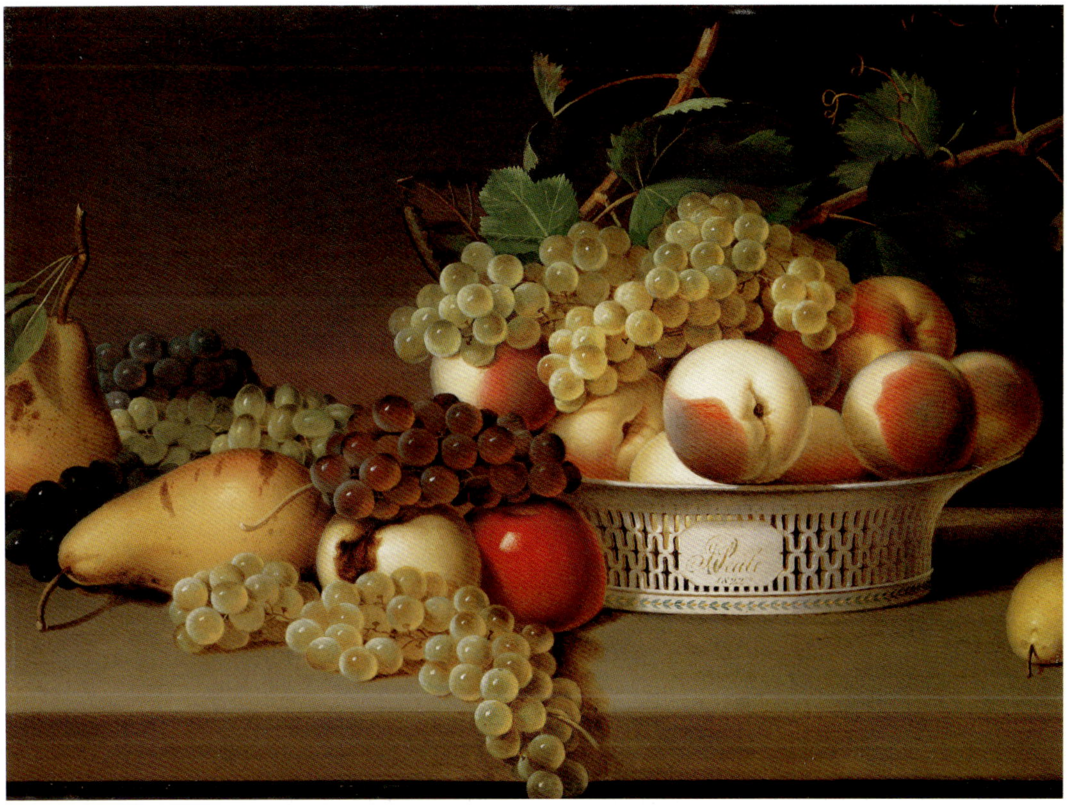

Fig. 40. James Peale, *Fruit in a Chinese Export Basket,* 1822. Oil on canvas laid down on cradled panel, 16 5/8 x 21 3/4 in. (42.2 x 55.2 cm). Private collection. Courtesy of the Kennedy Galleries, New York

psychological tensions apparent in Raphaelle's work, both James's signature and his composition retain a relatively decorative character. At the same time, his name here is a proud statement of the artist's handiwork.

Just as Raphaelle's and James's still-life paintings were reaching the high point of their maturity, landscape was emerging as the foremost subject of American artists. Thomas Cole has the distinction of being the country's first significant painter to be born in the new century (1801) and the leader of its first national landscape school, focused on the Hudson River Valley. Born in England, Cole emigrated as a youth. After some travel through the frontier landscape of western Pennsylvania and Ohio, Cole made his way to the art centers of Philadelphia and then New York in the mid-1820s. With the opening of the Erie Canal and the founding of the National Academy of Design in 1825, New York City was poised to ascend to national economic

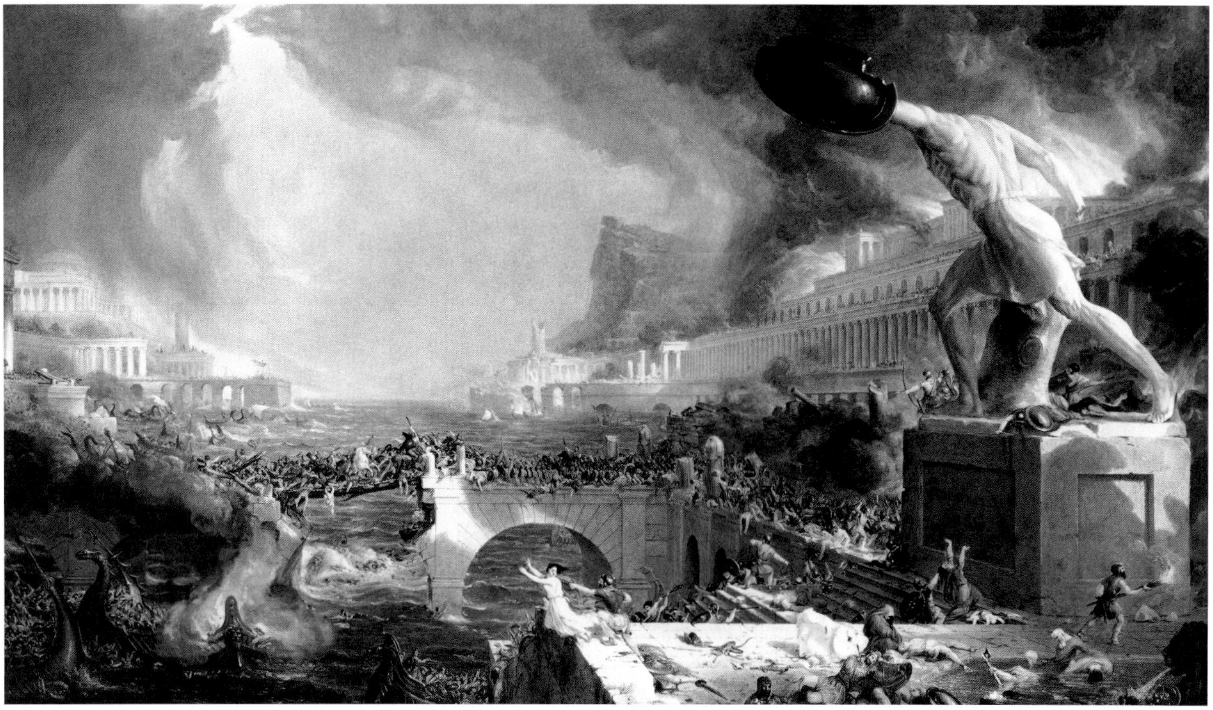

Fig. 41. Thomas Cole, *The Course of Empire: Destruction*, 1836. Oil on canvas, 33 ¼ x 63 ¼ in. (84.5 x 160.6 cm). Collection of the New-York Historical Society

and artistic prominence. Like his literary contemporaries in Boston, Ralph Waldo Emerson and Henry David Thoreau, Cole, along with Asher B. Durand, William Cullen Bryant, and others in New York, now embraced nature as the distinctive embodiment of national identity and destiny.

After his first exhibitions and sales of landscape paintings in the late 1820s, Cole soon established his reputation as the leading interpreter of American scenery with his idealized, allegorical views of nature. During the early 1830s he returned to England and Europe, reacquainting himself with the traditions of English painting and theory, and pondering the contrasts between the purity of the American wilderness and the crumbling ruins of ancient architecture he saw across the Italian landscape. When he returned to America, he immersed himself in two alternative approaches to landscape: the ideal and the real — moralizing narratives and exacting records of identifiable scenery. Consummate examples of these dualities can be found in two of his greatest images, both produced in 1836: *The Course of Empire: Destruction* (fig. 41) and *View from Mount Holyoke, Northampton, Massachusetts, after a Thunderstorm*, familiarly known as *The Oxbow* (fig. 42). In

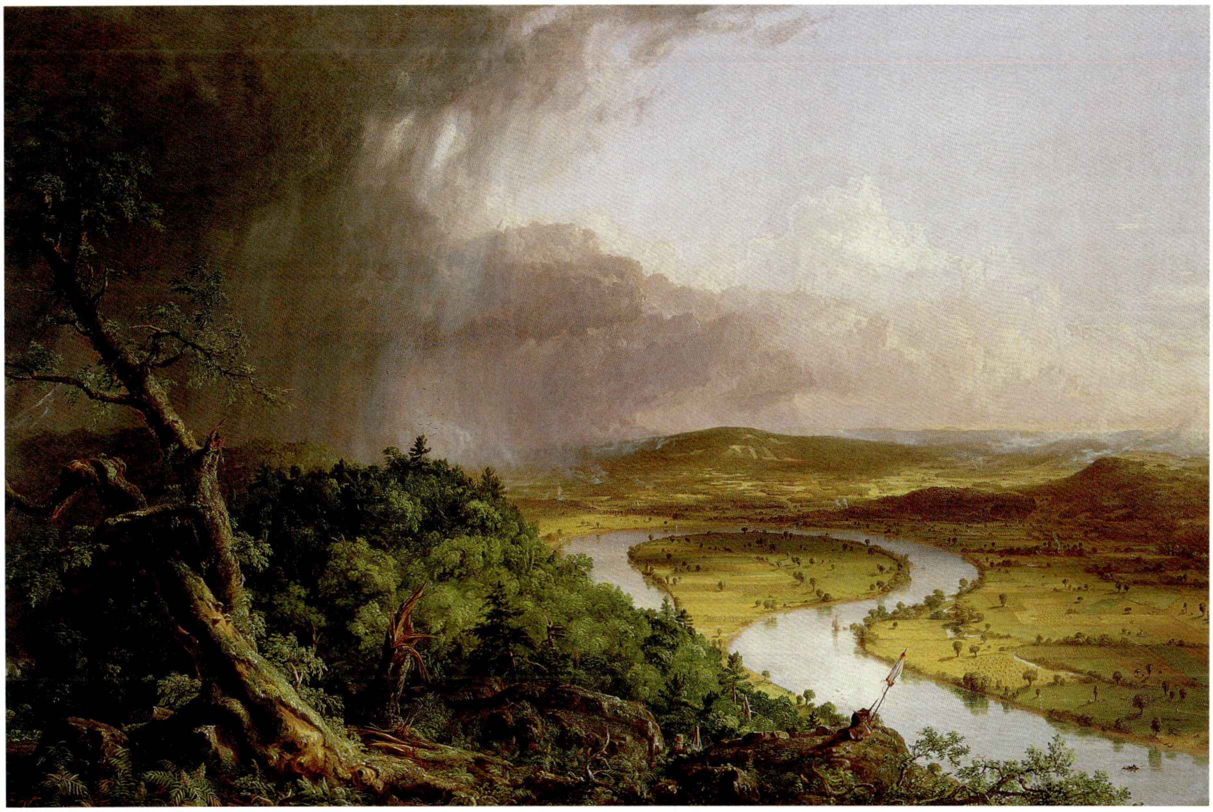

Fig. 42. Thomas Cole, *View from Mount Holyoke, Northampton, Massachusetts, after a Thunderstorm (The Oxbow)*, 1836. Oil on canvas, 51 ½ x 76 in. (130.8 x 193 cm). The Metropolitan Museum of Art, New York. Gift of Mrs. Russell Sage, 1908

a different way in each of the two, Cole introduced his signature cleverly within these scenes.

Destruction is the fourth painting in Cole's *Course of Empire*, an expansive five-canvas series promoting a cautionary moral about the rise of empires and their fall, brought about by vainglorious self-indulgence and disregard for nature's virtues. One of the lessons to be learned from Europe, Cole intimated, was how the architecture of civilization erodes nature's power. In its rise to prosperity and political glory, lest America's course result in romantic ruins, it should draw upon the spiritual sustenance of Edenic nature. Cole chronicled this imaginary story in his five canvases, moving from a state of creation to maturity and culmination to destruction and collapse. Correspondingly, his colors shift from soft to bright and glaring to turbulent and brooding; the times of day from dawn to mid-morning and noon to afternoon and evening;

and a landscape of primitive peoples and buildings to the crowding of modern civilized architecture and finally its crumbling ruins overrun by nature.

Destruction is, appropriately, a scene of violent contrasts, as thunderstorms and fires bring chaos and disintegration to the city's panorama, against a background of nature suppressed. The composition is the most turbulent and dynamic of the series, with its powerful diagonal forms and intense contrasts of light and dark, all suitable to the clamoring activity. Cole's signature appears prominently in the panel of the massive stone pedestal holding up the marble statue of a warrior (see fig. 41). As we look closely at the surrounding details, we see the tortured forms of figures being slaughtered, arms outstretched; the statue's head tumbled to the ground; and the pedestal chipped and cracked. As if echoing all this anguish, the block lettering of Cole's name and date is a distortion of pure classical carving, with an expressive crudeness of its own. Four years later, Cole painted a similar composition in *The Architect's Dream* (figs. 43 and 44), though the clarity and order are closer to the central panel of *The Course of Empire: Culmination*. The later work was a commission from his colleague Ithiel Town, an architect and designer prominent in New Haven and Hartford. Already an accomplished creator of buildings in the full variety of revival styles popular at mid-century, Town in Cole's vision reclines on a gigantic column. Spread out around and below him are enormous portfolios and architectural plans, while to the side and beyond are sequential examples of structures in Egyptian, Greek, Roman, and Gothic revival styles.[10] (In passing, we have to wonder if this was in part Cole's sly homage to his patron's name.) On the marble slab below the reclining figure, Cole carved, now in orderly classical letters, his inscription: "PAINTED BY T. COLE / FOR I. TOWN, ARCHt / 1840" (see fig. 44). Here Cole's name imitates the heroic marble edifices depicted, and he aligns his presence with his fellow professional. Ironically, although Town is presented as a grand visionary, the architect was upset with the picture, preferring instead one of Cole's pure American landscapes.

Among the greatest of Cole's American scenes is *The Oxbow* (figs. 42 and 45), which takes us back again to 1836. Here Cole's presence, as we shall see, is slightly different from the relatively decorative function of his name in *The Destruction of Empire* and *The Architect's Dream*, although the general composition of his diagonally organized landscape shares certain similarities with the narrative paintings. Now, stylistically, the left side of the painting represents the sublime, while to the right we have the embodiment of the beautiful. A dramatic clearing storm and blasted tree trunks occupy the left

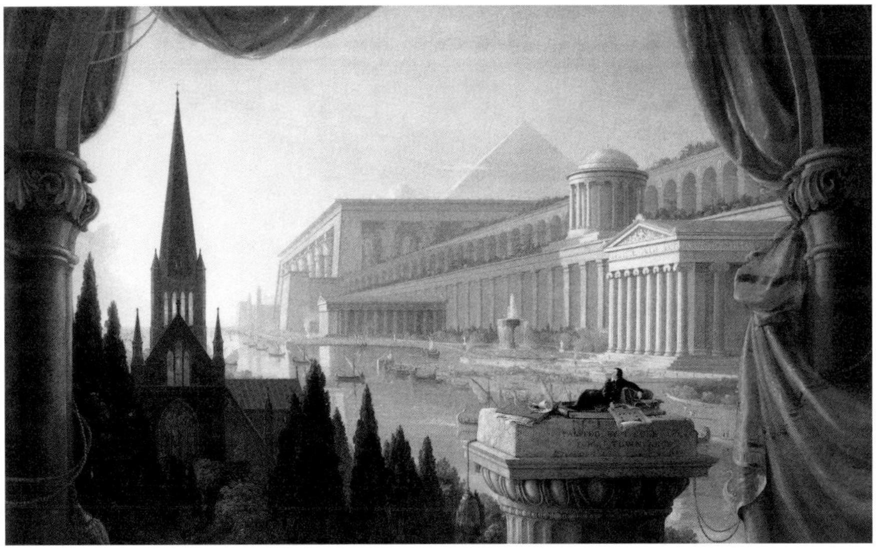

Fig. 43. Thomas Cole, *The Architect's Dream*, 1840. Oil on canvas, 53 x 84 1/16 in. (134.7 x 213.6 cm). Toledo Museum of Art, Toledo, Ohio. Purchased with funds from the Florence Scott Libbey bequest in memory of her father, Maurice A. Scott

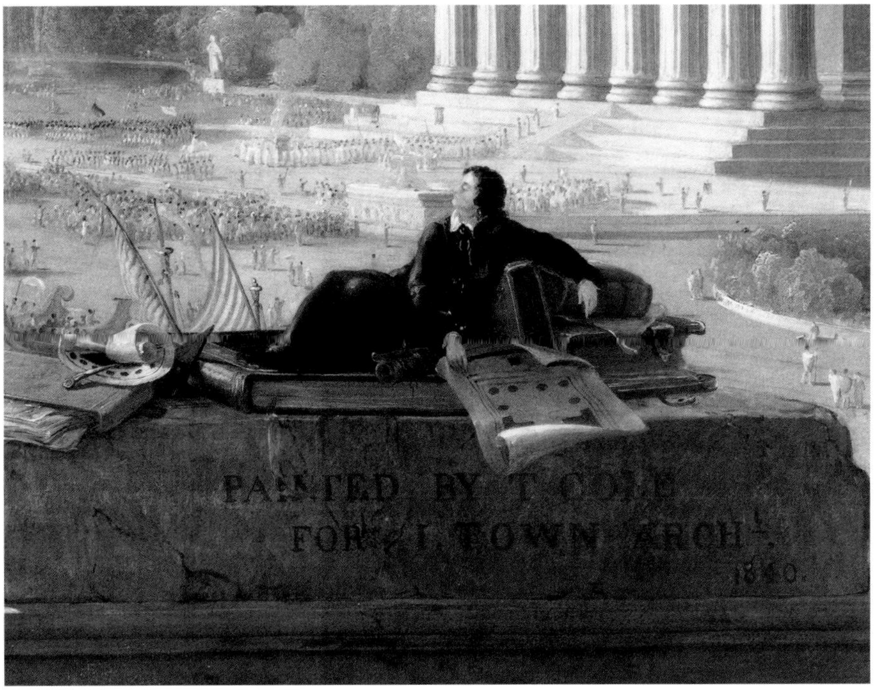

Fig. 44. Thomas Cole, *The Architect's Dream* (detail of fig. 43), 1840

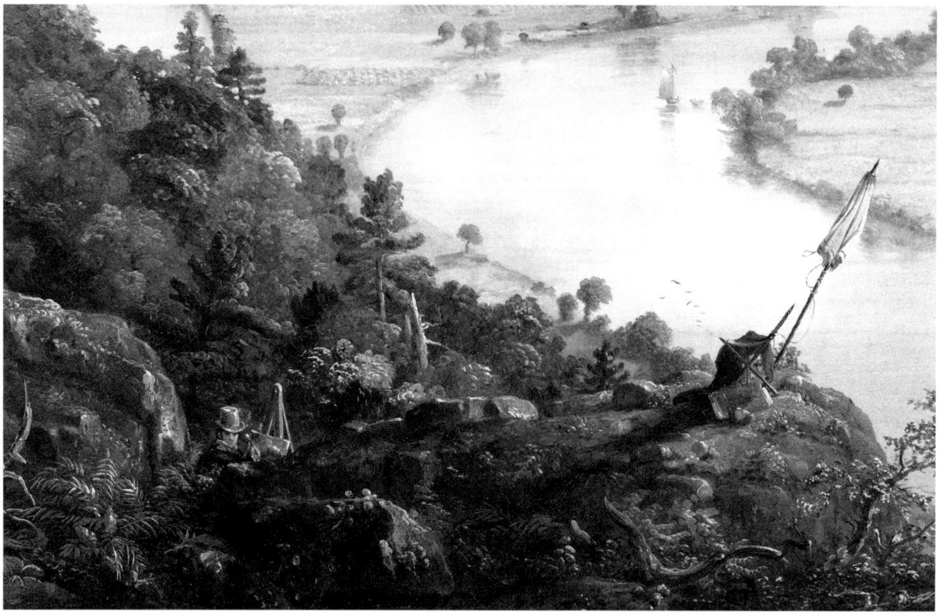

Fig. 45. Thomas Cole, *View from Mount Holyoke, Northampton, Massachusetts, after a Thunderstorm (The Oxbow)* (detail of fig. 42), 1836

foreground, in contrast to the bright sunlight and smooth agricultural landscape filling the right distance. Matthew Baigell is the first to have called attention to the cuttings on the far hillside, a possible inscription that could read "Shaddai" in Hebrew, or "Noah."[11] Cole may well have intended to underpin his specific local vista with spiritual and philosophical meaning, for the passing thunderstorm both highlights nature's destructive forces over time and unveils a safe and tranquil world, refreshed and renewed by God's power.

Where is the artist in all this? As we might anticipate, he is actually there in a tiny self-portrait, sitting amidst the rocks and foliage with his easel at lower center, in a sense halfway between the two conditions of nature around him. Even more at the juncture between dark and light, foreground and background, the waters of the biblical flood and the valley of prosperity is the mediating form of the artist's painting parasol, stool, and portfolio. It is here, on the side of his portfolio, that we find Cole's signature (see fig. 45), now another representation of himself in his landscape. Generally aligned with the writing on the distant mountainside, the artist's painting on canvas is analogous to God's hand in nature's creation.

This picture and its signature had a coda several years later in *The Temple of Segesta with the Artist Sketching*, ca. 1842 (fig. 46). A panoramic

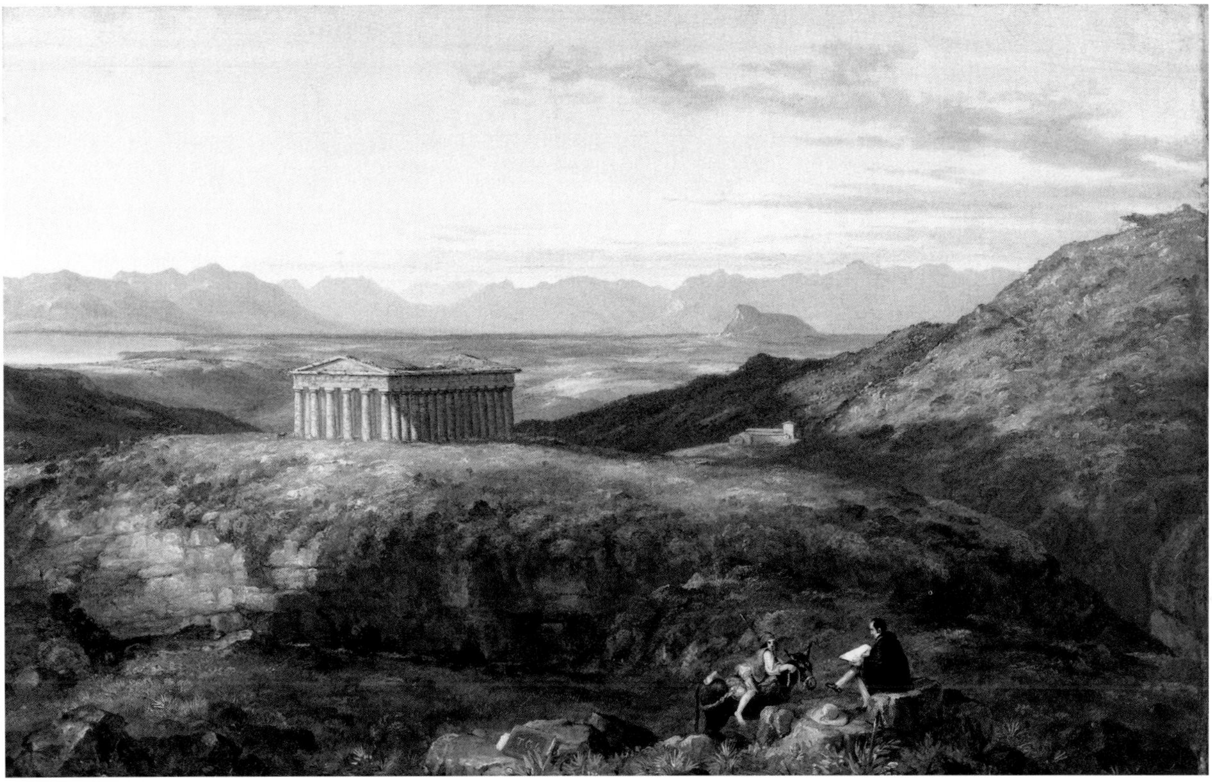

Fig. 46. Thomas Cole, *The Temple of Segesta with the Artist Sketching*, ca. 1842. Oil on canvas, 19 5/8 x 30 1/8 in. (49.8 x 76.5 cm). Museum of Fine Arts, Boston. Gift of Mrs. Maxim Karolik for the Karolik Collection of American Paintings, 1815–65

recollection of his trips to the Italian countryside, with its poignant ancient ruins bathed in golden sunset colors, it positions the artist painting in the foreground. Literally front and center we see his red-bound portfolio resting on a rock, with "T. Cole" written across it in large legible letters. Here, as before, the painter is present as an active professional, first journeying through the actual landscape and then recording it in drawings and sketches. Cole's signature affirms both his experience and interpretation of nature.

Cole's almost exact contemporary, America's first important marine painter, Fitz Hugh Lane, was born in 1804 in Gloucester, Massachusetts; in contrast to Cole's associations with the Hudson River Valley, the Catskills and Adirondacks, and Italy, Lane would pass virtually all of his career along the northern New England coast from Boston to Maine. Partially paralyzed in his legs as an infant, Lane found sketching and painting from a boat naturally comfortable, and much of his artistic output comprises shoreline views,

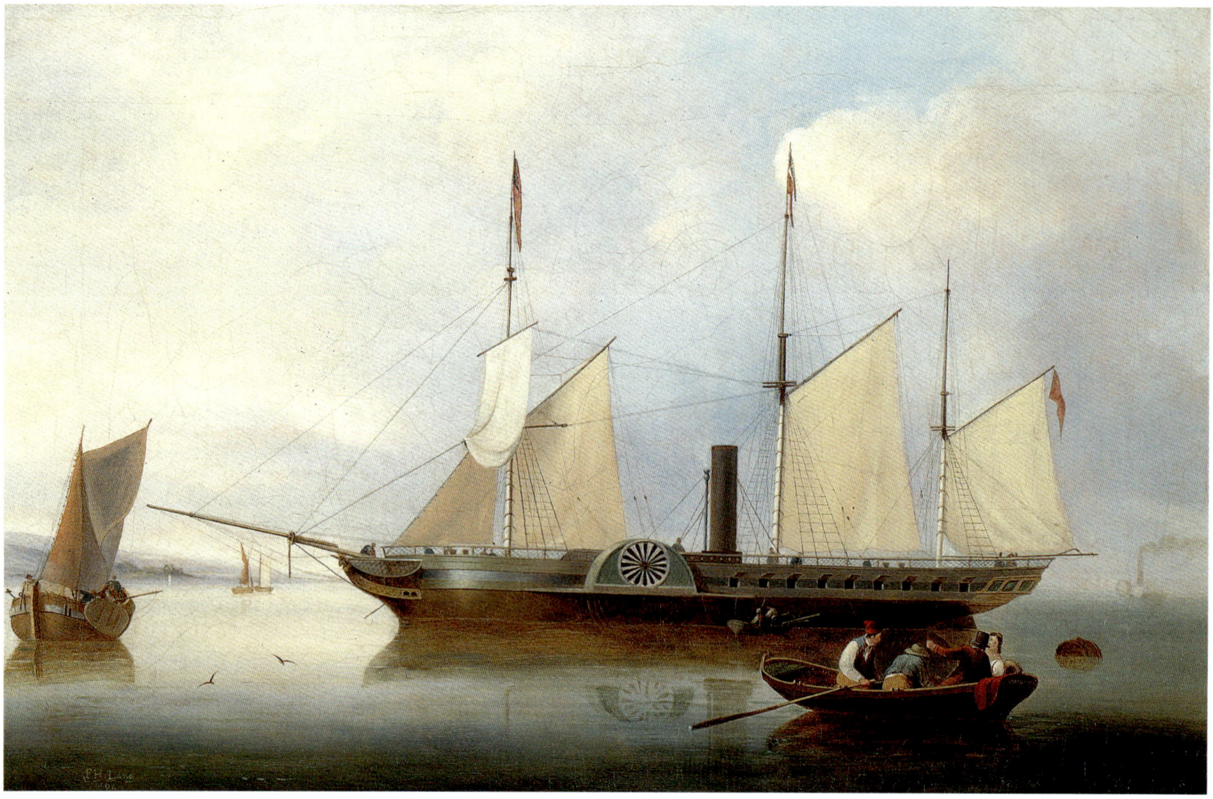

Fig. 47. Fitz Hugh Lane, *The "Unicorn" in Salem Harbor*, 1840. Oil on canvas, 16 x 24 in. (40.6 x 61 cm). Private collection. Courtesy of Sotheby's

often from off shore. Even as his style shifted from the narratives of the earlier works, filled with shipping activities or shorefront industry, to the poetic radiance and spacious serenity of his later images, now familiarly known as "luminist," Lane preferred to record his compositions from the middle of a harbor and with increasingly open vistas. For the most part he signed his canvases in the conventional manner, in block letters at one of the lower corners. But there are several occasions in early as well as mature paintings where the placement of his initials or name indicates either his engagement with the activities he depicts or his lifelong passion for sailing free of the shore.

Trained as a lithographer, Lane first turned to oil painting during the 1840s, composing small views in Gloucester and Boston harbors. These carry over the precision of drawing, detailing, and contrasts of lighting of his earlier graphic work. In Boston they record the variety of shipping activity

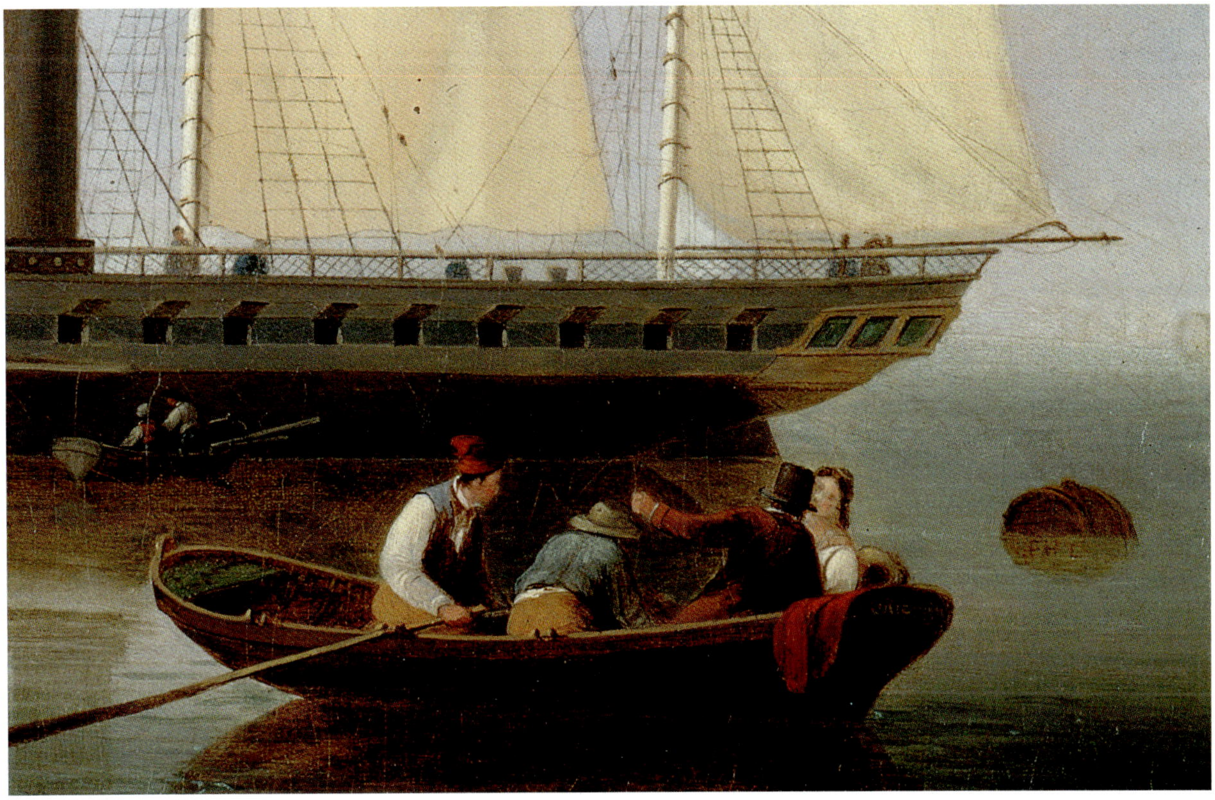

Fig. 48. Fitz Hugh Lane, *The "Unicorn" in Salem Harbor* (detail of fig. 47), 1840

to be seen in this increasingly prosperous and busy port, but Lane captured as well the new transatlantic traffic of oceangoing steamers, as in *The "Unicorn" in Salem Harbor*, 1840 (fig. 47) and *The "Britannia" Entering Boston Harbor*, 1848 (private collection). After the manner of Robert Salmon, an older English marine painter active in Boston during Lane's youth and much admired by the aspiring younger painter, Lane employed the familiar devices of receding bands of light and shadow across the water; tight, repeated rhythms of wave crests; and rowboats with outstretched oars and gesturing figures. The appearance of these vessels must have been exciting events for the population, and Lane indicates his firsthand presence by his signatures. In *The "Britannia" Entering Boston Harbor* he painted his name at the lower left, where it curves downward as if riding the small crest of a wave, while in *The "Unicorn" in Salem Harbor* his initials appear on the side of a barrel floating nearby in the water (fig. 48). The previous year he had begun a series of small pictures of the Gloucester waterfront, and in one, *On the Wharves,*

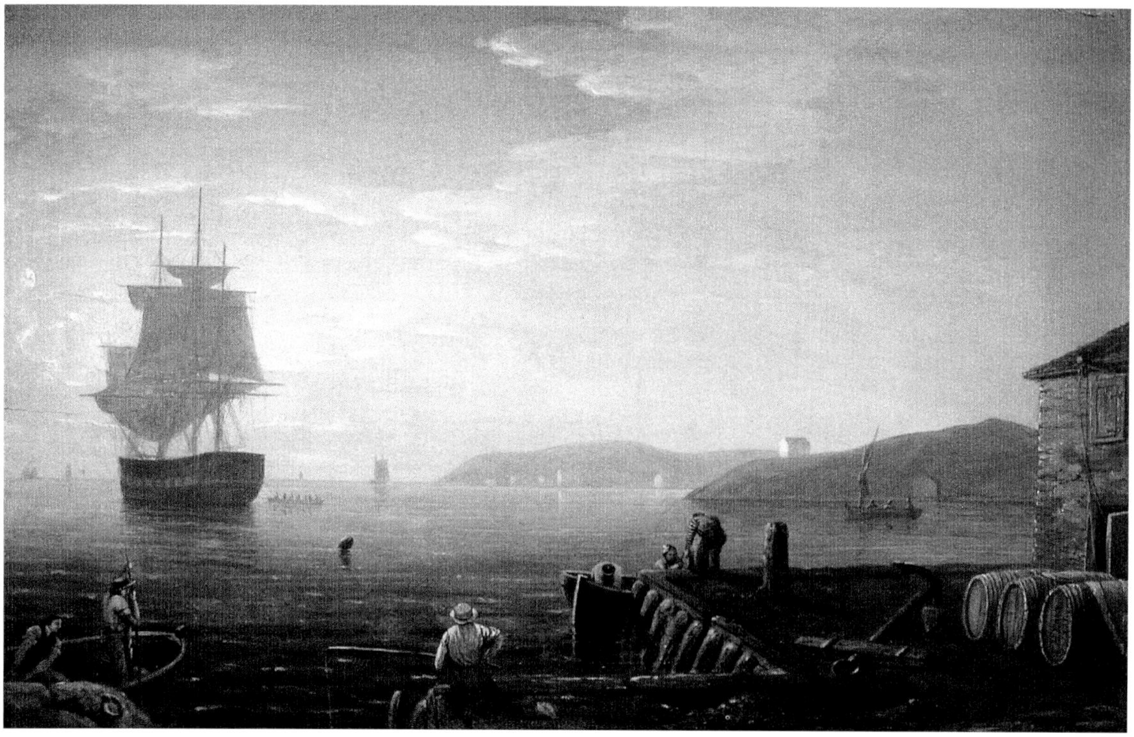

Fig. 49. Fitz Hugh Lane, *On the Wharves, Gloucester Harbor,* 1847. Oil on panel, 9 ¾ x 14 ½ in. (24.8 x 36.8 cm). Cape Ann Historical Association, Gloucester, Mass.

Gloucester Harbor, 1847 (fig. 49), he placed his signature on one of the barrels piled to the side. Like the adjacent figures looking out to the water, Lane shows himself to be an active observer and participant in his own scenes.

At the same time as he was painting these harbor views, Lane was also documenting the beachfront work of local fishermen and shipbuilders. One such scene, *Gloucester Harbor,* 1847 (fig. 50), looks outward from the inner shoreline over Five and Ten Pound Islands. Across the beach in the foreground we see myriad activities related to the local shipbuilding and granite industries: figures haul lumber, caulk a rowboat hull, and split logs. All these moments prepare for the launching and transport of the several schooners in the harbor beyond. At the lower right is a pile of recently quarried stone, presumably for building locally as well as in distant ports, and diagonally across the face of one block we find Lane's name. Lane regularly walked and sketched along these beaches, so putting his name at the site would have come naturally. He signed this way on other occasions throughout his career, most notably on a large boulder, also in the lower right corner, in the Gloucester beach scene

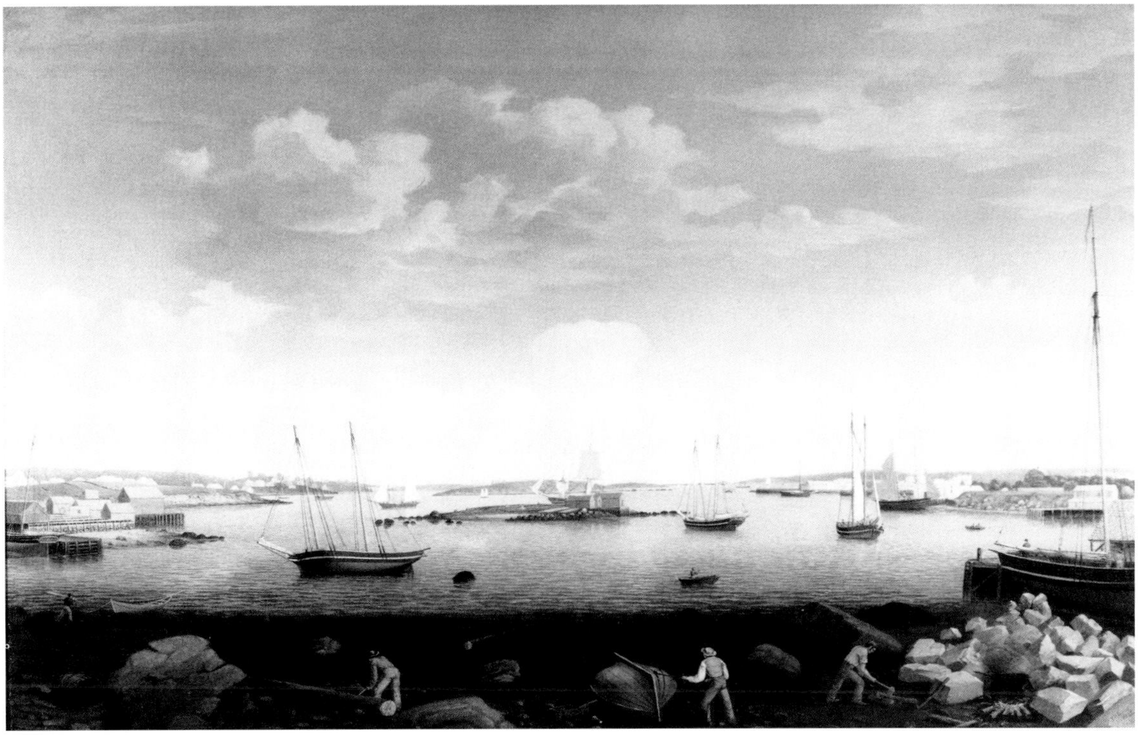

Fig. 50. Fitz Hugh Lane, *Gloucester Harbor*, 1847. Oil on canvas, 23 x 35 ½ in. (58.4 x 90.2 cm). Cape Ann Historical Association, Gloucester, Mass.

Stage Fort across Gloucester Harbor, 1862 (fig. 51), one of his last major canvases. His implied presence there is such that we can well imagine Lane sitting on that very rock at the high-water mark, sketching the scene before him.

Perhaps his most unusually placed signature is also among the most revealing. *Salem Harbor*, 1853 (figs. 52 and 53), is one of his most beautiful mid-career harbor views, characteristically sun-flooded and spacious in design. The sails of his vessels alternate in lively visual rhythms of light and dark across the canvas, with the center of the composition boldly empty, or, rather, filled just with nuances of shadowy light in the sky and on the water. Just left of this central axis a small schooner drifts placidly, its oars at rest and its limp sails in shadow. High up on the middle sail, Lane painted his initials and the date in bright red letters, a color used otherwise only for three of the red-shirted figures below or nearby. Not only does Lane implicitly place himself in a vessel in mid-harbor, he intentionally calls attention to the elevated viewpoint. We know from the notations on many of Lane's preparatory drawings and from the recollections of his cruising companion and, later, ex-

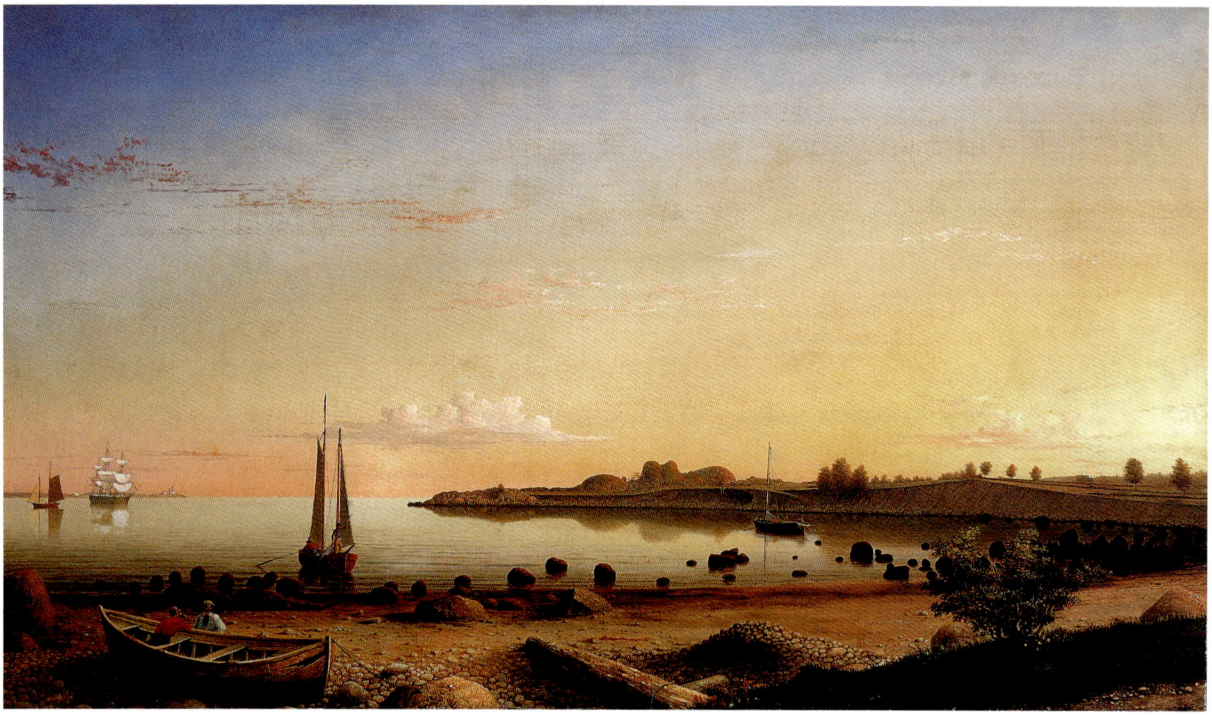

Fig. 51. Fitz Hugh Lane, *Stage Fort across Gloucester Harbor*, 1862. Oil on canvas, 38 x 60 in. (96.5 x 152.4 cm). The Metropolitan Museum of Art, New York. Purchase, Rogers and Fletcher Funds, Erving and Joyce Wolfe Fund, Raymond J. Horowitz Gift, Bequest of Richard De Wolfe Brixey, by exchange, and John Osgood and Elizabeth Amis Cameron Blanchard Memorial Fund, 1978

ecutor of his estate, Joseph L. Stevens, Jr., that Lane favored sketching his shoreline views from just such a modest sailing schooner. Stevens reported that on occasion the painter had himself hoisted by bosun's chair partway up a mast in order to secure a more panoramic view across the water. Certainly the size and placement of this vessel — and the presence of Lane's name on its sail — suggest the schooner was a stand-in for the artist at work in the scene.

Another contemporary of Thomas Cole's, Asher B. Durand, also walked, as it were, in the woods he painted. Upon Cole's early death in 1848, Durand assumed the mantle of leadership of the Hudson River School, and by mid-century had helped to establish nature as an essential spiritual as well as national experience. He intensified Cole's devotion to specific scenery and literalness of detail, textures, and conditions of light. Even a relatively early work, *The Beeches*, 1845 (fig. 54), with its somewhat sentimental shepherd in the distance, has a title of identifiable trees. In this regard, Durand was

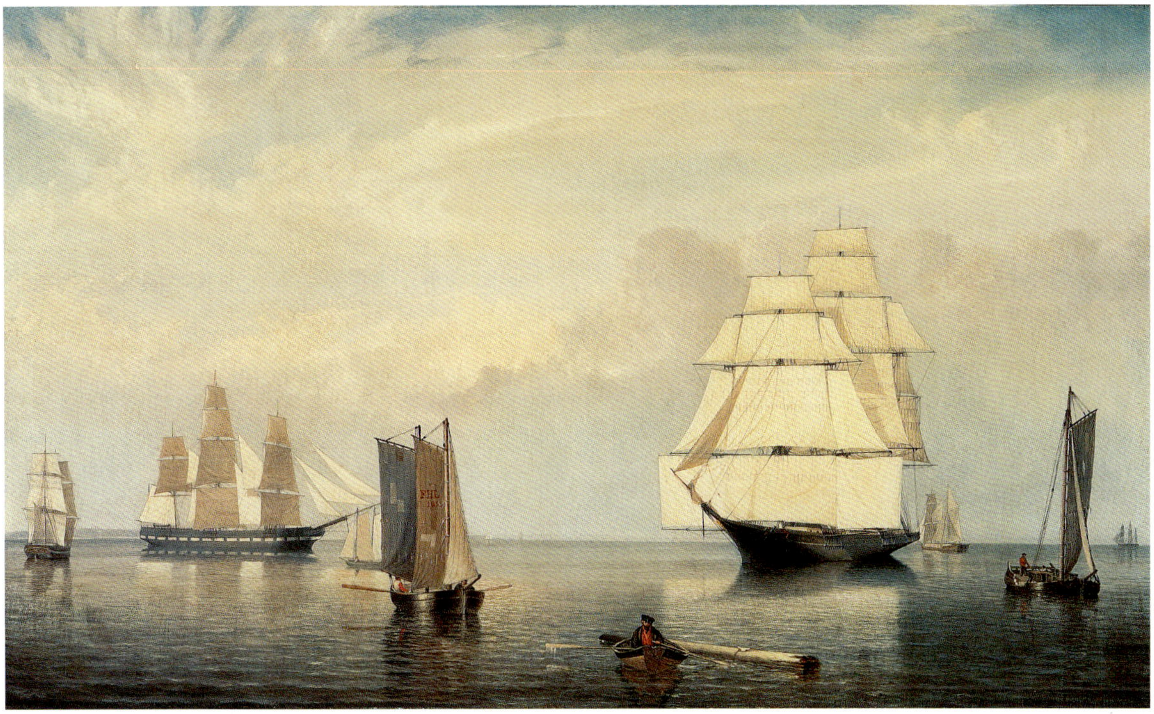

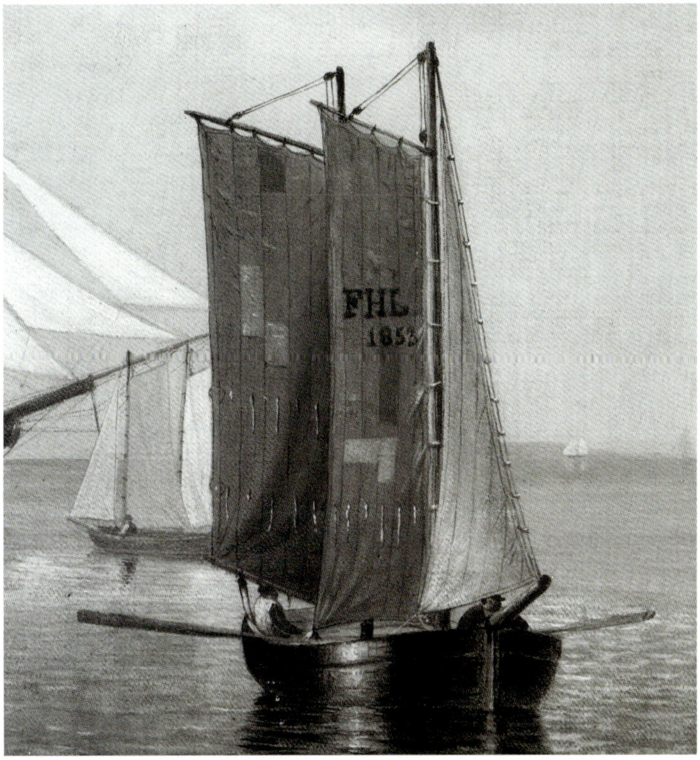

Fig. 52. Fitz Hugh Lane, *Salem Harbor*, 1853. Oil on canvas, 26 ⅛ x 42 in. (66.4 x 106.7 cm). Museum of Fine Arts, Boston. Bequest of Maxim Karolik, 1964

Fig. 53. Fitz Hugh Lane, *Salem Harbor* (detail of fig. 52), 1853

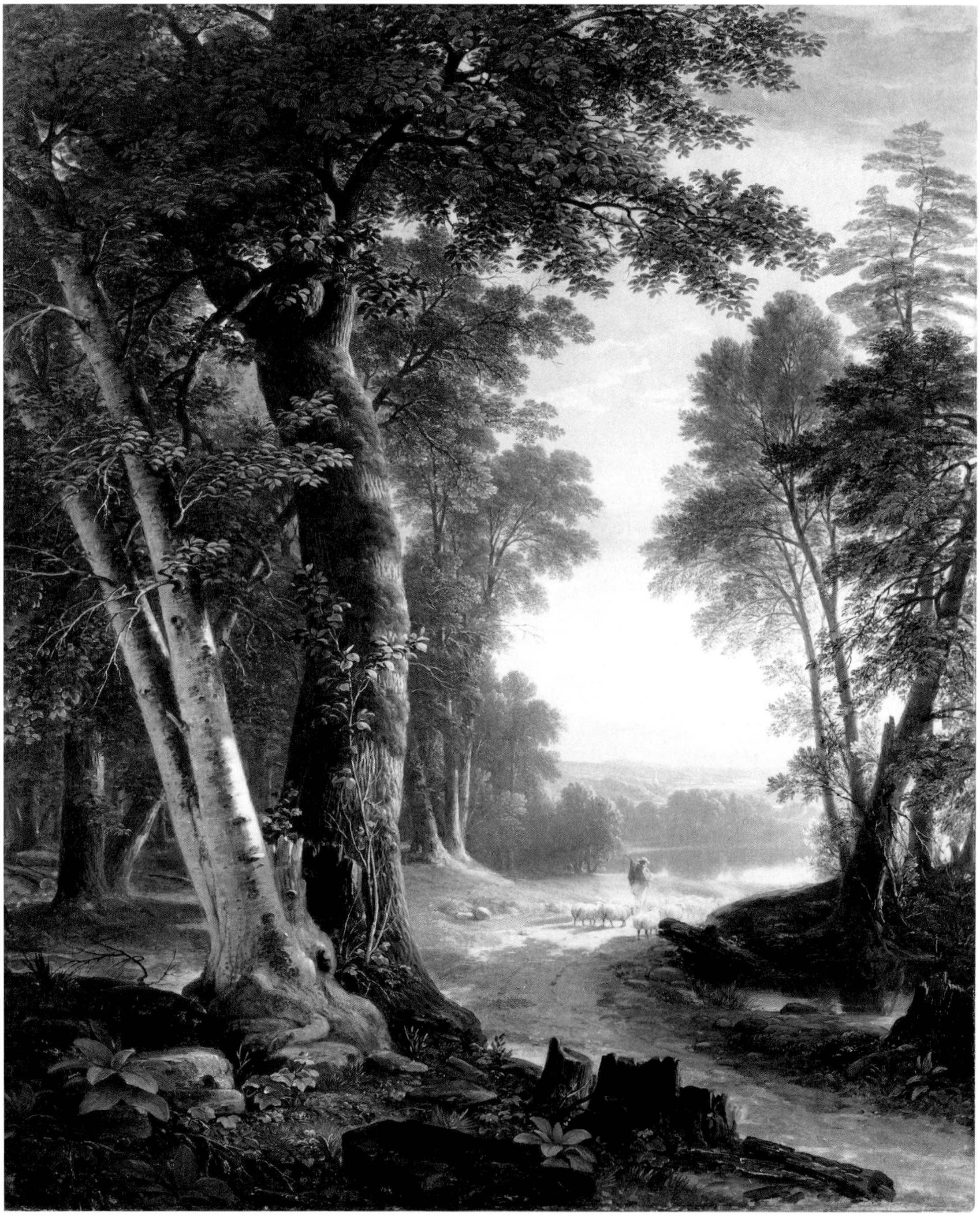

Fig. 54. Asher B. Durand, *The Beeches*, 1845. Oil on canvas, 60 3/8 x 48 1/8 in. (153.4 x 122.2 cm). The Metropolitan Museum of Art, New York. Bequest of Maria DeWitt Jesup, from the collection of her husband, Morris K. Jesup, 1915

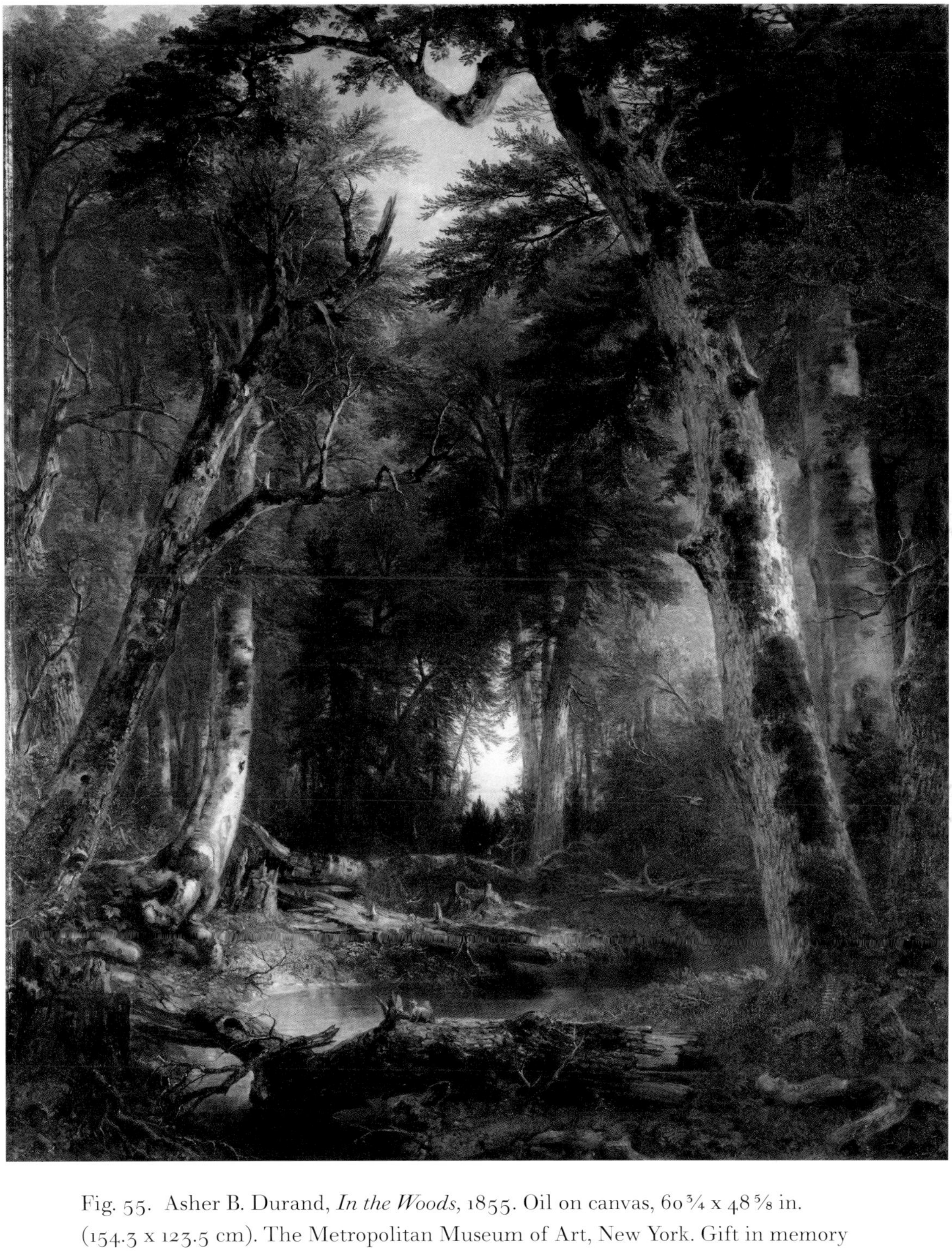

Fig. 55. Asher B. Durand, *In the Woods,* 1855. Oil on canvas, 60 ¾ x 48 ⅝ in. (154.3 x 123.5 cm). The Metropolitan Museum of Art, New York. Gift in memory of Jonathan Sturges by his children, 1895

an ardent follower and promoter of John Ruskin's new theories of landscape painting and drawing, which called for close observation and the depiction of nature immediately at hand and underfoot. In both imagery and execution Durand would advocate precision, and called for painters to "draw with scrupulous fidelity the outline or contour of such objects as you shall select, and . . . choose the most beautiful or characteristic of its kind. If your subject be a tree, observe particularly wherein it differs from those of other species."[12]

It should not surprise us to find Durand's signature in *The Beeches* on a boulder at the lower left, telling us that he has walked like a pilgrim or the shepherd through this landscape. He reprised this idea in a mature painting a decade later, by signing *In the Woods,* 1855 (fig. 55), along the fallen tree limb at lower right. Now the tall birches and other trees bow inward over the valley stream like the Gothic arches of a church nave, an intentional image of reverence understood by the artist and his public alike. As Durand led his colleagues and viewers into the glories of the American wilderness, so he inserted his name into these paintings as records of his experience.

This impulse to record one's pilgrimage through nature continued with Cole's most accomplished pupil and follower in the next generation. Frederic Edwin Church of Hartford studied and lived with Cole for two years in the late 1840s, and absorbed his teacher's practices and subjects intimately, gradually transforming them once he was on his own in the next decade. Church now emerges as America's leading painter, in the preeminence of his intellect and technical abilities. While his landscapes continued to possess Cole's allegorical and symbolic power, they soon became more explicit in location and the conditions of light and atmosphere. Church appears to have enjoyed rather clever and varied introductions of his name, both written and visual, into his canvases. *West Rock, New Haven,* 1849 (fig. 56), is one of the first works of his early maturity. Like that of C. W. Peale, Church's name denoted an object, and it is a fitting coincidence that this artist came to paint some of America's most expressive spiritual landscapes. Early on, he exploited the associations of his name with ecclesiastical buildings by highlighting the small detail of a church spire in the background of *West Rock, New Haven.* We know he intended this pictograph to stand as his signature from a couple of letters (now at Olana, his Moorish villa and studio in the upper Hudson River Valley) he wrote to A. C. Goodman during the preceding year (fig. 57), in which he wrote out his initials F. E., immediately followed by a small outline of a country church.

A year later Church followed in Cole's footsteps with the first of several

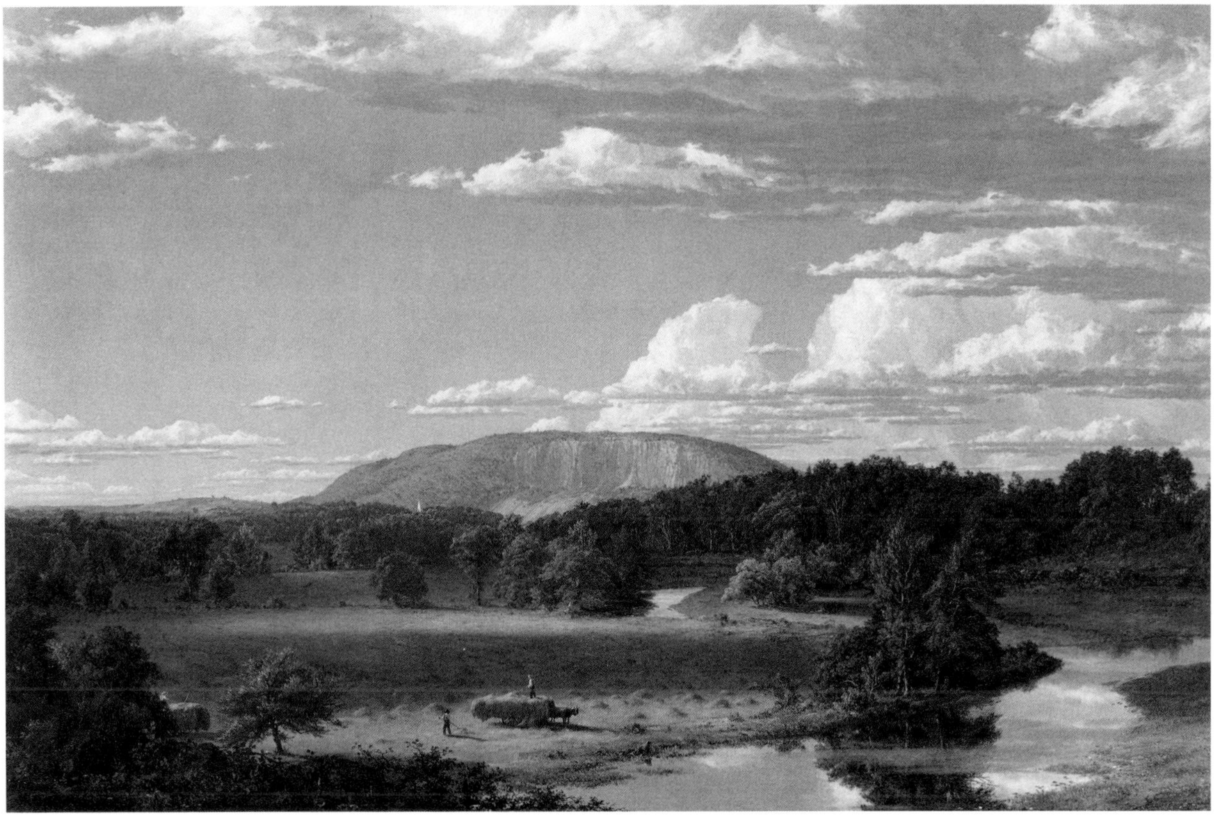

Fig. 56. Frederic Edwin Church, *West Rock, New Haven*, 1849. Oil on canvas, 26 ½ x 40 in. (67.3 x 101.6 cm). New Britain Museum of American Art, New Britain, Conn. John B. Talcott Fund

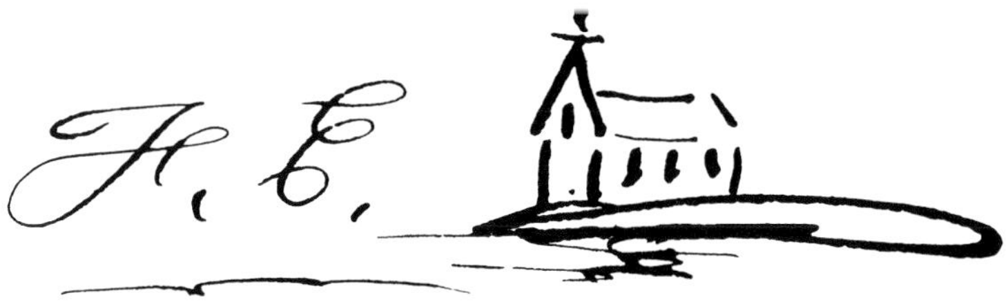

Fig. 57. Frederic Edwin Church, Signature on a letter to A. C. Goodwin, January 30, 1848. New York State Office of Parks, Recreation and Historic Preservation, Bureau of Historic Sites, Olana State Historic Site, Taconic Region

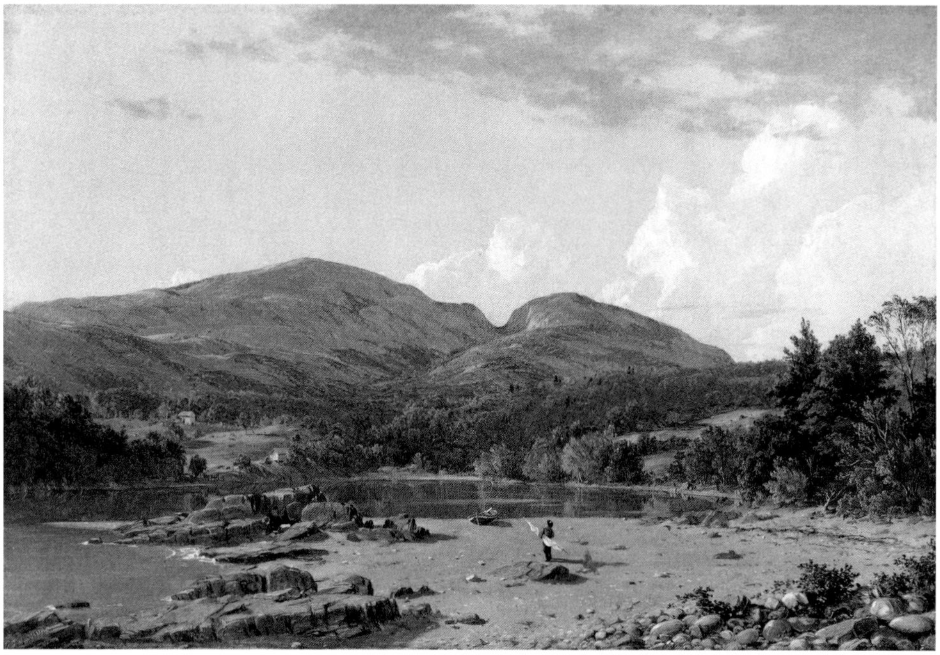

Fig. 58. Frederic Edwin Church, *Otter Creek, Mount Desert,* 1850. Oil on canvas, 16¾ x 24 in. (42.5 x 61 cm). Museum of Fine Arts, Boston. Seth K. Sweetser Fund, Tompkins Collection, Henry H. and Zoë Oliver Sherman Fund and Gift of Mrs. R. Amory Thorndike, 1982

trips to the Maine coast, where he painted for exhibition *Otter Creek, Mount Desert,* 1850 (fig. 58). Several historians have pointed out that the shadow cast by the foreground figure with a furled sail under his arm falls across the beach in a clear configuration of a cross. In one sense we may argue that this is an extended image of Church's name, but it was also appropriate to this sojourner in the American Edenic landscape. Certainly, the image of the church spire appears as a surrogate for the artist's name in a number of later New England landscapes. Church also used the device of signing his name on a rock, as he did with "F.E. Church/Mt. Desert 1851" on a half-submerged ledge in *Newport Mountain, Mount Desert,* 1851 (private collection). Like Lane and Durand, Church observed such details of nature with the care that Ruskin urged: "Look at your stone antagonist boldly in the face. . . . A stone may be round or angular, polished or rough, cracked all over like an ill-glazed teacup, or as united and broad as the breast of Hercules. It may be flaky as a wafer, as powdery as a field puff-ball; it may be knotted like a ship's hawser, or kneaded like hammered iron, or knit like a Damascus sabre, or fused like a glass bottle, or crystallized like hoar-frost, or veined like a forest leaf: look at it."[13]

Church expanded his travels during the mid-1850s to embrace much of the South as well as North American continents, and a number of his Andean landscapes have signatures prominently inscribed on foreground rock formations, often adjacent to where figures on horseback or burros are proceeding into the scene.[14] The most spectacular of his South American panoramas was the summary work *Heart of the Andes*, 1859 (figs. 59 and 60). As Stephen Jay Gould has shown, this represented the culmination of Church's optimistic vision of hemispheric grandeur and glory, an homage to the pioneering journeys to South America a half century earlier by the German natural scientist Alexander von Humboldt and to the expansive view of New World geography that Humboldt articulated in his book *Kosmos*. In his Andes vista Church found the full sweep of the earth's geology, from lowest valley to highest peaks, from tropical vegetation to glacial snows. His view expands in all directions, laterally from one quadrant to another, vertically ascending over all types of terrain, and in depth from nature underfoot to distant skies opening to endless horizons. This vision is as much spiritual as physical, with nature herself a holy church inspiring the faithful. Again, the artist is present in a couple of ways, as a pilgrim who pauses before the cross in the left foreground, and as the carver of his initials illuminated on the tree at the extreme left.

We know that Church sent the painting off to Europe upon completion for the aged von Humboldt to see, but coincidentally the German died before its arrival. Later that fateful year, Charles Darwin published his *On the Origin of the Species*, decisively undermining this heroic and celebratory image of nature, and introducing

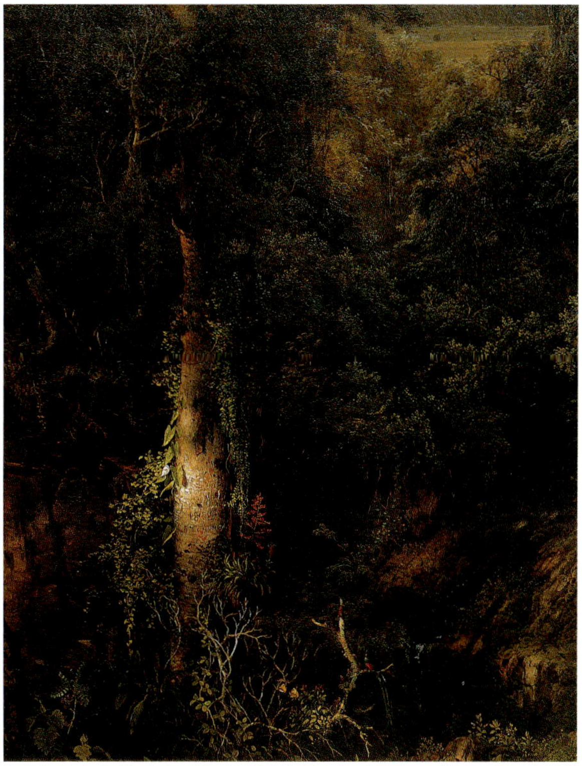

Fig. 59. Frederic Edwin Church, *Heart of the Andes* (detail of fig. 60), 1859

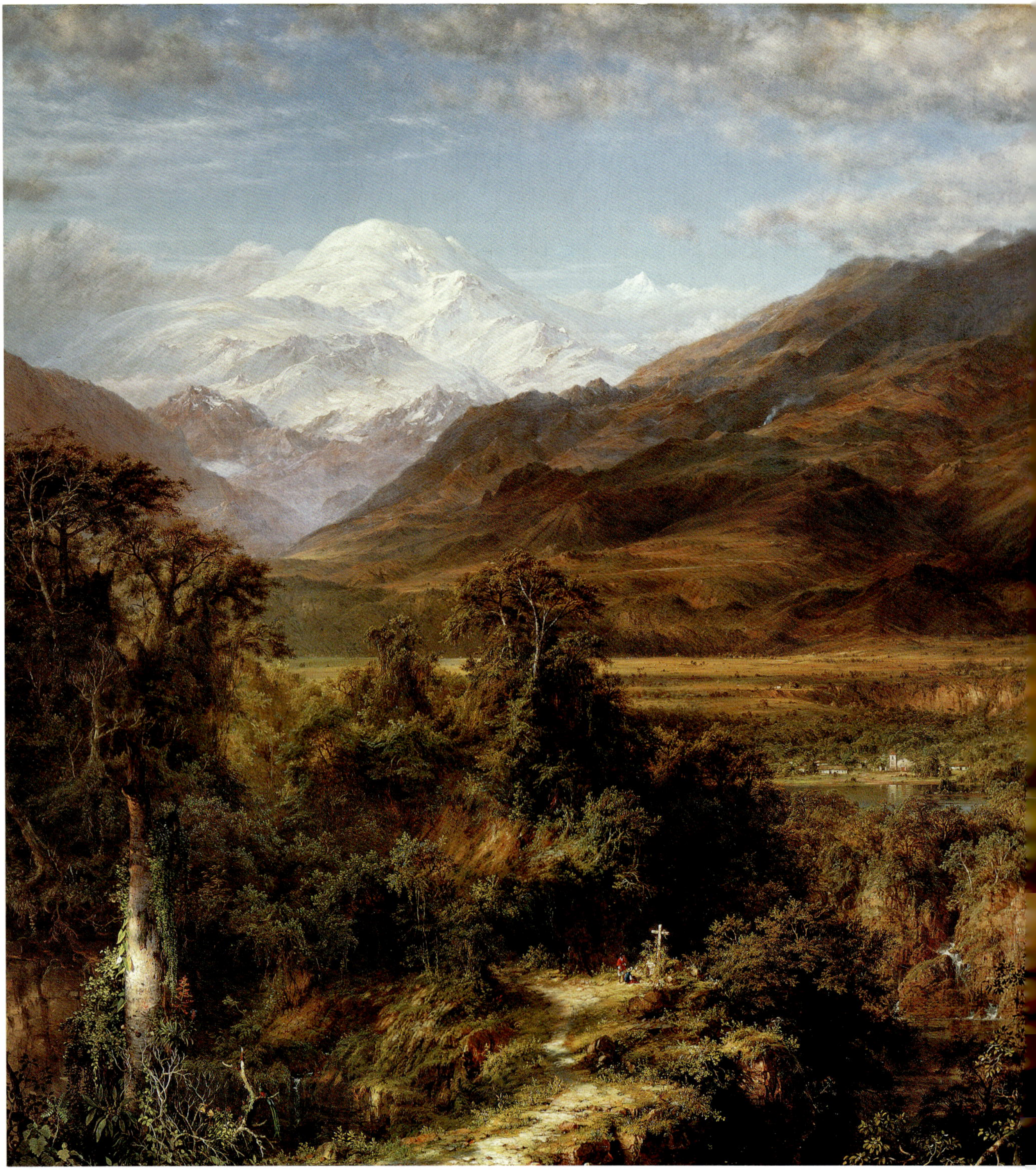

Fig. 60. Frederic Edwin Church, *Heart of the Andes*, 1859. Oil on canvas, 66 1/8 x 119 1/4 in. (168 x 303.4 cm). The Metropolitan Museum of Art, New York. Bequest of Margaret E. Dows, 1909

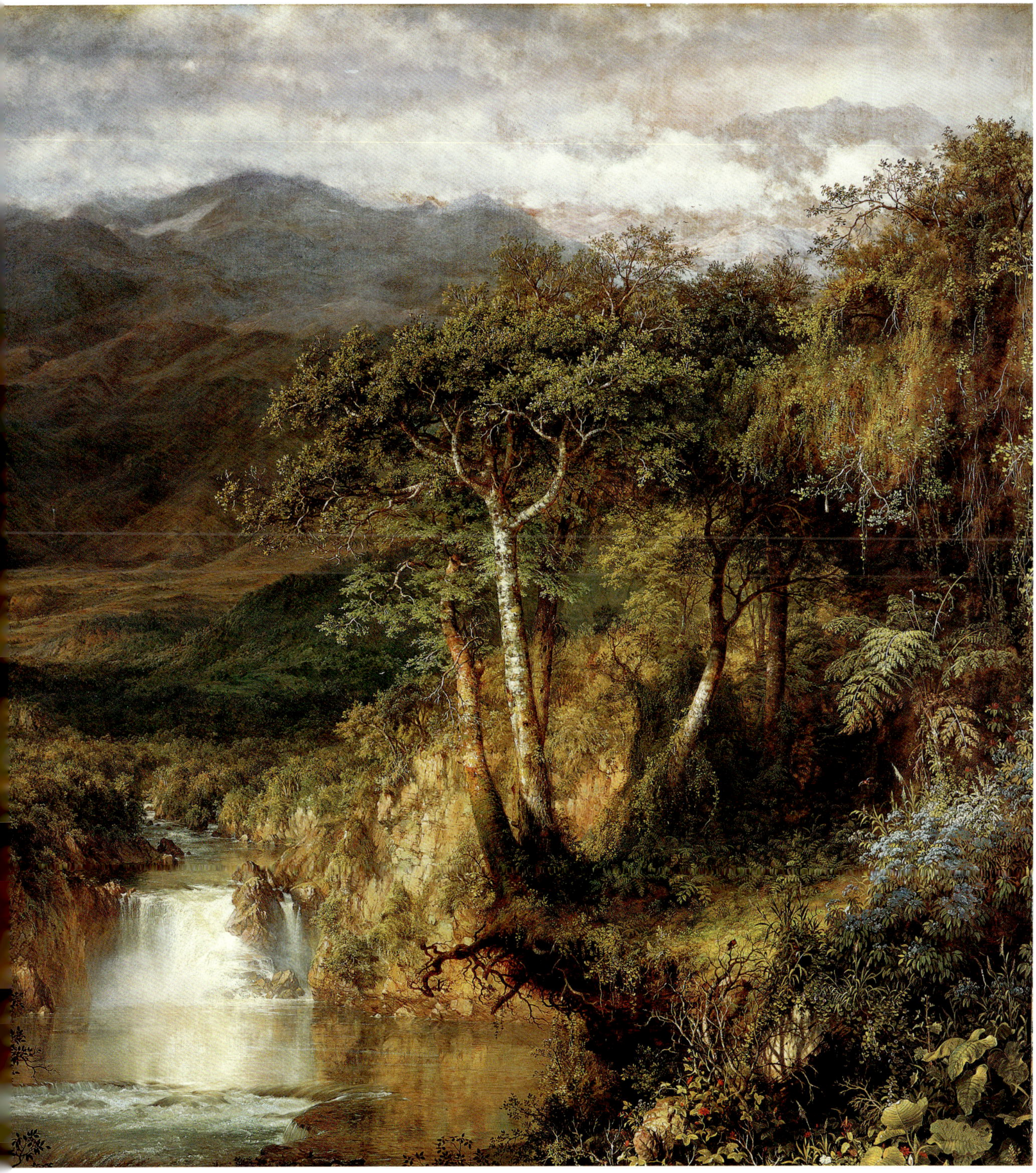

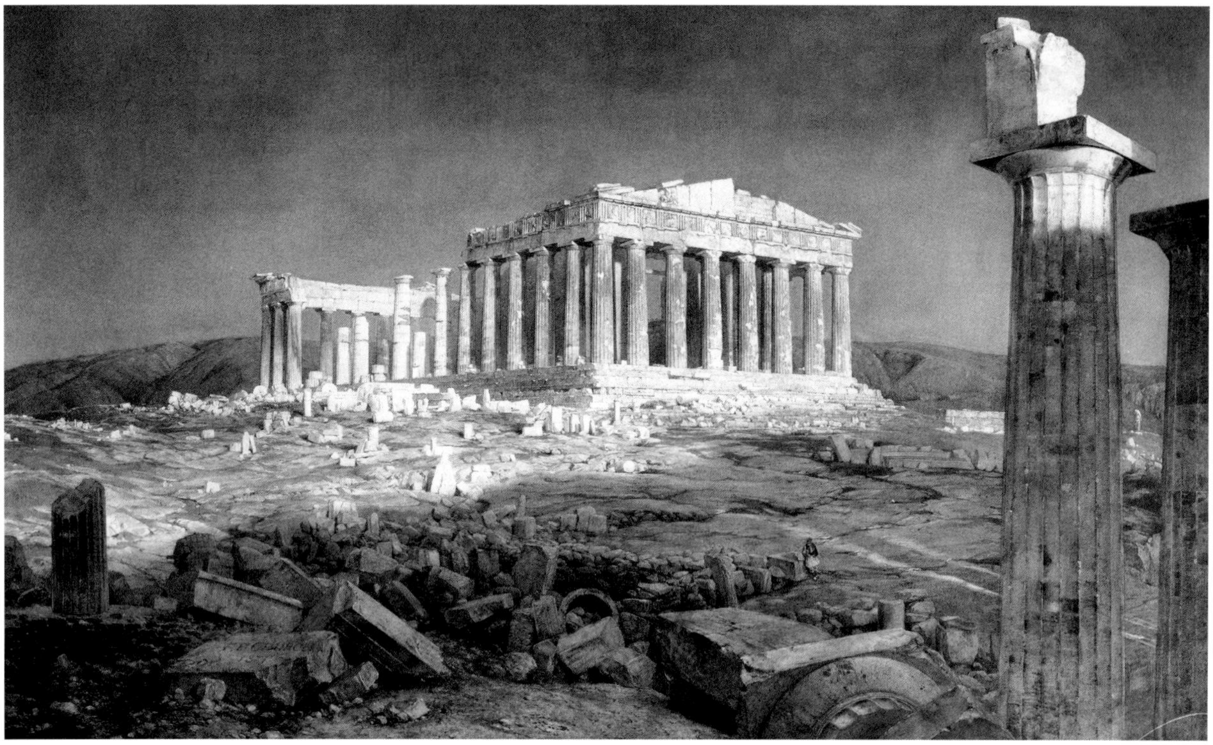

Fig. 61. Frederic Edwin Church, *The Parthenon*, 1871. Oil on canvas, 44 1/8 x 72 1/8 in. (112.1 x 183.2 cm). The Metropolitan Museum of Art, New York. Bequest of Maria DeWitt Jesup, 1915

a contradictory view of cruelty and accident in the natural world. Now, instead of that of God's guiding hand at work, such concepts as natural selection and survival of the fittest prevailed. Thus, *Heart of the Andes* represents the end of an era for Church and for America. Although Darwin forever changed the Western world's understanding of natural history, and contributed to Church's gradual withdrawal to his own landscape at Olana, high above the Hudson, Church still made voyages of faith to the Old World into the early 1870s. Some of the great later pictures resulting from these excursions to the sites of ancient Western civilization — notably, *Jerusalem from the Mount of Olives*, 1870 (Nelson-Atkins Museum of Art, Kansas City, Missouri); *Syria by the Sea*, 1873 (Detroit Institute of Arts); and *The Parthenon*, 1871 (fig. 61) — are all signed prominently on rocks or stones in the foreground. In the latter, his name lies across a large block of marble fallen from a building on the Acropolis; a shadow falls over it and much of the middle distance. Church, implicitly both tourist and amateur archaeologist, experi-

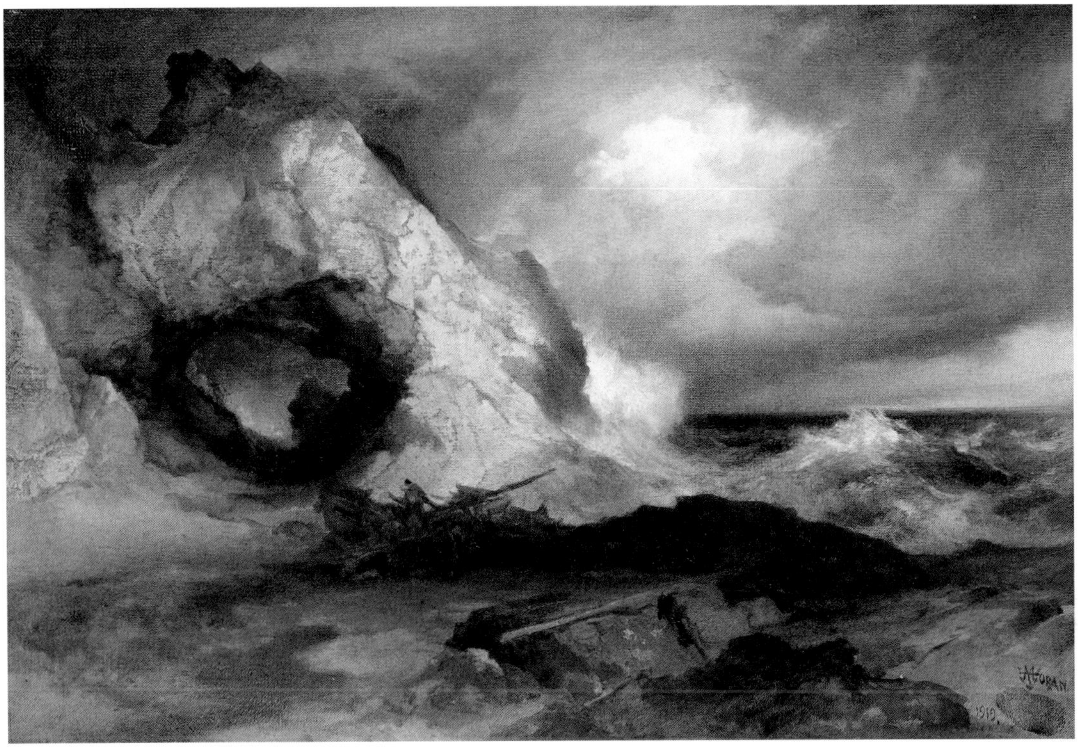

Fig. 62. Thomas Moran, *Sinbad Wrecked*, 1919. Oil on canvas, 20 ½ x 26 ⅝ in. (52.1 x 67.6 cm). Private collection, via Berry-Hill Galleries, New York

ences the poignant glories of the past across the ruins of time. He did not always sign his pictures this way, but as with his earlier American landscapes, when he entered a subject with deep personal meaning, he left his name behind as witness.

As a coda to this major American tradition of landscape painting through the middle of the nineteenth century, we should mention a final quirky example, actually dating from the early twentieth century, by an artist whose long life carried this subject matter into periods when tastes had markedly shifted elsewhere. Thomas Moran shared with Church an admiration for Joseph Turner, and this is evident in his *Sinbad Wrecked*, 1919 (fig. 62). In the lower right corner Moran signed his name with his traditional monogram, conventionally enough, but directly below he placed his fingerprint into the pigment, not to comment or gloss on his subject in any way, but literally to authenticate his canvas in the most modern of ways. It surely gives a new twist to the signature as evidence of the artist's presence in the work.

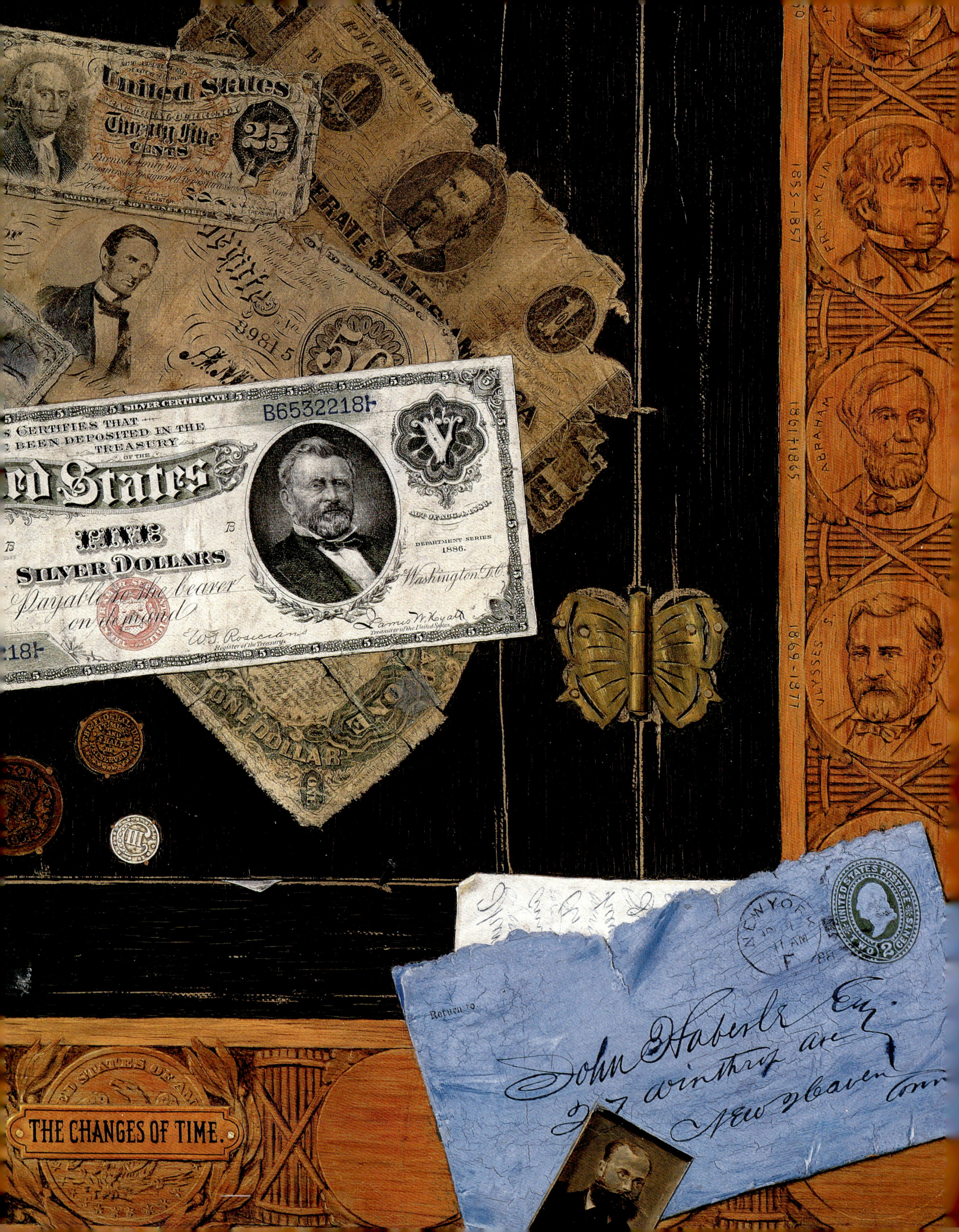

United States
Twenty five
CENTS
25
RICHMOND
39815
SILVER CERTIFICATE
B65322181
CERTIFIES THAT
BEEN DEPOSITED IN THE
TREASURY
States
FIVE
SILVER DOLLARS
Payable to the bearer
on demand
DEPARTMENT SERIES
1886.
Washington D.C.
ONE DOLLAR
FRANKLIN
1853-1857
ABRAHAM
1861-1865
ULYSSES S.
1869-1877
NEW YORK
Return to
John Haberle Esq.
27 winthrop ave
New Haven Conn
THE CHANGES OF TIME.

CHAPTER 3 Genre and Later Still-Life Painting

GENRE PAINTING is especially accommodating to the incorporation of the artist's presence, since its principal concerns are the incidents and vignettes of everyday life, frequently those familiar to the artist or in which he has taken part. The painter is often a narrator or moralist who observes, inhabits, or comments on the usually ordinary and humble subject matter around him. Drawing on the inherited traditions of Dutch seventeenth- and English eighteenth-century painting, genre emerged in America as a major subject type, along with landscape, during the second quarter of the nineteenth century. It perfectly suited the democratic national temperament, a generally practical, materialist, and Protestant culture not unlike that of Holland earlier, and it complemented the cult of the individual and of the "common man" in the age of Jacksonian democracy. Given genre painting's central emphasis on pictorial storytelling, its images naturally invited the artist to locate a signature strategically as an expression of involvement in the world depicted, or perhaps as critical scrutiny of some social or political situation of the time.

This framework exactly describes the apparently calculated placements of William Sidney Mount's name in many of his works. One of America's earliest major genre painters, Mount belonged to the same generation as Thomas Cole and Fitz Hugh Lane; he was born in 1807 on eastern Long Island, where, after training in New York as a youth, he returned to paint for most of the rest of his life. As a result, Mount's career and art were constantly influenced by the contrasts (and occasionally conflicts) between and mix of urban and rural, city sophistication and country naïveté, national politics and regional customs. His stories would also unfold indoors and outside, and involve negotiations between male and female, old and young, slickers and bumpkins, whites and African-Americans. He especially enjoyed making observations about the political foibles of his time, and thanks to Elizabeth Johns and others we know that many of his pictures are coded commentaries on vernacular slogans, campaigning behavior, and antebellum presidential elections. The United States, of course, and New York, in particular, were increasingly caught up in abolitionist politics, although neither Mount's imagery nor his letters provide a fully clear reading of his personal political sympathies.

Mount's production of major finished oils is not a large one — they number some three to four dozen important pictures — but at least half of them have clearly placed signatures, many painted illusionistically within the fictive scenes. In some instances they appear logically in open areas without carrying any heightened meaning or association; in others they seem to call special attention to a key element of the narrative or the artist's connection with the subject. We can actually group his signature locations into a few favored types. The first group includes his interior scenes, composed, as might be expected, after Dutch genre precedents. Seldom are more than two or three figures seated or standing together in the center of a small plain room; in these paintings, Mount used the perspective of the bare floorboards to create the spatial recession in the room. On the plane of the floorboard in the foreground he signed his name as if it were on the plane of the floor itself. From Mount's sketchbooks we know he practiced exercises in perspective, though he did not explicitly inscribe his lettering in receding perspective as Thomas Eakins would later in the nineteenth century. Sometimes the floorboard closest to the viewer in the foreground, at the bottom edge of the canvas, appears ambiguously to be both parallel to the picture surface and receding into space under the figures.[1] Elsewhere, when the boards recede perpendicularly to the lower edge, their perspectival recession is more convincing. One such example is particularly effective: *The Painter's Triumph,* 1838 (fig. 63), originally known as *Artist Showing His Own Work.*

The image is full of teasing ironies. Looking very much like Mount himself, the artist stands at the center of the composition, gesturing dramatically at his canvas. For a country dweller, he appears rather suave in his sophisticated dress and confident manner, in contrast to the bright clothing of his more rustic visitor, who holds a buggy whip. We can think of Rembrandt's self-portraits in the studio and other Dutch genre images that might have served as inspiration for this, where we have representations of paintings within a painting. Here, all the canvases are obscured, either turned to the wall or angled away from our view. The only image visible is on the back wall: a

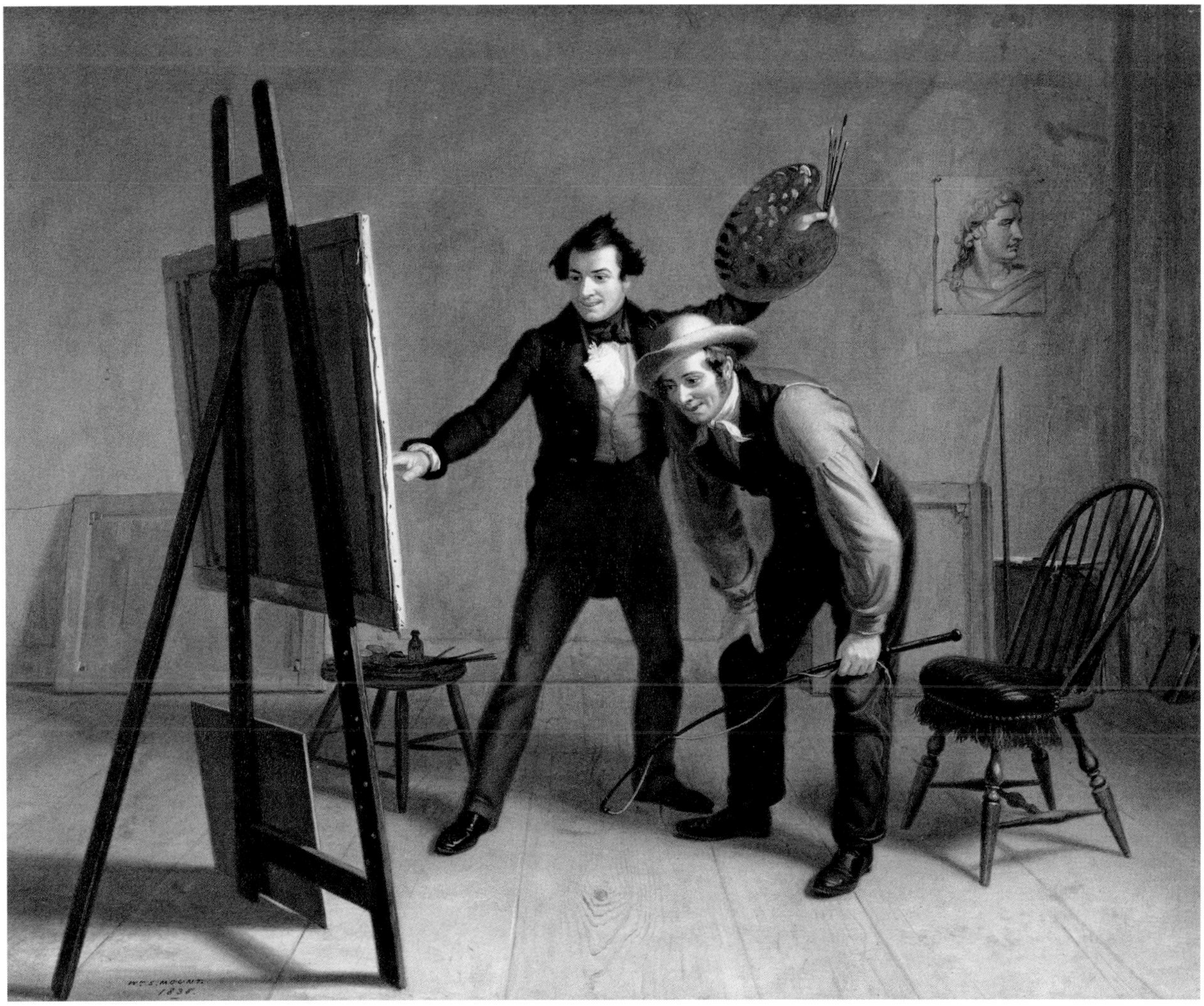

Fig. 63. William Sidney Mount, *The Painter's Triumph,* 1838. Oil on wood, 19 ½ x 23 9/16 in. (49.5 x 59.8 cm). Courtesy of the Pennsylvania Academy of the Fine Arts, Philadelphia. Bequest of Henry C. Carey (The Carey Collection)

drawing of Apollo's head, which turns away from the modern scene. The painter lunges at his canvas like Zeus hurling a lightning bolt or a fencer thrusting, while his guest eagerly focuses his attention in the same direction. The outstretched arms of the painter form a diagonal linking the ideal classicism of the past — the Apollo — with Mount's contemporary genre subject presumably on the easel.[2] This dichotomy represented in fact a critical dialogue in which Mount could well have been engaged at the National Academy of Design at the time. Thus, it would seem no accident that Mount painted

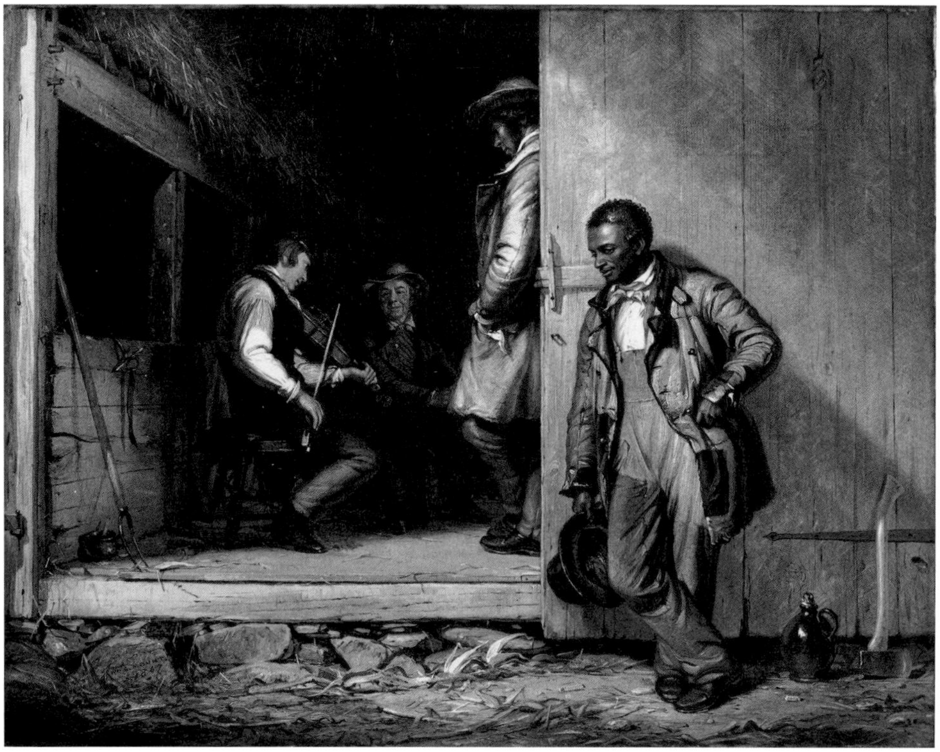

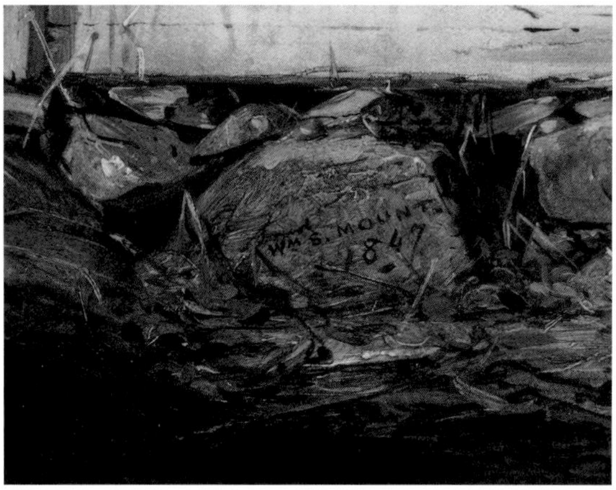

Fig. 64. William Sidney Mount, *The Power of Music,* 1847. Oil on canvas, 17 1/8 x 21 in. (43.4 x 53.5 cm). The Cleveland Museum of Art, 2002. Leonard C. Hanna, Jr. Fund

Fig. 65. William Sidney Mount, *The Power of Music* (detail of fig. 64), 1847

his name and the date on the floorboard just below the two canvases propped up on the easel, thereby associating himself a second time with the artistic enterprise in the scene.

A variation of this occurs in one of Mount's early outdoor genre paintings, *Dancing on the Barn Floor,* 1831 (Museums at Stony Brook, New York), where his signature appears on the foreground beam that supports the barn floor on which his figures dance. In later versions of this theme, most notably *Dance of the Haymakers*, 1845 (Museums at Stony Brook, New York), and *The Power of Music*, 1847 (figs. 64 and 65), his name is on one of the large rocks serving as a foundation for the barn floor. Mount himself was a proficient musician, and he used as his models for these paintings local neighbors and friends. We can wonder if he was subliminally aligning his place in the scene with the figure dancing or playing the fiddle above, or expressing sympathy with the black figure, who, like the artist, is on the outside of the barn listening to the music within. It is obviously impossible to know how explicit Mount's feelings were, except that his signature intimately ties him to his imagery.

The late landscape *Catching Crabs*, 1865 (Museums at Stony Brook, New York), also has a signature on a rock — in this case situated on the edge of the beach in the foreground — which is not so much a gloss on the narrative meaning as simply an indication of Mount's familiarity with this scenery. Yet another group of outdoor pictures displays signatures on a patch of dirt near the foreground. These include *Farmer's Nooning*, 1836 (Museums at Stony Brook, New York); *Ringing the Pig*, 1842, and *Eel Spearing at Setauket*, 1845 (both New York State Historical Association, Cooperstown); and *Loss and Gain*, 1848 (Museums at Stony Brook, New York), which again primarily indicate Mount's firsthand awareness of the subject matter. We know more about his explicit commentary on the political context in one picture, *Cider Making*, 1841 (Metropolitan Museum of Art, New York), which was occasioned by his Whig patron, Charles Augustus Davis, and the successful Whig campaign in the presidential election of 1840. Stuart Feld was the first to see that the theme was associated with the campaign slogan "Log Cabin and Hard Cider," and, indeed, one of the most prominent of the several cider barrels depicted in the foreground bears the date 1840.[3] This Indian summer is the time of both the election and the ripe apple harvest. Elizabeth Johns further notes that the voting citizenry often overindulged in hard cider, and that the barrels were emblematic of the Whig party. She has even identified most of the figures shown as prominent party politicians.[4] Although Mount leaned toward the Democrats, he included himself here as a detached observer by his signature and the second date of 1841 (the year of completion) on the flat rock in the left foreground corner.

There is a final grouping of Mount's signatures, also ranging in their associations from contemporary politics to personal activities, but all signed by him on some object usually central to the picture's theme. In *Catching*

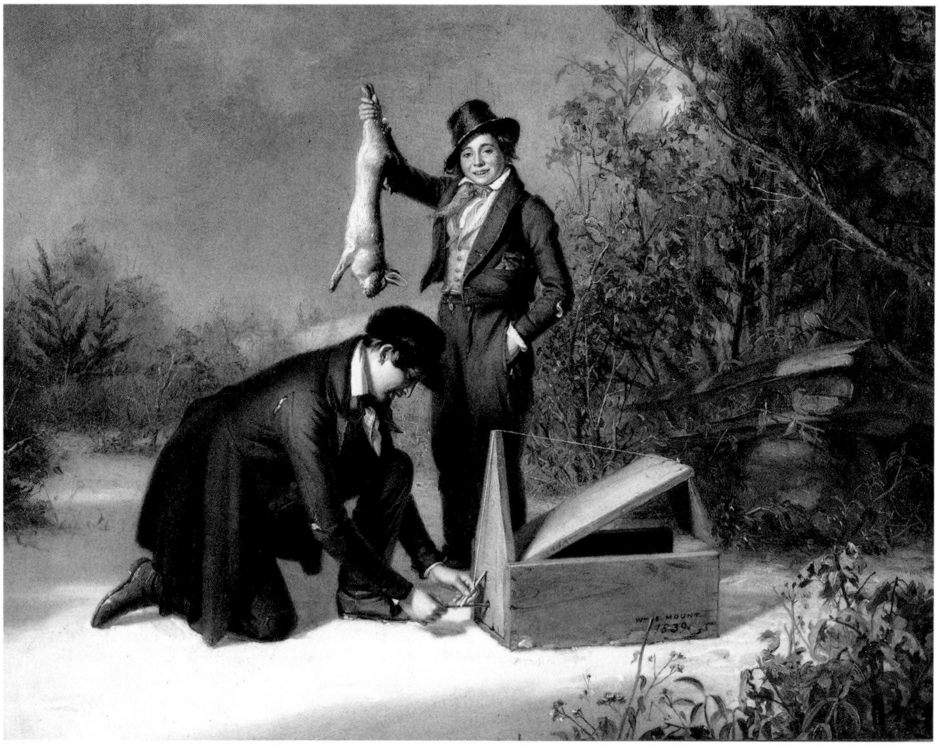

Fig. 66. William Sidney Mount, *Catching Rabbits*, 1839. Oil on panel, 18 ⅛ x 21 ¼ in. (46 x 54 cm). The Long Island Museum of American Art, History & Carriages, Stony Brook, N.Y. Gift of Mr. and Mrs. Ward Melville, 1958

Rabbits, 1839 (fig. 66), his name sits on the lower corner of the wooden trap. On the surface, this is a charming image of two jaunty youths in a playful winter scene, but, again according to Johns, on another level, one well understood by Mount's audience, this was a not so veiled reference to contemporary politics. First, there are the word associations with the central image in the composition, the plump trophy just retrieved from the trap and held up before us, which any learned observer would have appreciated: rabbit = hare = hair = wig = Whig. The painting would thus be alluding to the Whig efforts to trap votes in the campaign of 1840;[5] in this regard, we can read the rabbit trap as a precursor of the ballot box. With the placement of his signature, Mount established himself as a close observer of these tricks, a Democrat catching the opposition red-handed.

In 1848, Mount painted a non-political image, *Farmer Whetting His Scythe* (Museums at Stony Brook, New York), and, as if to associate himself with a familiar and commonplace activity of his local agricultural landscape,

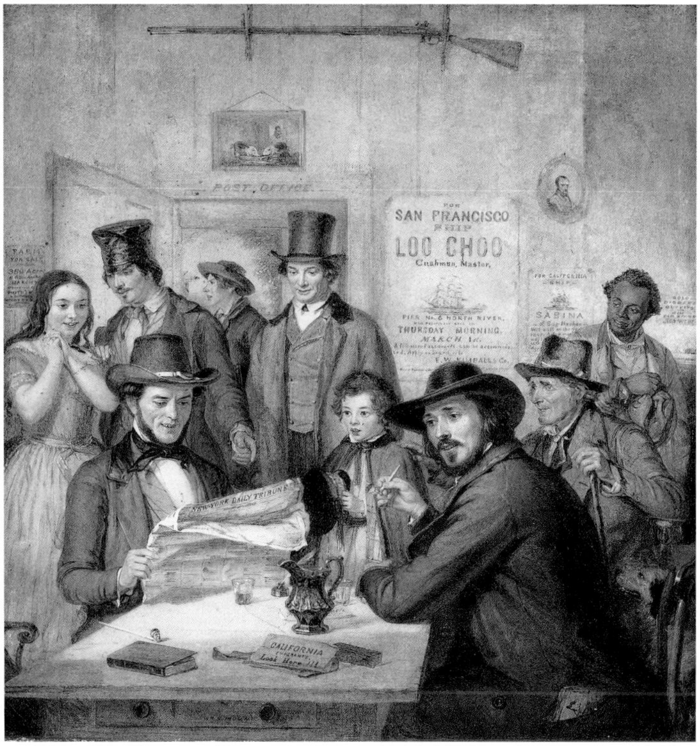

Fig. 67. William Sidney Mount, *California News*, 1850. Oil on canvas, 21 ½ x 20 ¼ in. (54.6 x 51.4 cm). The Long Island Museum of American Art, History & Carriages, Stony Brook, N.Y. Gift of Mr. and Mrs. Ward Melville, 1955

he signed his name on the farmer's bright red shirt cast down in the lower right foreground. Two years later, the artist turned his attention to two subjects of regional as well as national interest: the Mexican War of 1846 and, following almost immediately, the California gold rush of 1849. *California News*, 1850 (fig. 67), presents a number of individuals, varied in age, gender, class, and race, all gathered around the latest newspaper to arrive at the local post office. The rifle above the door is a reminder of the country's recent territorial expansionism, while the small painting of fat pigs below and the poster advertising travel to San Francisco suggest respectively the greed for gold and the allure of the western horizon. By implication, Mount again is present in this gathering, taking his place at the viewer's end of the table, where his name appears between the knobs on the table drawer in the immediate foreground. It even appears that the man at the right has turned to engage the unseen artist-as-journalist in conversation.

Around 1850, Mount began a series of portraits showing figures playing musical instruments; he is said to have used his brother Robert and local black neighbors and farmhands as models for some of these. These paintings display a combination of Mount's awareness of Dutch genre precedents and

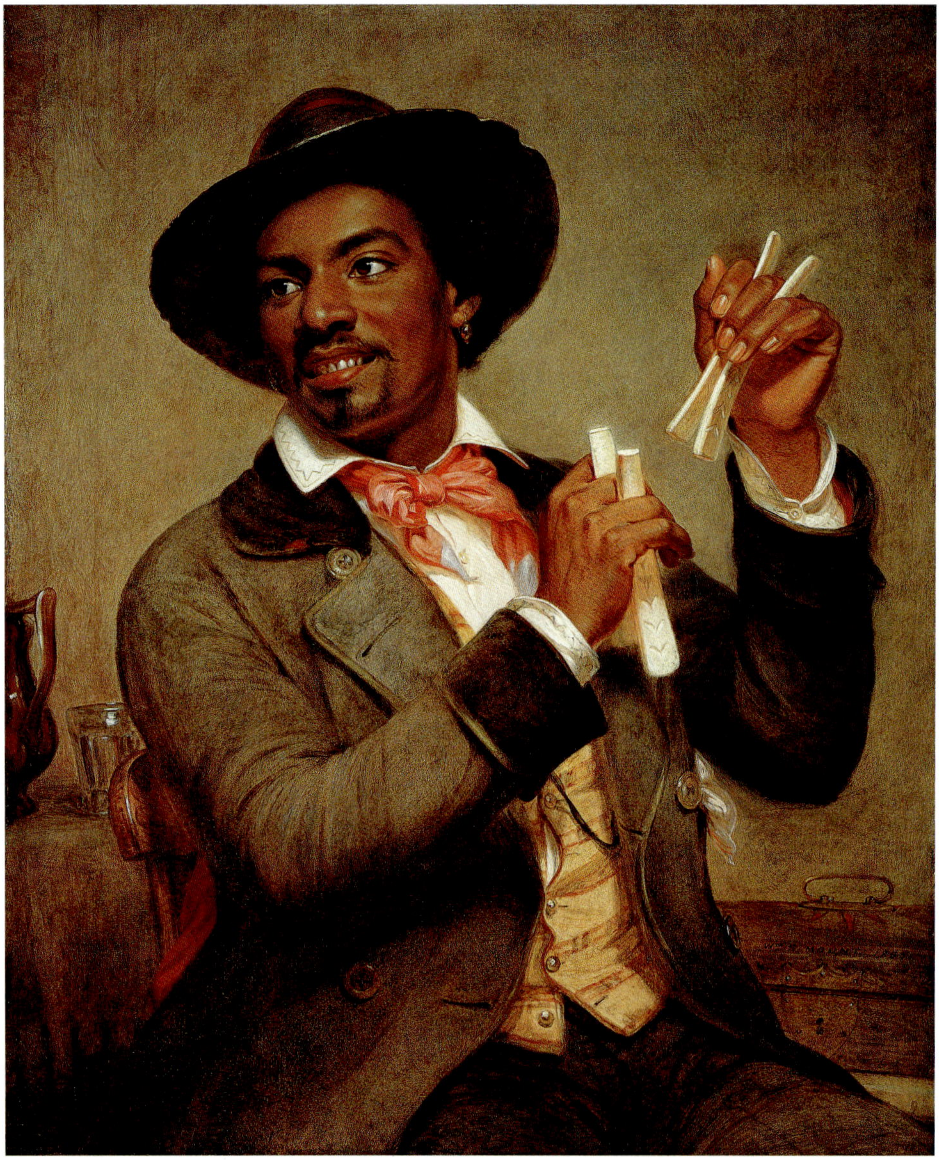

Fig. 68. William Sidney Mount, *The Bone Player*, 1856. Oil on canvas, 36 ⅛ x 29 ⅛ in. (91.7 x 73.9 cm). Museum of Fine Arts, Boston. Bequest of Martha C. Karolik for the M. and M. Karolik Collection of American Paintings, 1815–65, 1948

his own facility as a musician. Certainly his depictions of African-Americans at this time were among the rare sympathetic and unsentimentalized treatments by a white artist in antebellum America. Of this whole group, *The Bone Player*, 1856 (fig. 68), especially catches our attention, for Mount chose to place his signature on the top of the box just behind and to our right of the musician. The handle on the lid suggests that this is the carrying case for the fellow's musical instruments, elements both essential to the picture and personally familiar to the artist.

Such deep involvement with the subject matter has its counterpart, though less frequently or consistently, in Mount's slightly younger contemporary in the west George Caleb Bingham. The other major genre painter of mid-century America, Bingham was born in Virginia in 1811, but moved with his family eight years later to the Missouri frontier, where he grew up. As a youth, he received some early training as a portrait painter, which instilled in him a sense for human individuality that carried over into much of his later figure painting. A trip to the east first exposed him to the genre pictures of Mount, Joshua Shaw, and Emmanuel Leutze, whose work was being exhibited at the Pennsylvania Academy and elsewhere in the late 1830s. During the next few years, Bingham undertook his own first scenes of daily life, such as figures conversing in cottage yards or washing clothes along the riverbanks, subjects along or on the Missouri River he knew well. In the mid-1840s he became interested in politics, producing parade banners for the Whig candidates in 1844, and two years later actually running for the Missouri legislature. Observing firsthand the ferment and imperfections of politics on the frontier led him early in the next decade to undertake his large series of canvases devoted to aspects of the election process. Whether from life on the river or in the chambers of government, Bingham produced his best works out of direct personal experience.

His signature on a large rocky outcropping outside the front yard in *Cottage Scenery*, 1845 (Corcoran Gallery of Art, Washington, D.C.), signifies Bingham as a nearby observer, while his name in another picture of the same year, *Landscape: Rural Scenery* (private collection), appears on a rotting plank of wood in the foreground. Immediately adjacent, a mother with two small children does the family washing at the river's edge, a grouping that can easily stand for the beginnings of the artist's own family at this time. But it is in several of his important scenes of boatmen and settlers that he is at ease within his own landscape. In *The Squatters*, 1850 (figs. 69 and 70), his name reads across the foreground log just below the seated figure. His upright, rounded letters and the date have the careful clarity of a school blackboard exercise, but more importantly, Bingham's inscription up front is a reminder of the artist's actual viewpoint before the canvas and even suggests he is a visitor who has just engaged the squatters' attention. These people live off the

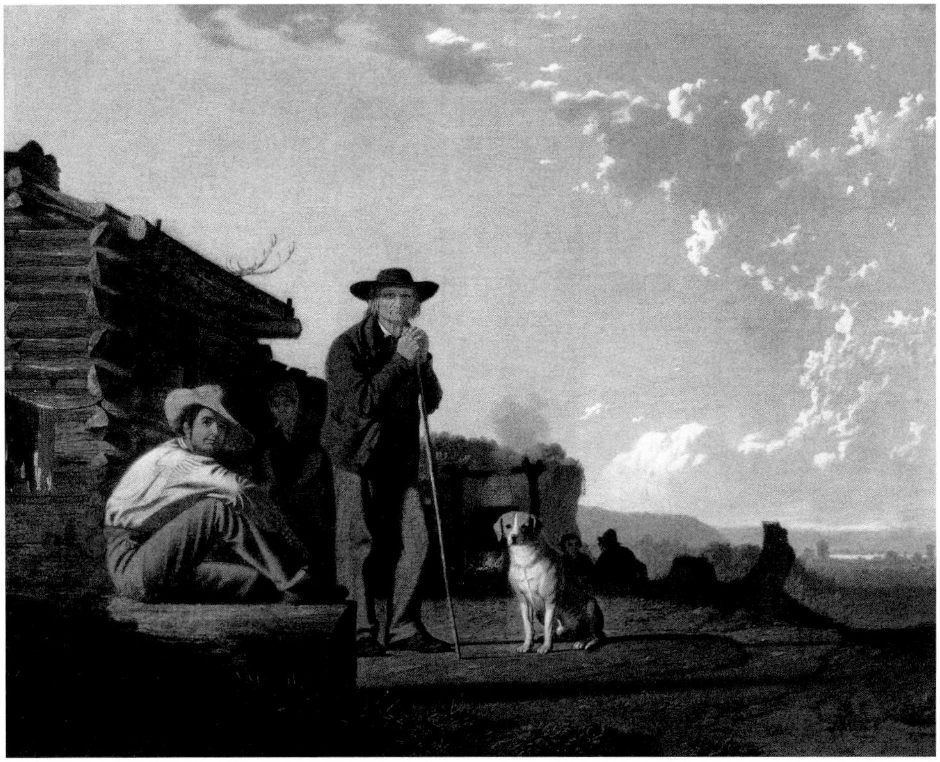

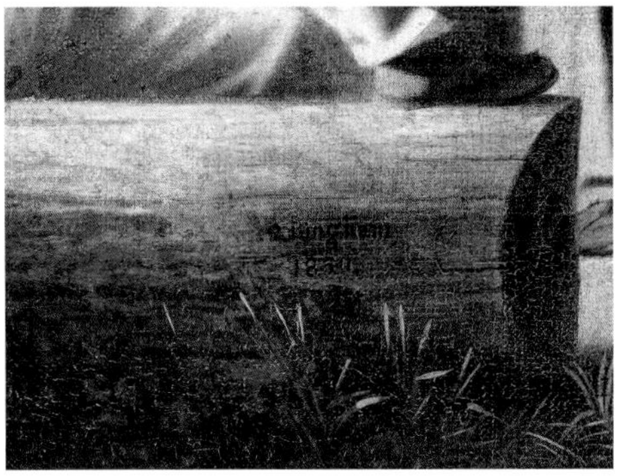

Fig. 69. George Caleb Bingham, *The Squatters,* 1850. Oil on canvas, 23 ⅛ x 28 ¼ in. (58.7 x 71.7 cm). Museum of Fine Arts, Boston. Bequest of Henry Lee Shattuck in memory of the late Ralph W. Gray, 1971

Fig. 70. George Caleb Bingham, *The Squatters* (detail of fig. 69), 1850

land, as the antlers above the cabin door attest, and after clearing this area, they will soon move on. His signature affirms Bingham's role as a witness.

The same is true of *Watching the Cargo,* 1849 (State Historical Society of Missouri, Columbia), in which he placed his name on the end of the barrel, again next to a boatman seated on the ground. This is the same gesture we have already seen in Durand's woods and on Lane's docks. In the second version of his famous *Fur Traders Descending the Missouri,* also known as *Trappers' Return,* 1851 (fig. 71), Bingham set his name on the stern of the

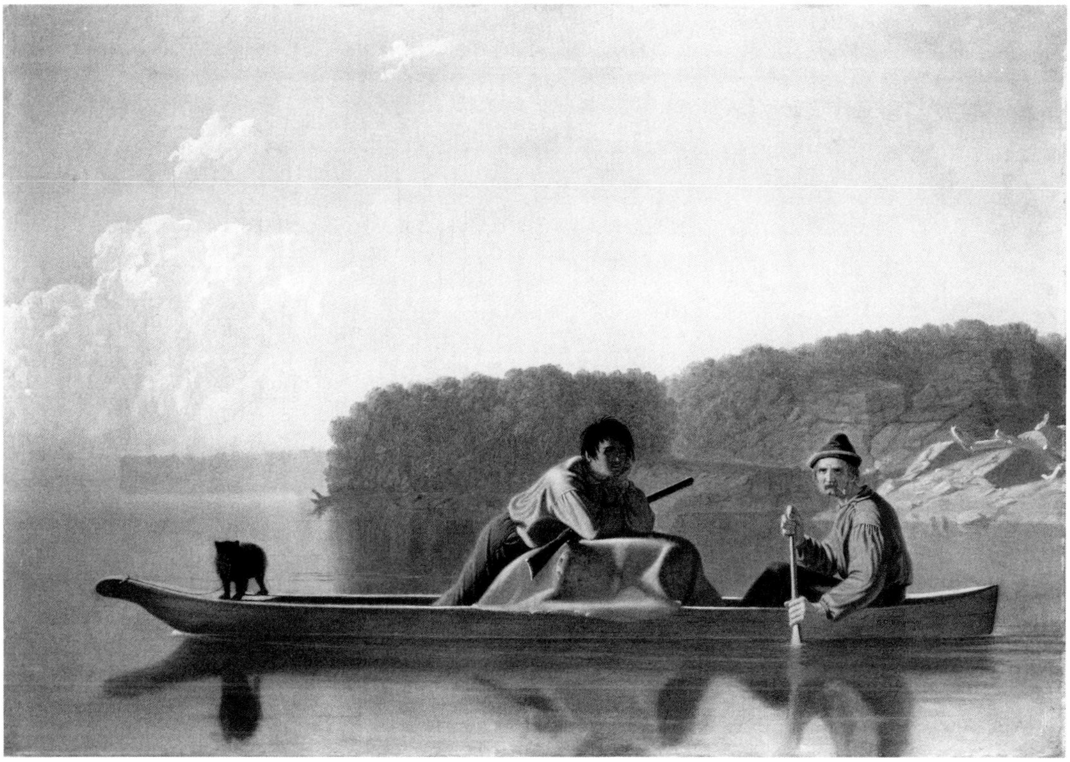

Fig. 71. George Caleb Bingham, *Trappers' Return*, 1851. Paint on canvas, 26¼ x 36¼ in. (66.68 x 92.08 cm). The Detroit Institute of Arts. Gift of Dexter M. Ferry, Jr.

canoe, just below the old French trapper paddling the boat. By doing so, Bingham identifies himself with the white man in control of the voyage, but the low placement also suggests the artist himself drifting and observing with the river at eye level.

If landscape and genre painting reflected something of America's expansive optimism and promise at mid-century, so too did the revival of still-life painting express nature's bounty and fruitfulness. Two of the leading exponents of this subject matter, both of them associated with the Philadelphia tradition established by Raphaelle Peale, were John F. Francis and Severin Roesen. Francis was a native of Philadelphia, who after beginning his career as a portraitist, turned to still life, likely aware of the Peales and of imported Dutch paintings. His abundantly packed tabletop compositions, such as *Still Life with Wine Bottles and Basket of Fruit*, 1857 (fig. 72), often display his signature along the front table edge — in this instance on the tablecloth —

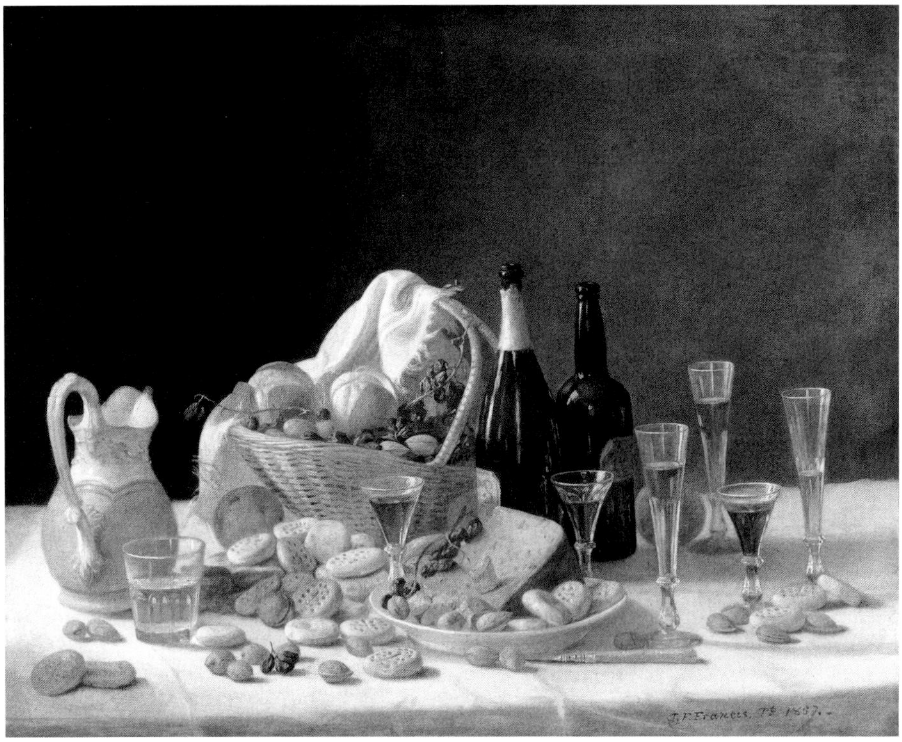

Fig. 72. John F. Francis, *Still Life with Wine Bottles and Basket of Fruit,* 1857. Oil on canvas, 25 ⅛ x 30 in. (63.5 x 76.2 cm). Museum of Fine Arts, Boston. Gift of Maxim Karolik for the Karolik Collection of American Paintings, 1815–65, 1947

recalling the examples of Cotán, Van Huysum, and later on Chardin. In the same way, the artist's name here calls attention to his role as designer.

Like Francis, Severin Roesen painted lavishly massed gatherings, usually of fruits or flowers. Trained as a porcelain painter in Germany, he emigrated to New York in 1848 and later moved to Pennsylvania, where he applied his technique of meticulous detailing, bright coloring, and polished surfaces to his still lifes. Of the several dozen works he produced, primarily over the decades of the 1850s and 1860s, a large number are signed in a highly personal way. While some bear his name in relatively conventional block lettering or in italic print, many display signatures in a script imitating vine tendrils, and extending from a grape or flower stem (fig. 73).[6] Like the leaves or buds often hanging over the front edge of the table, Roesen's tendril inscription floats out into the foreground air. His biographers believe he was aware of the German decorative-arts tradition, which may have directed him to floral themes. But he also likely knew the examples of Dutch still life, and especially

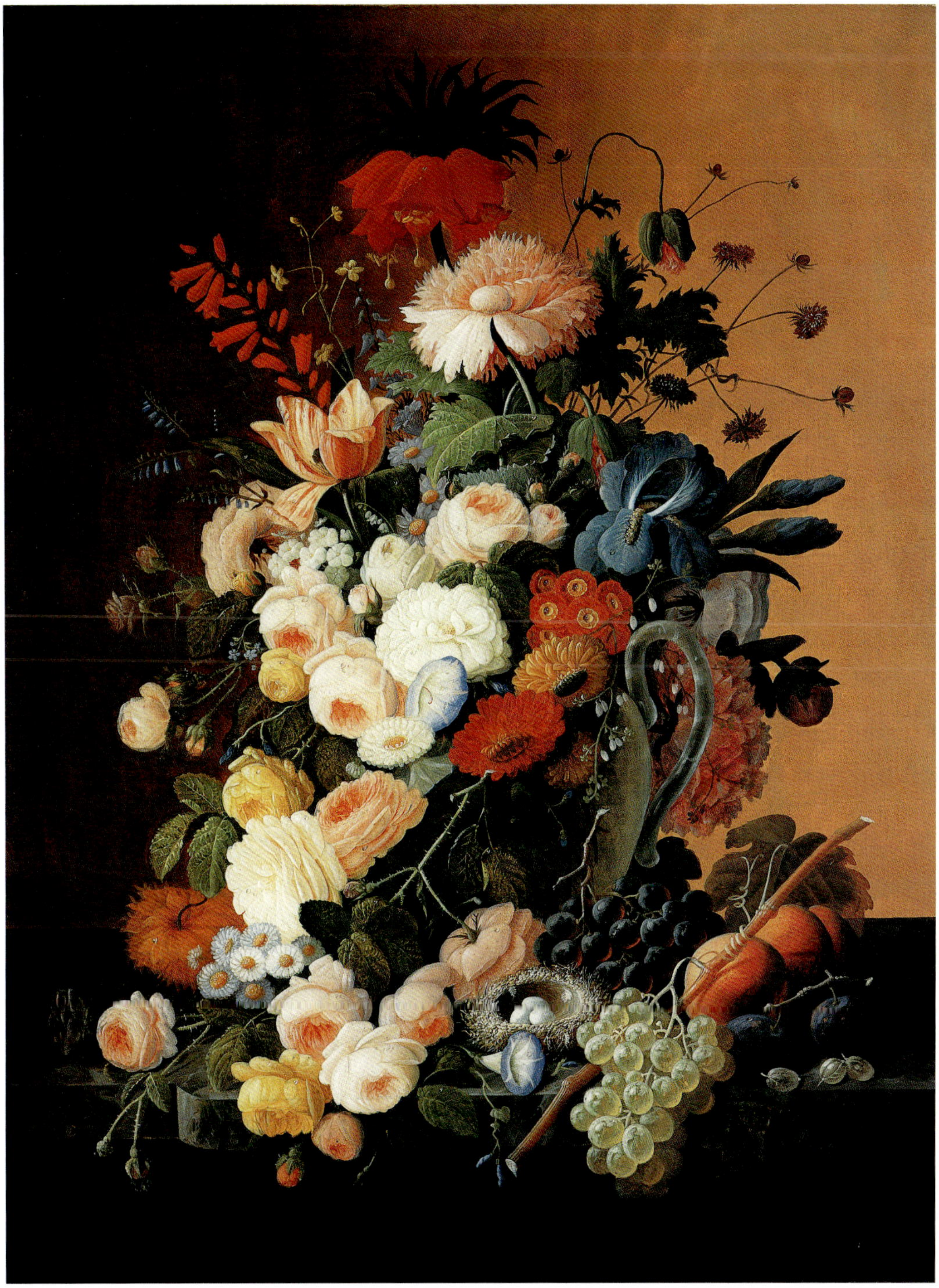

Fig. 73. Severin Roesen, *Still Life with Flowers*, ca. 1862. Oil on canvas, 40 x 30 in. (101.6 x 76.2 cm). Private collection, via Berry-Hill Galleries, New York

the work of Jan van Huysum, which would have provided him with models of both flower bouquets and flourishing vine-like signatures. We can well appreciate why Roesen employed inscriptions so organically identified with his subjects when we realize that in a larger sense his floral bunches themselves were emblematic self-portraits. After all, his name in German means "roses," the favored flowers that appear more than any other in his arrangements, constantly varied in size, massing, and coloring. His signature thus serves as a written footnote to the visual imagery above.

Another possible self-association with still-life subject matter occurs in Sanford Gifford's *Two Pears on a Tabletop,* ca. 1866 (fig. 74). This is a rare theme for an artist known foremost as a follower of Thomas Cole, a leading figure of the second generation of Hudson River painters, and later a key practitioner of luminist landscape views. At the same time, we can recognize Gifford's golden tonalities, more familiar in his radiant landscape paintings, applied here to the interior illumination softly surrounding the tawny pears and flickering in highlights on the crystal glasses behind. Gifford's name appears on the envelope at the left, in the manner of the Italian *cartellino* and Dutch calling card (see figs. 6 and 19), with his address, "15 10 St.," referring to his studio quarters in New York's famous Tenth Street Studio Building.

Gifford, one of the first to occupy space there, was soon joined by several other well-known colleagues of his generation, including Frederic Church, Jervis McEntee, William Hart, John Henry Hill, and Worthington Whittredge. (Later, other luminaries, such as Eastman Johnson, Winslow Homer, and William Merritt Chase, also worked there.) It was a collegial group, with strong artistic interchange and camaraderie among the tenants. Many traveled and sketched together, and in New York frequently met at the Studio Building for convivial dinners. In this light we can plausibly wonder if the envelope here is an invitation to such an evening, and the paired goblets and pears an intimate gathering by proxy of artistic friends at the table. Where it is, Gifford's name certainly places him in refined and mellow company.

In the following decades, American still-life painting would take markedly different directions, and during the second half of the nineteenth century the subjects shifted from luscious fruits and flowers to the inanimate realm of worldly possessions, presented often in a graver palette and mood. No longer distillations of a burgeoning landscape and spiritually optimistic expansiveness, later nineteenth-century still life became more introspective and materialist. It also embraced with a passion a different practice of seventeenth-century Dutch precedents: trompe l'oeil illusionism. Three painters

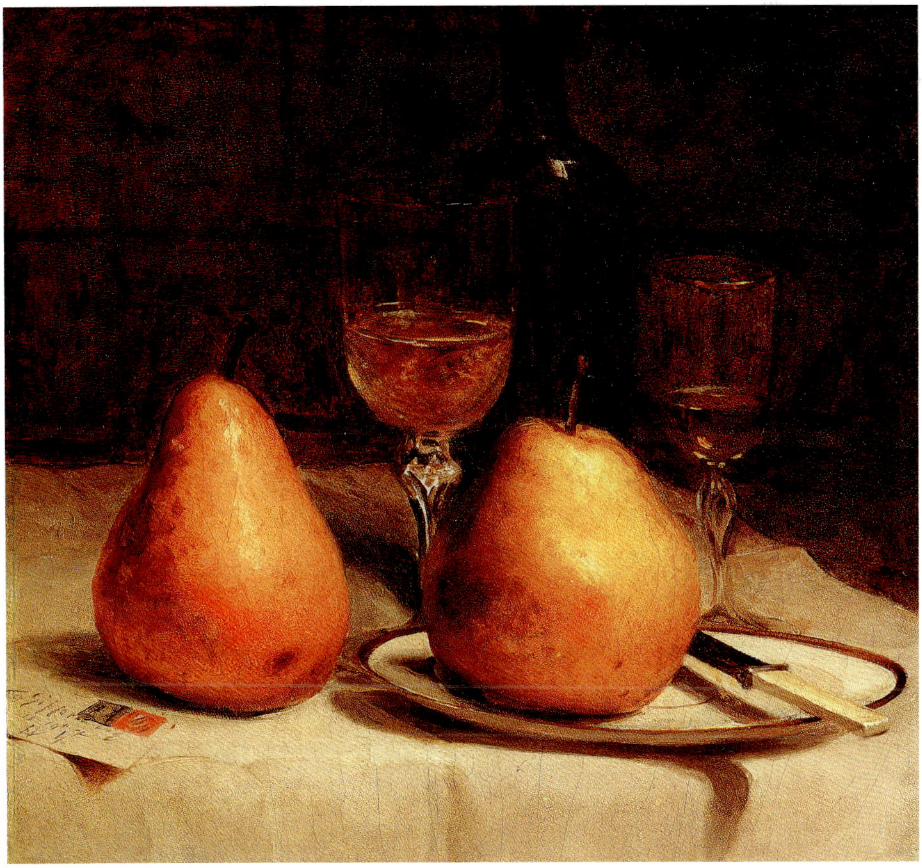

Fig. 74. Sanford R. Gifford, *Two Pears on a Tabletop*, ca. 1866. Oil on canvas, 11 ¼ x 11 ¾ in. (28.6 x 29.9 cm). National Gallery of Art, Washington, D.C. Gift (partial and promised) of William and Abigail Gerdts

in particular stand out in this tradition, each very different in the character of his work: John Haberle (1856–1933), William M. Harnett (1848–1892), and John F. Peto (1854–1907). Though they were aware of each other's art, and shared some subjects in common, their distinctive personalities emerge in their respective techniques and styles: Haberle the witty fabricator of visual puns, Harnett the worldly businessman and gregarious colleague, and Peto the introverted and long-suffering family man.

Haberle's principal biographer, Gertrude Grace Sill, has given us the major shape of his life and artistic production. Of German background, he was born in New Haven, and spent most of his life there. He began sketching early, then apprenticed with local engravers; during the early 1880s, he was employed as an exhibition preparator at the Peabody Museum at Yale

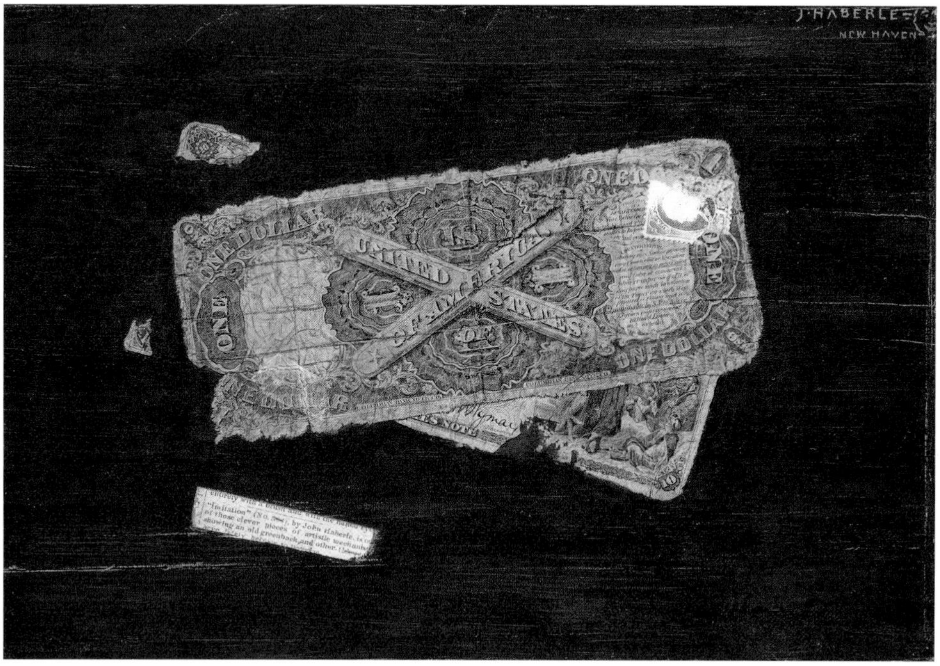

Fig. 75. John Haberle, *U.S.A.*, ca. 1889. Oil on canvas, 8 ½ x 12 in. (21.6 x 30.5 cm). Private collection. Courtesy of the Richard York Gallery, New York

University. We may legitimately speculate that the precision required in both these latter callings contributed to the meticulous detailing and complicated assemblages in many of his mature still lifes. Indeed, while still producing lithographs in the early 1880s, he undertook his first illusionist paintings. Significantly, the one he labeled "My first work in oil" was *Self-Portrait,* 1882 (private collection), which struck the central autobiographical note that would dominate his work over much of the following decade.[7] It was during this relatively brief period that he produced all of his major trompe l'oeil pictures, and signed most of them in clever or intricate ways. These signatures include painted newspaper clippings, frame labels, chalked names, caricatures, and tintypes of himself, all integrated into the flattened still-life array of ephemera displayed across his illusionist boards. Thus, his subjects were his prowess as an artist or events in his life, and his various signatures amusingly narrate Haberle's autobiography.

Since the chronology of his works has already received full attention, it is perhaps more revealing here to enumerate the typologies of his protean signatures — the multiple ways in which Haberle placed himself into his pictures. Quite possibly emulating devices he could have seen in contemporary examples by Harnett and Peto, one mode he employed on several occasions was the illusionist inscription of his name, as if carved in capital letters into the painted board on which his objects were hung or pasted. Typical is *Twenty Dollar Bill*, 1890 (Museum of Fine Arts, Springfield, Massachusetts), one of several similar currency pieces, in this instance signed and dated in the lower right corner of the board.[8] Two of the others include fragments of newspaper clippings pasted nearby, which add further autobiographical elements to the composition. In *U.S.A.*, ca. 1889 (fig. 75), the painted newsprint reads in part "entirely with the brush and with the naked eye. . . . *Imitation* (No. 3) by John Haberle is one of those clever pieces of artistic mechanics showing an old greenback and other. . . ."[9] *Reproduction*, ca. 1886–87 (private collection), depicts beneath the well-worn ten-dollar bill two clippings referring to counterfeiting (to which some felt Haberle came very close) and a tintype self-portrait. Other subjects signed in this manner were *Time and Eternity*, ca. 1889–90 (New Britain Museum of Art, Connecticut), which shows a hanging pocket watch, playing cards, and the artist's signature inscribed on an upper corner of the wood panel, and *Fresh Roasted*, 1887 (Yale University Art Gallery, New Haven), where his name is incised in the painted frame.

News clippings provided a natural form of self-representation for Haberle, and *Can You Break a Five?*, ca. 1888 (Amon Carter Museum, Fort Worth), displays the same newsprint he used in *U.S.A.*, which at once mentions his name and compliments his talents.[10] Perhaps his most obvious and visual form of signature was the tintype self-portrait he included with the news notice in *Reproduction*. This also appears in two of Haberle's most ambitious and complicated paintings, *Changes of Time*, 1888 (fig. 76), and *A Bachelor's Drawer*, 1890–94 (Metropolitan Museum of Art, New York), in both of which it is placed as if wedged into the lower edge of the picture frame. Both are dense assemblages of paper ephemera, in the former a variety of currency notes and postage stamps, and in the latter notes along with photographs, playing cards, and theater tickets. Clearly, Haberle loved to indulge in rendering all manner of printed lettering and figural images, often in counterpoint either to his own name in newsprint or his photographic portrait. *Changes of Time*, for example, reveals layers of presidential portraits on the several notes and surrounding postage stamps, and additional allegorical figures on coins nailed to the board. The frame, an equal tour de force, is painted to resemble a light blond wood into which have been carved in shallow relief presidential portraits from the Founding Fathers, beginning at the top center, going around the frame, and ending with the most recent presidents at the

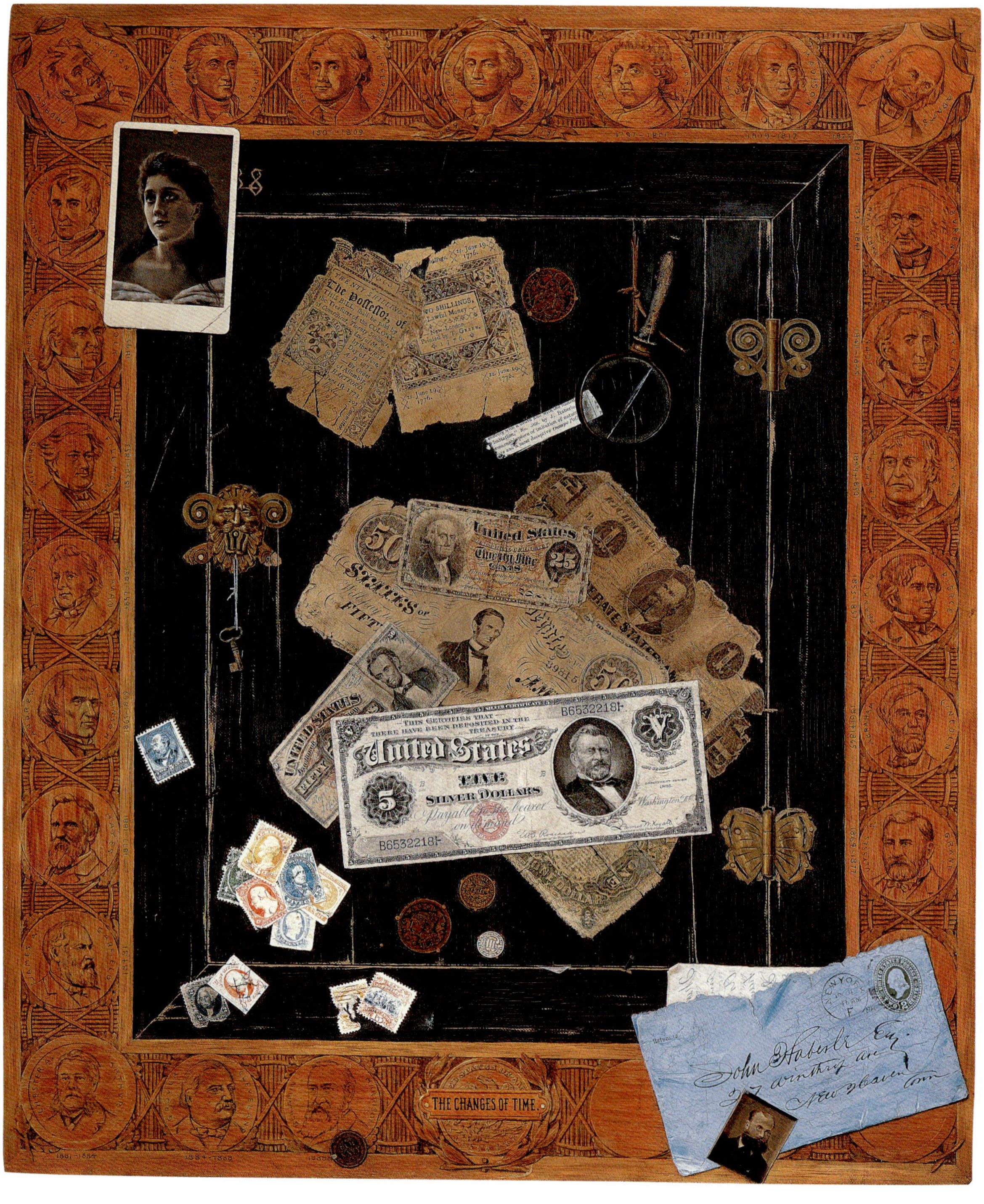

Fig. 76. John Haberle, *Changes of Time*, 1888. Oil on canvas, 23 ¾ x 15 ¾ in. (60.3 x 40 cm). Private collection

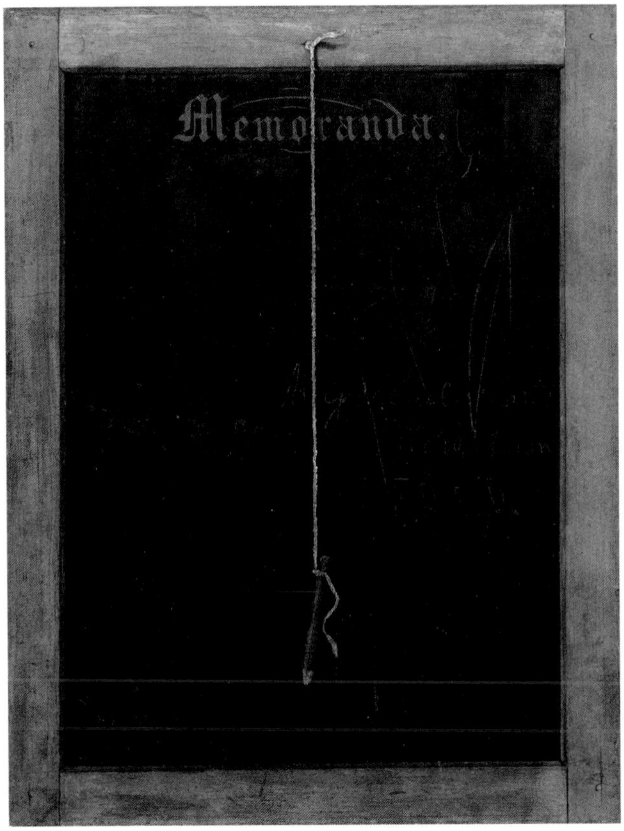

Fig. 77. John Haberle, *The Slate,* ca. 1895. Oil on canvas, 12 ⅛ x 9 ⅛ in. (30.8 x 23.2 cm). Fine Arts Museums of San Francisco. Museum purchase by exchange: Gift of Miss F. M. Knowles, Mrs. William K. Gutskow, Miss Keith Wakeman, and the M. H. de Young Endowment Fund

bottom. Tacked to the upper left is a photographic card of a woman, while diagonally across at the lower right we find Haberle's own tintype. This sits on a letter addressed to the artist, his name written out in a bold calligraphy that contrasts with the print typefaces above. *A Bachelor's Drawer* alludes to the playboy life prior to marriage, where money might be spent on girls, gaming, and theater. Again the colorful lithographed figures and photographic cards of models splay out above Haberle's portrait, which gazes out at us from the composition's lower edge.

One category of signatures involves the artist's name spelled out below a caricature of a head or stick figure — presumably another visual parody of a self-portrait. The scratched letters and crude profile of a face with a cigarette sign *A Favorite,* ca. 1890 (Museum of Fine Arts, Springfield, Massachusetts), with its hanging meerschaum pipe and matches affixed above. The subject is one that John F. Peto frequently painted around the same time, though Haberle delights in the illusionism of forms against a flat surface, whereas Peto's still lifes on the subject of smoking tend to be dark and even mysterious tabletop meditations on well-used objects. A stick figure drawn in chalk rather than "incised" (one more play on artistic techniques) appears to dance above Haberle's name on an illusionistic black slate (fig. 77), a format he variously repeated with the words "Memoranda," ORDERS, or LEAVE YOUR ORDER HERE written at the top of the slate. Gertrude Sill explains that the notation "My last slate at Watertown FRED" refers to the nickname of his son-in-law Anthony Fresneda, who lived in a nearby section of New Haven and to whom Haberle gave the picture. It is a charming conjunction of work, artist, and provenance as subject.[11]

Haberle's permutations of signing and placing his name seem endlessly clever, and obviously became an integral part of his artistic endeavor. A large painting titled *Japanese Corner*, 1898 (Museum of Fine Arts, Springfield, Massachusetts), shows an elaborate Japanese screen folded behind a still life on a bamboo table in the foreground. This is signed twice, once in imitation of Japanese characters at the bottom of the screen and again as a typed return address on an envelope attached at the left. A related still life, *Japanese Doll*, 1889 (private collection), depicts the title toy figure hanging from a nail on a small, framed panel. As if the greater number of signatures were in inverse ratio to the painting's size, Haberle entered his name in three places: on an attached metal label at the bottom, carved at the lower left, and integrated into the printed pattern of the doll's brocade kimono. If *A Bachelor's Drawer* represents one aspect of Haberle's interests, *Wife, Wine and Song*, 1889 (fig. 78), according to Sill probably alludes to another — his engagement and marriage, probably in 1890. The arrangement, with its partially pulled curtain, carved niche, and shallow shelf with objects, derives from obvious Dutch prototypes, but the subject matter appears to have veiled autobiographical elements. The cigar, violin, and champagne, along with the tintype, perhaps of an actress, suggest Haberle's bachelor tastes, while the carved roundel of a woman and child, and the block-lettered title below refer to the transition to domesticity. We note that the words are meant on the one hand to call to mind the old tune with the phrase "wine, woman, and song," and on the other, with the last letter obscured by the music sheet, to emphasize the new experience of a wife and son. An integral part of all this, Haberle introduces himself with the familiar tintype tucked in the lower corner and with his dashing signature on the woman's photograph, making him doubly present as an image maker.[12]

During the early 1890s, Haberle undertook a series of paintings called *Torn in Transit* (Memorial Art Gallery, University of Rochester, Rochester,

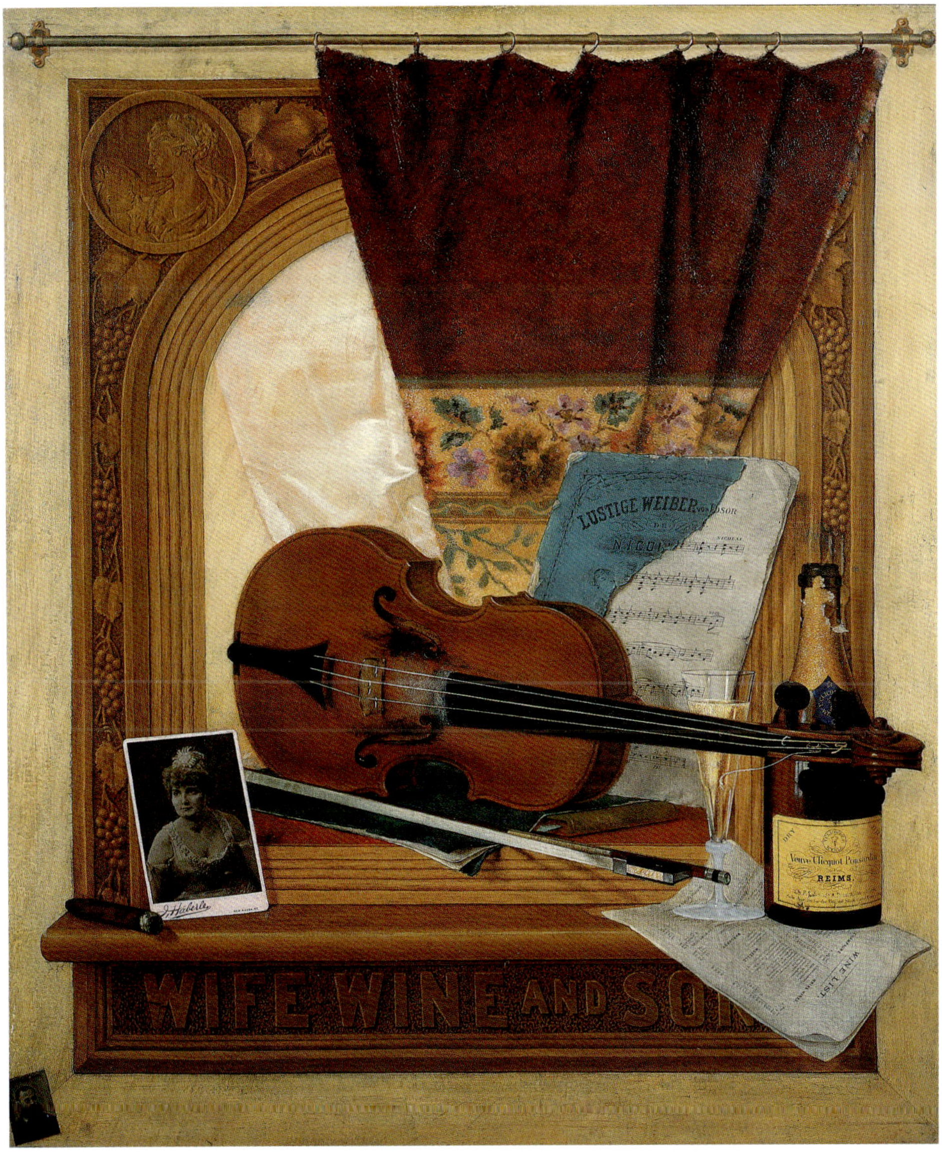

Fig. 78. John Haberle, *Wife, Wine and Song,* 1889. Oil on canvas, 30 x 25 ½ in. (76.2 x 64.8 cm). Courtesy of Berry-Hill Galleries, New York

New York), which show ostensibly wrapped landscape paintings with much of the paper ripped off the package. They bear the inscription "from Haberle" on one corner, presumably part of a return address. The looser style of the painting revealed within hints at the more painterly impressionist mode Haberle would soon take up, here still incorporated into a flat illusionist design. The theme of art about art informs a final set of paintings with signatures

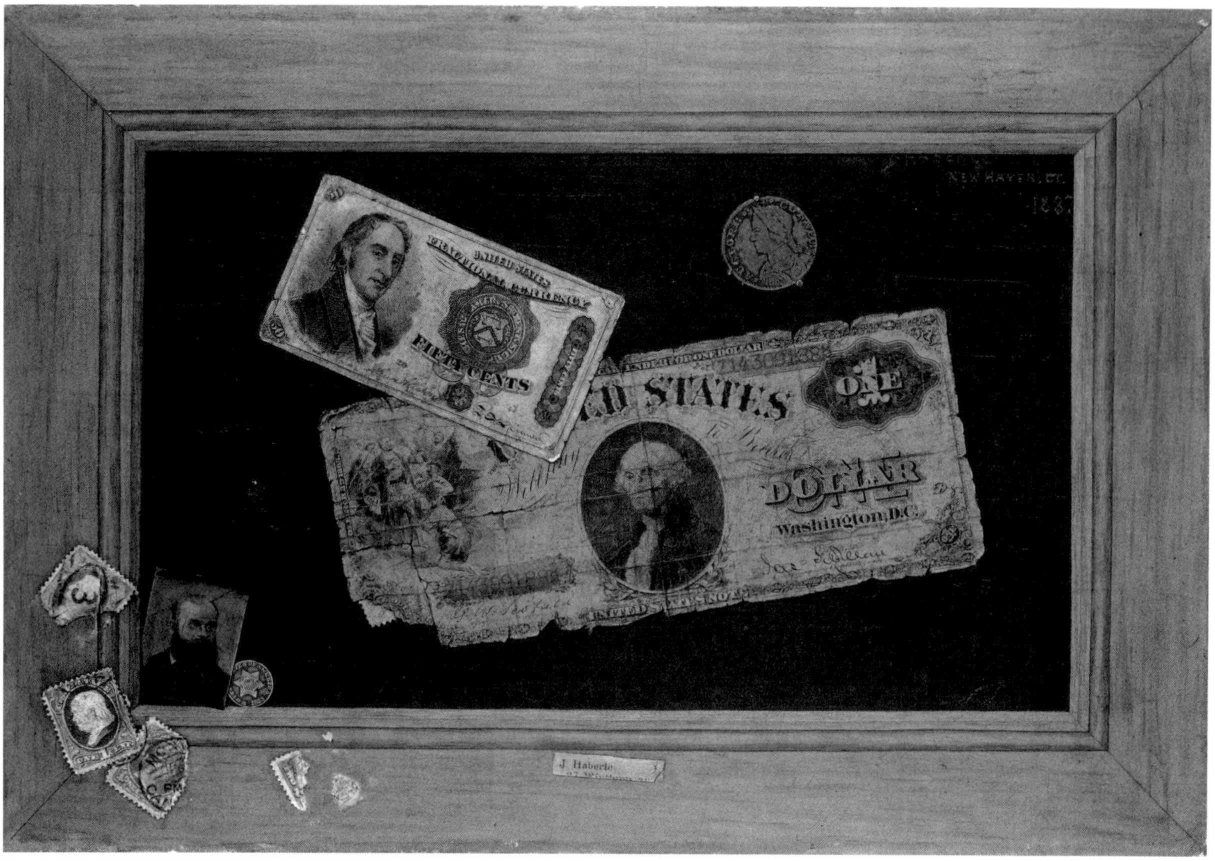

Fig. 79. John Haberle, *Imitation*, 1887. Oil on canvas, 10 x 14 in. (25.4 x 35.6 cm). National Gallery of Art, Washington, D.C. New Century Fund, gift of the Amon G. Carter Foundation

in the guise of labels on picture frames. *Imitation*, 1887 (fig. 79), gives us the usual assembly of currency, stamps, coins, and tintype self-portrait, with the artist now further identified by a clipped printed label on the center of the painted frame. An even more formal painted label bearing the artist's name appears on *The Palette*, ca. 1890 (fig. 80). In another version, Haberle actually attached real paintbrushes to a palette-shaped panel, heightening the ambiguity between the real and the artificial, and looking forward to a similar play with the imagery of palette and brushes by the Pop artist Jim Dine many decades later. Haberle's *Palette*, with its array of brushes, palette knife, and daubs of colored pigments, displays here both the source and end of the artist's work. In the ultimate act of imagination he uses paint to represent paint, a last and lasting reminder that the practice of art and the artistic pro-

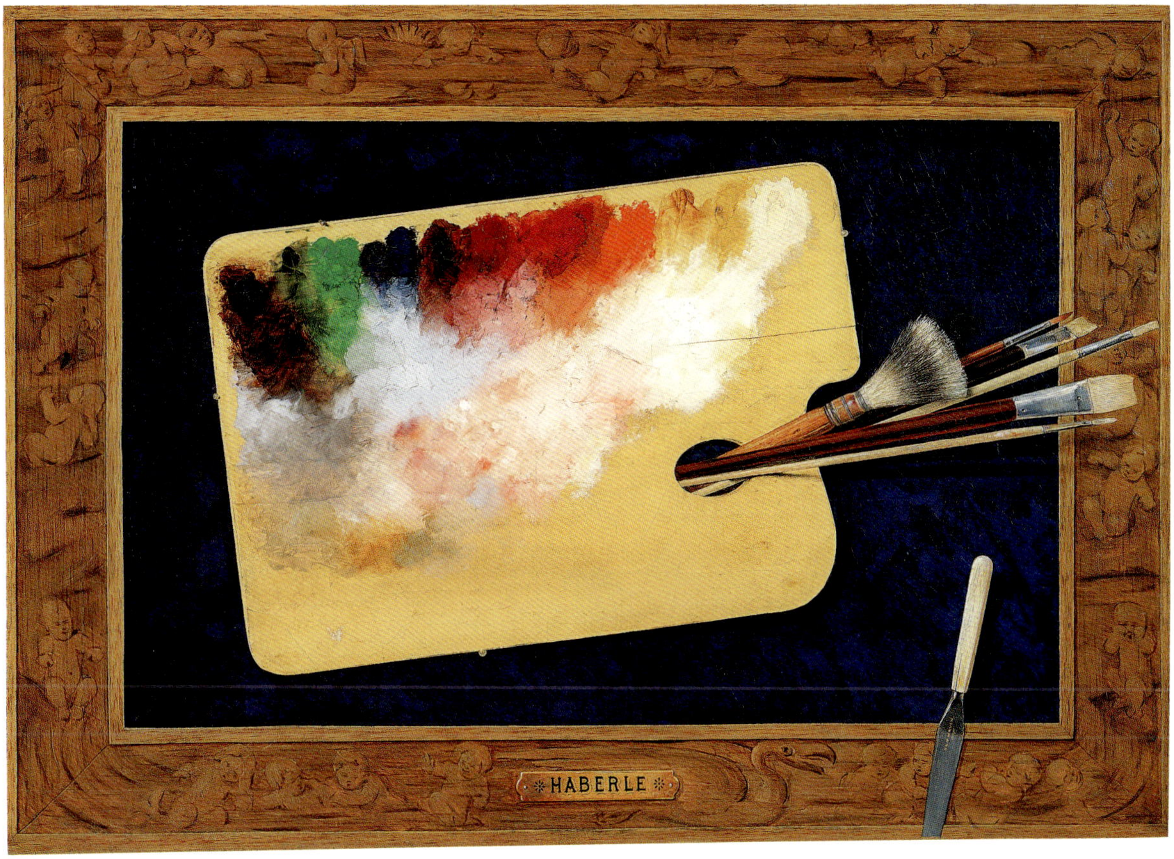

Fig. 80. John Haberle, *The Palette*, ca. 1890. Oil on canvas, 17 ½ x 24 in. (44.5 x 61 cm). Private collection, via Berry-Hill Galleries, New York

fession were an irresistible delight to him. We can only smile at his sly pun in a painted newspaper clipping, in which he referred to a picture as "a most deceptive trompe l'oil."[13]

A few years older than Haberle, William M. Harnett lived a life that seems as orderly, balanced, and compact as his art. His working career divides neatly into three six-year periods: in Philadelphia from 1874 to 1880, Munich from 1880 to 1886, and New York from 1886 to his death in 1892. Like Haberle, he was capable of great technical precision and the refinements of illusionism, though Harnett's manner tended to be more businesslike, his images often associated with commerce. Much of his meticulous style of sharp detailing and clarity of outline undoubtedly goes back to his early training in drawing at the Pennsylvania Academy of the Fine Arts in Philadelphia and the Cooper Union in New York, supplemented by some time employed as a silver engraver at Tiffany's. His turn to still life as the principal subject for his subsequent career in art probably had several causes: first, his study under Thomas Eakins, who taught still-life design in night classes at the Pennsylvania Academy, and whose paintings at the time included prominent still-life elements.[14] Second, Dutch still lifes were among some of the first old master paintings to come into New York collections then, with several listed as early acquisitions of the new Metropolitan Museum in New York. Philadelphia, of course, had its own venerable tradition of still-life painting, going back to the Peale family at the beginning of the nineteenth century as well as a number of seventeenth-century Spanish examples shown at Academy exhibitions (see, for example, fig. 10). It was in this context that Harnett took up his own practice of still-life subjects, frequently mindful of Dutch precedents (such as fig. 19), during the mid-1870s. And just as his teacher Eakins often painted himself and family into his work, so Harnett alluded to an autobiographical content in some of his pictures by the calculated inclusion or placement of his signatures.

For the most part, Harnett's compositions and signatures in his early work are relatively conventional, and follow modes we have already seen in seventeenth-century Dutch practice or later examples by Chardin in France, wherein the artist's name appears as an inscription along the stretcher panel or side edge of a tabletop (see figs. 18 and 30). Harnett did just this on some of his first food compositions and soon after on similar arrangements of books and writing implements.[15] Whereas in the first works he simply found appropriately flat surfaces at the bottom of his canvases for his lettering, when he turned to the imagery of handwritten letters and envelopes, newsprint, bookbindings, engraved postage stamps, and currency, we sense that his inscriptions enter into a visual dialogue with the typography and calligraphy above. This is especially evident in *Still Life with Letter to Thomas B. Clarke*, 1879 (fig. 81), and in its close variant, *Still Life with Letter to Dennis Gale*, 1879 (private collection). He had begun to explore the subjects of writing and printing two years earlier in a series of small canvases with generic titles like *The Banker's Table* and *The Secretary's Table*, in which he set off small geometric piles of books and letters or coins and folded notes. Usually an inkwell and quill pen either frame the design or unify it, implying a contrast between the spheres of private and public commerce. These were increasingly commissioned by well-to-do business patrons of Harnett, and became in effect stand-in portraits of his paintings' owners and records of the artist's transactions with his clients.

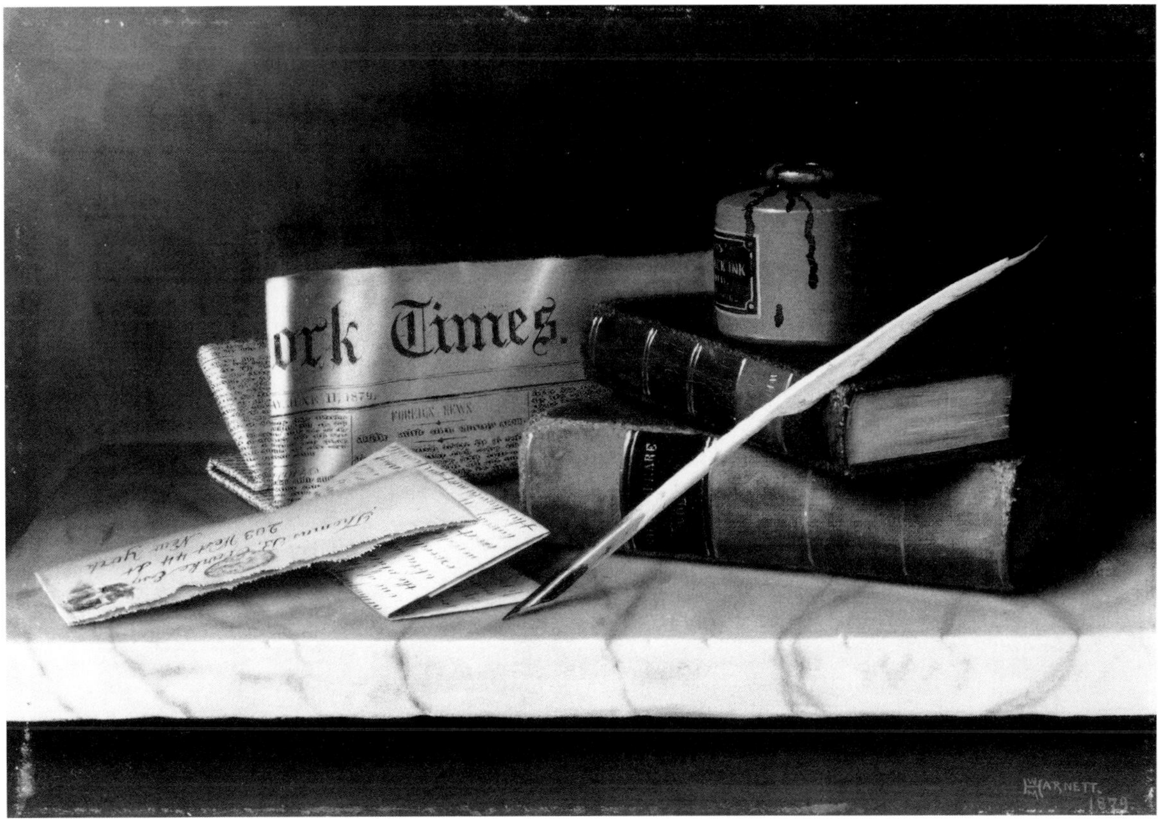

Fig. 81. William M. Harnett, *Still Life with Letter to Thomas B. Clarke*, 1879. Oil on canvas mounted on Masonite, 11 ⅛ x 15 in. (28.3 x 38.1 cm). Addison Gallery of American Art, Phillips Academy, Andover, Mass. Gift of Harold Clarke Durrell

Just as his subject matter now spoke to the materialism of the high Victorian era — the indulgence of foreign travel and acquisition of decorative arts abroad, the display of commodities and new personal wealth — so, too, many of the purchasers of Harnett's art were in the business world. Doreen Bolger's analysis shows that they included manufacturers and dry-goods merchants, entrepreneurs in department-store and other retail commerce, bankers and financiers, newspapermen and stationers. Moreover, while his paintings were displayed in drug and department stores, in offices and at industrial fairs, the objects he depicted were for sale in the new dry-goods emporiums flourishing after the Civil War.[16] But among his patrons were also collectors of bric-a-brac and decorative arts as well as picture dealers and early promoters of works by Harnett and his contemporaries. As such, this cross-section of buyers provides us with a collective portrait of his artistic enterprise.

The prominence of his inscribed signatures close to the artifacts of their world should be understood in this light. The two very similar compositions of 1879, devoted respectively to Dennis Gale and Thomas B. Clarke (see fig. 81), are particularly revealing in this regard. Gale was an English picture dealer who settled in Philadelphia around 1872; Clarke an art dealer in New York. In the first painting, a folded copy of the *New York Herald* is visible, along with a conical inkwell and blue envelope, seen upside down and receding, and addressed to Gale; in the second, we see instead the *New York Times,* a cylindrical inkwell, and a yellow envelope bearing Thomas B. Clarke's New York address. The diagonal axis linking Harnett's monogram and block lettering with the calligraphy for Clarke aptly crosses the sloping arc of the resting quill pen, a nice engagement of the two art professionals.

In one other variation of these still lifes from around this time, *Job Lot Cheap,* 1878 (Reynolds House, Winston-Salem), Harnett employed a more relaxed handwriting for his name, appropriate to the more casual and informal piling of old books in the wood box. In Germany a few years later, he continued his practice of signing on a side panel of a table supporting still-life objects. The panel that surrounds his inscription on *Still Life with "Le Figaro,"* 1882 (private collection), almost treats his name like a framed work of art within the larger canvas. That Harnett increasingly thought of his inscriptions as part of a larger typographical display was equally evident in his other major subject matter: trompe l'oeil arrangements on flat wall boards. These begin with a singular work painted just before his departure for Munich, *The Artist's Letter Rack,* 1879 (Metropolitan Museum of Art, New York), in which the envelopes refer to various individuals with whom Harnett did business. Altogether, the stamps, labels, engraved bill, business cards, clipping, and different types of writing in ink and chalk collectively depict a rich range of activities involving the hand and eye.[17] Harnett's strong monogram and date at the upper left assert his pride of craft.

Harnett's years in Munich during the early 1880s were in part a time of derivation and synthesis. He looked closely at mid-nineteenth-century German photography (notably the work of Adolphe Braun), and studied the old masters in the German museums. While he continued to paint his tabletop still lifes, his detailing and textures became more jewel-like. He began an extensive series of wall-board arrangements — presumably after seventeenth-century Dutch examples — the best-known of which were the variations on *After the Hunt* based on Braun's photographs. For a few years following his return to America in 1886, Harnett focused intently on single elements

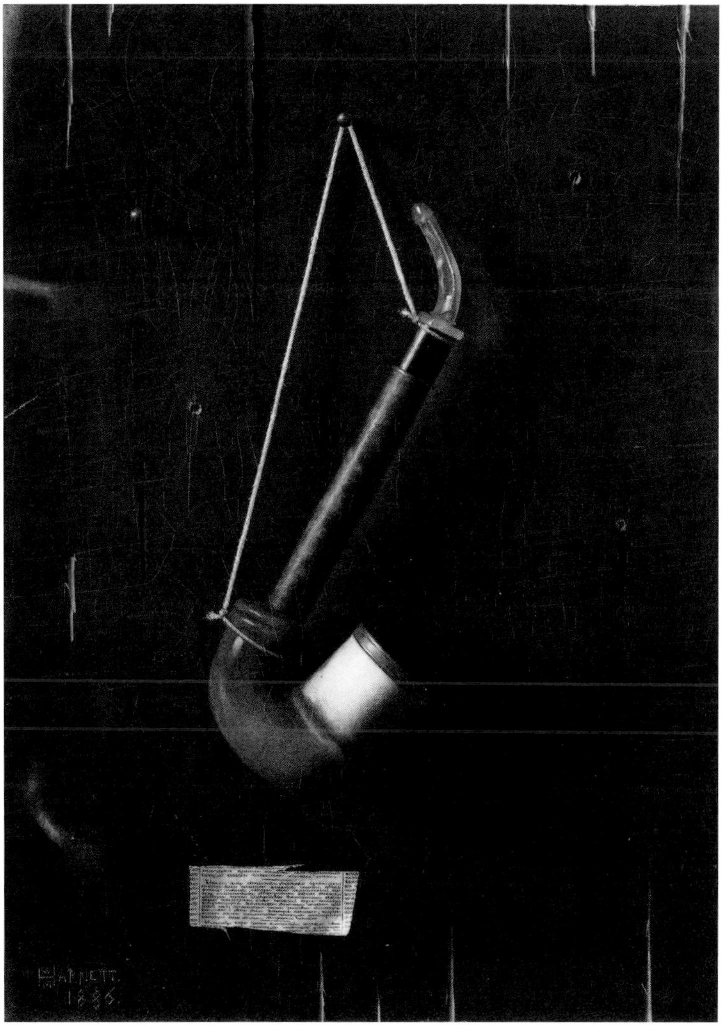

Fig. 82. William M. Harnett, *The Meerschaum Pipe*, 1886. Oil on canvas, 17 ⅛ x 12 ⅛ in. (43.5 x 30.8 cm). Fine Arts Museums of San Francisco. Gift of Mr. and Mrs. John D. Rockefeller 3rd

from those dense accumulations of hanging objects. Against near black or dark green panels he painted a dead hare, quail, or plucked chicken hanging from a nail, more intimate or witty variants of the early trophies of the hunt; single horseshoes fastened to a wall, possible emblems of his current professional fortunes; and the familiar *Meerschaum Pipe*, 1886 (fig. 82), an object once a part of the sociable men's-library still lifes of the 1870s, now displayed in monumental isolation. On all of these he painted his monogrammed signature to appear carefully chiseled into the grained and cracked wood surfaces. While on one level they were examinations of simplified forms and sophisticated illusions, they were surely also artifacts of his daily life and experience. His name only affirmed their autobiographical associations.

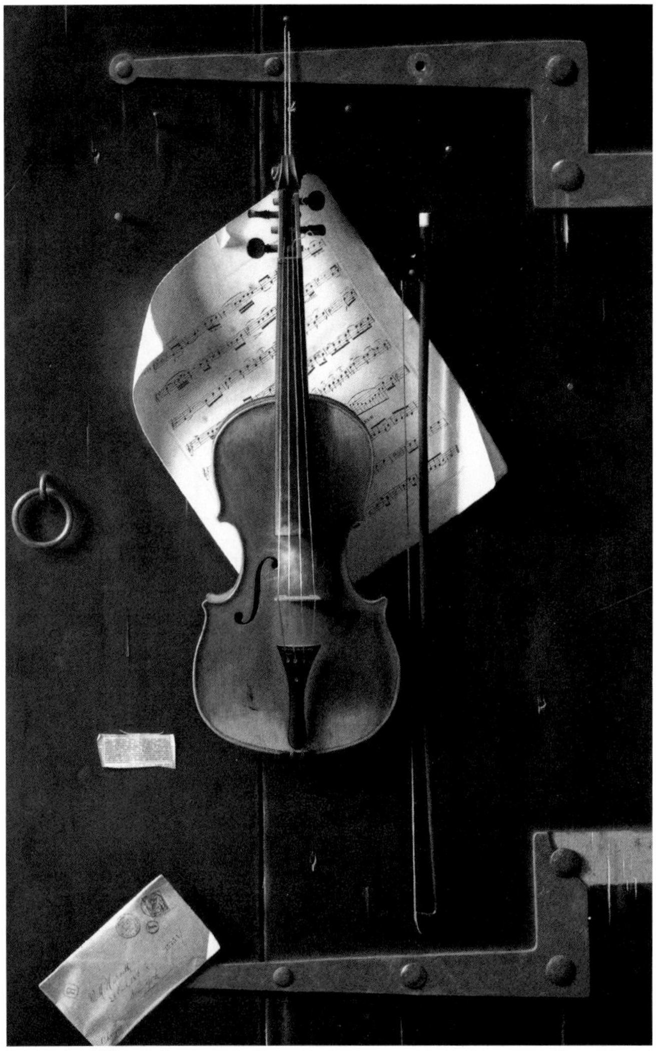

Fig. 83. William M. Harnett, *The Old Violin*, 1886. Oil on canvas, 38 x $23\frac{5}{8}$ in. (96.5 x 60 cm). National Gallery of Art, Washington, D.C. Gift of Mr. and Mrs. Richard Mellon Scaife in honor of Paul Mellon

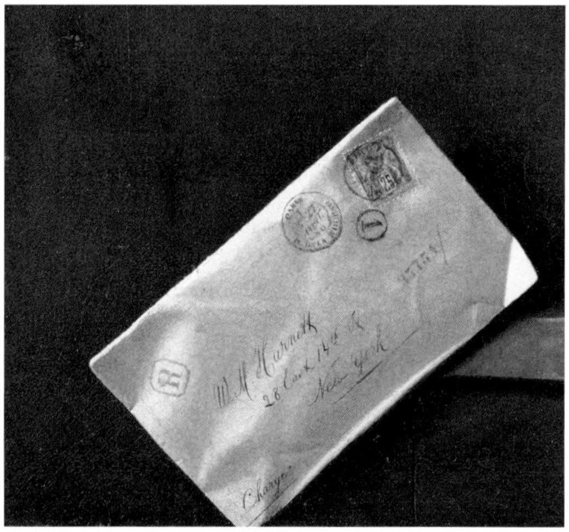

Fig. 84. William M. Harnett, *The Old Violin* (detail of fig. 83), 1886

This certainly was the case with his two major compositions featuring violins, one of the more important musical instruments Harnett owned and played. They are marvels of his illusionist dexterity, as well as showcases of his methodical sense of order. Unlike the visual tensions, depth of feeling, and threatened disarray that we shall see in his friend John F. Peto's work, rhythmic verticals and horizontals in restful near symmetries largely characterize the compositions of Harnett's *The Old Violin*, 1886 (figs. 83 and 84), and *Still Life — Violin and Music (Music and Good Luck)*, 1888 (fig. 85). He painted them at the peak of his career, when he was enjoying the confidence of success, popularity, and influence. That Harnett possessed a sense of control and clarity in his mature art we see in the placement of his name, on an

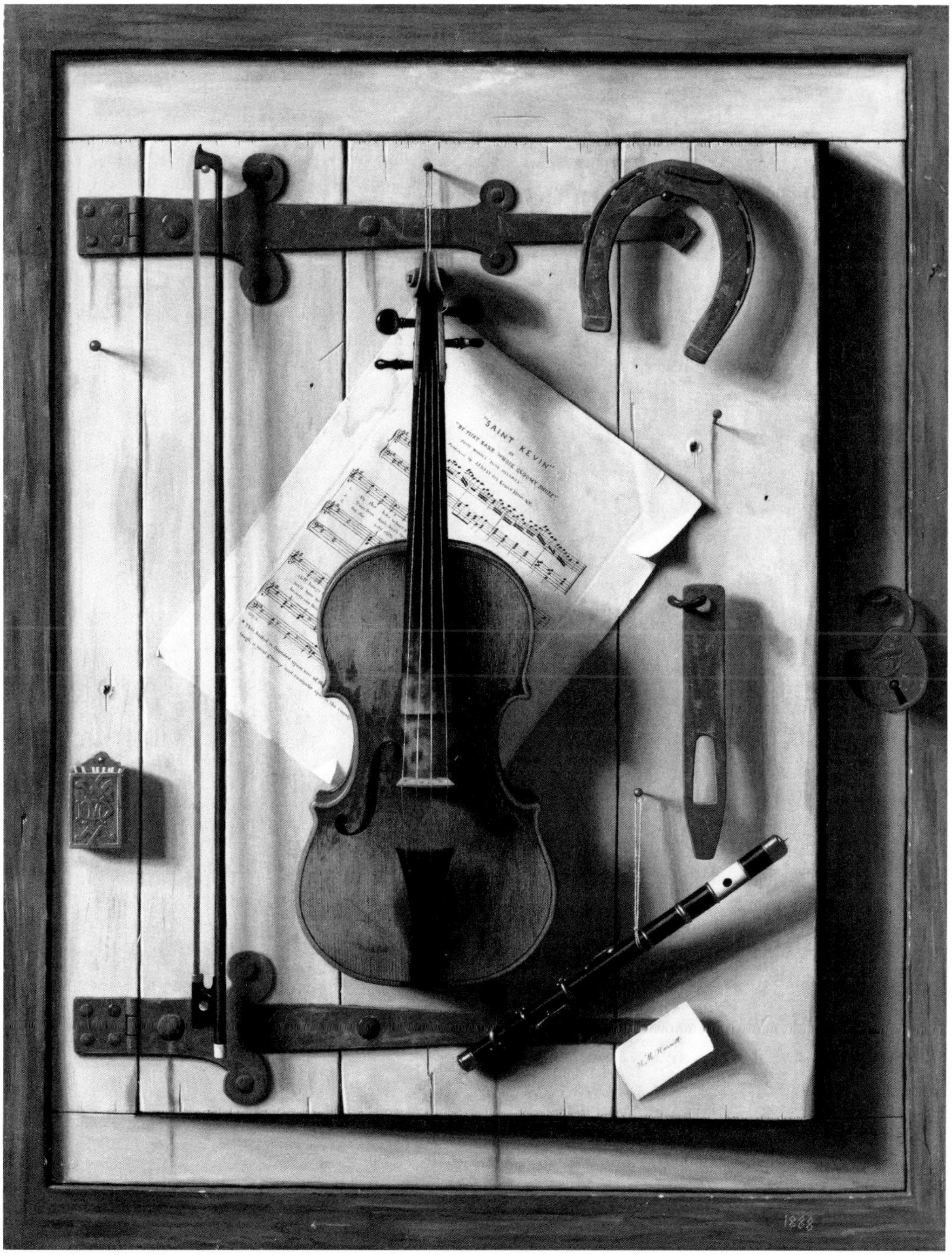

Fig. 85. William M. Harnett, *Still Life — Violin and Music (Music and Good Luck)*, 1888. Oil on canvas, 40 x 30 in. (101.6 x 76.2 cm). The Metropolitan Museum of Art, New York. Catherine Lorillard Wolfe Fund, 1963; The Catherine Lorillard Wolfe Collection

envelope in one and a calling card in the other, each oriented diagonally to echo or counterpoint the sheet of music tacked above.

His summary work of biography is *Mr. Hulings' Rack Picture,* 1888 (fig. 86), his second and only other rack picture after *The Artist's Letter Rack* of a decade earlier. During the interim his fellow painter and friendly competitor Peto had taken up rack painting and office board designs almost obsessively, and we sense that it is almost in rivalry that Harnett returns to the format, in a bravura demonstration of technical one-upmanship. Be that as it may, the canvas also gathers visual references to many of his patrons' business and social associations, and it was all too fitting that he sign it in two incarnations, an incised inscription at lower left and — even more appropriately — near the compositional center, with a business card teasingly revealing the last letters of his name under the ribbon. George H. Hulings (1844–1902) was yet another Philadelphia dry-goods merchant who was a friend of the artist and collector of his work. Hulings in fact had commissioned *The Old Violin,* but before he could take possession, Harnett had sold it to another client. His relationship with the original patron may have prompted the especially personal, even intimate quality of this rack picture, with its myriad letters and cards lifted from Hulings's desk and bearing his business address. But an equal number of items refers to other friends besides Harnett and to colleagues of Hulings: associates in his church, Masonic lodge, and former Civil War regiment.[18] The painting stands as a visual narrative of his life, a group portrait, as it were, of Hulings and his private and professional associations — along with the central card testifying to Harnett's artistic commission.

Intimations of this generation's participation in the Civil War seem to have been a larger concern to Harnett, as well as to Peto, Alexander Pope, and other artists and writers of the period. In 1890, Harnett painted and exhibited together *The Faithful Colt* (fig. 87) and *Emblems of Peace* (Museum of Fine Arts, Springfield, Massachusetts), often considered meditations on that wrenching American conflict, heightened at century's end by an awareness of the accelerated rate of deaths among Civil War veterans. We can also cite Walt Whitman's late poetry and *Specimen Days* (1882), Peto's many Lincoln pictures, and Stephen Crane's realistic *Red Badge of Courage* (1895) as anguishing memoirs of the violence.[19] Harnett's *Faithful Colt* is a relic of the Civil War era, hung up now as a trophy on the wall, but we may speculate that it also has meaning for the time when he was painting it. Guns were emblems of the American frontier and the winning of the west. But in 1890 that western frontier, so symbolic of the nation's exploration and expansion to the

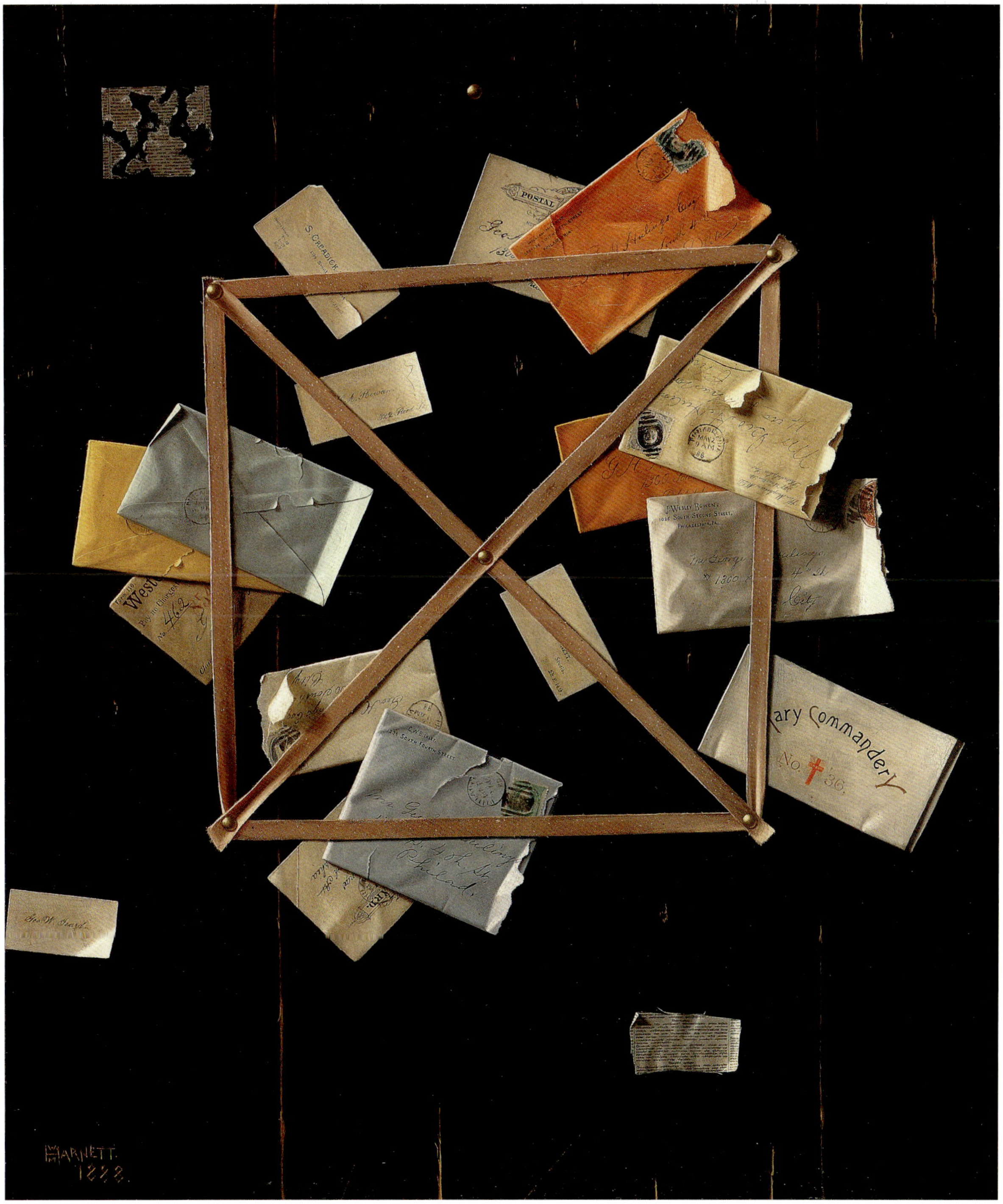

Fig. 86. William M. Harnett, *Mr. Hulings' Rack Picture*, 1888. Oil on canvas, 30 x 25 in. (76.2 x 63.5 cm). Collection of Jo Ann and Julian Ganz, Jr., Los Angeles

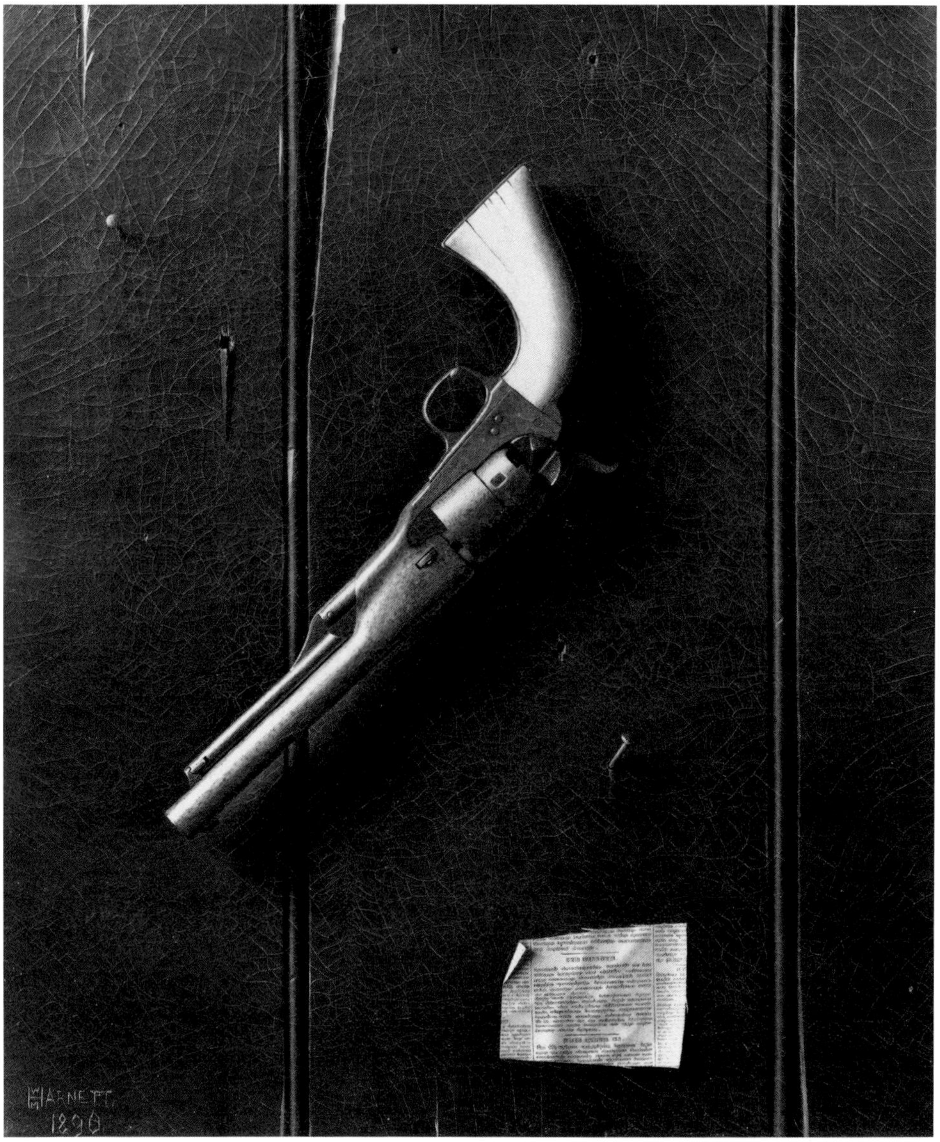

Fig. 87. William M. Harnett, *The Faithful Colt,* 1890. Oil on canvas, 22 ½ x 18 ½ in. (57.2 x 47 cm). Wadsworth Atheneum, Hartford, Conn. The Ella Gallup Sumner and Mary Catlin Sumner Collection Fund

California coast, was about to be declared closed, as Frederic Jackson Turner would argue in Chicago three years later. The gun was an agent for another presidential assassination at the turn of the century and a sign of renewed American militarism in the years around the Spanish-American War.

Finally, on a personal level this gleaming revolver seems to have been a haunting reminder of mortality and the end of an era for Harnett himself. Even though his style continues to isolate a single object against the largely blank wooden planks, in the manner of his 1886 series, there appears to be a new starkness here, a severity of theme as well as of execution. Now we are more aware of the small gashes and splintering in the panels, the nails that seem to puncture and tear the wood, the greater austerity in the contrasts of light and dark. In 1890, in fact, Harnett had reason to feel in a graver state psychologically and physically. As early as 1886 he had been hospitalized for rheumatoid arthritis, and over the following couple of years he returned to the hospital several times with kidney pain, due to complications (probably Bright's Disease) that led to his death in 1892 at the age of forty-four.[20] Whatever associations he attached to the old Colt, we have to wonder how intentional was the placement of his gouged signature at lower left, "cornered," we might say, in the revolver's line of fire.

Harnett's fellow student and friend John Peto, who was younger by a few years, would take up a number of the same themes in his work. He outlived Harnett, painting into the early twentieth century, but coincidentally dying from the same torturous kidney disease. His style ranged from the teasing visual wit of Haberle to the poignant gravity of Harnett, especially as Peto faced his own mortality in his last years. Peto signed only a fraction of his works (perhaps twenty-five percent), partially, we suspect, because he was more withdrawn from the mainstream — he exhibited only half a dozen paintings in his lifetime, and rarely executed formal commissions. But in those pictures he did sign, as his career matured, the nature and location of his signing took on ever greater significance. He overlapped Harnett by a year at the Pennsylvania Academy, where he, too, was registered in Eakins's night classes on still life in 1877. About this time, Peto turned out his own first paintings, initially tabletop arrangements of fruits and soon after library compositions with books, pipes, and mugs. He continued to make dozens of variations of these up to the 1890s, sometimes with an inkwell, ginger jar, nuts or candy, a wine bottle, candlestick, or, infrequently, a newspaper or letter. Like the signatures on Harnett's earlier work, Peto's appear logically on patches of flat open surfaces such as tablecloths or edges, but without any particular autobiographical connotations or conscious visual interaction with the objects depicted.

Although both artists had attempted their first rack pictures in the summer of 1879, Peto was quite likely influenced by the door and wall-board paintings that Harnett made after his return from Europe in 1886 when he turned to an extensive series of images of objects hanging against painted planks. In the late 1880s, when Peto married, he moved his family from Philadelphia and built a house on the New Jersey shore at Island Heights. He maintained his artistic rivalry with Harnett in painting similar subjects, such as letter racks and *The Old Violin*, ca. 1890 (fig. 88). Close as it seems to Harnett's version, its mood and technique are different enough that it is now hard to imagine the longtime confusion between the two artists' work. Although Peto's violin hangs near the center, its diagonal tilt is in tension against the vertical symmetries; one string is broken and falls to the side. The lower hinge is broken, the sheet of music extensively torn along all of its edges, and the painted wooden support is badly worn, with splintered losses and widened cracks. Where Harnett's music sheet displays a legible, identifiable song, Peto's bears the single word VIOLIN, as if its primary purpose is to play off the object as word versus image. His textured surfaces are rough and suggestive; the colors connote deep feeling.

The total effect of this painting hints of a material world subject to deterioration and assault. While the work in part conveys an interest in the play of pure forms, and celebrates music as a sister art to painting, the unsparing wear and tear are melancholy suggestions of a vanitas. In this regard Peto was articulating many of the anxieties and uncertainties that were haunting America toward the end of the century. By the 1890s the bitter failures of Reconstruction had led to the rise of new racism at home and abroad. Currency disputes and market failures roiled the political and business worlds. New inventions and technologies signaled both the possibilities and unknowns of a new era. Peto's initials at the upper left express something of this disruptiveness. Unlike Harnett, with his crisp calling cards and elegantly inscribed envelopes, Peto scraped his letters into the green board with a roughness matching the mood of the time.

He brings an alternative persona to *The Cup We All Race 4*, ca. 1900 (fig. 89), one much like Haberle's visual trickster and technical show-off. As with Peto's earlier violins, here we have the juxtaposition of the cup as a word and an image on a trompe l'oeil wooden board (which is in fact canvas), surrounded by a real wooden frame, which in turn is painted with illusionistic carving, a torn card, and Peto's attached nameplate at the top, serving as his signature and notice of his witty engagement in the whole artifice. The whole is a game of shapes and meanings. First there are the multiple variations of quadrants and rectangles: the planks of wood, fragments of the card, nameplate, and the full canvas in its frame. The cup suggests both the

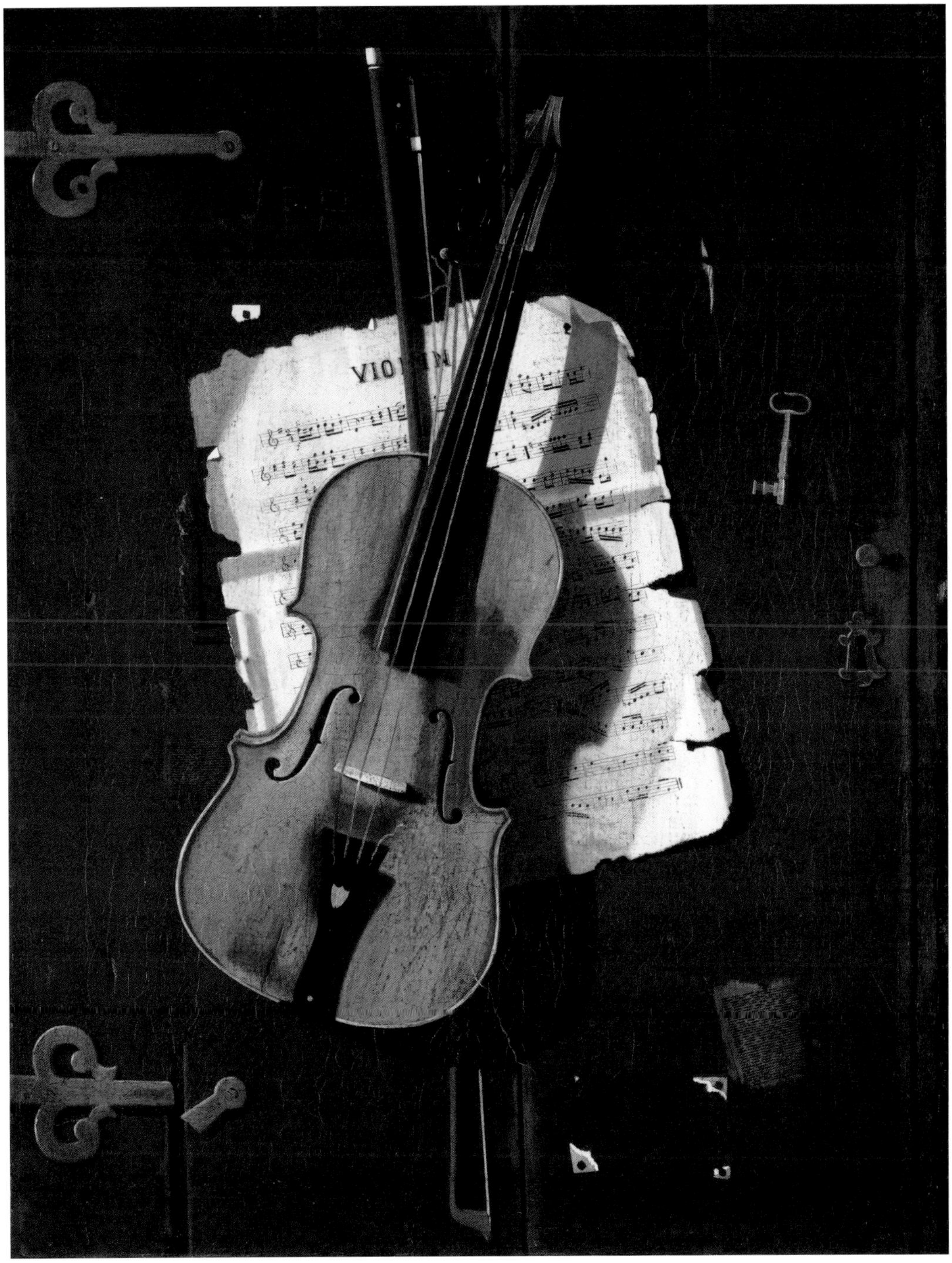

Fig. 88. John F. Peto, *The Old Violin,* ca. 1890. Oil on canvas, 30 ⅜ x 22 ⅞ in. (77.2 x 58.1 cm). National Gallery of Art, Washington, D.C. Gift of the Avalon Foundation

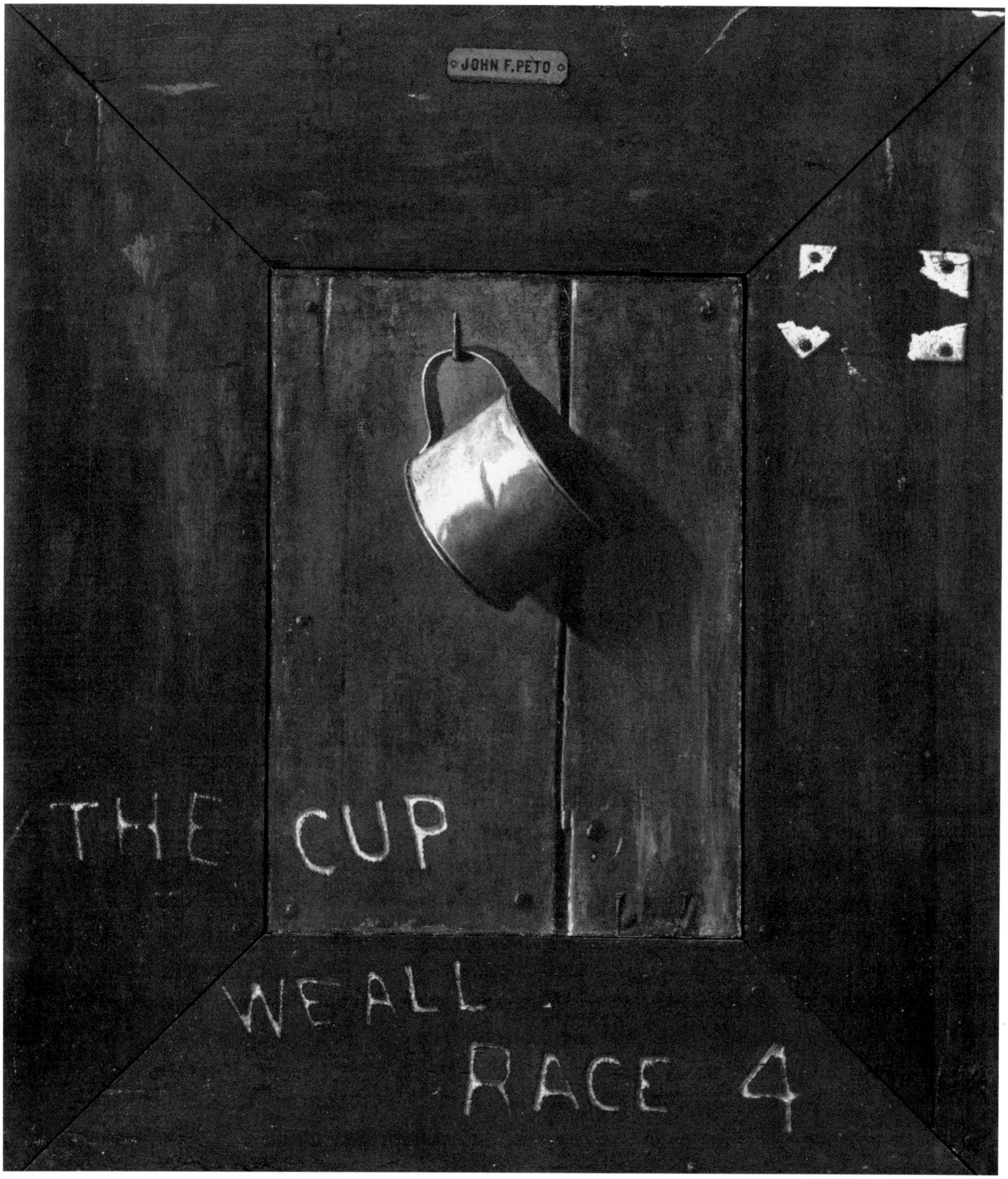

Fig. 89. John F. Peto, *The Cup We All Race 4*, ca. 1900. Oil on canvas and wood panel, 25 ½ x 21 ½ in. (64.8 x 54.6 cm). Fine Arts Museums of San Francisco. Gift of Mr. and Mrs. John D. Rockefeller 3rd

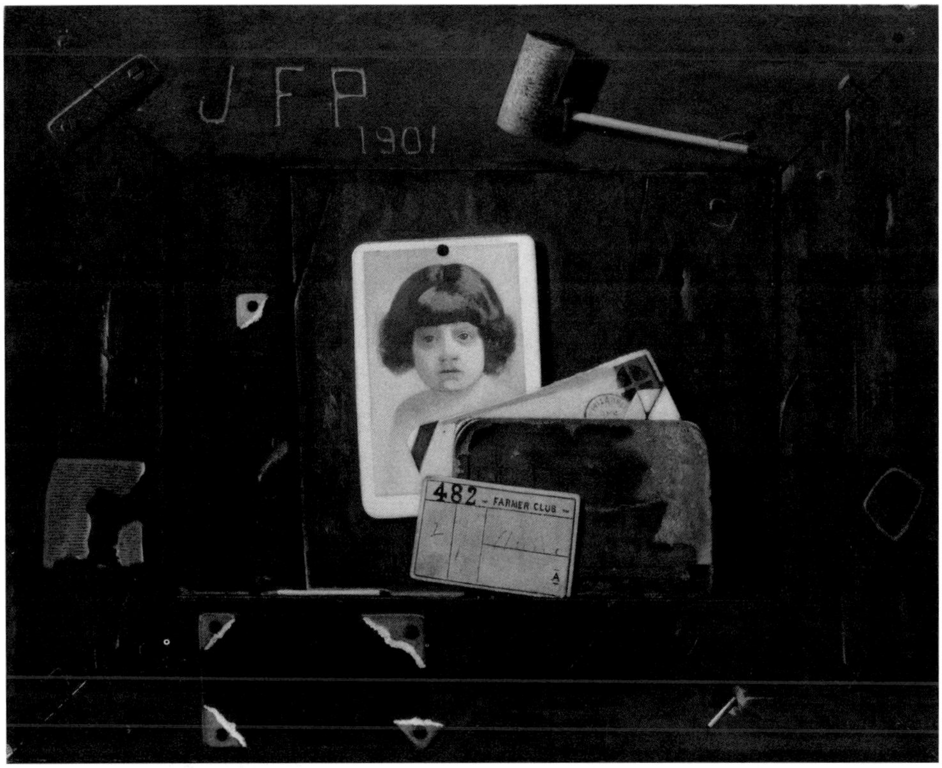

Fig. 90. John F. Peto, *Portrait of the Artist's Daughter,* 1901. Oil on academy board, 17 5/8 x 21 1/2 in. (44.8 x 54.6 cm). Mr. and Mrs. Meredith J. Long

goal of life's pursuits but also the trophy of the local racetrack. Finally there is the linguistic interplay of number, noun, and preposition, which, along with the format, adds up to a quadruple entendre.

In 1893, Peto's only child, his daughter, Helen, was born, bringing him great pleasure during his final years. In contrast, sometime during the later 1890s he began to experience intermittent and then near constant pain from the kidney stones that would lead ultimately to kidney failure. These conflicting events found expression in a series of letter-and-office-board "portraits" done during the first few years after 1900. Some incorporated old scraps and a letter addressed to a family member. *Sign Painting for Helen S. Peto,* 1904 (private collection), with the year 1893 scratched in the wood and an envelope bearing a cancellation dated 1904, was a present to the artist's daughter on her eleventh birthday. Her name, along with her parents' initials, is also gouged into the boards. In an almost identical layout of the same year Peto painted an office board for himself, but here the illusionistic carving cuts

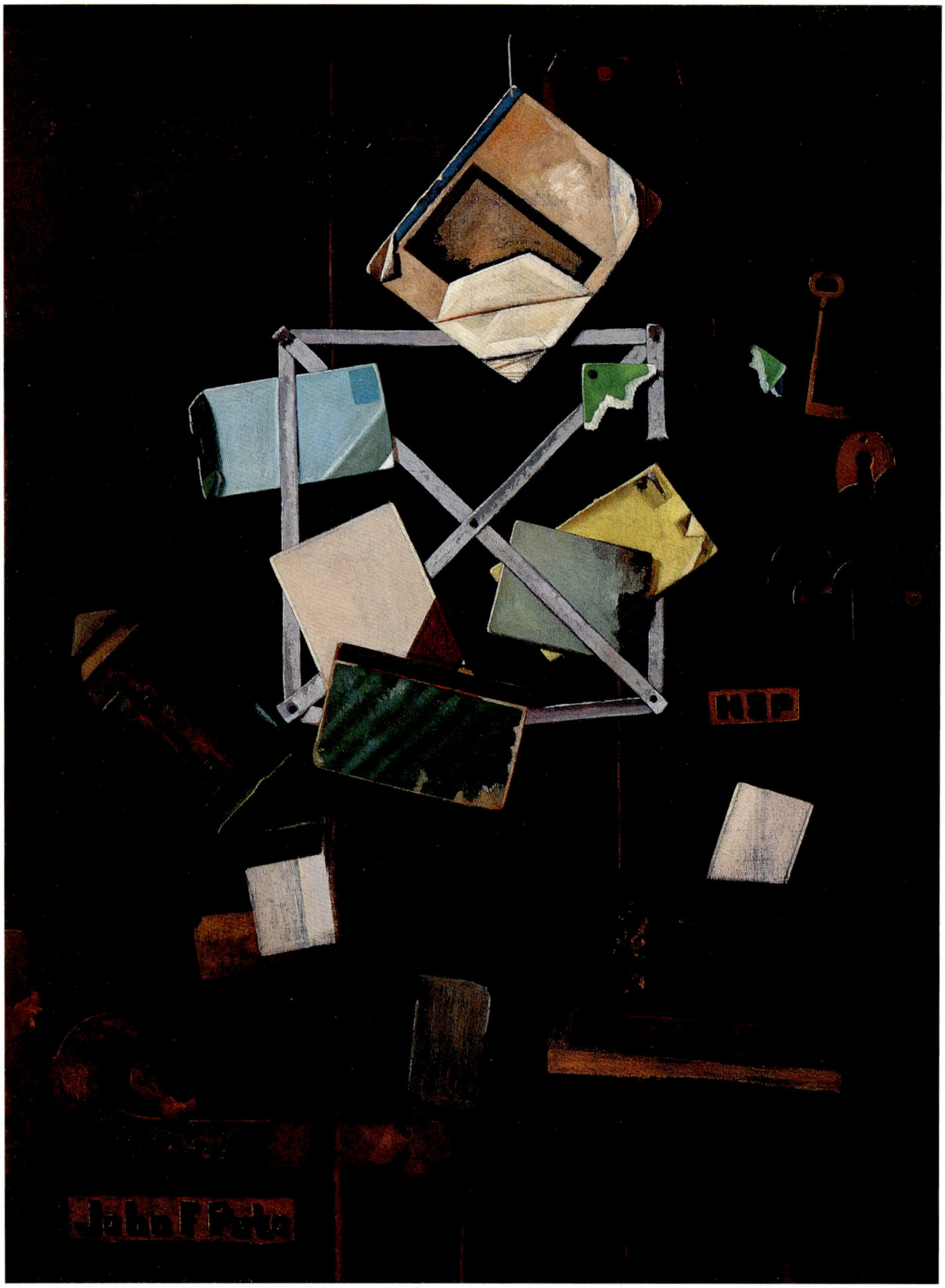

Fig. 91. John F. Peto, *HSP's Rack Picture*, ca. 1900. Oil on canvas, 40 ¼ x 30 in. (102.2 x 76.2 cm). Los Angeles County Museum of Art. Purchased with funds generously provided by Cecile Bartman

out the areas surrounding the block letters of his name as if in raised relief. He used this same carved signature in his final rack picture, known as *A Closet Door*, 1904/6 (private collection). The strong, large lettering appropriately serves as an advertisement of the artist's talents; indeed, Peto went on to paint a self-portrait of himself seated, palette in hand, and *A Closet Door* hanging behind him, as if it were doubling his artistic self-image.

The most poignant and tender of this group of paintings were devoted to Helen, the daughter who gave him much happiness in the midst of his bouts of kidney pain. In addition, he had to cope with the advancing senility of the aunts he cared for, one of whom had to be confined to an upper room in the Island Heights house. Helen's mounted photograph is the center of attention in *Portrait of the Artist's Daughter*, 1901 (fig. 90), although a few other scraps fan out below. Above the photograph Peto's corncob pipe rests adjacent to his gouged initials. The sadness in Helen's face is matched by the torn fragments of cards and battered old boards. A haunted, almost ghostly mood marks *HSP's Rack Picture*, ca. 1900 (fig. 91), where the tattered and broken objects seem in a state of dissolution, as Peto leaves numerous details only suggestively finished and more sickly in coloring. Using "raised" block letters for both, he links his name with his daughter's initials. In both of these types of signatures we feel the pressure and resistance of a knife or chisel digging into the wood. Unlike the clean, orderly calligraphy of Harnett's envelopes and business cards, Peto's letters bear his life's pain and travail. In the long tradition of Dutch precedents and other American counterparts, they remain deeply personal expressions.

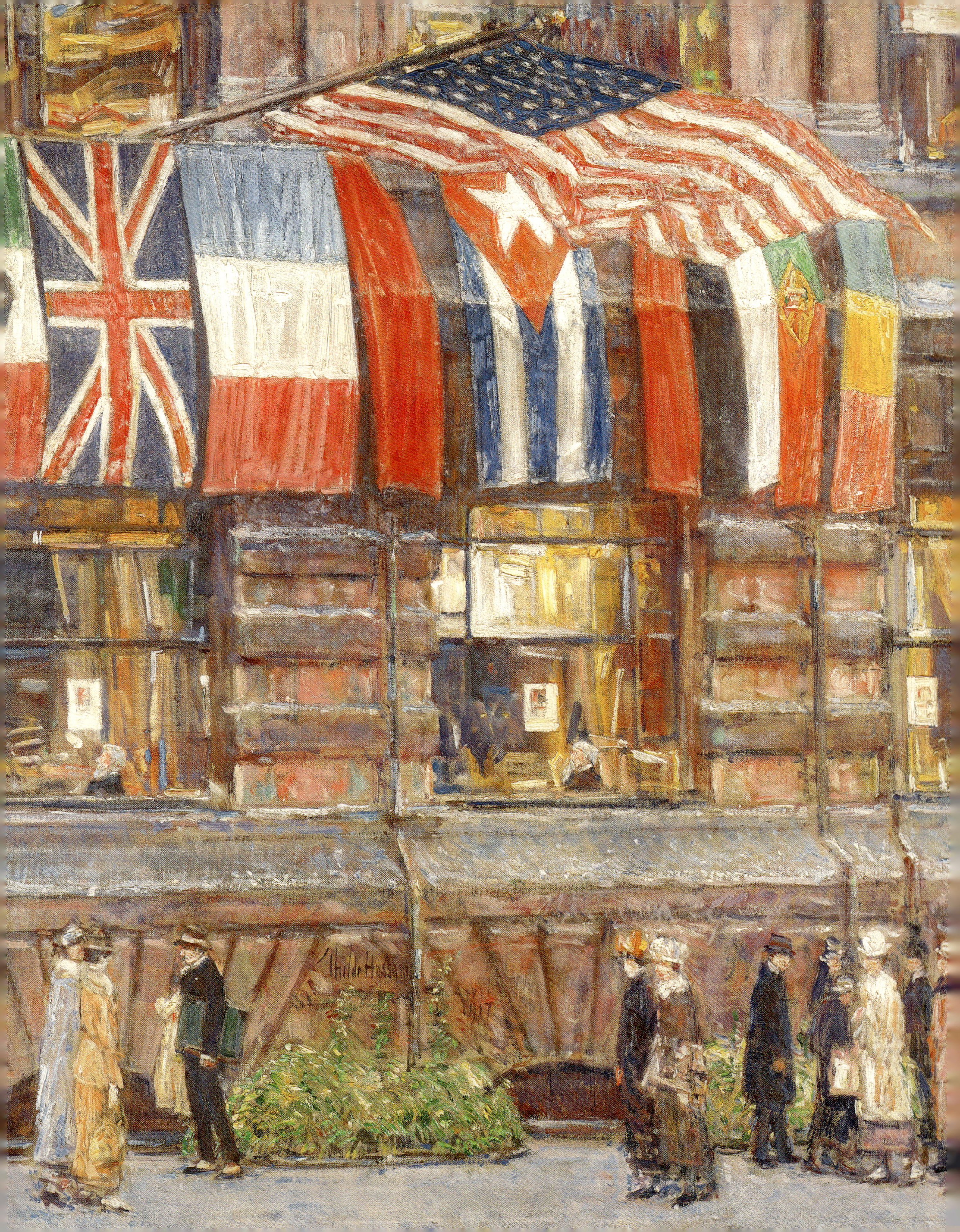

CHAPTER 4 Impressionism and Realism

BY ITS NATURE, the impressionist style, with its looser brushwork and often patchy color, is not especially conducive to incorporating artists' signatures or inscriptions within its depicted spaces. It seeks to suggest rather than define its subjects, in contrast to the conscious illusionism of trompe l'oeil, which can naturally embrace the clever placement of a name. Still, some painters of the American impressionist generation at the end of the nineteenth century found ways of situating themselves within their views or identifying themselves with their painted images. A good example is Childe Hassam, who at least once devised telling signatures in each of the major media that he mastered — watercolor, graphics, and oil. A Bostonian by birth, he left school to work for the publishing company of Little, Brown in the 1870s, then trained as a wood engraver and found employment as a freelance illustrator. Trips to Europe during the next decade introduced him to French impressionism, and he soon rose to eminence as one of the foremost American practitioners of the style, depicting landscapes of the New England coast, the colonial architecture of its picturesque villages, and New York City at the height of the Gilded Age.

Perhaps because pure landscapes do not readily accommodate inscriptions in their spaces, the few times Hassam called attention to himself through his name, he used the flat, ostensibly solid surfaces of urban architecture. An intimate watercolor of 1890, *Woman Leaning on Parapet* (fig. 92), almost certainly shows his wife relaxing along a walkway in Central or Prospect Park. Painted on the wall below the figure is the large letter "H" with "4 ft." below it, surely not just a reference to the street or some standpipe beneath, but a sign of the artist's name. With the outbreak of World War I and America's eventual entry into it, Hassam undertook his well-known series of flag paintings between 1916 and 1919, celebrating the Allies' collaboration and ultimate

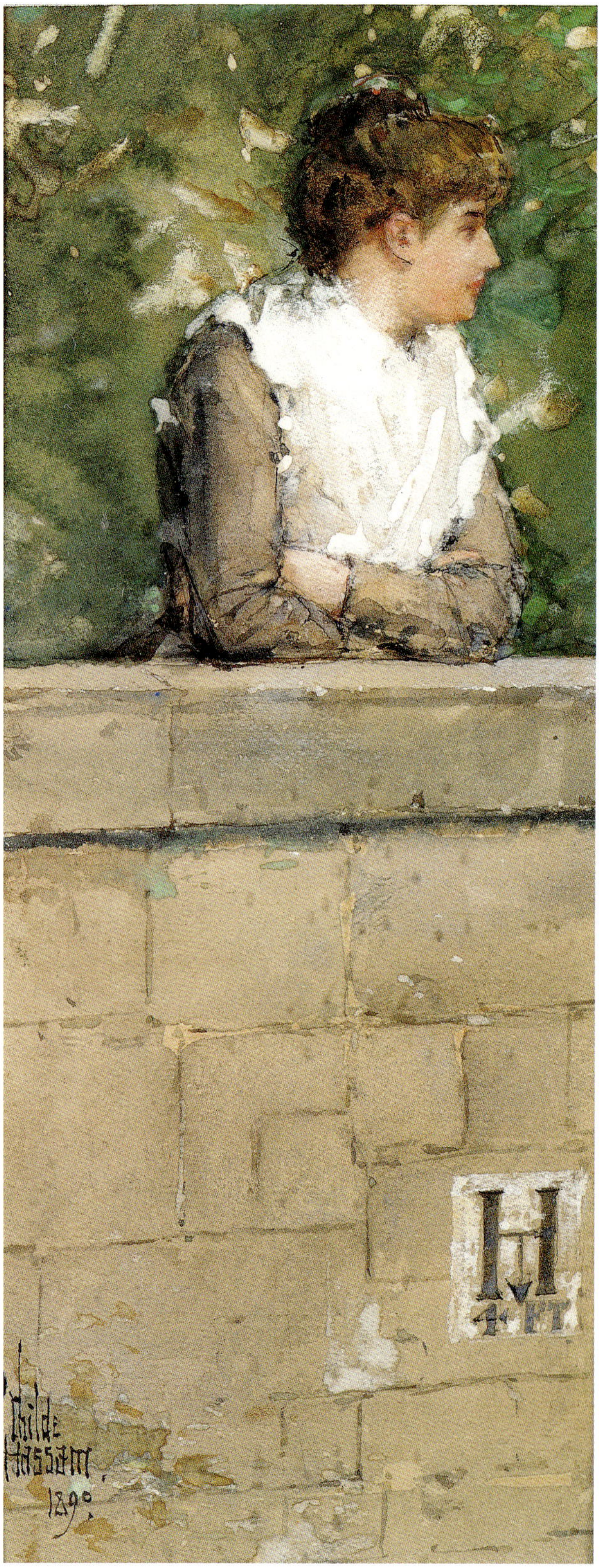

Fig. 92. Childe Hassam, *Woman Leaning on Parapet (Portrait of the Artist's Wife)*, 1890. Watercolor, 6 7/8 x 2 3/4 in. (17.5 x 7 cm). Collection of Mrs. George M. Kaufman

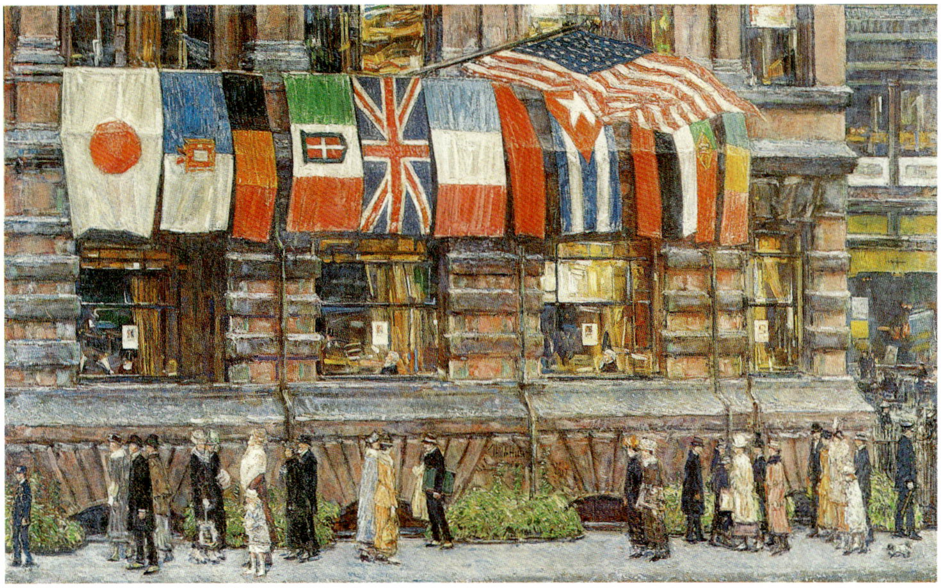

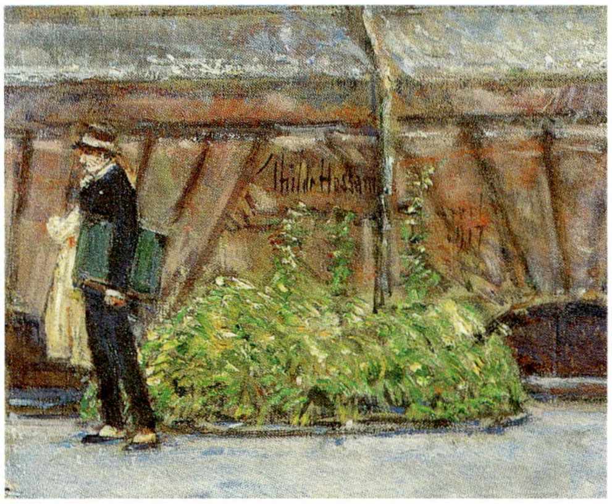

Fig. 93. Childe Hassam, *Allied Flags*, 1917. Oil on canvas, 30 ½ x 49 in. (77.5 x 124.5 cm). Private collection. Courtesy of the Kennedy Galleries, New York

Fig. 94. Childe Hassam, *Allied Flags* (detail of fig. 93), 1917

victory. These depicted colorful displays of the national banners seen along Fifth Avenue on various occasions and under different weather conditions. The intensity and number of the group (some two dozen) give an indication of both Hassam's fixation on the decorative and design possibilities of these scenes and his absorption in the patriotic passions of the time. We can see this devotion explicitly in one of the larger canvases and a related lithograph. In the print titled *Lafayette Street*, 1918 (Metropolitan Museum of Art, New York), Hassam's inscription is visible on the stone wall below a shopfront window, while the figure walking by is the artist carrying his portfolio. Almost the same configuration appears in *Allied Flags*, 1917 (figs. 93 and 94), where the painter, in dapper dress with his green portfolio under his arm, and his nearby signature, affixed to the rusticated stone base of the Union League Club, are literally almost at the center of our attention. (The notion of Hassam walking with his portfolio finds a later echo in several of Norman Rockwell's New York street scenes.) The imagery signals how much at home Hassam was among these fashionable promenaders and in this refined urban landscape at the turn of the century.

James McNeill Whistler's is quite a different presence in his pictures, so often marked with his famous butterfly monogram, that visual metaphor of his artistic ego. He seems to have enjoyed shaping the artifice of his personality as much as that of his pictures: just as a butterfly represents a mysterious transformation into a colorful and delicate flying creature, so Whistler from the outset was an elusive creation. He would select his birthplace to suit a given audience, declaring once, "I do not choose to be born in Lowell." Moving frequently as a child, he grew up in Saint Petersburg, where his father was employed by the Russian railroad. After his father's early death, he returned to the United States at mid-century, and enrolled at West Point Military Academy, where, fortuitously, he learned drawing and map making under the artist Robert W. Weir. He failed chemistry and so was discharged, but with the determination to become an artist. Whistler left for Paris in the mid-1850s, and was thereafter constantly on the move, residing nowhere for long. He embraced the avant-garde in Paris and London, producing pictures indebted variously to Pre-Raphaelitism, realism, and early impressionism. Over his career he managed to irritate the public, his patrons, and critics alike. One historian summarizes his personality traits as follows: "[H]e affected a style of self-conscious eccentricity, projected an aura of confident self-importance, and gave off a cultivated air of aesthetic arrogance."[1]

The butterfly image that came to embody both the quirks of his character and the decorative originality of his paintings evolved out of the rising fashionable taste for Japonaiserie and Chinoiserie during the latter half of the nineteenth century in France and America. Whistler collected Chinese porcelain and Japanese prints. Some have suggested that he used Japanese dolls to refine his figure arrangements, and Japanese screens appear in his works as objects as well as influences in their decorative flatness. It is said that the potter's marks on Chinese pots inspired him to sign his paintings with his initials, which by 1869 he had modified into the butterfly monogram.[2] As it evolved over his career (fig. 95), this sign with its petal shapes bears an obvious visual kinship with his frequent floral patterns, while elsewhere it seems to relate to the image of the peacock, itself another expression of his dandy's

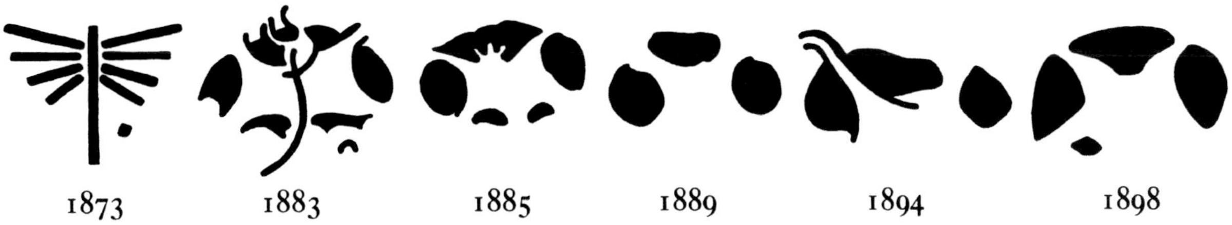

Fig. 95. James McNeill Whistler, Signatures. From Andrew McLaren Young et al., *The Paintings of James McNeill Whistler* (1980)

Fig. 96. James McNeill Whistler, *Arrangement in Grey: Portrait of the Painter*, 1872. Oil on canvas, 29 ½ x 21 in. (74.9 x 53.3 cm). The Detroit Institute of Arts. Bequest of Henry Glover Stevens in memory of Ellen P. Stevens and Mary M. Stevens

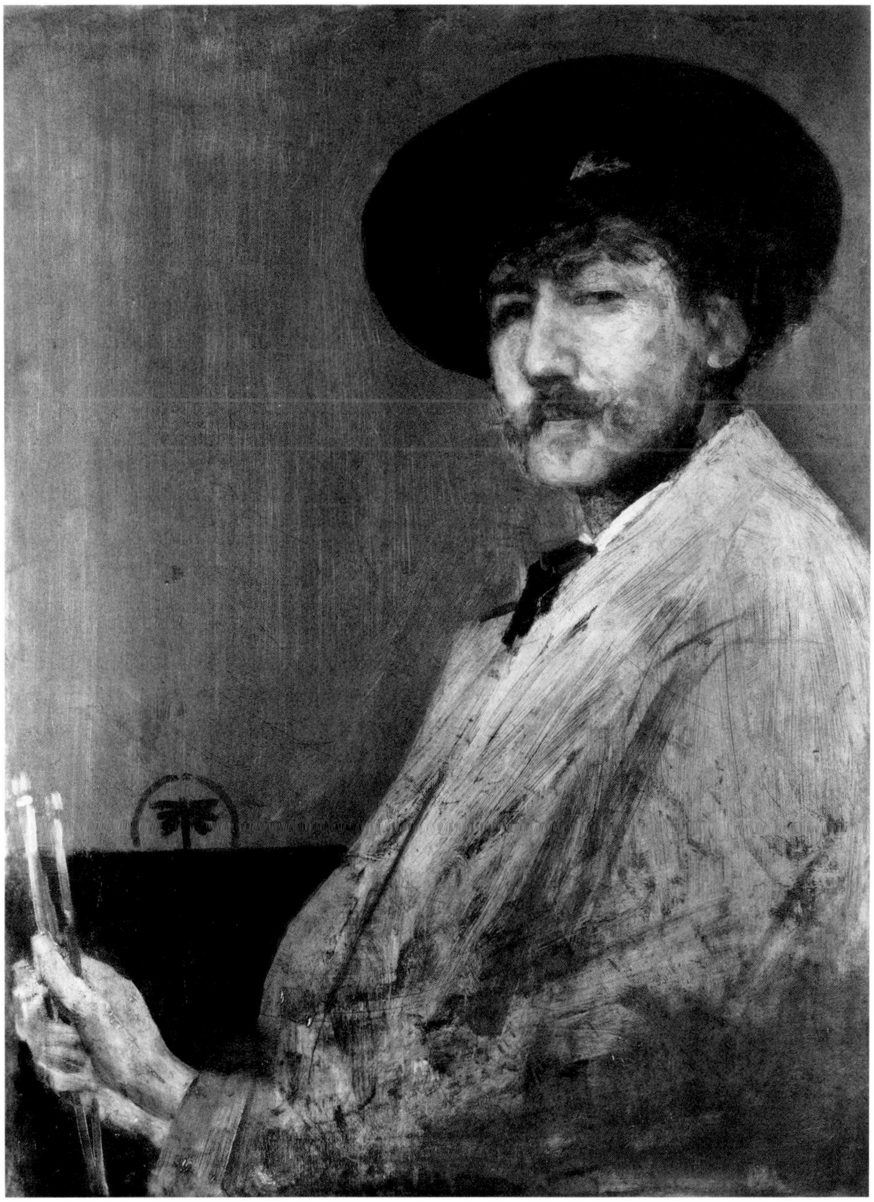

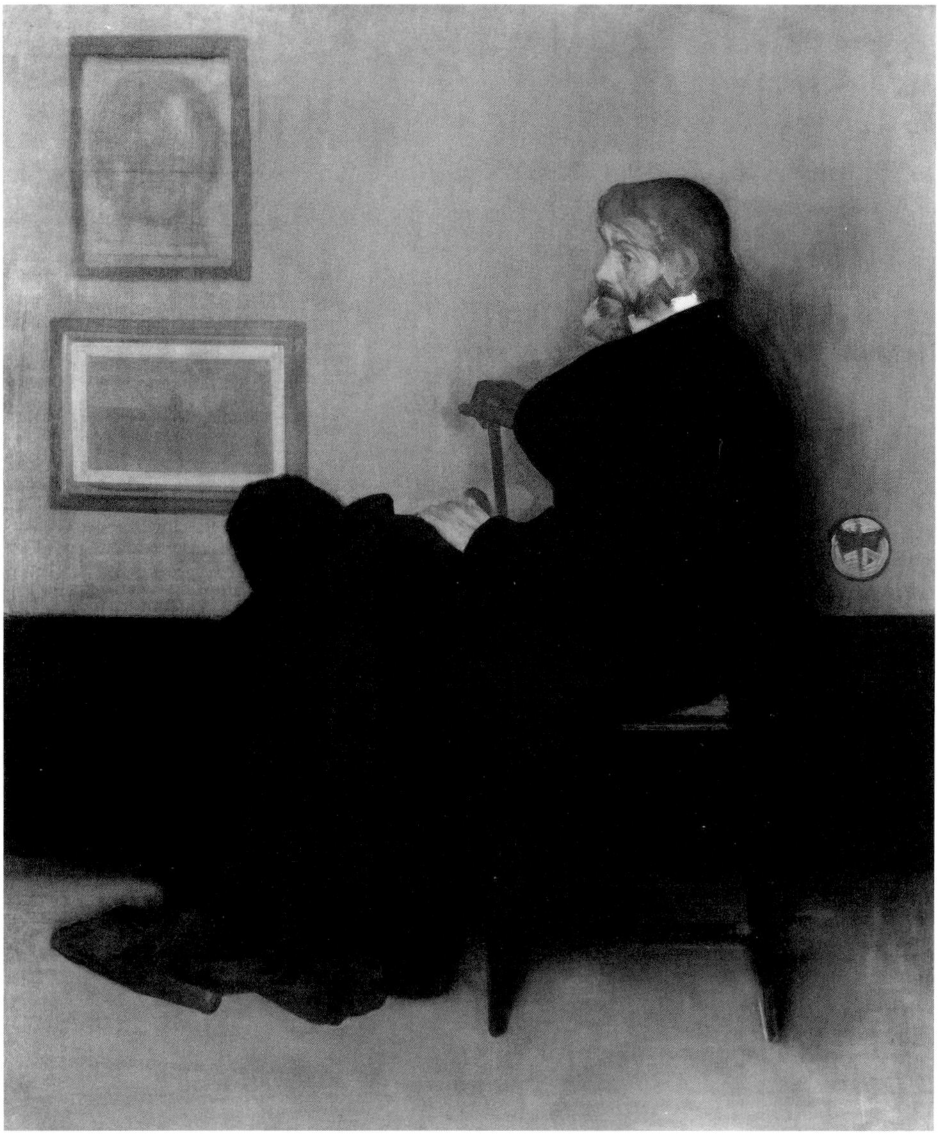

Fig. 97. James McNeill Whistler, *Arrangement in Grey and Black, No. 2: Portrait of Thomas Carlyle*, 1872–73. Oil on canvas, 67 ⅜ x 56 ½ in. (171 x 143.5 cm). Glasgow Museums: Art Gallery & Museum, Kelvingrove

manner and dress. Not only did the form of his monogram mutate over his career, it took on different associations as the subject or context varied.

It would be natural that in his self-portrait, *Arrangement in Grey: Portrait of the Painter*, 1872 (fig. 96), the painter's marks would emulate the potter's marks in the large butterfly or dragonfly form at the lower left. Partly

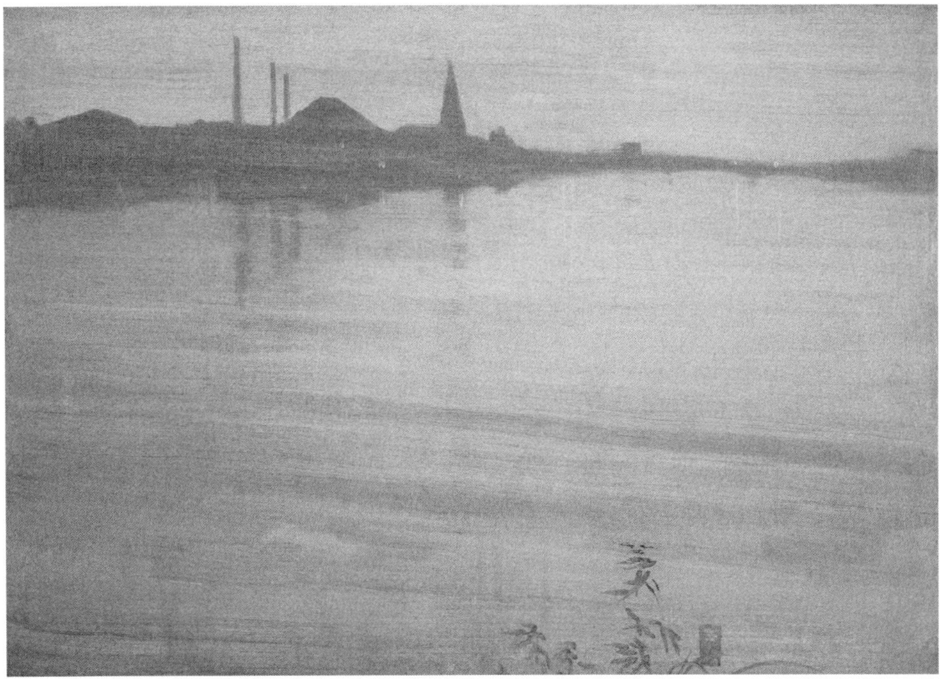

Fig. 98. James McNeill Whistler, *Nocturne in Blue and Silver*, ca. 1871–72. Oil on wood panel, 17 3/8 x 24 in. (44.13 x 60.96 cm). Courtesy of the Fogg Art Museum, Harvard University Art Museums. Bequest of Grenville L. Winthrop

enclosed in a painted circle, its silhouette echoes the shape of the artist's head nearby, itself framed by the dark, encircling hat. Significantly, the three prominent elements that extend above the dark chair railing along the wall are Whistler's brushes, his signature, and his head, all interrelated images of his self-portrait. A similar but more emphatic monogram rests on the wall in *Arrangement in Grey and Black, No. 2: Portrait of Thomas Carlyle*, 1872–73 (fig. 97). Here it reinforces the adjacent silhouettes of the hanging prints and the seated figure of Carlyle, respectively. But aside from its formal compatibility, we have to ask about its possible psychological connections to the sitter. The first important fact to note is that Carlyle's portrait immediately followed as a companion composition the famous *Arrangement in Grey and Black: Portrait of the Painter's Mother*, 1871 (Musée d'Orsay, Paris), and therefore had some intentional relationship to the parental image in Whistler's mind. Jonathan Weinberg analyzes this issue thoroughly, showing that the earlier picture followed a long tradition of artists painting their mothers that went back especially to similar poses drawn by Rembrandt and Dürer, and continued in contemporary examples by Mary Cassatt and Henry O.

Tanner.[3] Whistler's father had died more than two decades earlier, so that his mother's aged figure dressed in black is partially a reminder of mourning and mortality. With his patriarchal presence, Carlyle reunites the family, in Weinberg's view, and becomes a visual surrogate father. Whistler stamped his self-image only on the portrait of Carlyle: was it to identify with the male figure or to complete the pairing?

If we can imagine the links between the artist's signature and his direct or indirect imagery of himself, his presence in many landscape paintings and prints varies. *Nocturne in Blue and Silver*, ca. 1871–72 (fig. 98), is typical: at the lower right the framed butterfly form appears to float against the water, the yellow brush strokes in contrasting harmony with the nearby stalks of reeds at the edge of the water. In *Variations in Flesh Color and Green: The Balcony*, 1865 (fig. 99), the same form sits at the lower left, painted in the same rose and pink colors as the women's dresses and the spray of flowers. As a further conceit, a white butterfly intersects the monogram panel. In his 1880 etching *The Doorway* (Metropolitan Museum of Art, New York) the butterfly appears as a roundel on the building facade. On several beach scenes, such as *Low Tide*, 1883/84 (Freer Gallery of Art, Washington, D.C.), Whistler rounded his form as if it were a hand- or footprint in the sand. In just such evanescent and variable ways did he enter his work, adapting his imprint to each different subject, fusing the inventions of self and of art.

The great realist Thomas Eakins, who by contrast spent most of his life in his native Philadelphia, would seem to be the antithesis of Whistler. Yet for all of his wish to paint the objective world with uncompromising accuracy and unembellished truth, Eakins constantly treated his art as subjective and autobiographical. Among the elements that recur throughout his work, three of the most important are anatomy, calligraphy, and perspective, all basic aspects of his early training and significant parts of his life. Eakins gained his first grounding in mathematics and the sciences, including drawing in perspective, at Philadelphia's Central High School. Although he never developed much of a taste for literature, he did learn Latin, and subsequently at the Pennsylvania Academy drew from casts of antique sculptures. At the same time, he studied anatomy at Jefferson Medical College, soon complementing these studies with life classes at the Academy. Finally, his father taught him the art and practice of calligraphy, which would result in his elegant and disciplined handwriting as well as his frequent predilection for carefully calculated inscriptions on and in his paintings. Eakins brought together these various pursuits in his art, which almost entirely privileged the human figure.

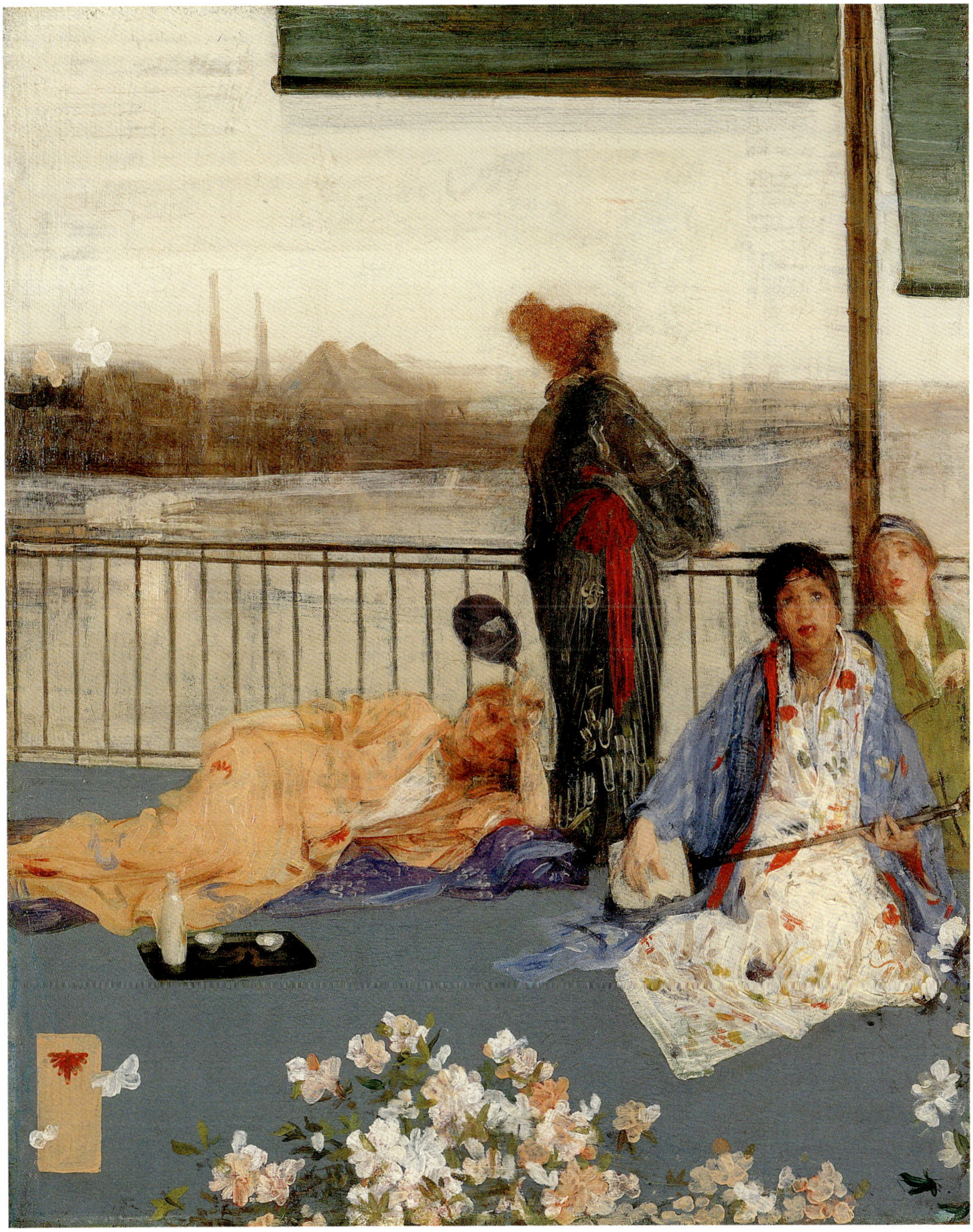

Fig. 99. James McNeill Whistler, *Variations in Flesh Color and Green: The Balcony*, 1865. Oil on wood panel, 24 ⅛ x 19 ¼ in. (61.4 x 48.8 cm). Freer Gallery of Art, Smithsonian Institution, Washington, D.C. Gift of Charles Lang Freer

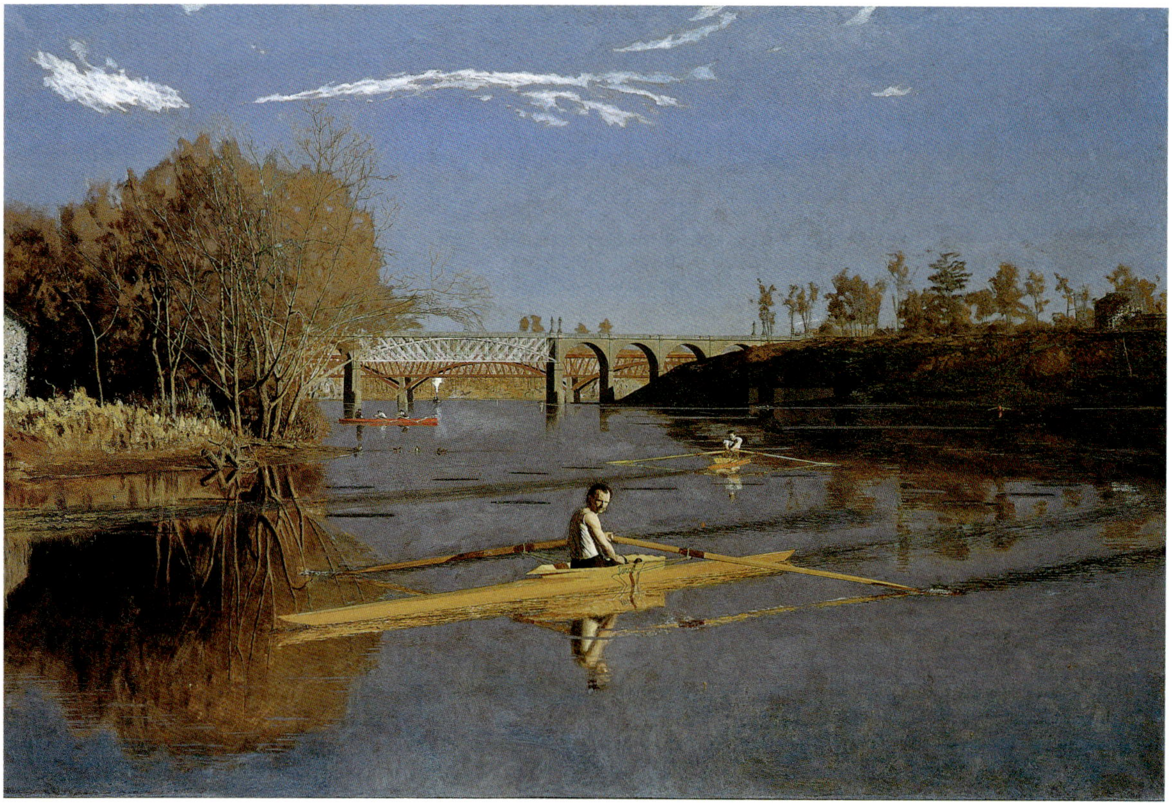

Fig. 100. Thomas Eakins, *The Champion Single Sculls (Max Schmitt in a Single Scull)*, 1871. Oil on canvas, 32 ¼ x 46 ¼ in. (81.9 x 117.5 cm). The Metropolitan Museum of Art, New York. Purchase, 1934, The Alfred N. Punnett Endowment Fund, and George D. Pratt Gift, 1934

But just as he saw and understood the human form as an integrated, organic whole, he also placed his figures within a clearly delineated spatial envelope, often carved out by perspective and illuminated by rational lighting. In turn, he linked perspective to calligraphy as kindred types of inscriptions, both on the picture surface and within the pictorial space. All this facilitated Eakins's disposition not only to identify with his subjects but to enter their depicted terrains as well.

In fact, into three of his most famous pictures he literally introduced his own self-portrait: sketching at the right in *The Gross Clinic*, 1875 (Thomas Jefferson University, Philadelphia); observing at the right in *The Agnew Clinic* (his figure here painted by his wife, Susan MacDowell Eakins), 1889 (University of Pennsylvania, Philadelphia); and rowing a scull in the middle

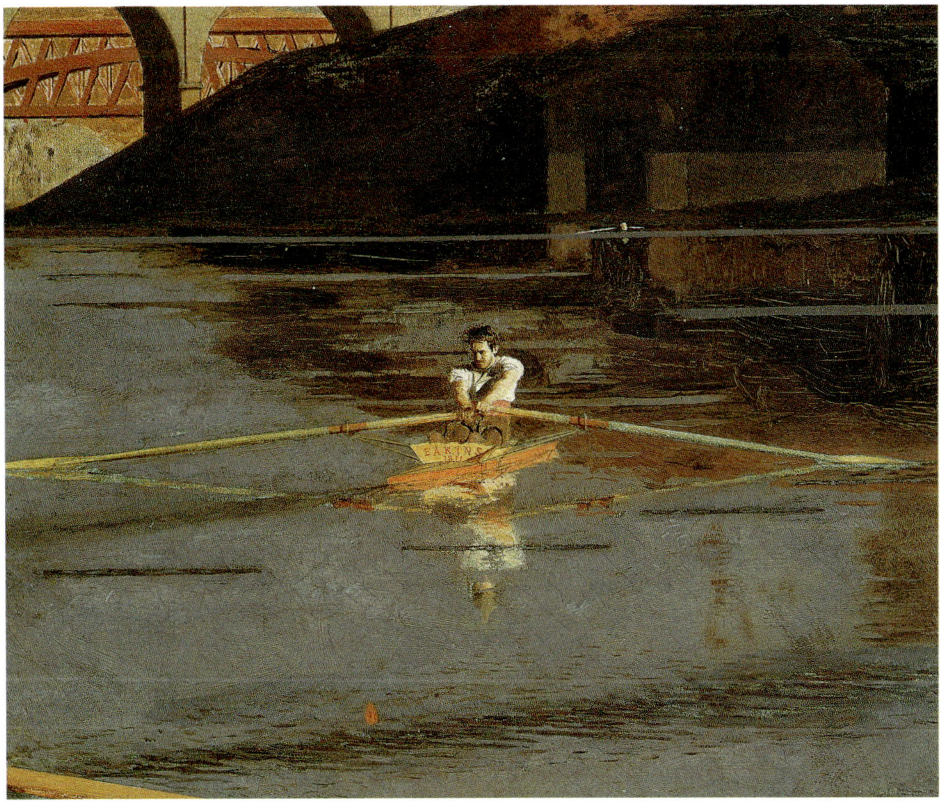

Fig. 101. Thomas Eakins, *The Champion Single Sculls (Max Schmitt in a Single Scull)* (detail of fig. 100), 1871

ground of *The Champion Single Sculls,* 1871 (figs. 100 and 101). Several historians have persuasively asserted that the figure of the sculptor in his series *William Rush Carving His Allegorical Figure of the Schuylkill River* (1877 and 1908) was a surrogate self-portrait, especially in the facial features drawn in the later canvases (see fig. 104). Over the four decades of his artistic production Eakins would bring his life, through his family, into nearly two dozen paintings. During the early 1870s there are several variants of one or two of his sisters gathered at the piano; his niece is the center of attention in *Baby at Play,* 1875 (National Gallery of Art, Washington, D.C.), seen in the bricked courtyard of the family's Philadelphia house; his wife, Susan MacDowell Eakins, posed for two important pictures, the first a sad image known as *Lady with a Setter Dog,* 1885 (Metropolitan Museum of Art, New York), set in the informality of the studio with the family dog, Harry, at her feet. A handful of portraits of his father-in-law, William H. MacDowell, date from

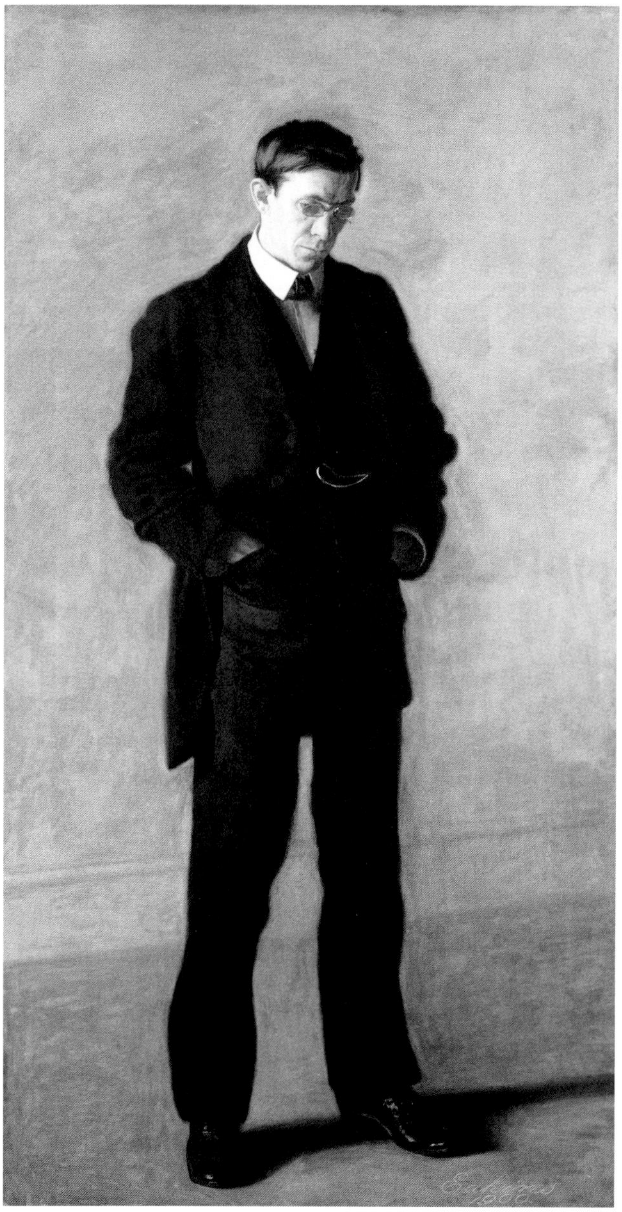

Fig. 102. Thomas Eakins, *The Thinker: Portrait of Louis N. Kenton*, 1900. Oil on canvas, 82 x 42 in. (208.3 x 106.7 cm). The Metropolitan Museum of Art, New York. Kennedy Fund, 1917

throughout the 1890s, and the full-length depiction of his sister-in-law's husband, Louis Kenton, *The Thinker*, 1900 (fig. 102), is one of the memorable works of his late career. Beyond family, deep collegial friendship is evident in several of the portraits, such as *William Merritt Chase*, 1899 (Hirshhorn Museum, Washington, D.C.), and *Henry O. Tanner*, ca. 1902 (Hyde Collection, Glens Falls, New York). And of course, in the faces of the many students and professors he painted we see the embodiments of Eakins's professional pride and anxiety, his confidence and hurt. Similarly, the extensive number of portraits of singers and musicians, physicians and scientists, provided a kind of continual self-examination in the faces of others. He saw them as fellow professionals, accomplished in their respective pursuits, often at the peak of their powers, sometimes past their prime, but self-accepting of their frailties along with their abilities. To such images he brought a critical sympathy, celebrating the commonality of the artistic and scientific imagination.

Of all Eakins's family relationships, that with Benjamin Eakins, his father, was one of the most complex and important. The young aspiring artist relied on his father's support during his early study and travel in France, and

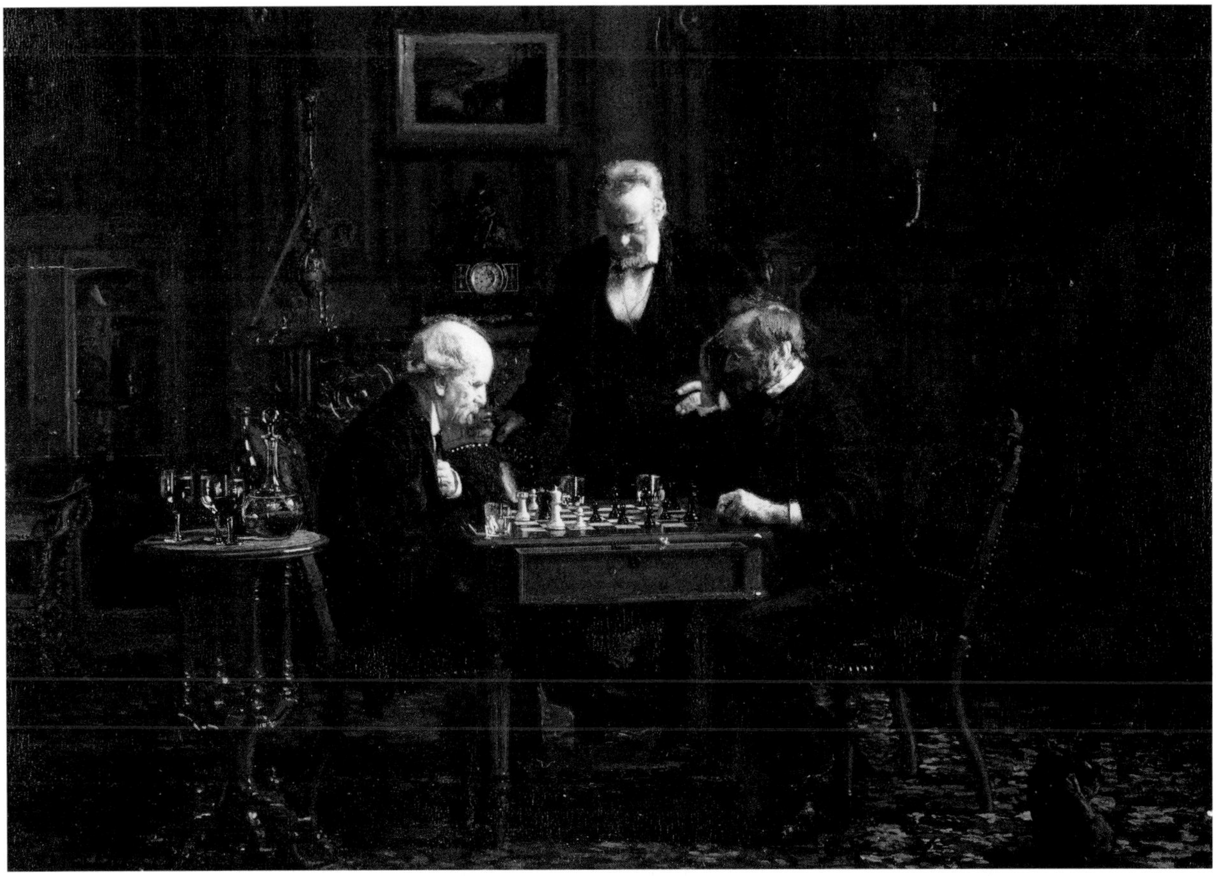

Fig. 103. Thomas Eakins, *The Chess Players,* 1876. Oil on wood, 11¾ x 16¾ in. (29.8 x 42.5 cm). The Metropolitan Museum of Art, New York. Gift of the artist, 1881

lived in his father's house until middle age. Later, after Thomas married, he moved back to the family home with his wife, and ultimately died there. He painted the elder Eakins on several occasions, depicting father and son together in one of the first such works, *The Artist and His Father Hunting Reed Birds on the Cohansey Marshes,* 1874 (Yale University Art Gallery, New Haven). Two years later, Benjamin Eakins is the central standing figure in *The Chess Players,* 1876 (fig. 103), and appears in the background crowd of a late boxing picture. He is of course the subject of *The Writing Master,* 1882 (Metropolitan Museum of Art, New York), where the old man is at work inscribing an elaborate document before him. Finally, we may argue that Eakins's students at the Pennsylvania Academy represented in effect an extended family, to whom he was at once mentor, friend, and father figure. There has been much analysis dedicated to these mostly all-male relationships, pictured most vividly in *Swimming*, 1885 (Amon Carter Museum, Fort Worth), again a key painting in which Eakins included himself as a central participant.

From this summary it is clear how constantly this artist projected his autobiography — both his personal relationships and his artistic fortunes — into his art. This enumeration provides the necessary background to an analysis of how Eakins's signatures provide explicit insights into the ways he made himself a part of the physical and imaginative spaces of his canvases. With the first masterpiece of his career, *The Champion Single Sculls*, 1871 (see figs. 100 and 101), he placed his name in a prominent and strategic location: on the sternboard of the scull he himself rows in the background. While Schmitt rows a boat whose name, *Josie*, is inscribed next to him on the sideboard, that name carries no further meaning for the oarsman. But Eakins not only painted his friend in a familiar activity on the Philadelphia River, he enjoyed such outings himself, and so the scene pictures both biography and autobiography. He is doubly there, in image and in name, much as Peto juxtaposed the visual and verbal in his violin and old cup. The letters Eakins painted are at once on the surface of the canvas and on the shell within the picture space, but the inscriptions also echo the marks made by Eakins's and Schmitt's oars on the placid river surface. The plane extending illusionistically to the horizon, the sculls, and their component details all result from the painter's manipulations of perspective, just as the two figures are demonstrations of Eakins's early mastery in observing and rendering human anatomy. All this is finally held together by another fundamental theme, which the artist would employ throughout the rest of his career, namely the link between head and hands. As superlative rowing requires the integrated harmony and coordination of the whole body working with the oars and shell, so intelligence and technique are necessary to the artist's job. This painting equally declares admiration for the abilities of a champion sculler and celebrates the painter's analogous ambitions for art. Eakins affixed his name to a document of both physical and mental activity.

A very different signature appears in *The Chess Players*, 1876 (see fig. 103). Just below the center of the painting Eakins inscribed in Latin on the open drawer of the chess table the words BENJAMINI. EAKINS. FILIUS. PINXIT. 76, meaning, "Benjamin Eakins's son painted this." Above and directly behind the table stands the senior Eakins, while the unseen artist faces him, the signature a stand-in for this implied observer at the fourth side of the table. That he identifies himself not by his own first name but as his father's son suggests something of the financial dependency, even emotional subordination, the artist may have felt in the paternal household.[4] To be sure, the Latin was a natural expression of Eakins's classical learning as well as of his father's instruction in calligraphy, but the sturdy block letters neatly centered in the design also recall ancient architecture and an enduring past. Eakins senior and his elderly companions seem as set in place as the chess figures they contemplate, their fragility of age matched by the decanter and glasses arranged nearby. In contrast to Eakins's rowing pictures of a few years before, the balance of coordination between their heads and hands here tilts toward the cerebral rather than the muscular.

Stung by the pervasive criticism of *The Gross Clinic*, his largest and most ambitious effort to that time, and by its rejection for the art building at the Philadelphia Centennial fair, Eakins turned inward. Over the next year or two he undertook smaller, more concentrated pictures, exploring themes of family and artistic production. The first canvas in the series *William Rush Carving His Allegorical Figure of the Schuylkill River* called attention to this Philadelphia artist of an earlier age, with whom Eakins felt an affinity. *The Chess Players* pursued a more familiar variation of *The Gross Clinic*'s theme: a further scrutiny of age, wisdom, and authority. It seems no accident that, like Dr. Gross, Benjamin Eakins stands alone in concentration, his seated colleagues engaged in the activity before them, and his balding head receiving a focal glare of light. Whatever Oedipal conflict may have existed between father and son, Eakins felt moved to recognize the paternal exemplar, whether in modern imagery or ancient words. Throughout his body of work, he would hold up men of accomplishment to emulate and if possible to equal.

A third type of inventive signature appears in the *William Rush* series. In an earlier version of 1876–77 (Philadelphia Museum of Art), Eakins signed his name as if carving it into a piece of wood at the lower right of the canvas. The signature sits diagonally across the composition from Rush himself carving his wooden figure of the Schuylkill, and thus reinforces Eakins's presence in the studio and identifies him with his predecessor — both made images from nude models. Eakins further charges his scene with an underlying sexuality, emphasizing the sensuosity of the discarded clothes at left center. The balancing of this almost erotic still life with the chaperone on the other side of the model — each placed on an identical Chippendale Revival chair, one turned blatantly outward, the other facing inward — suggests the Victorian tensions between revealing and concealing flesh.[5]

With the later versions painted in 1908, sexual innuendoes appear even

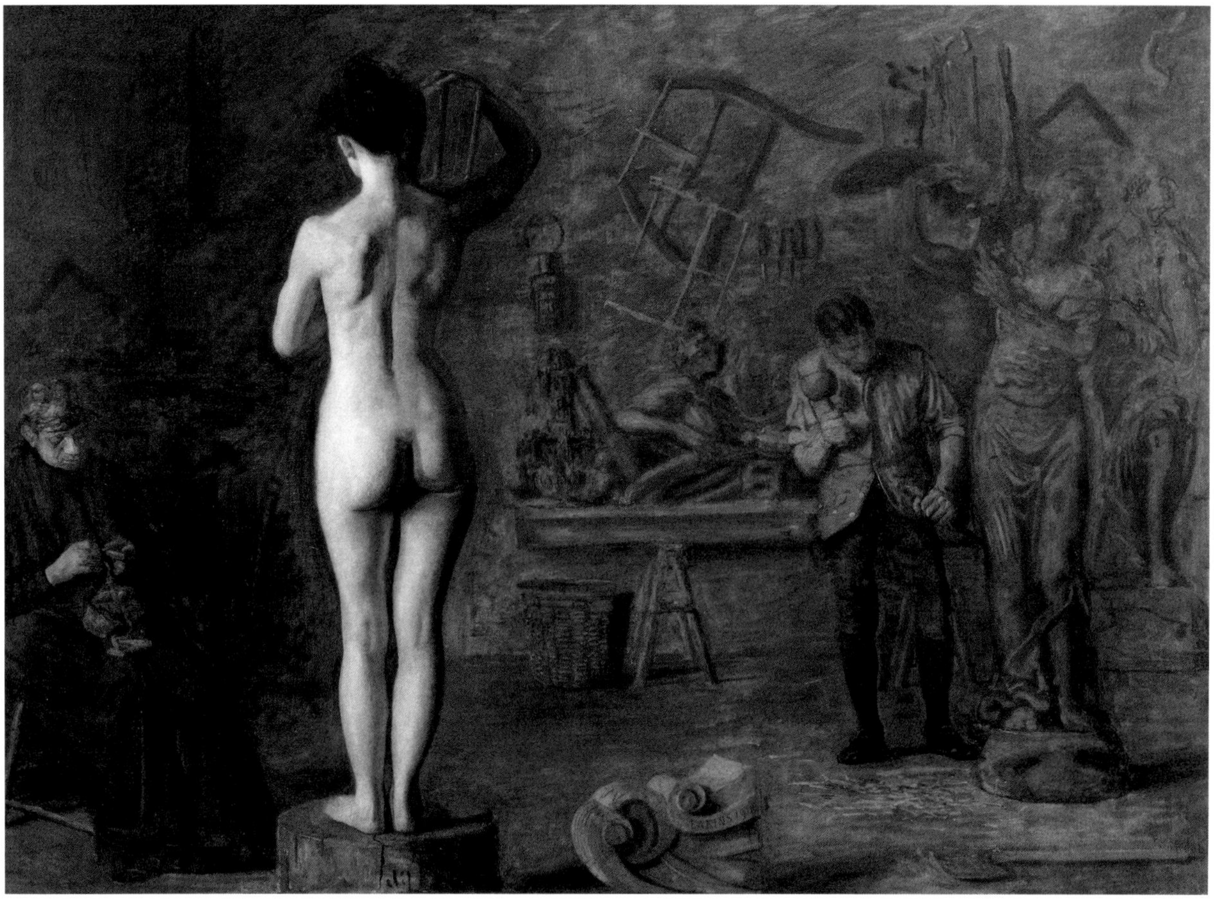

Fig. 104. Thomas Eakins, *William Rush Carving His Allegorical Figure of the Schuylkill River*, 1908. Oil on canvas, 36 7/16 x 48 7/16 in. (92.5 x 123 cm). Brooklyn Museum of Art, New York. Dick S. Ramsay Fund

more explicit. *William Rush and His Model*, 1908 (Honolulu Academy of Arts), is notable as Eakins's first frontal female nude. Although the figure appears uneroticized and painted straightforwardly, historians have noted the large, rather phallic form of the wooden ship's scroll intruding in front of Rush and the equally suggestive mallet held by the sculptor at crotch level. Also painted the same year was *William Rush Carving His Allegorical Figure of the Schuylkill River* (fig. 104), a reworking of the figures from the 1877 composition. But what is noteworthy here is the wooden scroll on the floor next to the nude model, its dual curves echoing her illuminated buttocks above, and bearing the artist's incised name. However we are to understand Eakins's attitudes toward female and male flesh, we should keep in mind the several pertinent incidents that occurred between the earlier and later versions of the subject: the severe criticism in the wake of *The Gross Clinic,* the dismissal from his teaching job at the Pennsylvania Academy for removal of a loincloth from a model in a class, family accusations of sexual abuse leading to a niece's suicide, and the rejection of a number of portraits by sitters unhappy with Eakins's unflattering realism. Finally, it is worth noting that in the years around the late *Rush* pictures he was simultaneously painting figures nude and sensuously clothed, embracing (as it were) imagery of men and of women, using palettes of reserved monochromy and brilliantly charged colors, depicting both intense physicality and spirituality. Some of these apparent contradictions are evident in the *Rush* imagery. With his signature Eakins enters his picture, where his chiseled name on the scroll associates him with the sculptor carving the female figure and wishfully places his hand on the curved forms of the real flesh.

The last type of internal signature Eakins employed appears in at least seventeen canvases. This is his calligraphic signature, written in perspective, usually on the floor plane beneath a depicted figure.[6] On a basic level these were demonstrations of his early training and lifelong experience in those two drawing techniques, parts of his life that had helped to define his art and now entered into it. More revealing, however, is the significance of those images so signed as expressions or extensions of his personality and interests. Kathleen Foster among others proposes that the series of large-format portraits from Eakins's last decades suggests self-portraiture.[7] That is, he identified most with the many teachers and other professionals he painted. Even more, it is possible to argue that in general he used the perspective signature — and thereby placed himself in the space with his subject — in cases where

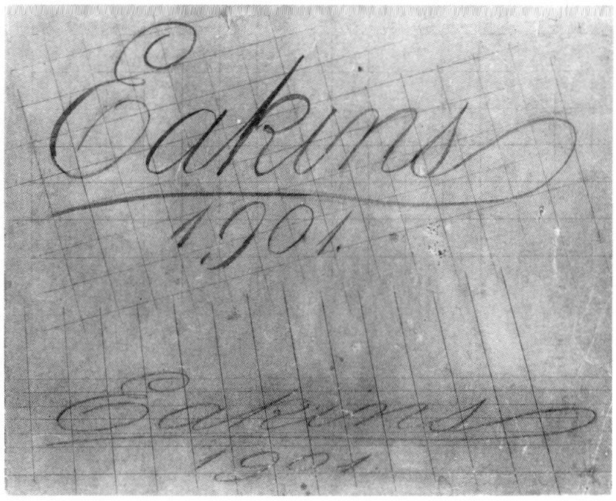

Fig. 105. Thomas Eakins, *Untitled (Perspective Study of Signature) (Study for Portrait of Professor Leslie W. Miller)*, ca. 1901. Pen and ink and pencil on paper, 13 7/16 x 16 7/16 in. (34.3 x 41.9 cm). Hirshhorn Museum and Sculpture Garden, Smithsonian Institution, Washington, D.C. Gift of Joseph H. Hirshhorn, 1966

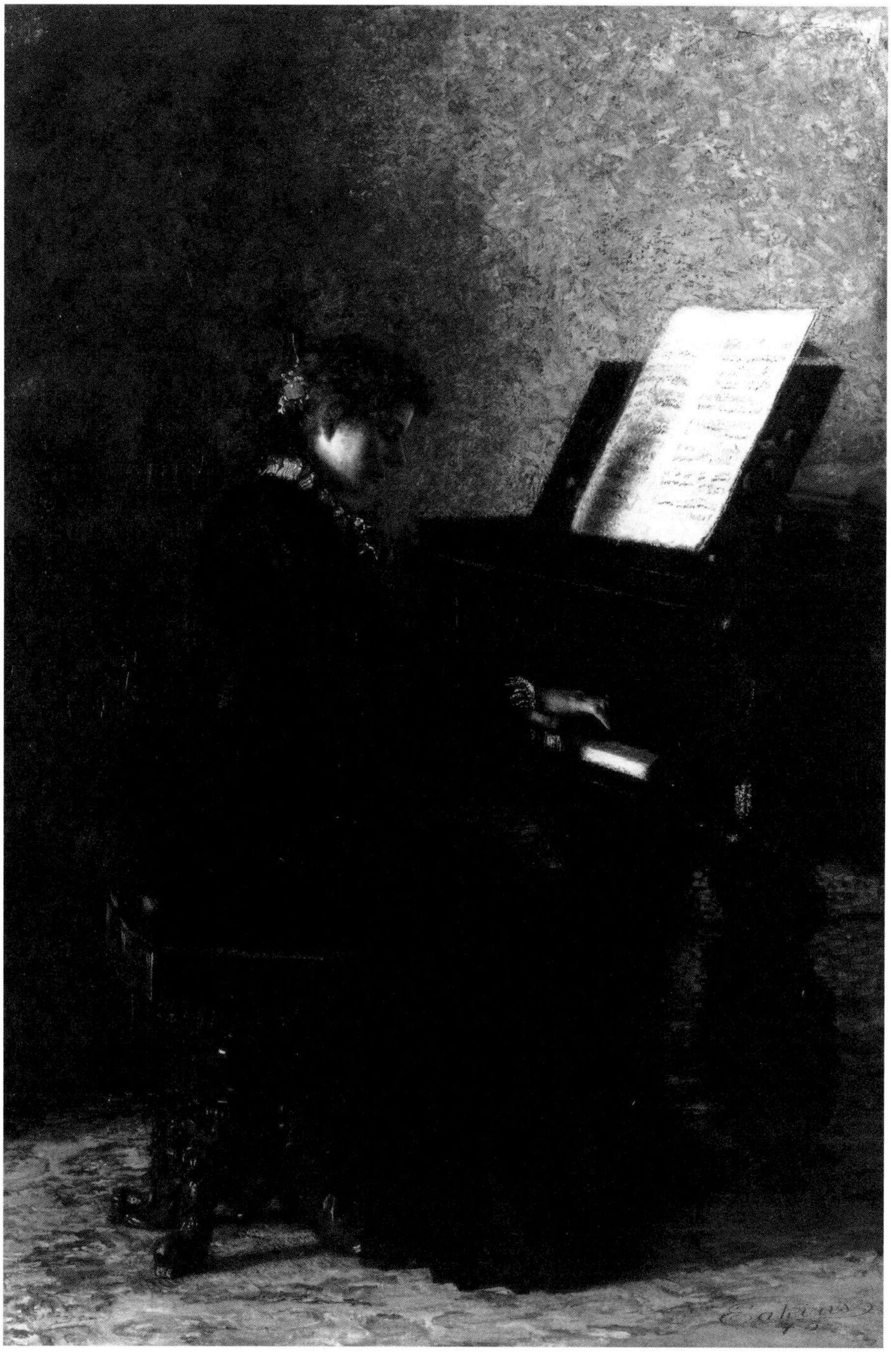

Fig. 106. Thomas Eakins, *Elizabeth at the Piano,* 1875. Oil on canvas, 72 1/8 x 48 3/16 in. (183.2 x 122.2 cm). Addison Gallery of American Art, Phillips Academy, Andover, Mass. Gift of anonymous donor

he felt a special sympathy or affinity. By contrast, he often signed his name in plain block letters on the picture surface of portraits of individuals he cared little about, such as bankers or industrialists. (One exception is *Salutat*, 1898 [Addison Gallery of American Art, Phillips Academy, Andover, Massachusetts], where Eakins placed his name on the arena wall in front of the boxer, as if he were in the crowd of observers himself.)

He often made preparatory drawings of his signature, as in the case of *Professor Leslie W. Miller*, ca. 1901 (fig. 105), for which he wrote out his name on a flat gridded surface that he then angled in order to translate them into a receding perspective. On the final painting, although the signature technically sits on the canvas surface, it illusionistically reads as if extending back on the depicted floor plane. In a further optical play Eakins sometimes wrote his name on a patterned rug, thus compounding the levels of figuration on a ground. In a few instances this internal signature not only associates the artist with his subject, it also plays off visually on key forms or details. It is instructive to note the principal portrait subjects that Eakins signed in perspective, works that date from as early as 1870 to as late as 1905. Among the first group were interior scenes with his sisters or friends, including *Elizabeth at the Piano*, 1875 (fig. 106), and *Home Scene*, 1870–71 (Brooklyn Museum of Art, New York). The latter shows his sisters Margaret and Caroline caught up in their respective reveries, the older sister pausing and turning from the piano, the younger on the floor drawing in chalk on her slate. The linking of thought and action in their contrasting creative pursuits becomes evident in the echoed poses of hands resting against cheeks. The vertical rectangle of Caroline's slate similarly matches the format of the music sheet above; both display artistic "marks" upon them and, as Martin Berger observes, are analogous to the larger canvas on which the artist paints.[8] Here Eakins has scratched his name in white on the floor at the lower right. If not inscribed by Caroline nearby, it at least associates the painter's work with the act of drawing in which his sister is engaged. It seems only natural that one so devoted to his family as Eakins would want to bind himself to the intimacy of his sisters at the outset of his career.

Besides family, a second major theme in these early images is music, an activity and a subject the artist would enjoy all his life. Some of his tenderest and most sympathetic music portraits bear his name — and presence — in perspective close by the feet of figures either singing or playing instruments. Examples include *The Zither Player*, 1876 (Art Institute of Chicago); *The Pathetic Song*, 1881 (Corcoran Gallery of Art, Washington, D.C.); and

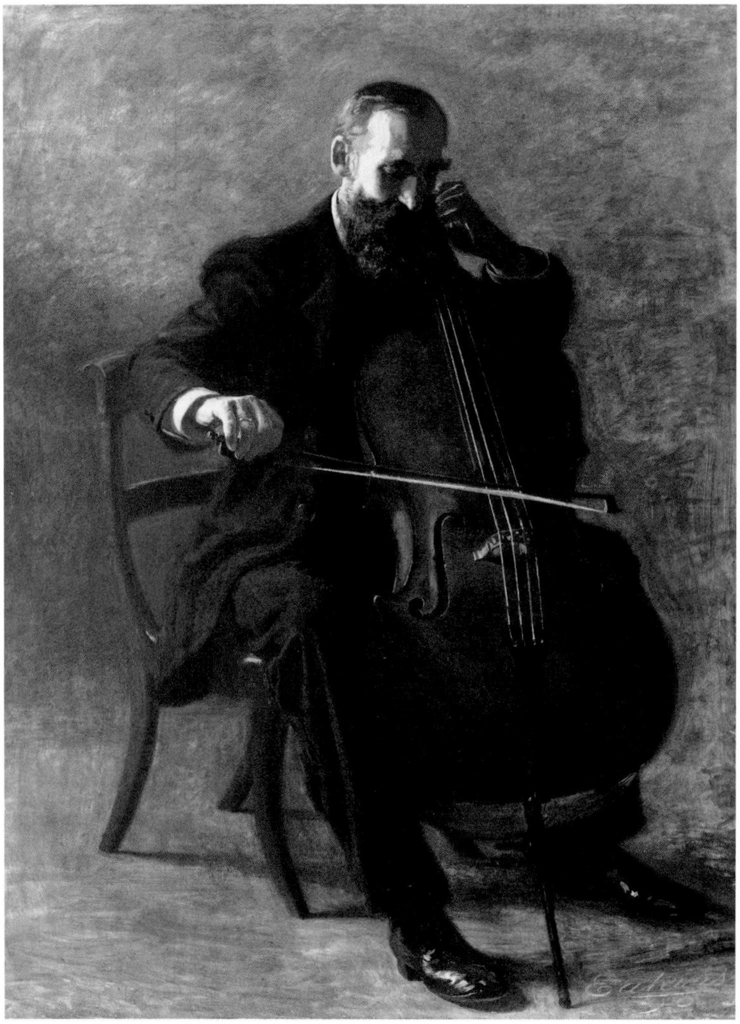

Fig. 107. Thomas Eakins, *The Cello Player*, 1896. Oil on canvas, 64 ¼ x 48 ⅛ in. (163.2 x 122.2 cm). Courtesy of the Pennsylvania Academy of the Fine Arts, Philadelphia. Joseph E. Temple Fund

The Cello Player, 1896 (fig. 107). In this last painting, the signature in large white calligraphy at the lower right is all the more forceful for residing at the end of the long diagonal that descends from Rudolph Hennig's concentrated glance down through the highlighted strings and the cello's supporting leg. By implication, painter and cellist occupy this same imagined space, complementary performers in these sister arts. One might imagine Eakins's fluid and disciplined lettering as analogous to notes on a music sheet or even to the melody being "drawn" within this mysterious space by Hennig's bow.

One portrait category where we might logically expect the insertion of Eakins's name as an expression of collegial admiration and association is

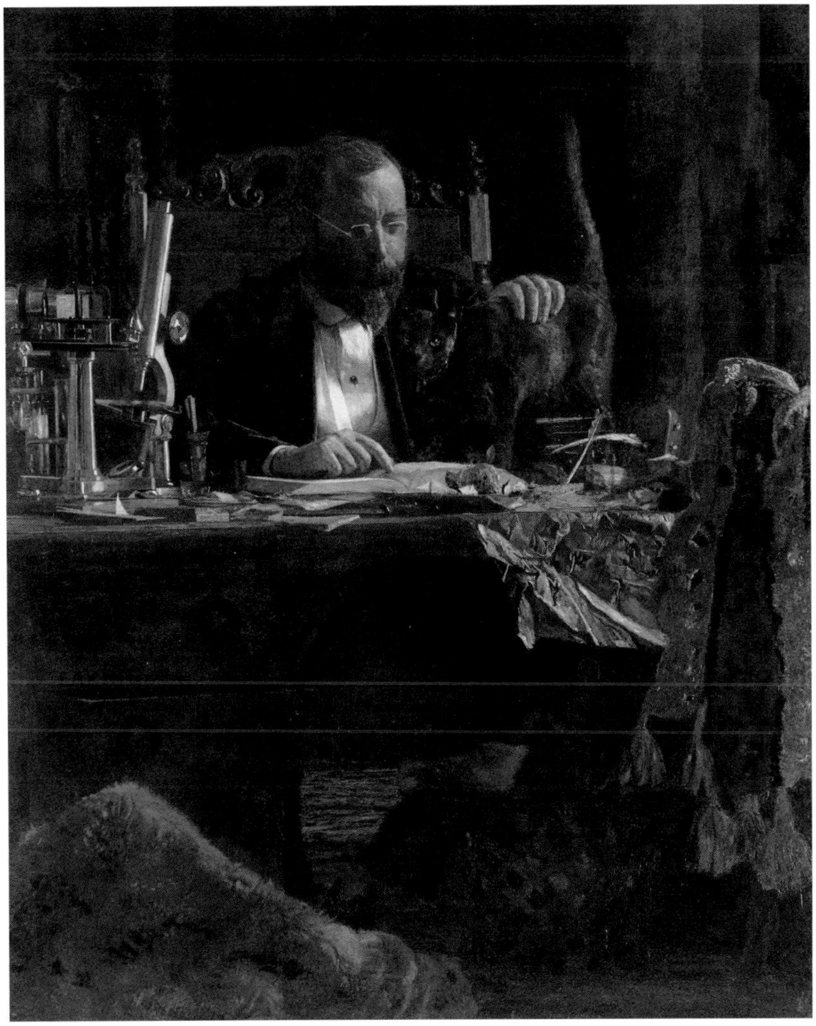

Fig. 108. Thomas Eakins, *Benjamin Howard Rand,* 1874. Oil on canvas, 60 x 48 in. (152.4 x 121.9 cm). Jefferson Medical College of Thomas Jefferson University, Philadelphia

that comprising physicians and scientists. So again the diagonal axis of the figure in *Dr. John H. Brinton,* 1876 (National Gallery of Art, Washington, D.C.), carries our eye downward to Eakins's name on the carpet. Although not in perspective, a parallel inscription appears on the near side of the desk in *Benjamin Howard Rand,* 1874 (fig. 108). A professor of chemistry, Rand sits absorbed in his reading, framed by the scientific instruments of his profession on the left, and by a more casual accumulation of domestic details on the right. Rand faces us from the far side of a partners desk; on this side Eakins affixed his name in the space, so to speak, where he painted his subject.[9] Its location invokes a partnership of professions, in which the aspirations and accomplishments of science and art mirror one another.

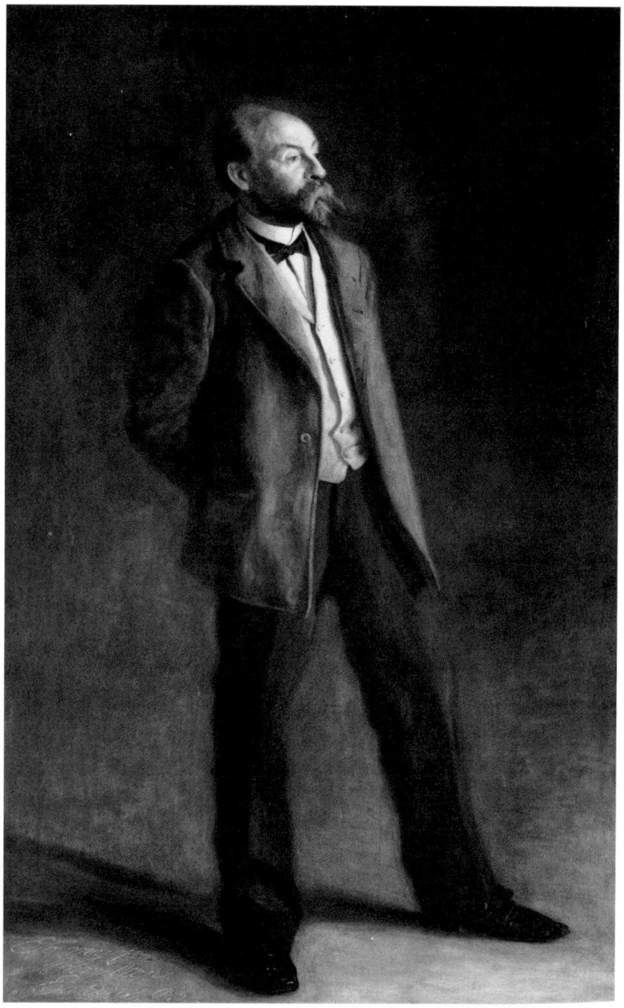

Fig. 109. Thomas Eakins, *Portrait of John McLure Hamilton,* 1895. Oil on canvas, 80 x 50 ¼ in. (203.2 x 127 cm). Wadsworth Atheneum, Hartford, Conn. The Ella Gallup Sumner and Mary Catlin Sumner Collection Fund

By the same token, Eakins saw sympathetic spirits in the subjects of several grand academic portraits, teachers and professors at Jefferson Medical College and the University of Pennsylvania. His name stands alongside them on the floor planes of their spaces. One of the best of this type is *The Dean's Roll Call,* 1899 (Museum of Fine Arts, Boston), portraying Professor James W. Holland reading the list of those graduating from medical college.[10] Fellow artists and intellects received equal attention: Eakins inscribed a literal statement of friendship and collegiality, written in perspective, into *John McLure Hamilton,* 1895 (fig. 109), "To my friend / J. Hamilton / Eakins '95." Hamilton was at the time a successful and recognized portraitist himself. Perhaps the most famous of these grand-format portraits was *The Thinker,* 1900 (see fig. 102), which depicts Louis Kenton, who was married to Susan MacDowell

Eakins's sister. Barbara Weinberg suggests that the title might have come from Auguste Rodin's recently popular sculpture, but the painting is also one of a series Eakins made of named individuals whom he also thought of as generalized types, such as "actress," "student," "bohemian," "veteran," "concert singer," and "cellist." These images, while capturing specific likenesses, also present something of the larger human condition.

The Thinker certainly gives us a person caught up in self-absorbed introspection. We feel a gravity both of thought and body, as if the individual is weighted down as much by a physical as an emotional burden. A mostly monochromatic painting, it conveys the somber mood of one whose marriage in the family would last only a short time. It mirrors tribulations both Eakins and Kenton must have felt. Kenton's glance carries straight down his torso and leg to Eakins's name and the year, in this instance written in boldly contrasting white letters on the floor. The location and brightness of the inscription, appropriately, match the starkly illuminated face and collar of Kenton above, tying together painter and sitter in form as well as meaning. It is striking that the year holds equal visual prominence, as if Kenton were standing metaphorically on the threshold of the new century and all its uncertainties.

It is quite possible that some of the poignancy and melancholy we see here was given added nuance by the death of the painter's father, Benjamin Eakins, at virtually the end of the old century, on December 30, 1899. The son, then fifty-five, was as we know close to his father and reliant on his support most of his life. This moment would have been an unsettling turning point in more ways than one. We also know that at about this time Eakins began bicycling out to suburban Philadelphia with one of his favorite pupils, Samuel Murray. Often on Sundays for exercise they went out the few miles from center city to the Saint Charles Borromeo Seminary on City Line Avenue in Overbrook. There, Eakins could converse in Latin with the well-educated clerics and listen to the music at Vespers. From his association and growing friendship with the Catholic clergy, he found stimulation and solace. After all, these were still years when criticism and rejection mixed with praise and acceptance, and we sense that the artist gained respite in that idyllic landscape. Between 1900 and 1906 he began to paint more than a dozen remarkable portraits of the clerics at the Seminary; some of these works are among the strongest and most moving of his late career.[11] We have to wonder if in their wise and intelligent faces, in their imposing and dignified poses, and in their demeanor of spiritual authority, the painter found surrogate father figures, replacements for his recent loss. At least two of the monumental canvases he produced in this period have his perspective signature, associating him with the imaginative spaces inhabited by these intellectuals.

One of these is *Archbishop William Henry Elder*, 1903 (Cincinnati Art Museum), which, according to Lloyd Goodrich, Eakins called "one of my best."[12] The other is *His Eminence Sebastiano Cardinal Martinelli*, 1902 (fig. 110). As in the portrait of Kenton, Eakins's name is inscribed in white on the floor, parallel to the diagonal edge of the patterned carpet beneath the cardinal's chair, and echoing his highlighted face and hands. Eakins frequently used chairs as crucial accessories reinforcing the character of his sitters: the Chippendale Revival chairs in his several Centennial subjects, the heavy Victorian chair emphasizing Amelia Van Buren's vulnerability or the stiff awkwardness of Helen Montanverde Parker in *The Old Fashioned Dress*, 1908 (Philadelphia Museum of Art), the expansive stage prop for Susan Santje posing in *The Actress*, 1903 (Philadelphia Museum of Art). Here we have an ample high-backed chair serving as a throne for a prince of the church. The rendering of the subject in profile, in a manner extending back to the early Renaissance, and the reserved color scheme suggest an intentional artificiality akin to that of Whistler's portraits of his mother and of Thomas Carlyle. While Martinelli is of this world, he has a combination of tranquility and detachment, as he looks toward the spiritual realm, that Eakins would have admired and wanted to identify with. The one major touch of color is the cardinal's hat, the biretta, painted in an intense raspberry red that signals specifically his position in the church and more allusively the Passion of Christ. Including the paneled wall behind, the chair frame, and the sharp outlining of Martinelli's figure, the composition relies on silhouetted and linear rhythms throughout. Most expressive are the wiry details of his face and hands, sympathetically complemented by Eakins's calligraphy. At his most engaged, Eakins repeatedly revealed his life in others, as his signature just as often affirmed.

Where Eakins was America's consummate painter of the human face and figure, his slightly older contemporary Winslow Homer was the great American landscape and seascape artist. Though both individuals shared earlier themes, such as genre subjects during the 1870s, Eakins increasingly isolated the figure indoors, while Homer turned more to nature, at the end often without human beings yet deeply mindful of the human condition. Around 1900, from personal impulses as well as larger intellectual forces, both painters moved toward a greater abstraction and psychological content. Like Eakins, Homer invested his presence in many of his works in all media,

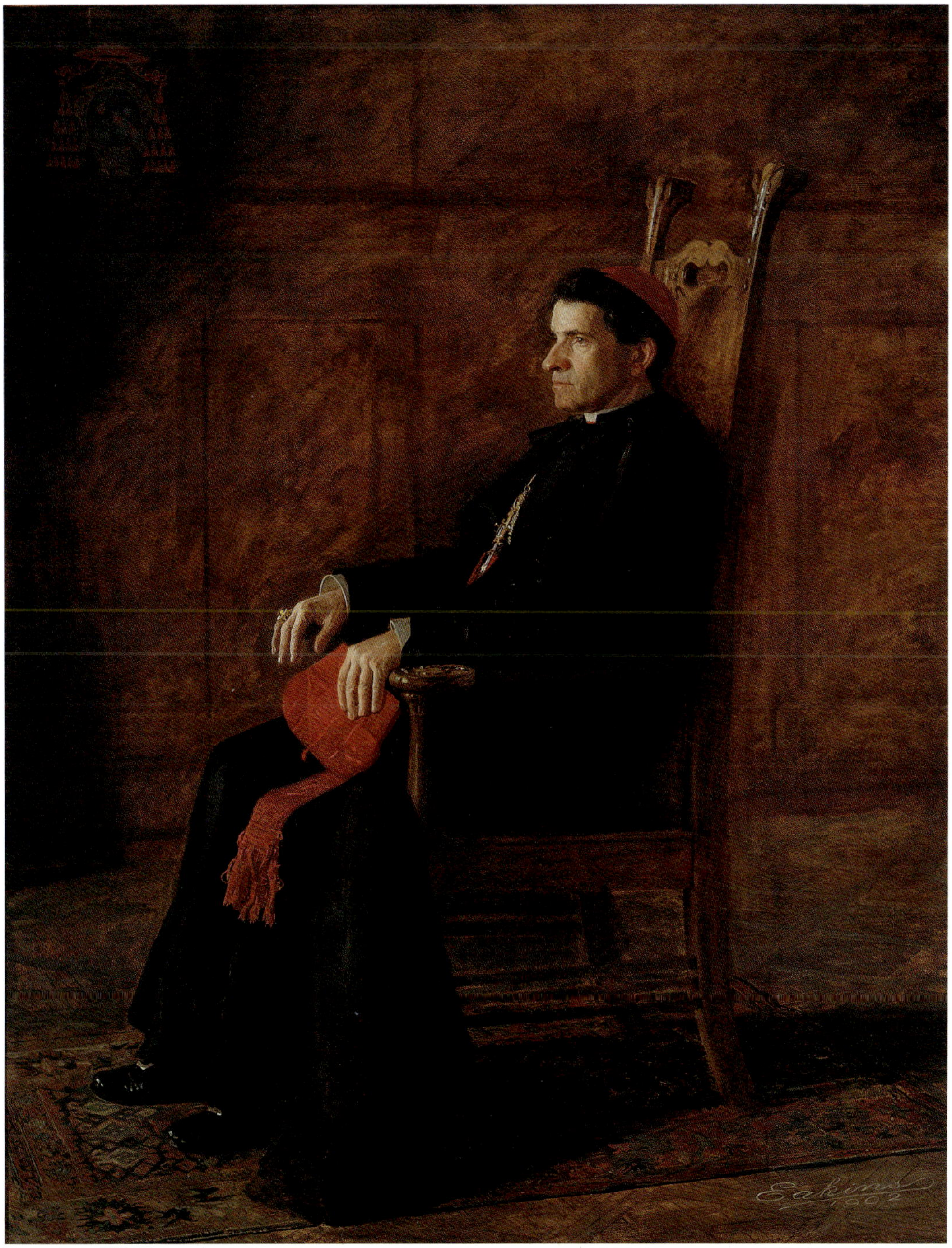

Fig. 110. Thomas Eakins, *His Eminence Sebastiano Cardinal Martinelli*, 1902. Oil on canvas mounted on panel, 78⅜ x 60 in. (199.1 x 152.4 cm). The Armand Hammer Collection. Gift of the Armand Hammer Foundation, UCLA Hammer Museum

from the beginning to the end of his career. In recent years, important initiatives in psychosexual and gender studies have probed a variety of aspects of Homer's art in efforts to get at his personal motivations and the intended as well as subconscious meanings of his images. He was a reticent Bostonian, born in 1836, who once stated, "Don't let the public poke its nose into my picture," and flatly told his first biographer, William Howe Downes, that "as the most interesting part of my life is of no concern to the public I must decline to give you any particulars in regard to it."[13] He was speaking of the famous *Gulf Stream*, 1899 (see fig. 133), even as he prepared to send it off for public exhibition. Such statements have fueled the efforts of Homer scholars to examine his art for signs of the artist within. Not surprisingly, one rich area for analysis has been a number of his signatures and inscriptions, which here deserve a much fuller accounting than they have heretofore received for their wealth and suggestiveness of meaning.

Several Homer scholars have commented on Homer's projections of self into his imagery and sometimes into his signatures. In particular, there are the intriguing analyses by Henry Adams on *Fox Hunt*, Jules Prown on *The Life Line*, and Nicolai Cikovsky on the schoolhouse series.[14] What we do know is that, probably more than any other American artist, Homer employed over his career the widest variety of initials and signature forms in his oils, watercolors, drawings, and prints. Nearly two dozen variants, all recognizably his, have been identified (fig. 111).[15] The question is why did he continually modify the appearance of his name — his self-representation — and what might these multiple identities tell us?

The story begins with his earliest body of work, his extensive production of graphic arts — specifically lithographs and wood engravings — from the mid-1850s to the mid-1870s. Homer was born in Boston, and, with the exception of two relatively short trips abroad and a period of work in New York, would remain a New Englander for most of his later life. As a youth, he went to work for a Boston lithographer, learning the craft of drawing in black and white, expressing forms in terms of line, outline, and tonal contrast. On his twenty-first birthday in 1857 he declared his independence from the job secured by his father, and asserted that henceforth he would work only for himself. For the next two decades he worked as a freelance graphic artist, making wood engravings for several illustrated New England magazines. His longest and best-known association would be with *Harper's Weekly*, which lured him to New York before the Civil War, then sent him to the front as a war correspondent. With the end of hostilities Homer shifted his

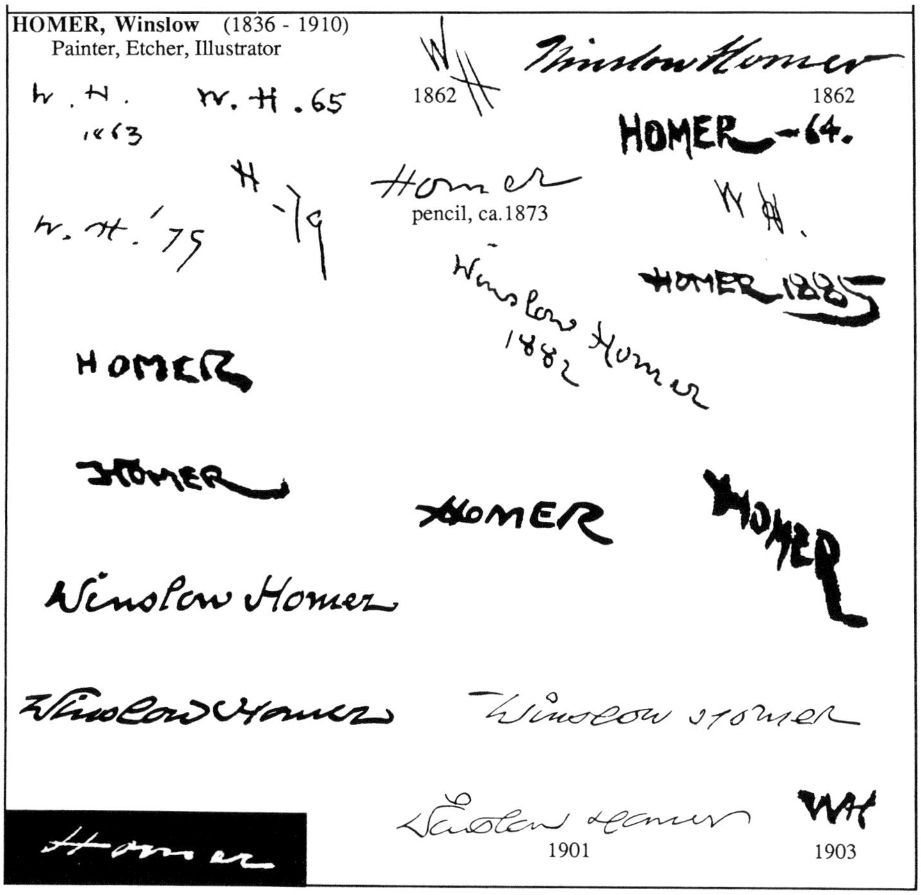

Fig. 111. Winslow Homer, Signatures. From Peter Hastings Falk, *Dictionary of Signatures and Monograms of American Artists* (1988)

reportorial eye to the new themes of domestic leisure and the vacation retreats of the Atlantic shore. During this period he grew into a successful and self-supporting artist, and produced more than two hundred prints. Many of these images are signed with either his initials, name, monogram, or inscription. They vary in their cleverness, purpose, and expressiveness, and a summary of their types is revealing.

The overall number suggests how conscious Homer was of referencing himself in his scenes and how much his images depicted personal experiences. In some instances his initials simply imitate surrounding forms or details, the best example being when he set his spiky letters among foreground grasses. He did this as early as June 1868 in *Green Apples* for *Our Young Folks,* and later in *Raid on a Sand-Swallow Colony — "How Many Eggs?,"* in the June 13,

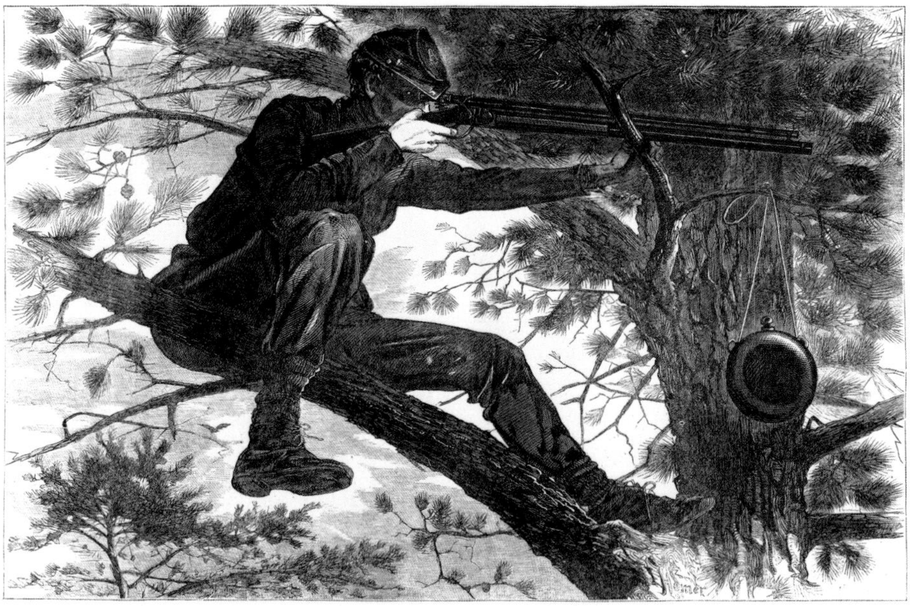

Fig. 112. Winslow Homer, *The Army of the Potomac — A Sharp Shooter on Picket Duty*, in *Harper's Weekly* (November 15, 1862). Courtesy of the Beinecke Rare Book and Manuscript Library, Yale University

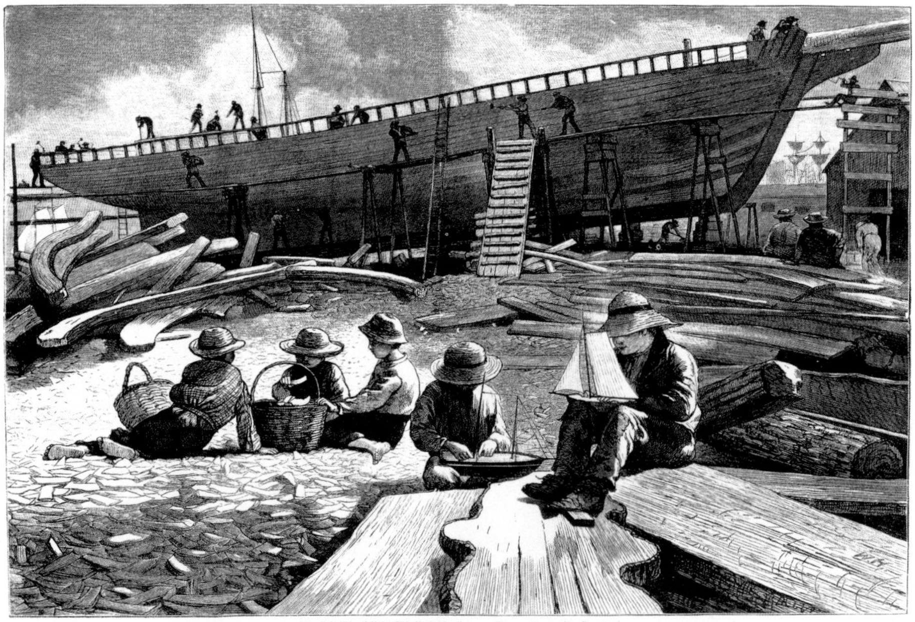

Fig. 113. Winslow Homer, *Ship-Building, Gloucester Harbor*, in *Harper's Weekly* (October 11, 1873). Library of Congress

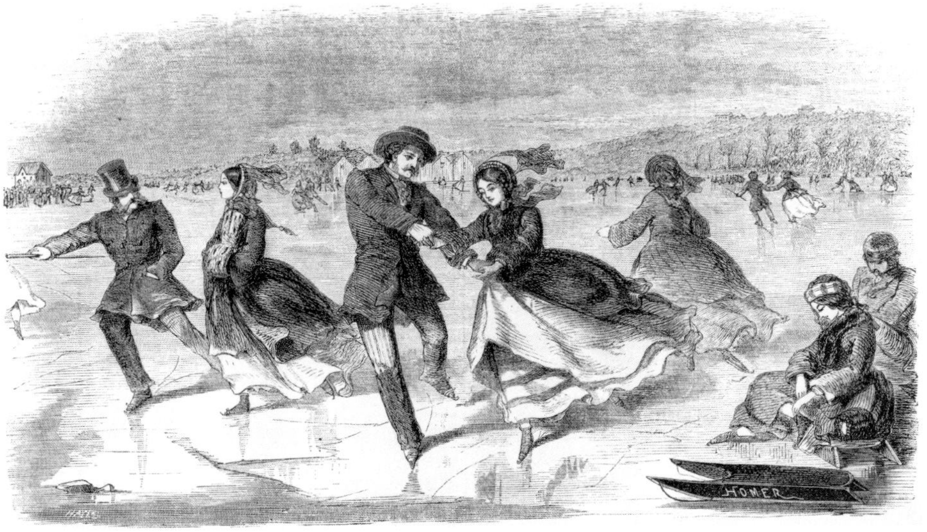

Fig. 114. Winslow Homer, *Skating on Jamaica Pond, near Boston*, in *Ballou's Pictorial Drawing-Room Companion* (January 29, 1859). Portland Museum of Art, Portland, Maine. Gift of Peggy and Harold Osher

1874, *Harper's Weekly*, where his initials also follow the upward contour of the sand bank.[16] A related type shows his letters imitating a wooden ground, such as a tree trunk or floor board. *The Army of the Potomac — A Sharp Shooter on Picket Duty* (*Harper's Weekly*, November 15, 1862) (fig. 112) has "Homer" set at the juncture of the tree limb and trunk, its lines seeming to curl out of the surrounding knot of wood.[17] By far the most imaginative signature in this grouping is in *Ship-Building, Gloucester Harbor*, 1873 (fig. 113): here Homer's initials appear cut into the plank of wood receding diagonally into the right foreground. The artist synthesized the scene, a composite of sketches done in watercolor, pencil, and oil, into a visual narrative of older men and younger boys engaged in the serious versus lighthearted making of boats for work and play at sea. We see wood in a range of forms and conditions from natural to finished filling almost the entire image. Homer clearly saw such vignettes often along the Gloucester waterfront, and visibly incorporates himself through his carefully placed initials. But these are a visual double-entendre, for he presents himself both as observer and as artist: after all, the work itself is technically a *wood* engraving, which also required carving to complete.

Homer spelled out his name on other wood surfaces of objects within his prints, for example, several times on the sides of children's sleds (fig. 114) or sleighs carrying adults, again, pleasures he experienced firsthand.[18] Similarly,

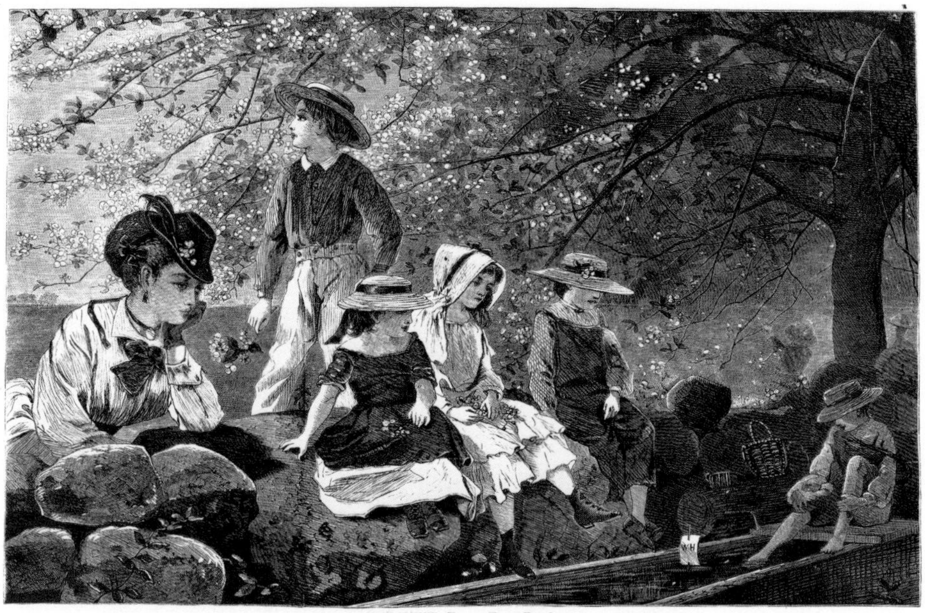

Fig. 115. Winslow Homer, *Spring Blossoms,* in *Harper's Weekly* (May 21, 1870). Courtesy of the Beinecke Rare Book and Manuscript Library, Yale University

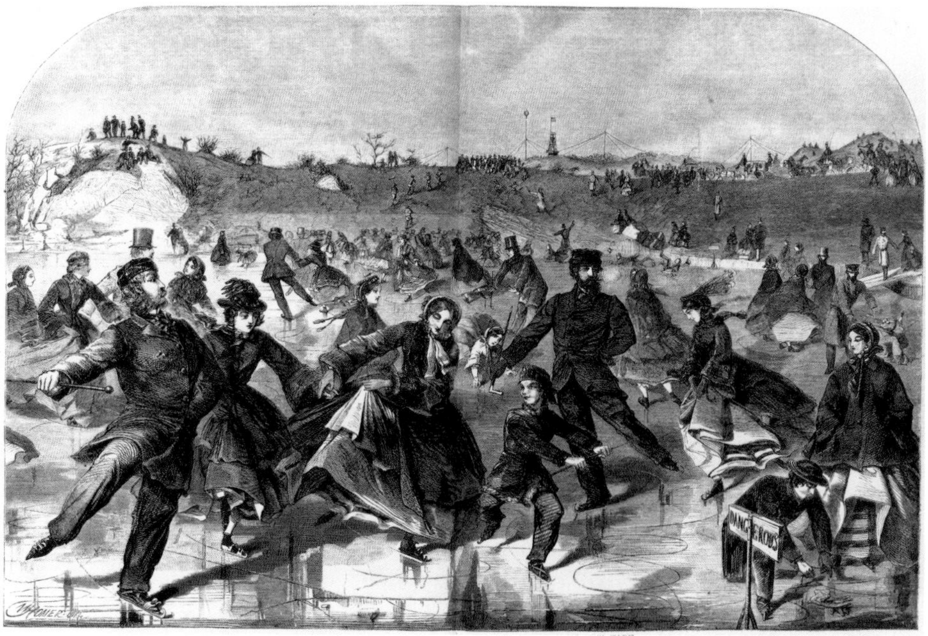

Fig. 116. Winslow Homer, *Skating on the Ladies' Skating-Pond in the Central Park, New York,* in *Harper's Weekly* (January 28, 1860). Courtesy of the Beinecke Rare Book and Manuscript Library, Yale University

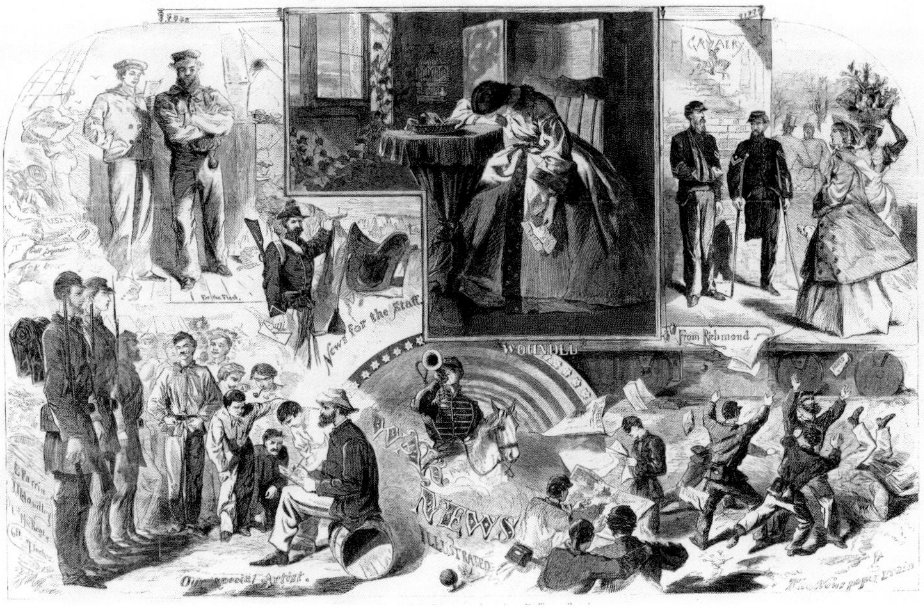

Fig. 117. Winslow Homer, *News from the War*, in *Harper's Weekly* (June 14, 1862). Courtesy of the Beinecke Rare Book and Manuscript Library, Yale University

he might put his name on a box within a picture, as in *A Bivouac Fire on the Potomac* (*Harper's Weekly*, December 21, 1861) or *The War — Making Havelocks for the Volunteers* (*Harper's Weekly*, June 29, 1861), although the former is more likely the one he witnessed personally. Other tricky locations for his initials include the side of a step in *What Shall We Do Next?* (*Harper's Weekly*, July 31, 1869), the inside rim of a large dishpan in *The Dinner Horn* (*Harper's Weekly*, June 11, 1870), and the sail of a toy boat in *Spring Blossoms*, 1870 (fig. 115), all images of familiar activities or nostalgic recollections. One winter pleasure that he enjoyed in New York was the popular new craze of ice-skating in the recently finished Central Park, celebrated in *Skating on the Ladies' Skating-Pond in the Central Park, New York*, 1860 (fig. 116). Homer's signature at the lower left appears to have been carved in the ice surface by a turning skate. Like others, this conceit is suggestive in more than one way: besides being a mark in the ice, it is also analogous to cutting a wood block — and to the artist drawing in the first place.

It is such subtler meanings that have to do with the practice of art, learning, and reading that emerge as a theme in a small core of his illustrations, and that would carry over into a more extensive and conscious exploration in many later oils. Two *Harper's Weekly* wood engravings eight years apart

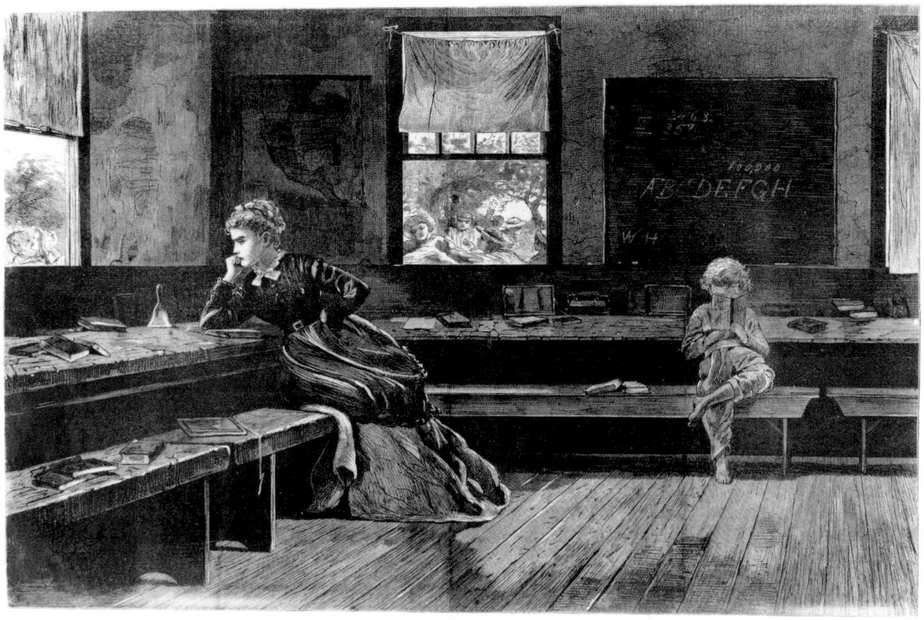

Fig. 118. Winslow Homer, *The Noon Recess*, in *Harper's Weekly* (June 28, 1873). Portland Museum of Art, Portland, Maine. Gift of Peggy and Harold Osher

have formats similar to half a dozen small vignettes of Civil War themes. *News from the War* (fig. 117) mixes scenes at home and at the front; prominent in the lower left corner is a bearded young illustrator, quite possibly Homer himself, seated on a barrel and sketching a line of soldiers. The title below reads: "Our special Artist." The later print, which appeared on January 8, 1870, is simply captioned *1860–1870*, and shows incidents at the war's end, along with subsequent peacetime activities. These refer to recent paintings in oil, a medium Homer had just taken up, showing veterans harvesting wheat and a schoolteacher with children in front of a blackboard. On a second board, letters from half the alphabet are spelled out, below which Homer signed his name. The subject of learning and literacy was one that interested him during the postwar years, but in placing himself in this imaginary schoolroom, he was linking writing to his own practice of drawing images on a page or canvas. This linkage is more explicit in *The Noon Recess*, 1873 (fig. 118), where we see on the blackboard in the schoolroom the alphabet written out up to the letter "H," a sly self-reference repeated by Homer's initials below in a second self-placement in the scene.

Two other illustrations of this time play on his initials as his marks within a landscape or interior. In *The Beach at Long Branch* (fig. 119) a woman

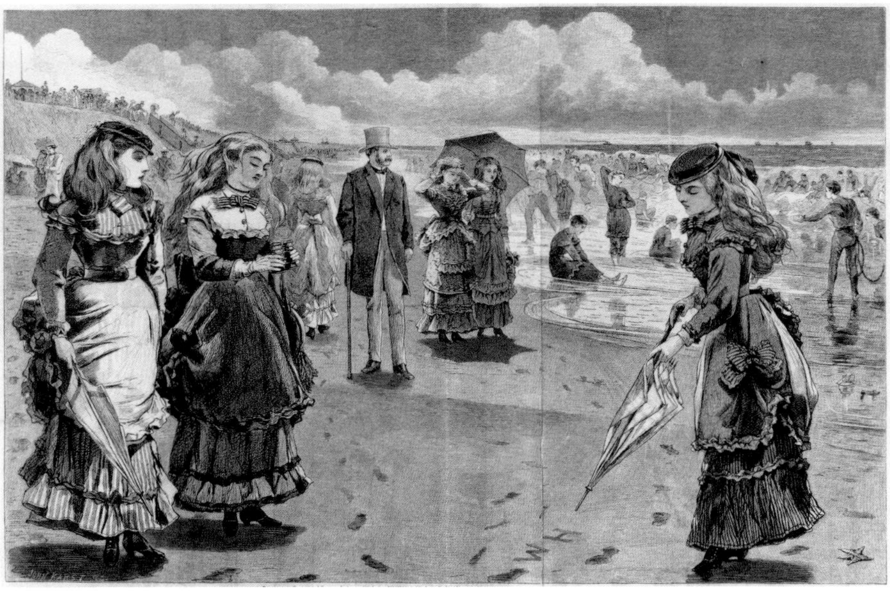

Fig. 119. Winslow Homer, *The Beach at Long Branch,* in *Appleton's Journal of Literature, Science and Art* (August 21, 1869). Portland Museum of Art, Portland, Maine. Gift of Peggy and Harold Osher

promenading on the beach points her umbrella to the letters W H drawn in the sand. We do not know if she or Homer has written them, but in pointing them out to her nearby lady friends and to us, the gesture calls attention to his presence and his work. Homer had sent several of his early paintings to Paris for display in the Universal Exposition of 1866, and made his first trip abroad then to see how they fared in an international setting. Little evidence of his travels exists beyond some two dozen modest oils and sketches. These do indicate he traveled into the French countryside and saw something of contemporary Barbizon and early realist painting. Equally important, one engraving he published in *Harper's Weekly* after his return demonstrates he visited the Louvre and saw its collections of old master paintings. *Art-Students and Copyists in the Louvre Gallery, Paris* (fig. 120) shows students filling the Grande Galerie with their palettes, easels, and canvases. Prominent in the left foreground, one female copyist is at work on a large picture bearing the faint outlines of Christ carrying the Cross, while a companion painter stands behind her looking in the direction of the white canvas, signed sharply at the upper left W H. While Homer would make little direct use of European old master precedents in his own work, he clearly looked at and absorbed the examples of other contemporaries. This was but one early indication of his

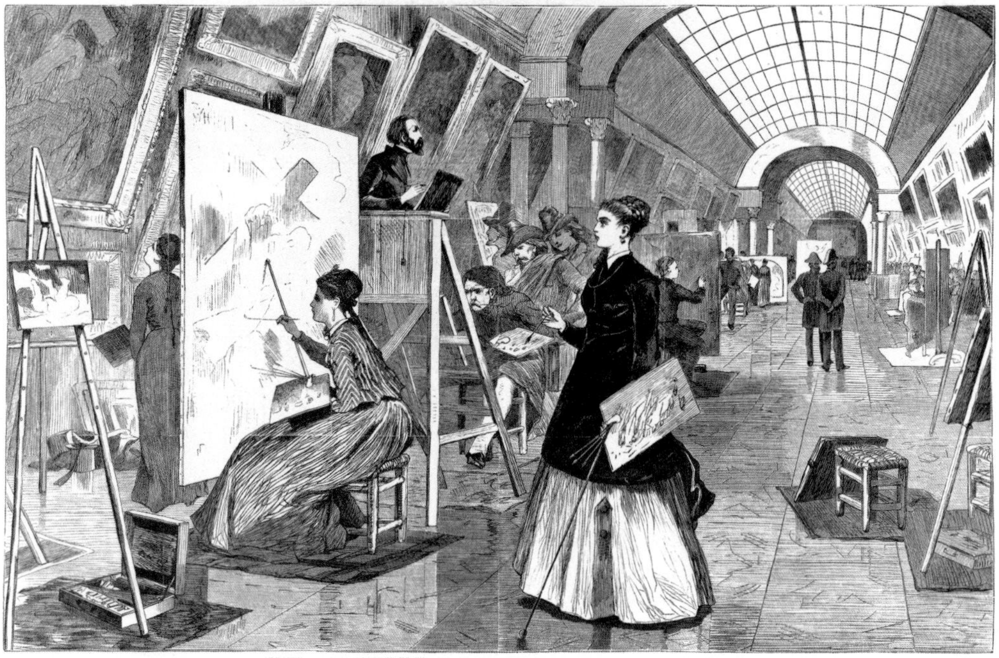

Fig. 120. Winslow Homer, *Art-Students and Copyists in the Louvre Gallery, Paris,* in *Harper's Weekly* (January 11, 1868). Courtesy of the Beinecke Rare Book and Manuscript Library, Yale University

interest in depicting the life and practice of the artist and in giving us teasing hints of his own artistic autobiography.

These themes immediately found their way into his first paintings in oil, a medium he took up toward the end of the Civil War. With the end of hostilities, artists and public alike could enjoy the countryside again, and Homer set off to paint in upstate New York and New England. As if to commemorate his new pleasure in oil painting — now usually out of doors thanks to his recent exposure to plein air French landscapes — he painted *Artists Sketching in the White Mountains,* 1868 (figs. 121 and 122). With his fellow artists at their easels on a hillrise, the scene shows us landscapes within a landscape as painters make art out of nature. We recognize Homer himself occupying the near center of the composition, the figure nearest to us: his curving mustache is just visible, silhouetted against the distant white cloud. But he is also embodied here a second time in his signature: his name appears legibly on the backpack behind him in the left foreground. (More conventionally on the corner of the canvas he inscribed "White Mts. 1868.")

If this picture was a veiled self-portrait, several schoolhouse paintings

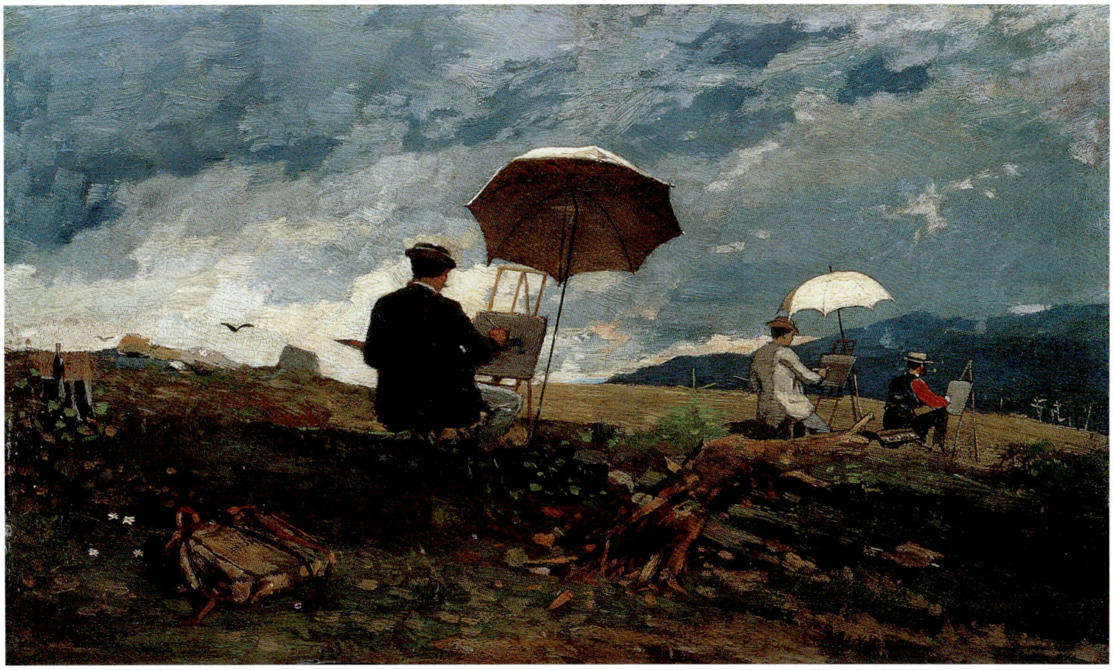

Fig. 121. Winslow Homer, *Artists Sketching in the White Mountains*, 1868. Oil on panel, 9 ½ x 15 ⅞ in. (24.1 x 40.3 cm). Portland Museum of Art, Portland, Maine. Bequest of Charles Shipman Payson

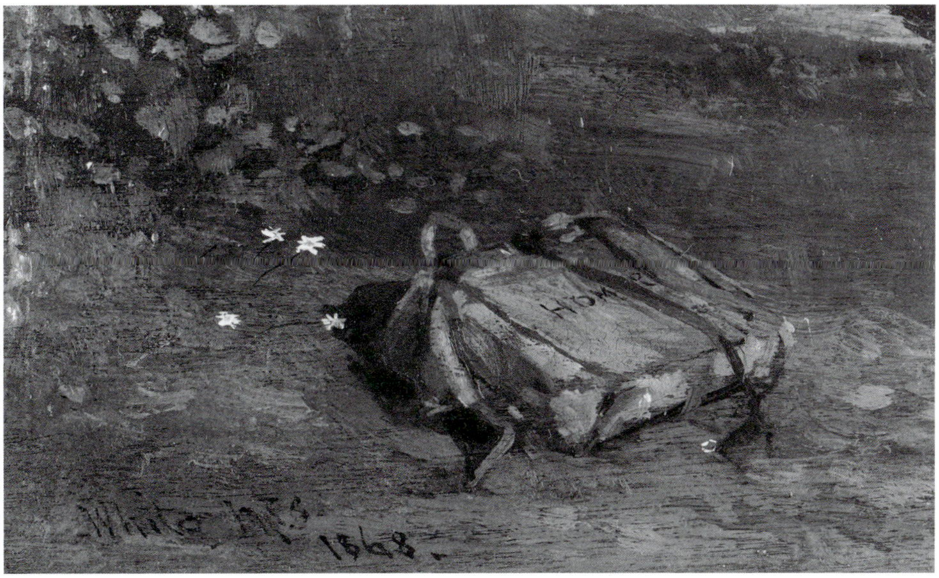

Fig. 122. Winslow Homer, *Artists Sketching in the White Mountains* (detail of fig. 121), 1868

that followed in the next few years played with images of writing, lettering, and inscribing — all closely related to the pointed placement of his signatures. These are less explicitly autobiographical, though indirectly they may carry certain personal associations. Not least, the blackboard, which appears in a number of the schoolhouse interiors, is visually akin to the landscape on the easel in *Artists Sketching*. On it and elsewhere on boards inside and out Homer affixed his name or initials, the blackboard being a surface where marks and images take on shape and meaning. Early biographers talk about the possibility of Homer having become interested in a pretty schoolteacher in upstate New York at about this time, and this may have been one impulse for taking up this subject. Now in his thirties, he may also have been nostalgic about his own receding youth, as well as the disappearing charms of the rural one-room schoolhouse. Further, Nicolai Cikovsky argues that his attention to women teachers in the schoolroom and to the disciplines of writing and drawing was a response to the new reforms in education and art arising after the Civil War.[19]

The whole sequence of paintings embraces a number of contrasting themes: the interior and exterior of the red school building, the schoolteacher as an isolated figure and as a part of the larger clustering of schoolchildren, the disciplines of learning and the conventions of play, architecture and landscape, and the spheres of male versus female activities. Probably the best-known image of the group is *Snap the Whip*, 1872 (Butler Institute of American Art, Youngstown, and The Metropolitan Museum of Art, New York), in which we see mostly the boys at their game during a recess. As Jules Prown shows, there is an implicit hierarchy of older and younger boys, of domination and subordination, of social interdependence and individual independence, of nature's roughness and its beauty. The composition is largely one of gentle but animated diagonals and curves, appropriate to the general tension between control and spontaneity. Both group and personal learning is going on, though it is informal and unplanned. All this in turn contrasts with *School Time*, early 1870s (fig. 123), where the children are in more casual small groups, while at the center the teacher guides two girls and a small boy toward the schoolhouse door. On the right, an independent older boy is painting Homer's initials on the clapboard siding. We cannot know if this is the artist imagining himself in his youth, but it certainly conveys his involvement in the subject. *Country School*, 1871–72 (Addison Gallery of American Art, Phillips Academy, Andover, Massachusetts), takes us through the door into the schoolroom, now centered on the standing schoolmistress and the large blackboard behind her. Through the windows we see pieces of the hilly landscape where the

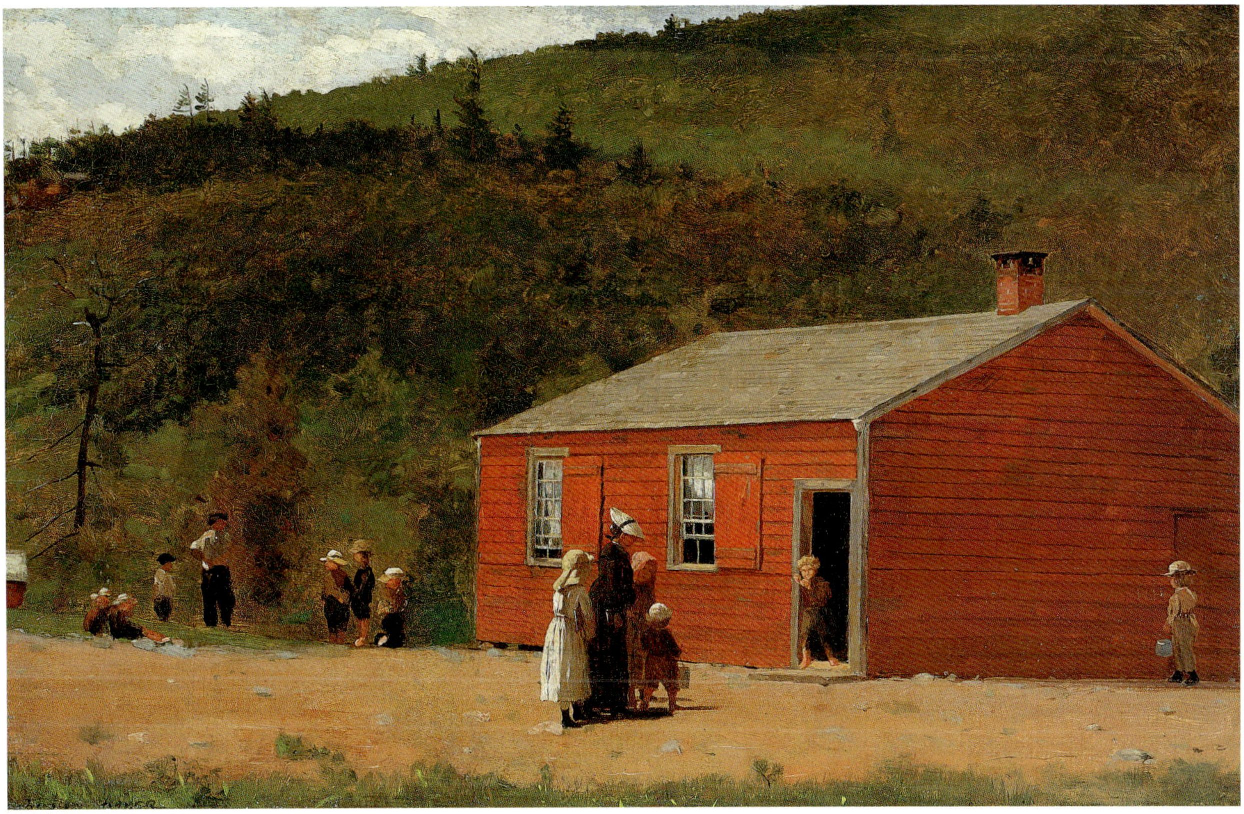

Fig. 123. Winslow Homer, *School Time,* ca. 1874. Oil on canvas, 12 ½ x 19 ¼ in. (31.8 x 48.9 cm). Collection of Mr. and Mrs. Paul Mellon

boys played outside, but now the emphasis is on the more formal rigors of academic learning. Virtually the entire composition is organized into austere planar — and plain — rectangles, from the floor, walls, and ceiling, to the windows and blackboard, and the room's furniture. How appropriate these interrelated and integrated shapes are to the mental processes of learning varied bodies of knowledge! Again Homer expresses his sympathetic interest and engagement by placing his signature on the bench at the right.

Other connected pictures in the following years extended to different concerns of the period. For example, *Taking a Sunflower to the Teacher,* 1875 (fig. 124), reveals Homer's sensitive awareness of race during the Reconstruction period, but a subtext of this watercolor is hinted at in his initials and the year signed as if in chalk on a slate in the lower right corner, namely the possibility for schooling and literacy for blacks in the postwar years. The new learning is evident in *Blackboard,* 1877 (fig. 125), which calls primary attention

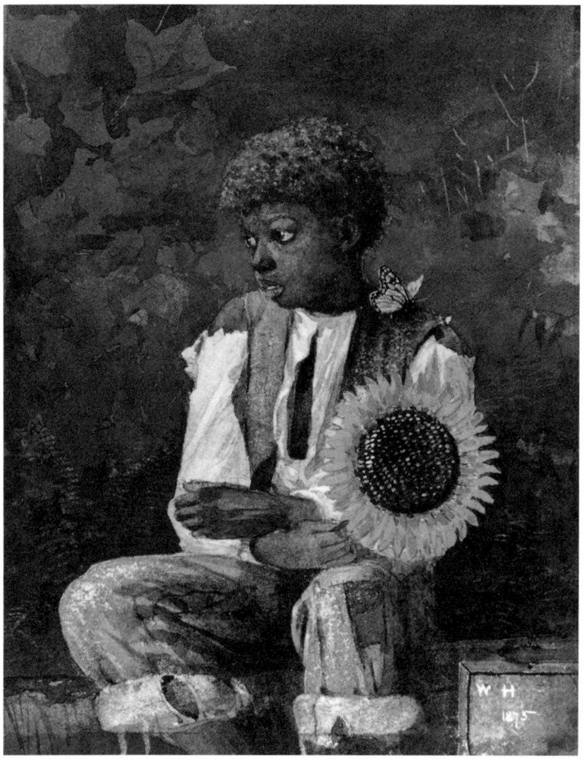

Fig. 124. Winslow Homer, *Taking a Sunflower to the Teacher,* 1875. Watercolor on paper, 7 x 5 ⅞ in. (17.8 x 14.9 cm). Georgia Museum of Art, University of Georgia, Athens, Ga. Eva Underhill Holbrook Memorial Collection of American Art, gift of Alfred H. Holbrook

Opposite:
Fig. 125. Winslow Homer, *Blackboard,* 1877. Watercolor on wove paper, 19 ¾ x 12 ¾ in. (50.2 x 32.4 cm). National Gallery of Art, Washington, D.C. Gift (partial and promised) of Jo Ann and Julian Ganz, Jr., in Honor of the Fiftieth Anniversary of the National Gallery of Art

to the taut and controlled pose of the teacher standing against a blackboard filled with basic geometric shapes. According to Cikovsky, she is giving instruction in the newly introduced drawing curriculum; this interpretation is affirmed by Homer's signature at the lower right corner of the board, seemingly treating these drawings as his own — another instance of an image within an image. These simple, legible forms allude not just to forms of art but also to architecture, and to letters and numbers. The whole palette of near-monochrome pale blues, grays, black, and white, along with the proportioned rectangles throughout, from the checkered apron and designs on the blackboard to the planes of wall and floor, all capture the authority of the mind and the rigors of intelligence. These works may have begun because of a personal acquaintance, but they ended with an artistic investigation of deep purpose.

Not all of Homer's signatures were so strongly visually inserted into his subject matter. As he had done occasionally with his wood engravings, he continued through much of his career to adapt the shape of his painted name or initials to elements or textures within his images. So in *The Mill (The Morning Bell; The Old Mill),* 1871 (Yale University Art Gallery, New Haven), his name in sharp black letters sits among the branches of a dark

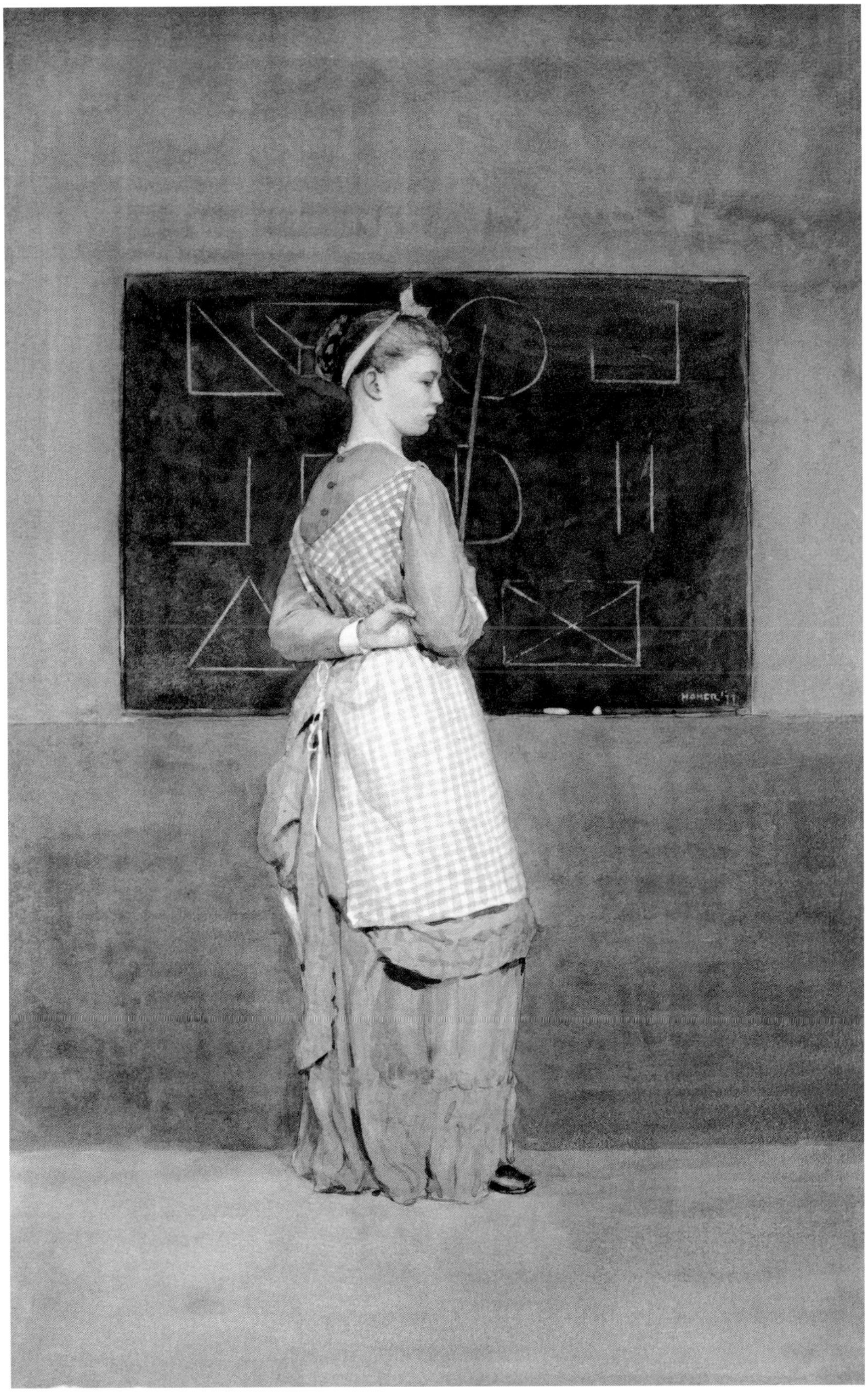
HOMER '77

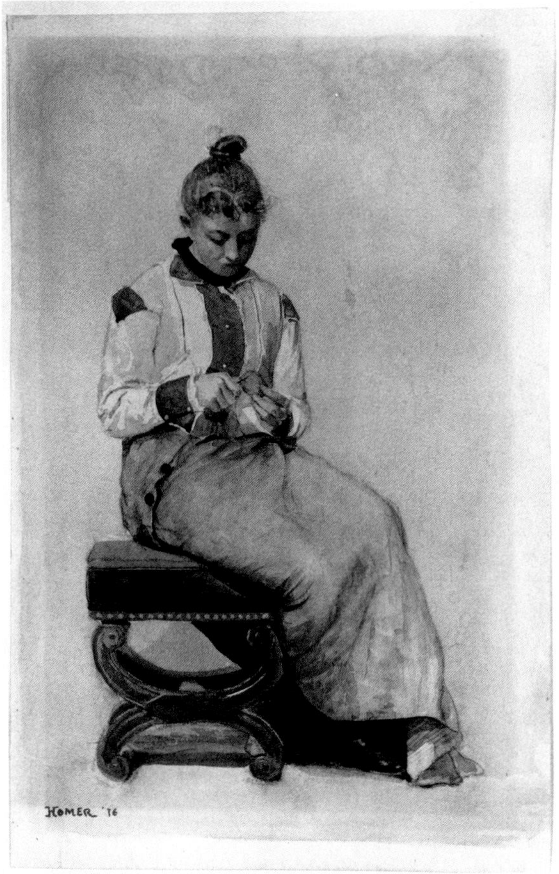

Fig. 126. Winslow Homer, *Woman Peeling a Lemon*, 1876. Watercolor over chalk sketch, 18 7/8 x 12 in. (47.9 x 30.5 cm). Sterling and Francine Clark Art Institute, Williamstown, Mass.

bramble bush in the lower right-hand corner. In other landscapes it follows the sloping lines of a hillside, the contours of a plow's handles, or the position of a reclining figure.[20] Several of Homer's consciously decorative watercolors of the later 1870s, with their stylistic indebtedness to Japonaiserie, have signatures that explicitly echo elements of the seated figures. The elaborate bars on his capital H visually play on the H-like form of the stool in *Woman Peeling a Lemon*, 1876 (fig. 126), while his vertically oriented name parodies the sofa's arms and legs in *Backgammon Game*, 1877 (Fine Arts Museums of San Francisco). Occasionally in later watercolors it seems plausible that the placement of his name directly aligns his presence with the activity depicted: in *Hudson River, Logging*, 1897 (Corcoran Gallery of Art, Washington, D.C.), it runs along a log in the right foreground, not far from the logger poised above; in *Shooting the Rapids*, 1902 (fig. 127), it curves with the rushing water over a submerged rock at lower right, parallel to the canoeists paddling nearby. These were familiar experiences to the artist on his regular hunting and fishing trips in the north woods of New York and Canada.

More intriguing is the subliminal association between Homer's inscription, half in, half out of the water, and the shot deer in *A Good Shot*, 1892 (fig. 128). The deer, just hit, is also poised on the large boulder with the hind legs still caught in the water. The stricken animal and the artist's signature are both painted with a combination of black, tan, and blue washes. Similarly, Homer's last watercolor of 1905, *Diamond Shoal* (fig. 129), bears his signature in the water at the lower right in the same black pigment used for the crests

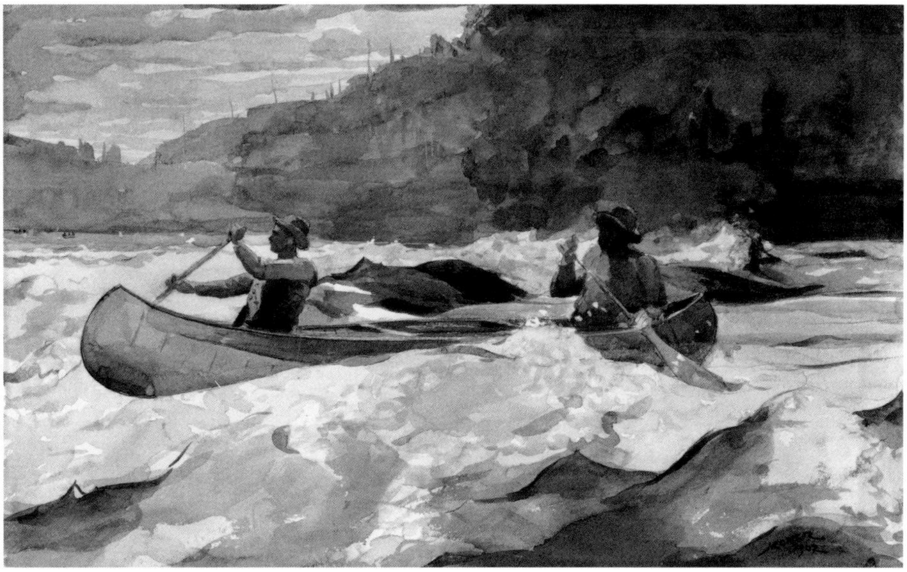

Fig. 127. Winslow Homer, *Shooting the Rapids,* 1902. Watercolor over pencil. 14 x $21\frac{13}{16}$ in. (35.5 x 55.4 cm). Brooklyn Museum of Art, New York. Museum Collection Fund and Special Subscription

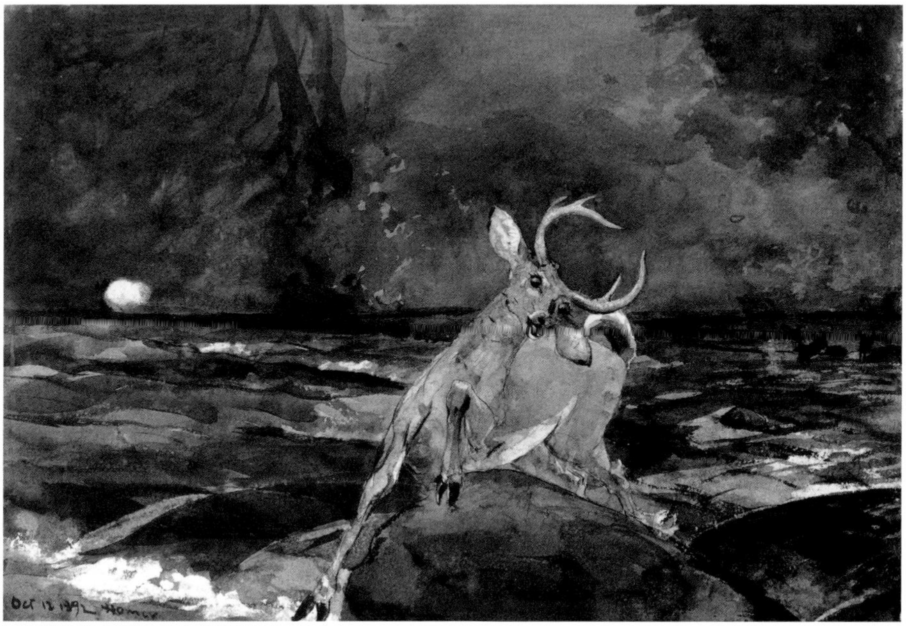

Fig. 128. Winslow Homer, *A Good Shot,* 1892. Watercolor. 15 x $21\frac{7}{16}$ in. (38.2 x 54.5 cm). National Gallery of Art, Washington, D.C. Gift of Ruth K. Henschel in memory of her husband, Charles R. Henschel

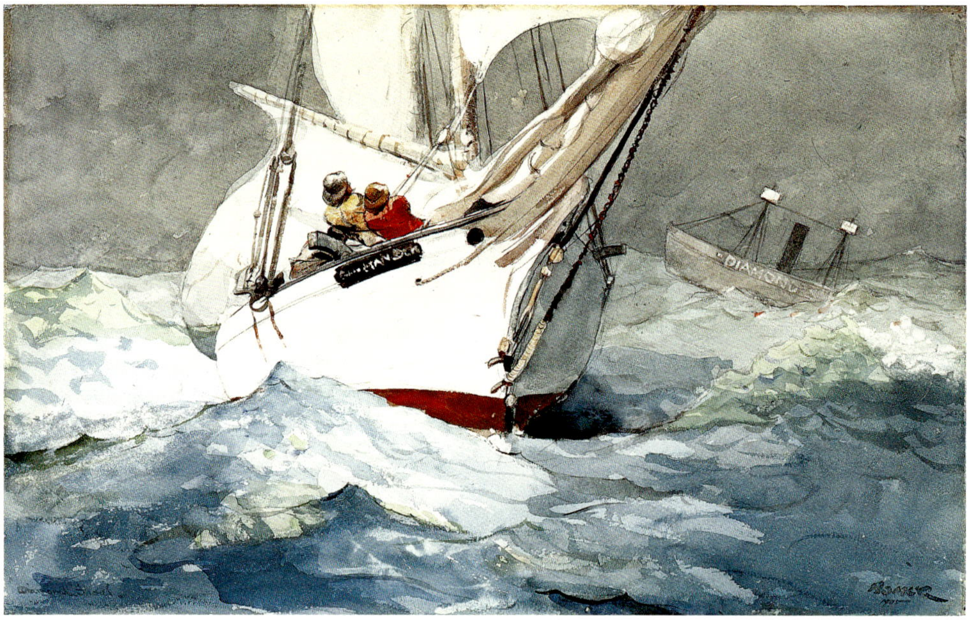

Fig. 129. Winslow Homer, *Diamond Shoal*, 1905. Watercolor on paper, 13 7/8 x 21 3/4 in. (35.2 x 55.2 cm). Private collection

of the waves across the foreground. These — like the vantage point of the viewer and Homer's presence — are directly in the way of the oncoming schooner bearing down in a storm. This dramatic perspective, employed to heighten the sense of imminent danger, is among the various expressive devices we often find in the works of Homer's late career. About this time the first signs of his heart or stroke troubles began to appear, leading to a slowing down in his artistic production; his final paintings date from 1909, the year before his death from an internal hemorrhage. His letters to family and friends in these years are filled with references to his illness and infirmities, and we are left to speculate to what extent his last somber images and these precariously placed signatures reflect his anxieties as he faced his own mortality.

Just as provocative are the signatures in a few watercolors of the late 1880s and 1890s set in the Caribbean. Not yet images of mortal struggle, they depict the opposite in their renderings of virile black masculinity. Homer seems to monumentalize the Bahamian natives with their lithe musculature and glistening deep brown flesh, as he presents them chasing or catching huge turtles and diving for coral or sponges. Three in the series are especially noteworthy. *The Sponge Diver*, 1898–99 (Museum of Fine Arts, Boston), shows a West Indian diver standing in shallow water and reaching to the stern

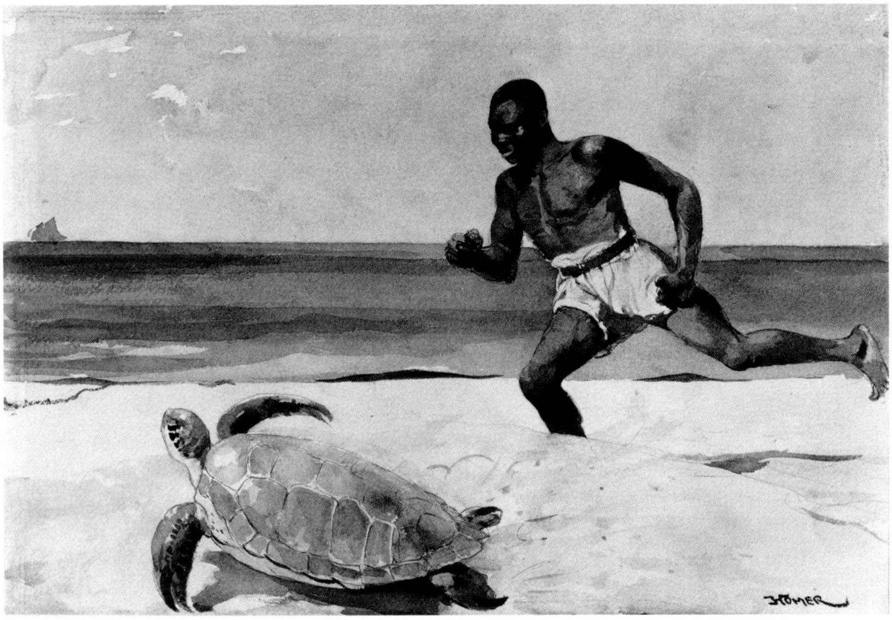

Fig. 130. Winslow Homer, *Rum Cay*, 1898–99. Watercolor, 14 7/8 x 21 3/8 in. (37.8 x 54.3 cm). Worcester Art Museum, Worcester, Mass.

of his boat, while just to the right is Homer's name, painted in the same brown pigment, almost floating in the water. Executed at the same time, *Rum Cay* (fig. 130) has a black figure racing across a beach in chase of a giant turtle. Two aspects of the signature seem to be unmistakable emulations of the native's running pose: the bars of Homer's capital "H" reach forward like the figure's right arm and leg, and the attenuated tail of the "R" curves back like the outstretched leg directly above. Finally, in *The Turtle Pound*, 1898 (fig. 131), one of the fishermen holds up a turtle to hand into the boat. He stands in a few feet of water with the brown skin of his lower torso partially visible in the clear ripples, his chest and arms above the surface. To the right in exactly the same position and with the same coloring, Homer's signature matches the fisherman, half in, half out of the water. It is as technically clever as it is psychologically suggestive.

How are we to read the significance of these inscriptions? Cumulatively, the visual connections are apparent. What meaning could Homer reveal or conceal in aligning himself with these powerful black male figures? To get at this, some context may be helpful. All three of these watercolors, along with the iconic *Gulf Stream* (Metropolitan Museum of Art, New York), come at the very end of the 1890s, a decade in which increasing attention was

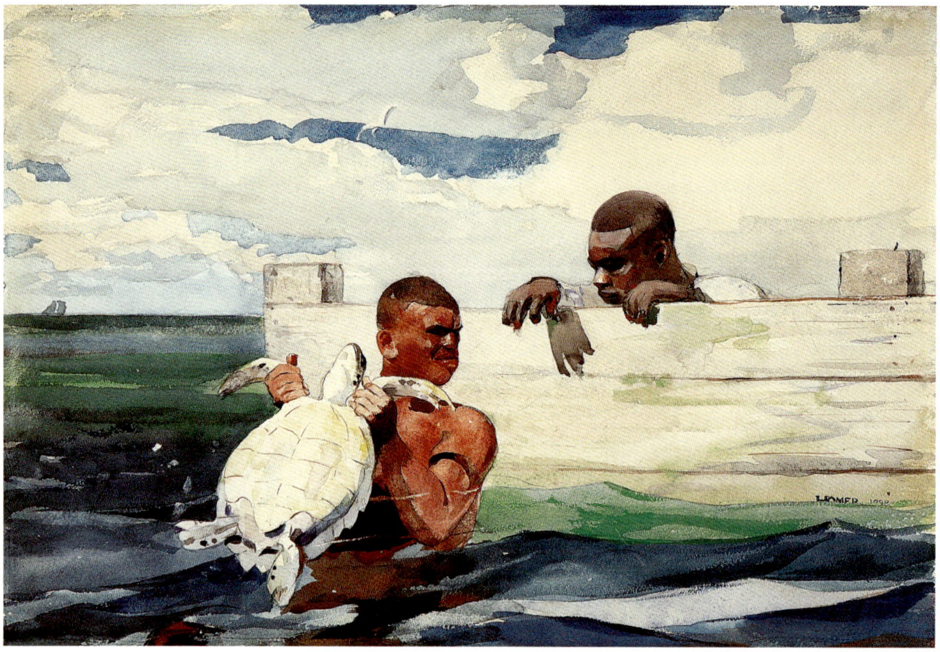

Fig. 131. Winslow Homer, *The Turtle Pound,* 1898. Watercolor over pencil, 14 ⅞ x 21 ⅜ in. (38 x 54.2 cm). Brooklyn Museum of Art, New York. Sustaining Membership Fund; A. T. White Memorial Fund; A. Augustus Healy Fund

going to racial issues at home and in the Caribbean. Major African-American spokesmen, such as Booker T. Washington, Frederick Douglass, and W. E. B. Du Bois, were addressing the relationship between people of African descent and American society at large. Congressional and judicial decisions were reviving the tensions of the Reconstruction era by encoding policies like "equal but separate." And a revived American imperialism saw national interests move into several Hispanic countries of the Caribbean, among them Puerto Rico, Cuba, Dominica, and ultimately Panama. Theodore Roosevelt's engagement in the Spanish-American War over Cuba exemplified this nationalist zeal, which extended elsewhere in the non-white world to American occupation of the Philippines.

While Homer, like most Americans at the turn of the century, was probably aware of such racial concerns, his paintings, including *The Gulf Stream* (see fig. 133), have little to do with overt political or social matters. Nor as Helen Cooper observes do they depict the standard tourist interests in exotic figures and settings. At the same time they come as close as Homer ever did to showing the nude figure. Only with *The Gulf Stream* do we have the mus-

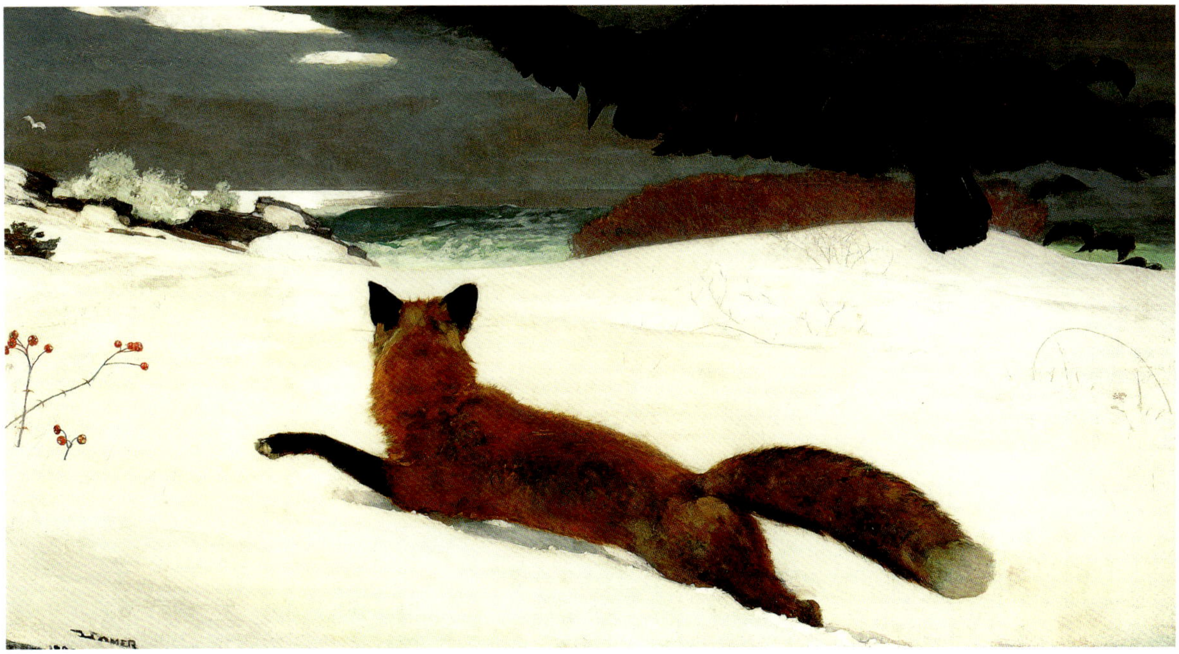

Fig. 132. Winslow Homer, *Fox Hunt,* 1893. Oil on canvas, 38 x 68 ½ in. (96.5 x 174 cm). Courtesy of the Pennsylvania Academy of the Fine Arts, Philadelphia. Joseph E. Temple Fund

cular black male placed in a new context, one of vulnerability in the shadow of threatening danger and the prospect of death. That notion of human life in the balance appears earlier in Homer's treatment of the animal world, most notably his deer-hunting series of the early 1890s, and later in the decade with the fishing watercolors. The most powerful painting of this theme, one of his greatest works, and as it happens the one bearing the most charged and discussed signature of his career is *Fox Hunt,* 1893 (fig. 132). Henry Adams receives the principal credit for first calling attention to the placement, shape, and coloring of Homer's name in the lower left-hand corner of the canvas.[21] It very visibly sinks halfway into the snow, like the fox; its diagonal follows the animal's form, the bar of the "H" protrudes forward, mimicking the outstretched foreleg and the tail of the "R" curves out like the tail against the snow; finally, the rusty red color is the same for both.

The painting embodies a number of elements increasingly apparent in Homer's later work, among them his consciousness of Japanese prints and their exploitation of flattened designs and asymmetrically balanced forms. Here, we see the fox starkly silhouetted against the field of snow, its diagonal line echoed by the looming crows above. We also view the scene from a slightly elevated vantage point, associated with the menacing predators. The cropping of the dark wings at the top serves to enlarge their presence in the foreground, while the rather high horizon line tends to compress the distance and close off visual escape, though the fox looks to the white field's edge. This is a Darwinian landscape, in which life is precarious, and nature's fortunes are cruel and haphazard. This was a subject Homer began to explore at Prout's Neck after his return from England in the 1880s, and it preoccupied him with increasing drama for the remaining decades of his life. The bold tonal contrasts of light and dark convey the equally powerful contest of forces engaged here. The one touch of bright color — the blood-red berries, hinting of food and survival — is an ironic lure: the fruit on this thorny bush is most likely poisonous. Moreover, the fox is slowed by the deep snow to the point of being trapped. His role as predator is poised at the point of reversal, where he may become prey to the waiting crows.

Given the obviousness and intentionality of Homer's signature in this picture, it is amazing that it caught no one's attention before, although Adams does cite one other crucial discussion of the painting, by Thomas Hess in 1973.[22] This was in a review of the comprehensive Winslow Homer exhibition organized by Lloyd Goodrich, then dean of Homer biographers, for the Whitney Museum of American Art. Hess's was an irreverent and at the time shocking analysis, asserting Homer's "dread of sexuality," with the black birds representing "the nightmare of the flying penis."[23] Most Americanists took offense at Hess's tone and conclusions, as coming from a modernist curator who was a champion of abstract expressionism. But since then numerous biographers and historians have approached the possibility of Homer's repressed homosexuality. At the least, the visual evidence offers some linkage between the artist's self-identification in his signature and the fox as vulnerable, a potential victim. Regardless of the extent to which we accept a psychological reading here, we need to return to Homer's explicit images of blacks at the end of this decade, and particularly *The Gulf Stream.*

This summary 1899 painting in fact brings together the dual themes of powerful black masculinity and mortal danger, as if Homer simultaneously was attracted to and fearful of black flesh. In light of the points discussed above, we have come to see the picture as touching on the anxiety raised by various finalities and endings. Its date coincides with the close of the century, a time of traumatic transition for many. Its undertaking immediately follows the death of Homer's father the year before. (It is interesting to note that

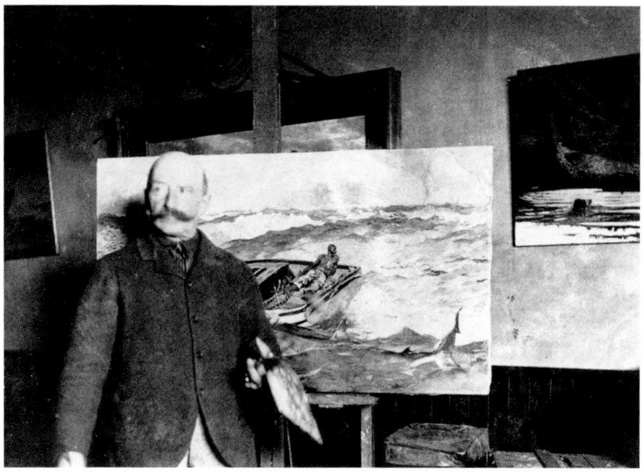

Fig. 133. *Winslow Homer with "The Gulf Stream" in His Painting Room at Prout's Neck,* ca. 1900. Albumen print. Bowdoin College Museum of Art, Brunswick, Maine. Gift of the Homer Family

the fathers of Peto, Eakins, and Homer all died in the 1890s, and the work of each artist took a darker psychological turn thereafter.) The muscular black man on the deck appears alert and composed, even though he is under assault from all sides: the sharks and the waterspout, which he sees, and the potential rescue ship, which is outside his range of vision. The very title indicates a setting of natural violence, where warm and cold water collide, spawning hurricanes. The black man as victim should not be a surprising subject at a time of America's invasion of Cuba, of renewed racial tensions at home, and of rising fears of mixing the races.

Although the setting of *The Gulf Stream* moves us to a very different temperature and part of the hemisphere from *Fox Hunt,* the compositions of the two canvases are strikingly similar, and so, we might argue, are their meanings. But how might we perceive that Homer identified with the plight of this black man? As an unmarried man, solitary on the rural Maine coast most of his later life, and sexually repressed, did he subconsciously identify with the "other," the oppressed and the marginalized in American society? In *The Gulf Stream* there is no internal signature (only a conventional one at the corner) to emphasize such an association. However, a surviving visual document conceivably offers the evidence we need. Some dozen photographs taken of Homer in his lifetime are known, the most famous of which shows him in his studio at Prout's Neck around 1900 (fig. 133). It is the only photograph to show him as an artist, with his brushes and palette in hand. And it is the only photograph to show him posing next to a painting, and that painting is *The Gulf Stream.* The two principal figures visible in the image, counterpointing each other, are Homer and the black man on the deck in his painting. Homer actually stands here in place of his signature, linking himself, whether by intention or happenstance, to one of the most fraught works of his inner and outer life. No wonder he said of it, "Don't let the public poke its nose into my picture."[24]

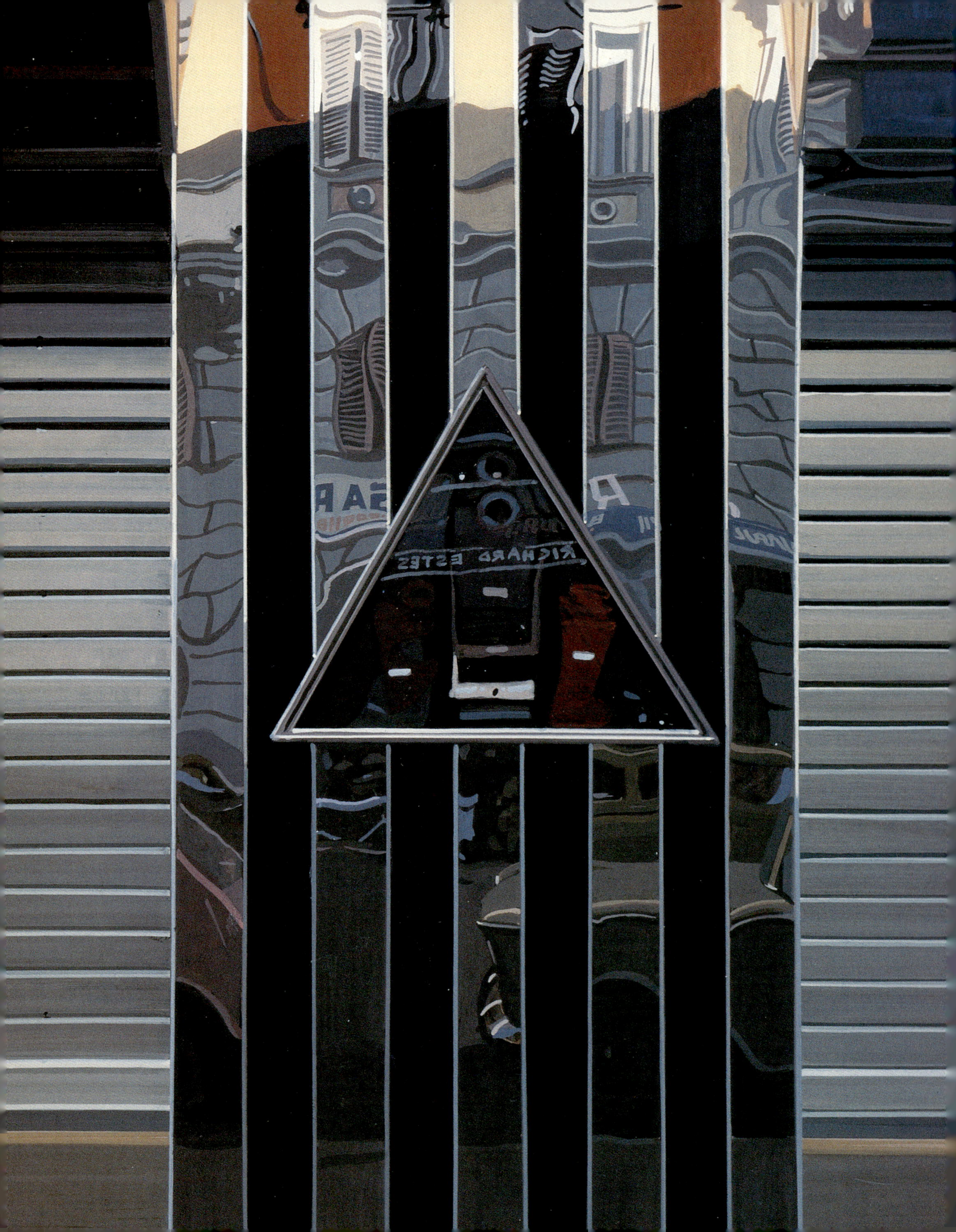

CHAPTER 5 Modernism

With the rise of modernism during the twentieth century and its embrace of abstraction, many artists turned away from creating illusionist three-dimensional spaces on their canvases. Other treatments of picture space and surface predominated over the fictive worlds into which they had projected themselves. At the same time, there were a number of moments in various forms of realism when painters toyed with their names and presence in their works. One of these artists was Charles Demuth, a member of Alfred Stieglitz's circle and of the early American avant-garde at the beginning of the century. Like most of his colleagues, Demuth gained exposure to modernist ideas in Paris and at the 1913 Armory Show, a controversial survey of contemporary art in New York City. Born in 1883, Demuth trained at the Pennsylvania Academy, but was soon drawn to New York and association with Stieglitz. A painter of delicate still lifes in watercolor, and later of oil and tempera paintings of midwestern industrial architecture, Demuth undertook during the 1920s a series of nearly a dozen so-called poster portraits of friends and associates working in the avant-garde in art, literature, and theater.

One that exists only in the form of a watercolor study from 1923–24 (fig. 134) was devoted to his friend and fellow painter Marsden Hartley. This has received a detailed analysis by Robin Frank, a précis of which is worth giving as a framework for seeing how both individuals are incorporated into the imagery.[1] Hartley's name, which runs vertically down the left-hand side, is parallel to the potted plant alongside. The heart-shaped flower at the top plays off the sound of the adjacent first syllable of Hartley's name. But stem and blossom are also a highly phallic form, which Frank interprets as an allusion to the shared homosexuality of the two artists. The stage-like setting of the composition flanked by curtains probably refers to their interest in

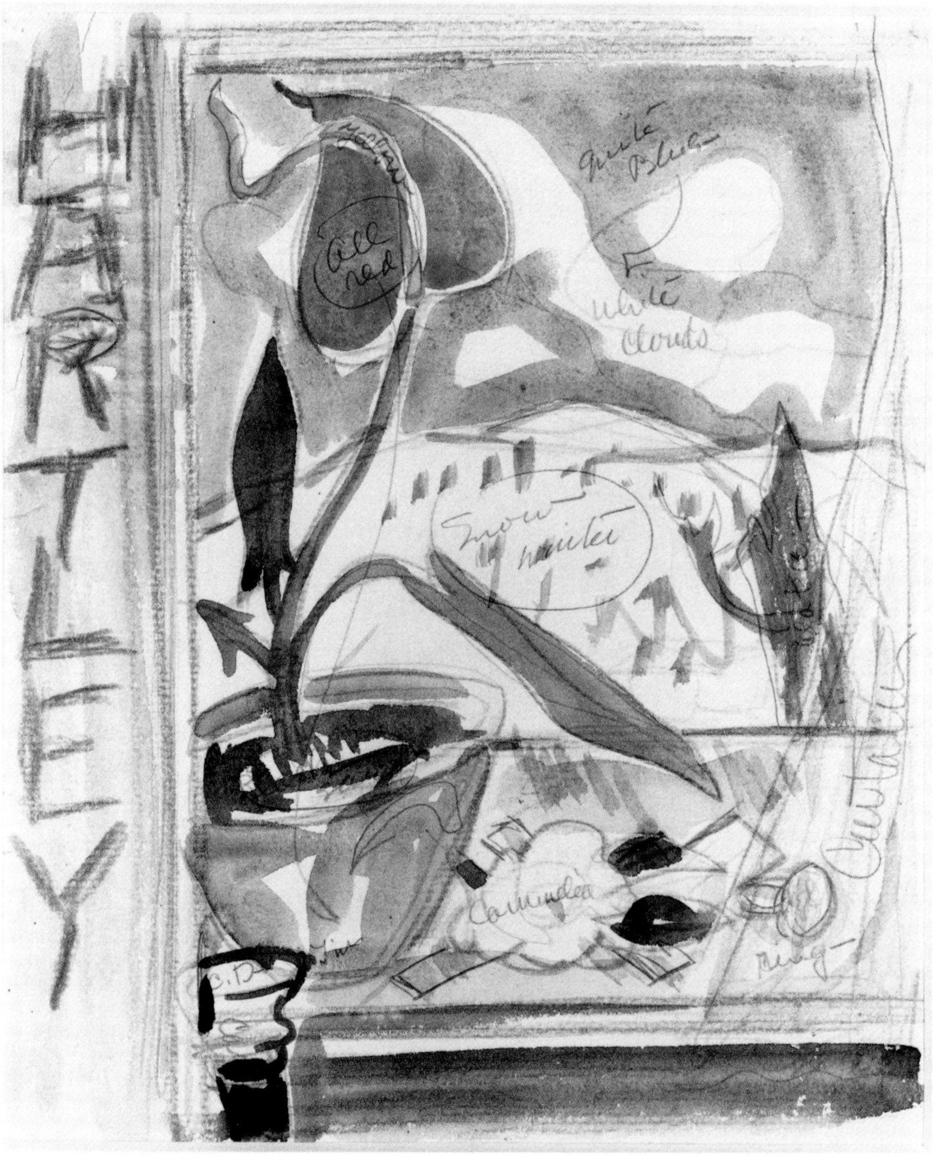

Fig. 134. Charles Demuth, *Study for Poster Portrait: Marsden Hartley*, ca. 1923–24. Watercolor and graphite on laid paper, 10 ⅛ x 8 ⅛ in. (25.7 x 20.6 cm). Yale University Art Gallery, New Haven. Stephen Carlton Clark, B.A. 1903, Fund and Everett V. Meeks, B.A. 1901, Fund

the theater, in both New York and Provincetown. The window "landscape," pays direct homage to Hartley's still lifes of the period, especially paintings completed a few years earlier in Bermuda, where he shared a studio with

Demuth during the winter of 1917. Prominent at the lower left is the head of a cane, on which Demuth placed his initials. It is aligned with and overlaps Hartley's plant, serving as an attribute of and stand-in for Demuth, who suffered from severe diabetes and needed a cane to walk. Thus, by his presence in this assemblage, Demuth rendered a double portrait, one of a close friendship and common experiences.

Considered his finest poster portrait, and certainly his best-known, *The Figure 5 in Gold*, 1928 (fig. 135), is a tribute to the poet William Carlos Williams. But its rich complexity within the seemingly obvious precisionist forms suggests much more. It is a visualization of a poem, the circumstances and occasion for which reveal a larger, metaphoric group portrait. Williams was a doctor in northern New Jersey who helped to care for Demuth, as well as a poet experimenting in the modernist idiom in his spare time. Around 1919, Williams came into New York for medical studies, after which he made his way to visit Marsden Hartley's studio at Fifteenth Street near Ninth Avenue. In the dark of a rainy night a fire engine suddenly roared by; the aural and visual effects spontaneously inspired a short poem of quick fragmented impressions:

Among the rain
and lights
I saw the figure 5
in gold
on a red
firetruck
moving
tense
unheeded
to gong clangs
siren howls
and wheels rumbling
through the dark city.[2]

Since the poem is the initial subject of Demuth's painting, it comes to stand for the doctor, whose experience provides the substance for the "portrait." The dark, transparent slashes of color indicate both night and rain, as well as the perspectival recession of street and sidewalks. The multiple fives capture the golden number quickly glimpsed on the truck as it approached and rushed by, that is, several different sequential views passing in time and

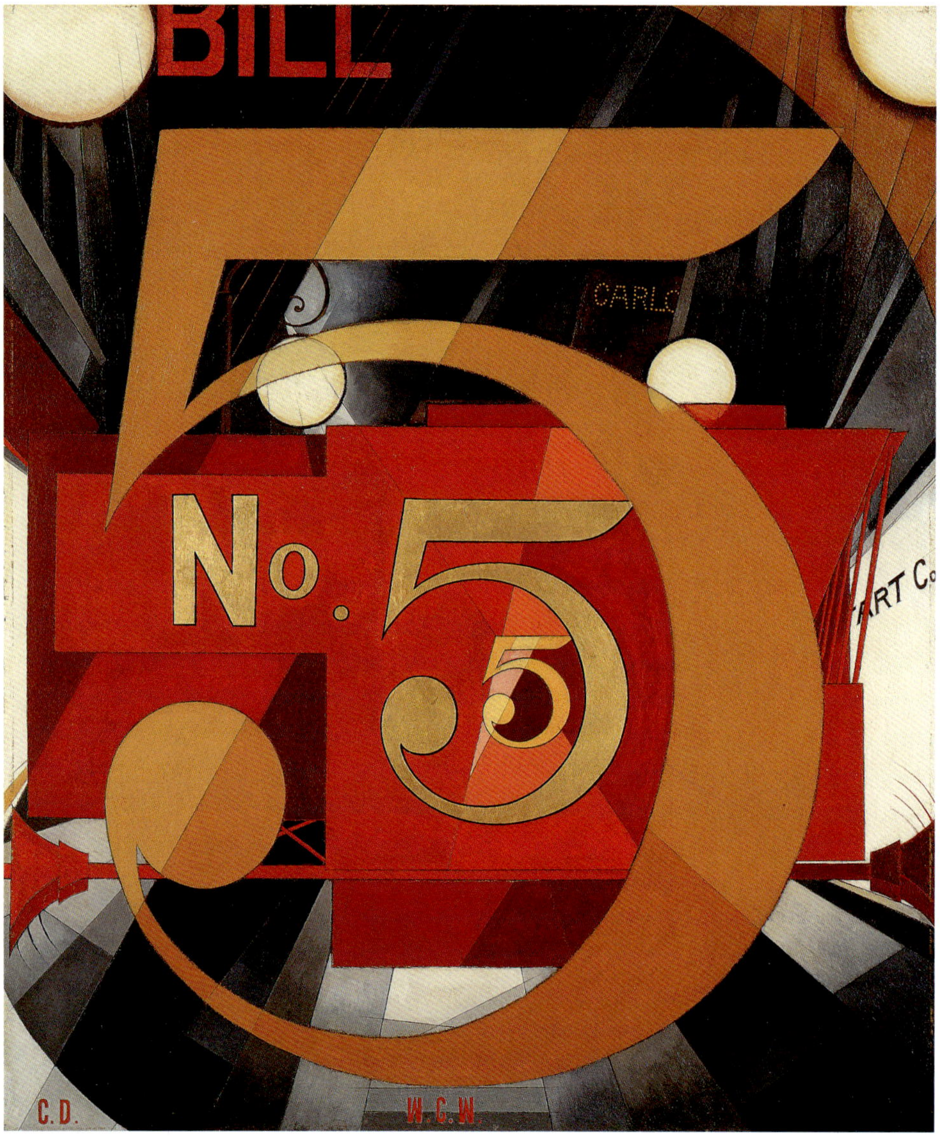

Fig. 135. Charles Demuth, *The Figure 5 in Gold*, 1928. Oil on composition board, 36 x 29¾ in. (91.4 x 75.6 cm). The Metropolitan Museum of Art, New York. The Alfred Stieglitz Collection, 1949

space. (Formally, this work may have taken a cue from Marcel Duchamp's infamous *Nude Descending a Staircase*, 1912 [Philadelphia Museum of Art], exhibited at the Armory Show in 1913.) We see the turning axles of the truck near the bottom, while, above, the repeated lights appear to belong both to the fire trucks and to streetlamps on the sidewalk. The white panel with the words [T]ART CO. could be the side of a passing truck or a shopfront window. If these elements constitute a primarily visual translation of the occasion via the poem, then the signage speaks to other aspects and participants in this portrait. As we know from the discussions of Robin Frank, Wanda Corn, and others, the word BILL at the top first refers to Williams. Its alternative meanings include: currency, an invoice, a theater playbill, and a building billboard. The doctor is additionally present with most of his middle name — CARLO[S] — spelled out in marquee light bulbs, and his three initials centered at the lower edge.

On the same line and in red paint at the left corner, Demuth placed his initials. The sharply colored capital letters tie this personal association to his friend and to the general scheme of a commercial, mechanical environment. In this regard the words ART CO. at the right hint at a larger company of colleagues. (Some have argued that adding the cutoff "T" barely visible at the beginning of the phrase gives the words TART CO., perhaps alluding to the prostitutes in the nearby theater district.) It is not farfetched to think of ART CO. as both a business company and one of common pursuits, such as those of the Stieglitz group. In this context the portrait is not just about Williams, "The Great Figure" (the actual title he gave the poem) in Demuth's eyes, but also about the painter and Williams's other friend Marsden Hartley. Remember that Hartley's studio was Williams's destination, and Demuth honored his fellow painter's art in the overall format and color scheme here. The combination of strong reds, golds, and blacks and the abstraction of numbers and letters recall Hartley's German Officer series of the mid-1910s. So, in his corner initials Demuth took his place in this constellation of avant-garde figures at work in the dynamic urban landscape of early twentieth-century New York.

Exactly the same age as Demuth, with similar experience in Europe and art training at the Pennsylvania Academy, Charles Sheeler came to be known by the 1920s and 1930s as a consummate painter of American industrial power in the wake of World War I. He was equally accomplished as a photographer, concentrating on architectural forms and details both in the vernacular structures of his native Bucks County, Pennsylvania, and in the mechanical forms of urban industrial plants. With a common style in both media of tonal contrasts, precise details, and meticulous, smooth finishes, Sheeler celebrated America's love and mastery of the machine during the interwar decades. Although an intense realist, he seems, with very few exceptions, to have been untempted by any imaginative intrusion of his signatures into his pictorial

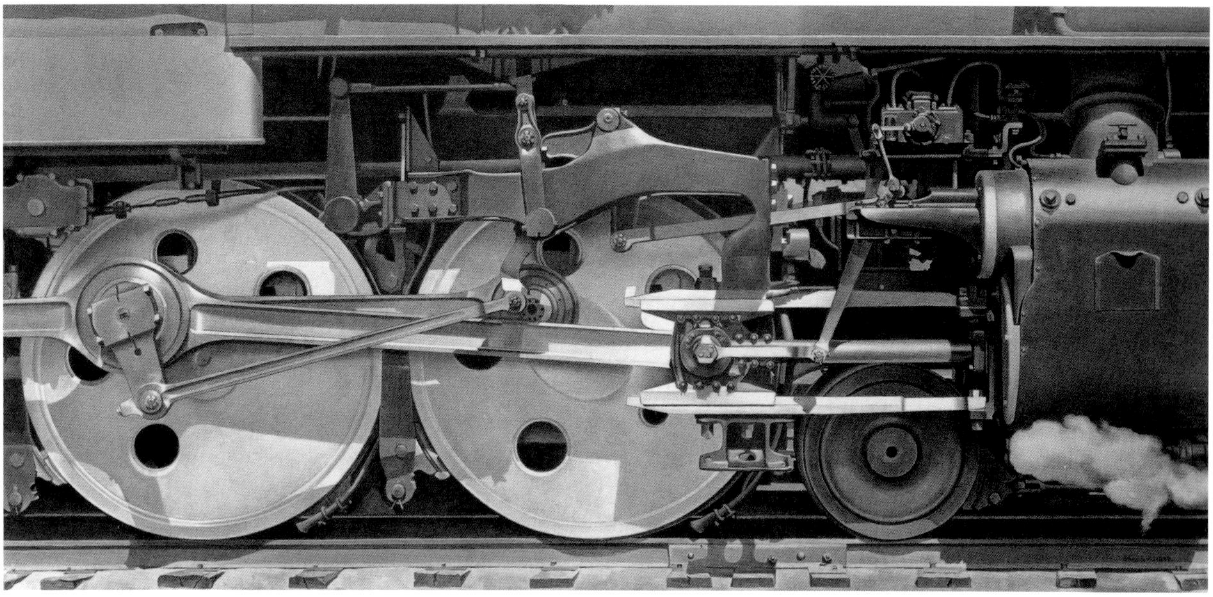

Fig. 136. Charles Sheeler, *Rolling Power*, 1939. Oil on canvas, 15 x 30 in. (38.1 x 76.2 cm). Smith College Museum of Art, Northampton, Mass. Purchased, Drayton Hillyer Fund, 1940

spaces. On one occasion he painted his self-portrait in the form of a telephone, a modern instrument he loved, and on another, in a key, summary work of his career he introduced a subtle and extremely witty play on his signature. *Rolling Power*, 1939 (fig. 136), depicts a close-up of the engine wheels of the Twentieth-Century Limited as its gleaming machinery gathers momentum. Like the partial view of the pristine shapes of a transatlantic ocean liner seen in his *Upper Deck*, 1929 (Harvard University Art Museums, Cambridge, Massachusetts), this is a visual song of praise to America's rising industrial power at home and abroad. Sheeler shows his admiration by emulating the mechanistic purity of his subjects in his very style and technique. In *Rolling Power* he chose to include himself in this landscape twice, first by setting his conventional signature on the railroad track at the lower right. Secondly, just above this, the puff of steam, ostensibly issuing from the engine, appears to rise from some valve in the letters. John Davis describes its shape as a cartoon dialogue balloon, as if it were being spoken or puffed out by his name.[3] We learn that Sheeler was an inveterate smoker, who here delights in exhaling smoke along with the machine.

The year Sheeler painted this work, Jasper Johns was a nine-year-old boy in Georgia; Johns would later serve a term in the army, and make his way to New York at the high moment of abstract expressionism. Setting a course to free his art from the domination of this movement, he was among the first of a younger generation to reintroduce representational imagery and signage into painting, and thereby come to be associated with the rise of the next major movement of realism — Pop art. Taking up painting in encaustic, a medium in which the pigment is mixed with wax, Johns created a highly tactile and even sensuous brushwork on his canvases, more solid in effect than the kinetic energies of abstract expressionism. He also sought to make his compositions more structured and calculated compositions, less embodiments of pure emotion and physical energy. As he said, "I didn't want my work to be an exposure of my feelings."[4] Still, his paintings do reflect his wry, intellectual sensibility, and periodically we can see his direct involvement with his process and image making. Upon occasion he makes a gesture or mark as a form of self-portraiture, for example, his skin- and hand-prints of the early 1960s.

Among his now well-known early works are the Target images in brushy, monochromatic fields, to which he added three-dimensionality by attaching small casts of body parts in compartments. Increasingly interested in signs made by stencils, he soon turned to paintings of the alphabet, numbers, a map of the United States, and the U.S. flag. Some of these were executed in all white or gray fields, others in the three primary colors, often with the words RED, YELLOW, and BLUE spelled out in the pigment. These follow in the tradition of John F. Peto's mental game-playing in juxtaposing verbal and visual representations (see fig. 89), at the same time that they speak to the modernist investigations of linguistics and semiotics. It is as if Johns were aiming to get at the basics of painting by asserting brushwork for its own sake and working only with the primary colors. Likewise, he began to call attention to the shape and structure of the canvas support, adding objects to its surface or edges, thus blurring the line between painting and sculpture.

One such early work was *Painting with Two Balls*, 1960 (fig. 137), consisting of three horizontally joined panels; between the upper two are wedged two balls. Most critics have discussed this and related pieces in formalist terms — how his imagery and materials pay homage to the Dada tradition of Marcel Duchamp, or the ways in which his inventions reformulate what a work of art is. Kenneth Silver is one of the first to have offered a sexual reading of Johns's production.[5] Silver suggests, for example, that this painting refers to issues of masculinity, including the masculine aggressiveness of abstract expressionism and the codes of homosexuality among Johns and his

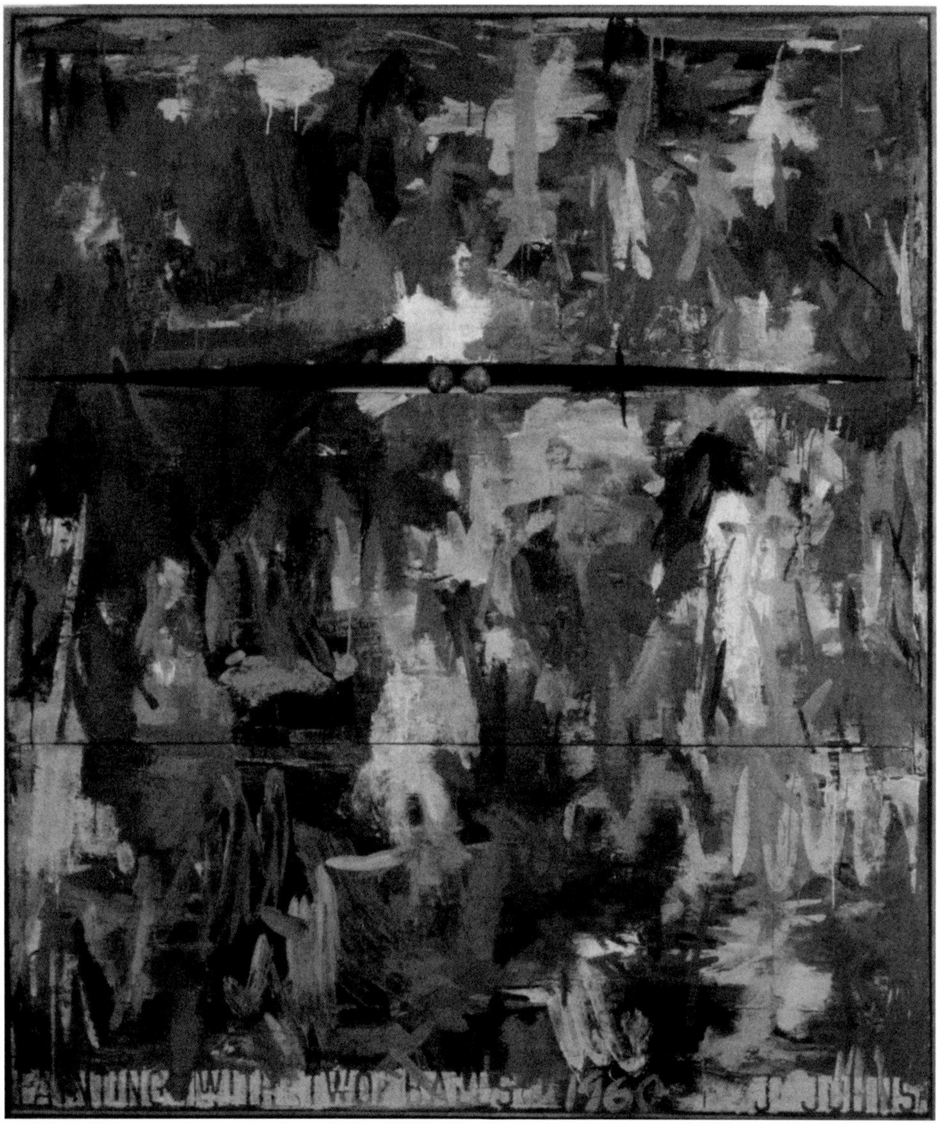

Fig. 137. Jasper Johns, *Painting with Two Balls,* 1960. Encaustic and collage on canvas with objects, 65 x 54 in. (165.1 x 137.2 cm). Collection of the artist

peers, such as Robert Rauschenberg and Andy Warhol. However we are to interpret Johns's imagery, this painting is among the first to incorporate the stenciled lettering at the bottom with his title, date, and name. This inscription is a signature that becomes a part of the work's subject matter. It plays off the freer brushwork nearby with the more mechanical execution of the letters; it is a verbal statement of fact, complementing the physical and visual

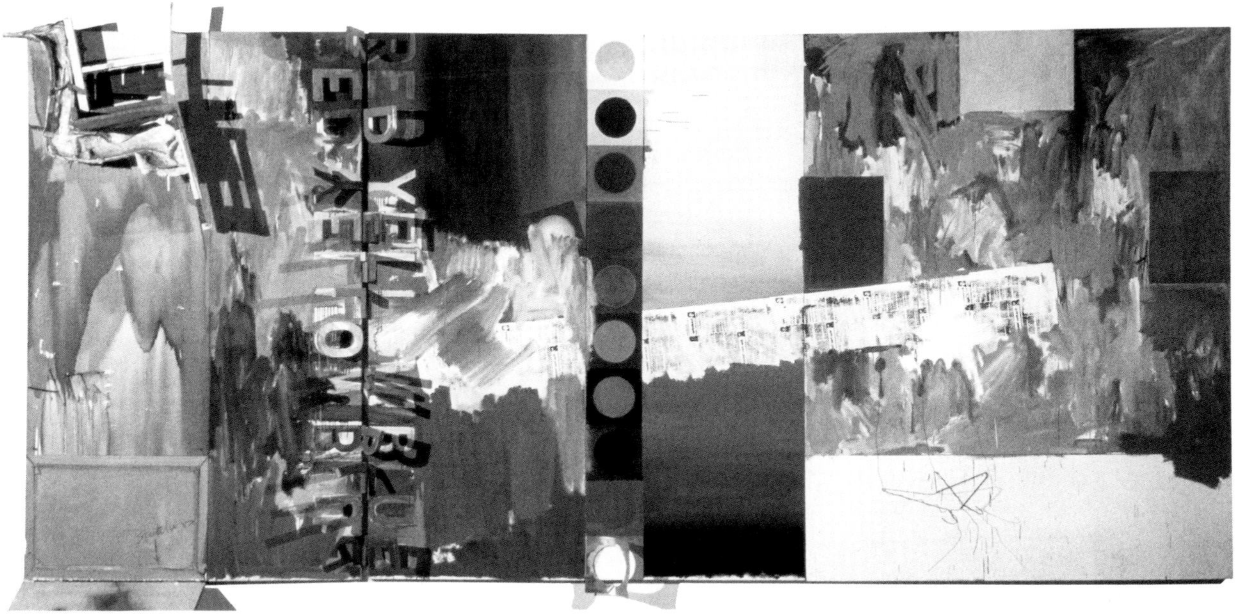

Fig. 138. Jasper Johns, *According to What*, 1964. Oil on canvas with objects, 88 x 192 in. (223.5 x 487.6 cm). Private collection

expressions above. Johns signed the work, making himself a part of his artistic process and mental inquiry. It was a format he would employ in several related works of the next couple of years, all signed similarly in stenciling along the bottom edge: *In Memory of My Feelings — Frank O'Hara*, 1961 (private collection); *The News*, 1962 (Kunstsammlung Nordrhein-Westfalen, Düsseldorf); and *Zone*, 1962 (Kunsthaus Zurich).

Two years after this group, Johns would undertake even larger and more complex constructions, with signatures that elaborate even further their multiple identities in the composition. *According to What*, 1964 (fig. 138), is one of a number of very large canvases consisting of contiguous panels with objects attached. Believed by critics to be partially a response to Marcel Duchamp's *Tu m'*, 1918 (Yale University Art Gallery, New Haven), in its mix of painting and sculptural elements and spectrum of colors, it is one of the artist's most ambitious and summary works to that time.[6] The column of color circles running down the center suggests an urban landscape of streetlights but more explicitly the range of pure and mixed pigments. To the right we find the free expression of what looks like a square, quasi–abstract expressionist painting within the larger field, while to the left an echoing column of hinged letters spells out the primary colors. These three-dimensional letters have

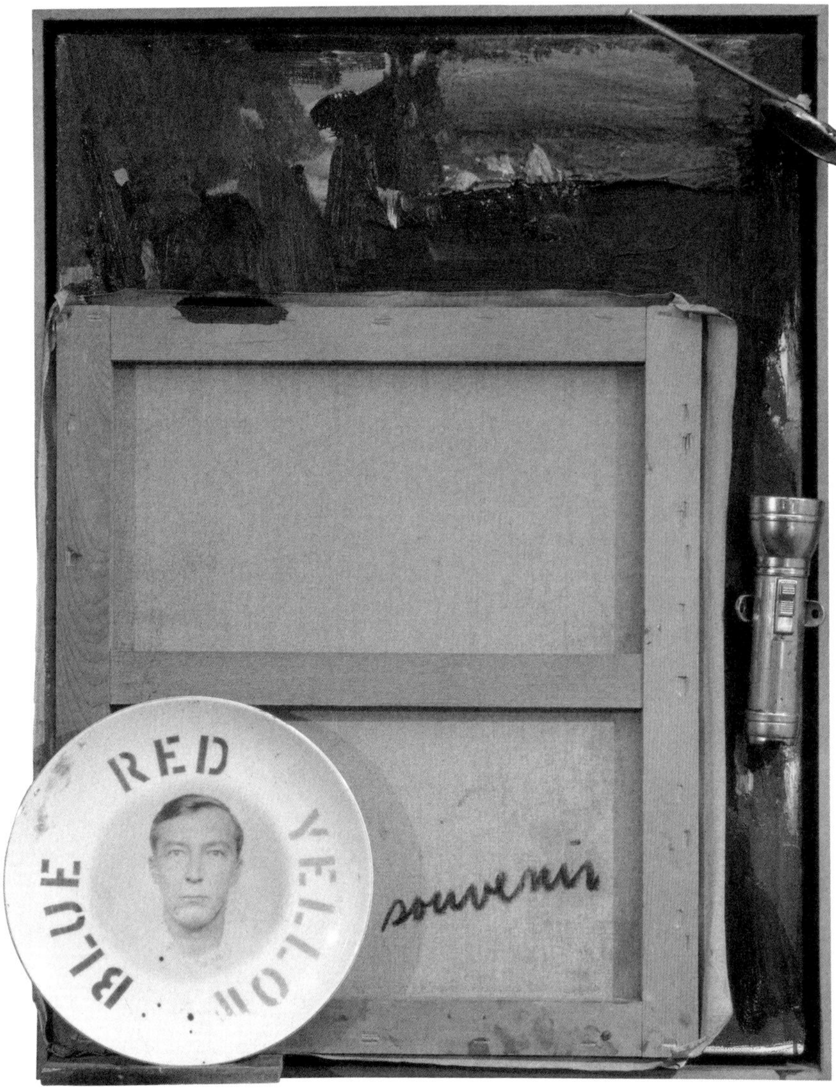

Fig. 139. Jasper Johns, *Souvenir 2*, 1964. Oil on canvas with objects, 28 ¾ x 21 in. (73 x 53.3 cm). Private collection

their own counterparts in the same painted shapes, front and back, appearing on the adjacent panels on either side of the hinges. Part of a chair holding the inside of a leg cast — the ghost of a body — hangs at the upper left corner of the canvas. Directly below, in the lower left corner, is a small canvas on a stretcher, seen from the back and hinged at the bottom edge. When unfolded from the big field, it completes the homage to Duchamp by revealing his painted profile. More to the point here, the back of this little canvas contains Johns's title and signature in two forms, stenciled and handwritten. The second is upside down and appears to have been partially erased, again a play with ghost and mirror versions. The whole is a rich investigation of self-referential art and artist.

Similar in spirit is *Souvenir 2* (fig. 139), one of two versions completed the same year.[7] Attached to a dark encaustic surface are a flashlight, which points up to a mirror, which is in turn aimed at a plate with Johns's photograph printed on it and surrounded by the words RED YELLOW BLUE. The second version also has attached to its surface a smaller, reversed canvas on a stretcher with "souvenir" written out by hand. Within a relatively simple assemblage of objects there is a complex play of rectangular and round shapes, an equal interest in both sides of a canvas, the primary colors seen as mechanically reproduced words as well as freely brushed pigments, and a juxtaposition of media from painting, construction, and found objects to photography. By directing our attention counterclockwise around the canvas from flashlight to mirror to plate, the work casts light, indirectly, on the artist, and raises questions about what we see and understand. Here Johns's image, printed on a cheap plate like a commercial souvenir, represents all at once maker and made, subject and object, title and signature. He has elaborated on many of these ideas over the decades of his prolific and inventive career, though seldom signing himself in his work the same way again. The 1970s took him into new explorations of abstraction, which he then fused with some of his earlier imagery. In 1983, *Racing Thoughts* (Whitney Museum of American Art, New York) brought together fragments from previous canvases; references to other art, including Barnett Newman and *Mona Lisa* via Duchamp; and objects in his house.[8] This is one of the few later works to include his name stenciled in a corner of the composition, serving dually as title and signature.

A near contemporary of Johns — Robert Clark was born in 1928 — would become Robert Indiana when he moved from his native midwestern state east to New York in the mid-1950s, and acquired a new identity. This reinvention was in the tradition of Arshile Gorky and Mark Twain, but for Indiana the shift was personal and spatial, as well as artistic: he wanted to distance himself from his divorced parents as much as define an artistic identity in a new place. He would soon come to be known as one of the core figures in the Pop art movement of the 1960s, taking for himself even more than Johns did the use of stenciling as an expressive technique for his paintings, constructions, and lithographs. He declared himself to be an American painter of signs. An American historical consciousness and an awareness of ubiquitous commercial signage were powerful formative forces shaping his art. Among his early works was a series he devoted to masters of American literature, designed, for example, around lines from Herman Melville's *Moby Dick,* Henry Wadsworth Longfellow's *Song of Hiawatha,* and Walt Whitman's *Leaves of Grass.* Indiana also referred to the signs painted on old buildings, trucks, and barges, and to the visual language of the street and highway. A third current that emerged strongly in his work of the 1960s and continued through his later career was an autobiographical narrative. Pictures recalled his grandfather's employment on the railroad and his father's marriage to his stepmother. Almost like an astrologer, he incorporated into his paintings numbers referring to key dates in his life or that of his subject. Several works just of numerals and numerical sequences allude to the calendar, and hence to the passage of time, or the modern voyage of life.

At the end of the 1960s, which had been an enormously productive period, defining his style and reputation, Indiana undertook two related series of canvases, in two sizes, each consisting of ten square panels and both called *Decade Autoportraits* (fig. 140). Although other numbers sequentially appear, a large numeral 1 recurs, a reference to "oneself," which in one canvas is further played off with the middle I in the artist's name. The changing color schemes refer to particular paintings executed in each respective year, while other cities or places of significance at the time appear throughout.[9] In the larger-format group Indiana repeated his name at the bottom — as much a signature as a reference to his birth state and artistic persona. In the smaller-format series the abbreviation IND dominates the center of the design. Beyond such specific associations, the various permutations of reds, yellows, and blues; the flattened, quasi-cubist fragmentations and overlappings; and the mix of letters, numbers, and words all pay tribute to Hartley's German Officer paintings and Demuth's *The Figure 5 in Gold* (see fig. 135). As a gay artist, Indiana felt both a personal and an artistic affinity with his predecessors, painting specific variations of their key works in his own idiom. Thus his incorporations of his name into the *Decade Autoportraits* transformed his signature into a more conscious artistic autobiography.

If Jasper Johns represents early Pop art and Indiana one of its mature expressions, the slightly younger Richard Estes has come to be identified as the preeminent figure in the photorealist movement of the late 1960s and 1970s. Born in Illinois and trained at the Art Institute of Chicago, Estes was in New York and exhibiting there from the late 1960s on. Like many painters

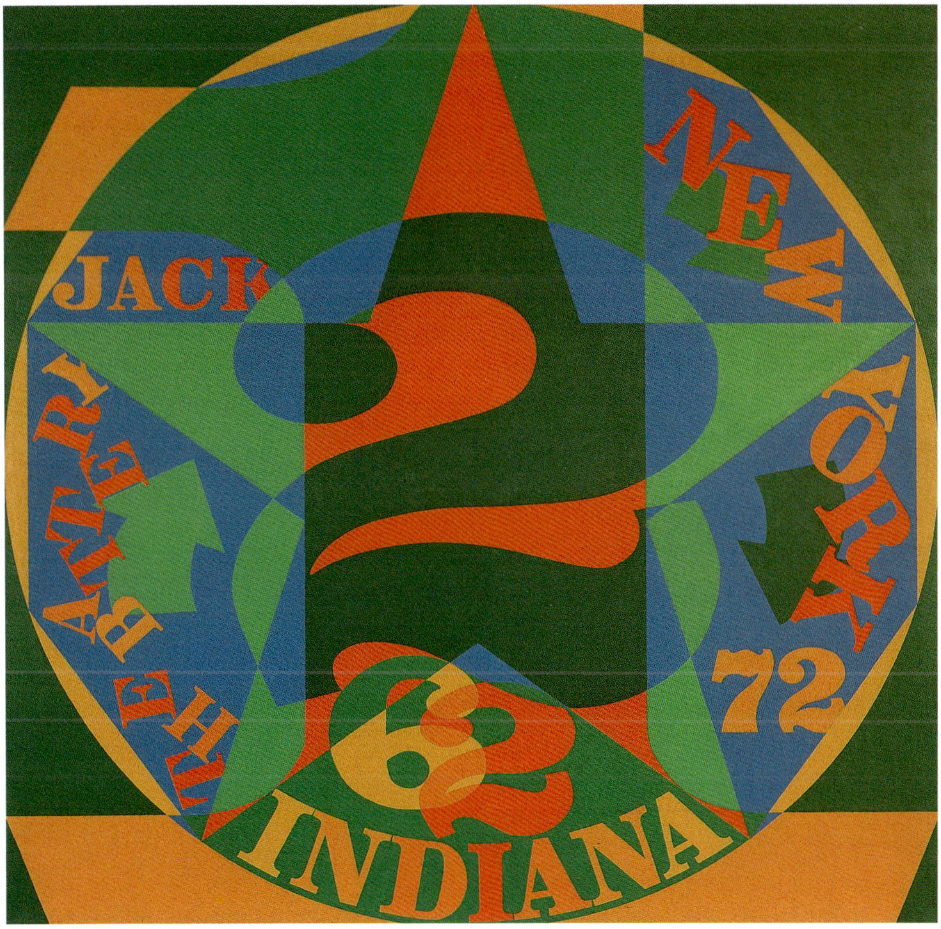

Fig. 140. Robert Indiana, *Decade Autoportrait 1962*, 1977. Oil on canvas, 72 x 72 in. (183 x 183 cm). Private collection. Courtesy of Simon Salama-Caro, New York, Morgan Art Foundation Limited / Art Resource, NY

of his generation, he worked his way beyond abstract expressionism by gradually tightening his brushwork and turning for subject matter to commonplace and commercial imagery. He concentrated for a decade or two almost entirely on the New York "streetscape," to use the term of one biographer.[10] Estes developed a personal approach that began with his taking multiple photographs of a view — details or fragments perhaps, different framings or croppings, shifted angles or spatial compressions. These would become memory aids in the studio, where he assembled and synthesized the seen and photographed experiences in such a way that a finished painting resembled rather than depicted a scene.

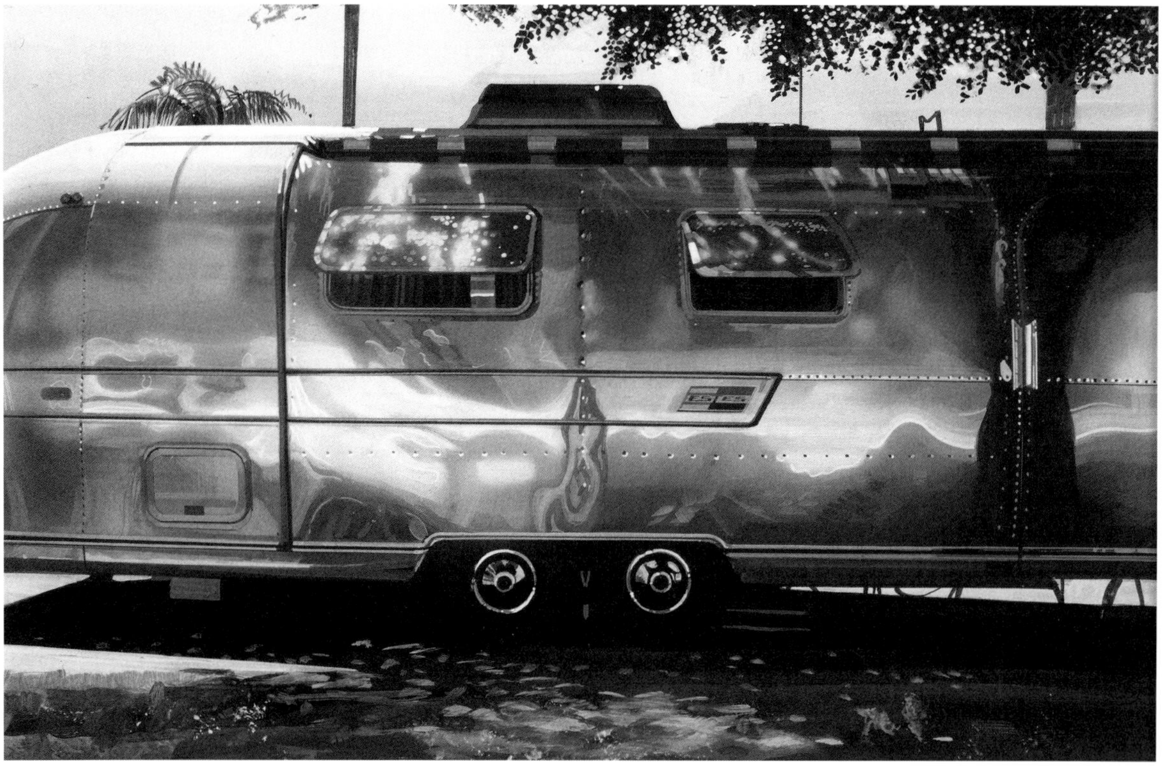

Fig. 141. Richard Estes, *Airstream,* 1974. Gouache on paper, 14 x 21 in. (35.6 x 53.3 cm). Courtesy of the Louis K. Meisel Gallery, New York

Although figures do increasingly enter his later work, Estes's principal subjects are light and reflections.[11] Critical wedges or segments of his cityscapes are given to brilliant passages of sky, while windows and multiple mirrored surfaces fill his compositions. We see this light and these reflections usually in two ways: they are either parallel to the picture plane or receding obliquely to deep vanishing points. Both set up highly complicated, often challenging depictions of spatial recession both behind and in front of the viewer. Sometimes we see objects in an interior behind a windowpane, overlapping reflections on its surface of objects in the space in back of us. Paradoxically, Estes's paintings both look like photographs and show his paint handling and touch of the brush; the result is ambiguous, visibly manipulated, even distorted. They force the eye and the mind to contemplate *how* we see, even more than *what* we see. They engage us in the facts of seeing and the fictions of perception.

Given all this, it should be no surprise that Estes regularly signed his pictures in locations well inside these contrived vistas. He has said there are

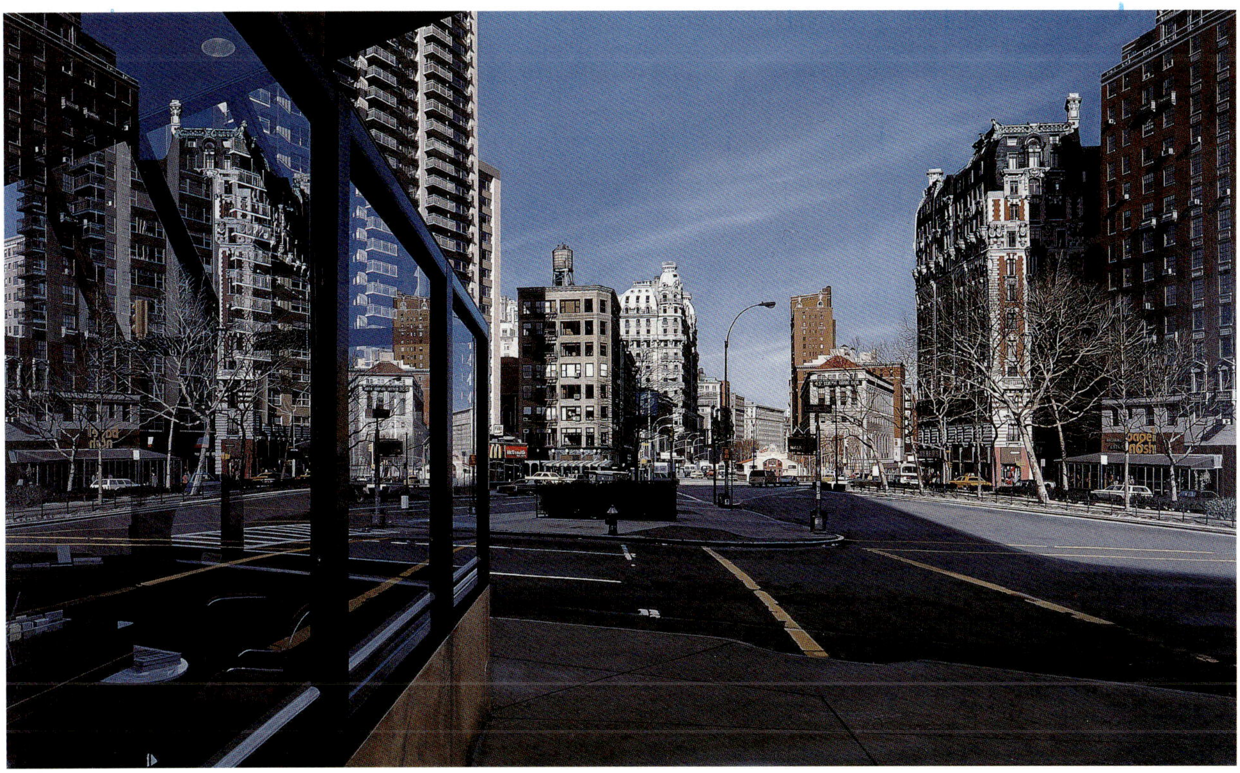

Fig. 142. Richard Estes, *MacDonalds*, 1981. Oil on canvas, 34 x 55 in. (86.4 x 139.7 cm). Courtesy of the Allan Stone Gallery, New York

certain types of paintings he usually would not sign: ones he intended to keep for himself or otherwise did not anticipate putting on the market, and natural (as distinct from urban and architectural) landscapes.[12] But within his urban streetscapes of polished automobiles, shopfronts, billboards, and street signs, he found countless places to insert his name. Typically clever examples include *Airstream*, 1974 (fig. 141), where it appears in place of the trailer maker's logo on the metal side panel; *MacDonalds*, 1981 (fig. 142), where it appears in raised letters next to "Bagel Nosh" over the cafeteria entrance on the far side of the street; and *Old Police Headquarters*, 1981 (Allan Stone Gallery, New York), where it reads as the street sign at an intersection in the center distance. Estes obscured the legibility of his name even more in *Andy Capp*, 1982 (fig. 143), in which it appears backward in reflection on a sign in Rome.[13] Surrounding the panel are numerous vertical and horizontal aluminum strips with their own distracting reflections, looking at once illusionistic and abstract. By contrast, Estes cropped off half of his name

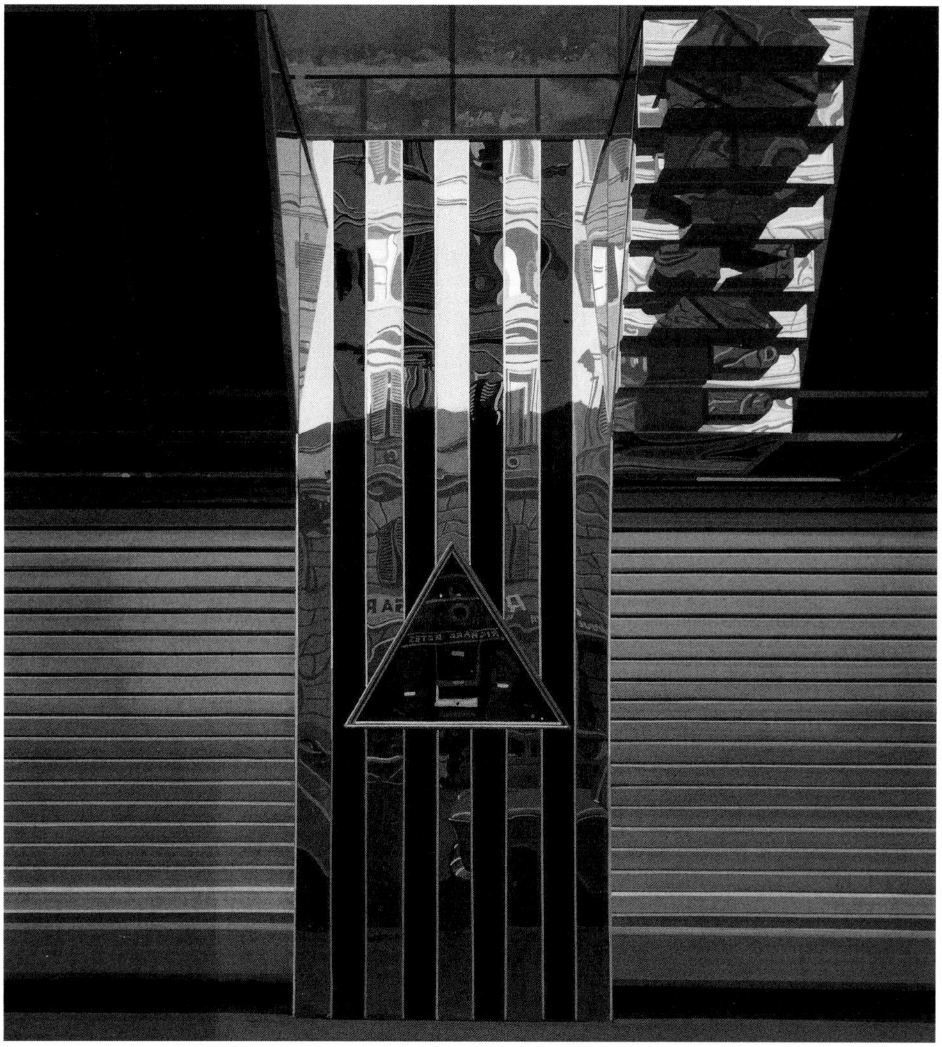

Fig. 143. Richard Estes, *Andy Capp*, 1982. Oil on board, 19 ½ x 17 ½ in. (49.5 x 44.5 cm). Courtesy of the Louis K. Meisel Gallery, New York

in *Shoe Outlet*, 1973 (Collection of Mr. and Mrs. John Belger, Missouri), where it is on part of the shopfront adjacent to the title store. These signatures are clearly a pleasurable ingredient in the artist's teasing optical effects. They represent both his actual sightings and his artistic conjurings.

Standing in contrast to the cool opticalities of Estes are the emotional undercurrents and what might be called the narrative realism of Andrew Wyeth. Born in 1917, he began painting under the tutelage of his father, the eminent illustrator N. C. Wyeth, and developed a style of realism tempered by imagination that has remained consistent into the twenty-first century. He was schooled at home, and drew on the example and support of his father as a shaping source for his own art. Early in his career the younger Wyeth also looked closely at the work of Winslow Homer, whose watercolors strongly influenced his own subjects and techniques. For his figure paintings and portraits Andrew Wyeth found further inspiration in the example of Thomas Eakins. Along with these major strains in the American tradition, he has also grounded his art deeply in the two principal landscapes he has inhabited almost his entire life — the Brandywine Valley around Chadds Ford, Pennsylvania, and the mid-Maine coast around Cushing.

Perhaps because so much of Wyeth's art is autobiographical, that is, stimulated and conditioned by deep personal responses to locations or people, he has seldom found it necessary to sign himself into his fictive spaces; instead, he places his signature conventionally in a corner of his temperas and watercolors. At the same time, both he and his biographers have more than once explained how he frequently employs objects or accessories to stand in for individuals, whether neighbors, friends, or even himself. A bucket, a bell, a blue shirt, old boots are only some of the emblems that turn many of his still lifes, interiors, and landscapes into forms of portraiture. Thomas Hoving's book on the artist, *Andrew Wyeth: Autobiography*, in fact consists of images matched up with Wyeth's personal commentary. In it, for example, Wyeth declares *Trodden Weed*, 1951 (private collection), "A self-portrait."[14] We look down at a close-up of old boots and just the hem of an overcoat moving through a rough brown field, a distillation of a particular experience. Another well-known example is *Alvaro and Christina*, 1968 (Farnsworth Art Museum, Rockland, Maine), a loving memorial tribute to his longtime models and friends in Maine: "I conceived this as a portrait of the whole Olson environment. . . . [T]he contents of that room seemed to express those two people — the basket, the buckets and the beautiful blue door with all the bizarre scratches on it that the dog had made. The Olsons were all gone but powerfully there nonetheless."[15]

Wyeth's art, like his life, is filled with contrasts of somberness and puckish wit, though the most comprehensive and critical biography of him to date leaves an overriding impression of the former, stressing the tragic, bitter, and brooding elements.[16] Certainly those currents have dominated important turning points in the family history, and found expression in many major pictures. But the love of costumes and games, the bursts of laughter, flights of imagination and fantasy, moments of affection and tenderness lead us in

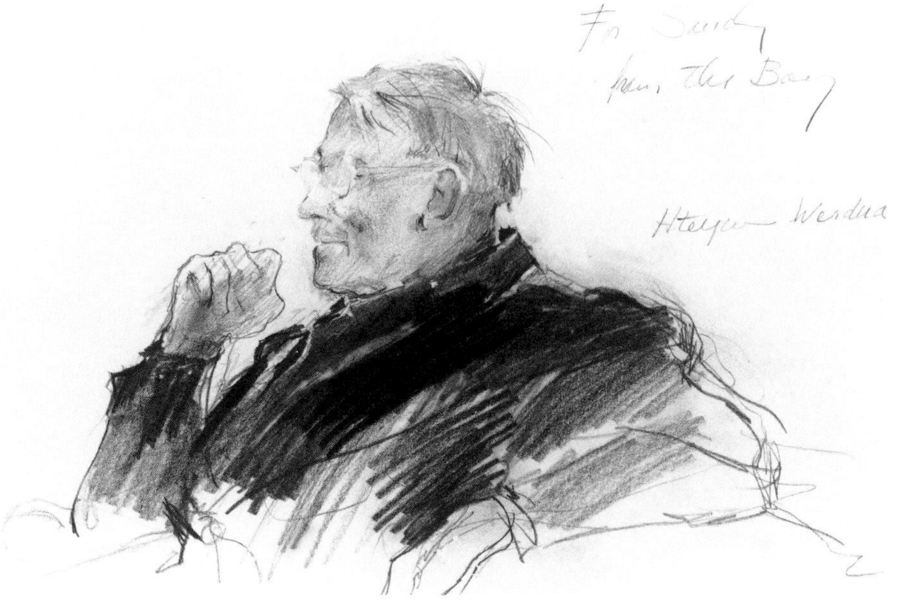

Fig. 144. Andrew Wyeth, *Portrait of Chris Sanderson,* ca. 1939. Charcoal on paper, 6¾ x 10½ in. (17.1 x 26.7 cm). Collection of the Brandywine River Museum, Chadds Ford, Pa. Museum purchase, The Dr. E. Douglas Vere Nicoll Memorial Fund

a different direction. And it is in this spirit that, appropriately, we encounter the occasional signature playfully located within a composition. Most of these are portraits of individuals with whom the artist has or has had some close association, and therefore his signature naturally draws him into their spaces. But a couple are views (a landscape and an interior) with which he has also had an intimate connection and so a reason to be present by implication.

On a very early portrait drawing, *Chris Sanderson,* ca. 1939 (fig. 144), Wyeth inscribed "For Sandy / from the Boy / Hteyw Werdna," the last his name spelled in reverse. Sanderson was a history teacher in the local school, and became a boyhood mentor and friend of the aspiring artist. Not technically a mirror image of his name, the signature is in a sense within the space of the sitter, as it were, written on an imaginary plane that only he can read from inside the picture space. What it is primarily, of course, is a youthful demonstration of cleverness, of showing off technically for a favorite teacher. More intriguing to both Wyeth's followers and critics are his initials in *Maidenhair,* 1974 (fig. 145). The scene depicts a young girl wearing a crown of flowers and seated at the front of a simple country church. This was a reworking of *Crown of Flowers,* 1974 (private collection), one of the strongest

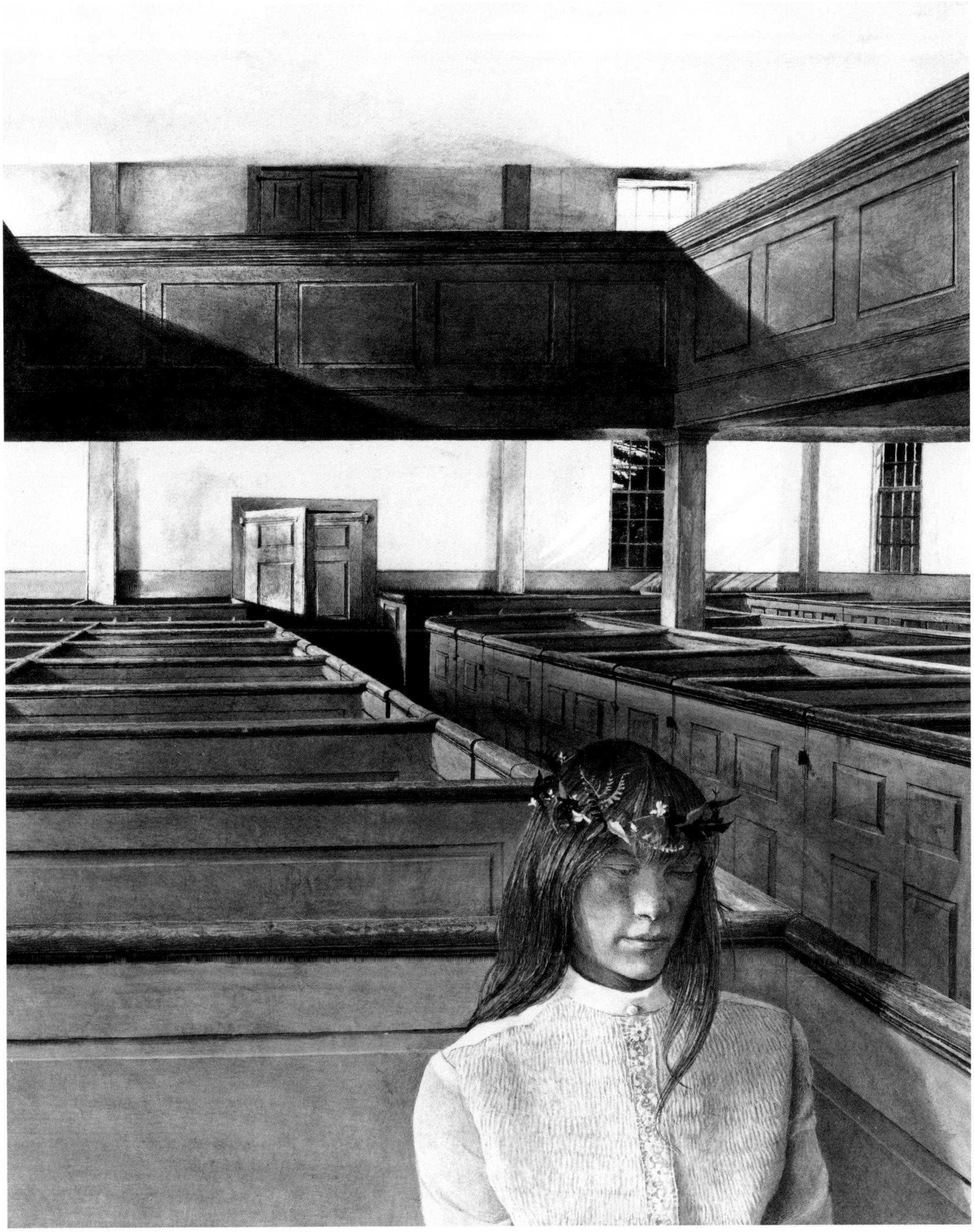

Fig. 145. Andrew Wyeth, *Maidenhair,* 1974. Tempera on panel, 29 1/8 x 23 in. (74 x 58.4 cm). Collection of Andrew and Betsy Wyeth

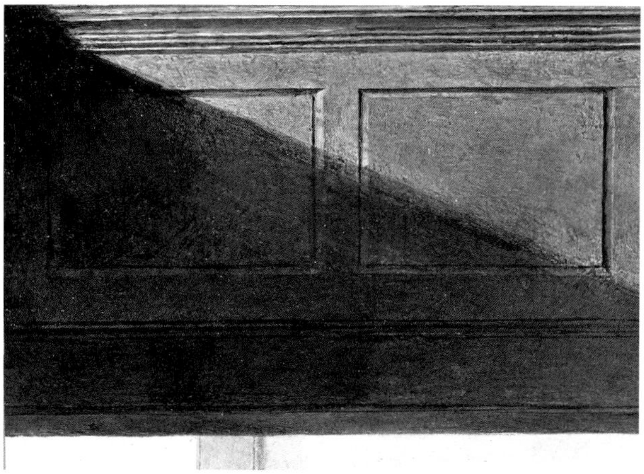

Fig. 146. Andrew Wyeth, *Maidenhair* (detail of fig. 145), 1974

drybrush watercolors in the infamous Helga series. Painted between about 1970 and 1985, the series focuses almost entirely on one model, Helga Testorff; the artist's wife, Betsy, was unaware at the time that the group included dozens of frank studies of Testorff in the nude, leading to much critical speculation and sensational press coverage.[17] In fact, Wyeth reworked some of the images in the series, occasionally using other models for variant pictures. For example, the white model for *Barracoon*, 1976 (private collection), became black in a later tempera, with hands modeled after the artist's own. *Maidenhair*, a similar variation of the central series, was painted in Maine after the Wyeths finished their winter season in Chadds Ford and the artist had suspended temporarily the sittings with Helga. The image of a girl with flowers in her hair stayed in his mind, and went through several transformations both in his imagination and in sketches. He used three more models before settling on a local Maine girl, Elaine Benner, who vaguely resembled Helga. Meanwhile, Wyeth had also seen a plain country church in nearby Waldoboro, and told his wife a story about happening into a wedding taking place there. He said he had hidden in the choir loft to watch, and later drew the bride seated alone in the front pew.[18] In any case, he placed his initials on the lower panel of the balcony in the picture's upper left, as a lone witness or voyeur (fig. 146).

Richard Meryman recounts the emotional fallout the Helga episode evidently had on Wyeth's relations not just with the press and critics but also with his wife. He describes the tensions surrounding the secrecy and intimacy of the project, the stories circulating about an affair, and the strains put on their marriage. Yet standing back from this prolific period of work, we might see, whatever else transpired, a rather traditional corpus of paintings of a nude model posing in an artist's studio, and a not especially surprising interest in the flesh on the part of a man reaching his sixties and the threshold of later life. In any event, well after the public and private imbroglios had subsided, Wyeth painted in *Love in the Afternoon*, 1992 (fig. 147), what might be described

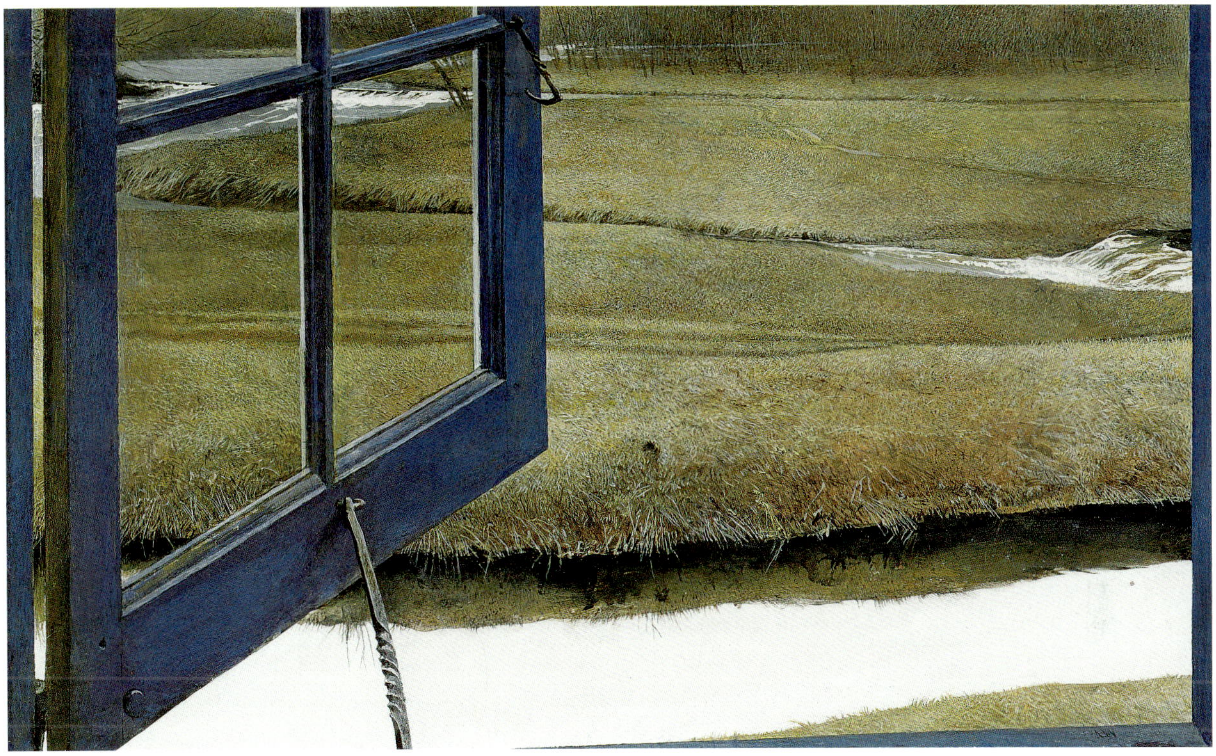

Fig. 147. Andrew Wyeth, *Love in the Afternoon*, 1992. Tempera on panel, 17⅝ x 28⅝ in. (44.7 x 72.7 cm). Private collection

(to use a term of Robert Motherwell) as a "reconciliation elegy." It is one of the more abstract and beautiful temperas of his late career. Interestingly, it has had two alternative titles, *Coming Together* and *Millhouse*. The former is said to refer to the merging of two streams in the view outside the window, but it also carries an unintended (perhaps) sexual innuendo. The latter title refers to the Wyeths' Pennsylvania house — the blue-framed window with this view is in their bedroom. We do not have to take the main title literally to sense a tranquility and order here, a balancing of architectural geometry and natural animation, a complementary play between the monochromatic tans of the fields and the periwinkle blue (a Wyeth favorite) of the window. There is an unusual distillation of form and sentiment in this image, which literally opens out to a breath of fresh air and a feeling of resolution.

Windows have been a crucial element in Wyeth's picture making throughout his entire career. They serve many purposes, from framing figures to lending personality to a building, from suggesting an imaginative escape for sitters confined inside to contrasting the man-made and natural worlds. Besides being a room's metaphoric eyes, windows can possess strong compositional power in their shape, color, and texture. It is possible to argue that Wyeth's windows are most expressive when placed somewhat asymmetrically in a design, slightly cropped, or set just a bit obliquely from the picture plane. All of which is so in *Love in the Afternoon*. Wyeth's own comments about it are rather shaded and diverting, understandably: "I was looking out of the window in the Mill at the bleached ground and the reflections of the race. I go to that window and open it in the morning and close it in the evening. . . . I was taken by the feeling of almost falling out of that window. I didn't want a frame around it. I didn't want a feeling of the inside of the room; I wanted the feeling of pushing this windowpane out and letting in the air. . . ."

Then he adds cryptically, "You'll recognize it as one of my most mature pictures if you really look at it."[19] Indeed, it is so deceptively simple that we almost do not look at it closely enough. There are his initials, AW, written on the lower corner of the blue window frame. The painter/husband is at the very juncture between the bedroom inside that he shares with Betsy and the landscape outside that he has always looked at. His signature sits just where he would lean to open that window, where the spaces of his personal and artistic life come together. Finally, there is the nice perceptual ambiguity of the landscape being doubly viewed, through the nearly contiguous boards of the painted window casing and through the actual picture frame. Like Jan Porcellis's in his *Tempest* of 1629 (see fig. 13) — though Wyeth probably did not know the painting directly — Wyeth's initials are at the point of a seamless transition from our space to the pictorial space.

Such intense color stands out in Wyeth's usually monochromatic work, and this blue carries associations with the sky and water, bringing an unusual vibrancy to this particular painting. More familiar in the artist's canon is his palette of whites, tans, and browns, exactly the combination in *Arctic Circle*, 1996 (Collection of Andrew and Betsy Wyeth). Snow scenes recur often in his career, and are occasions for almost Whistlerian medleys in white. The sitter here is Mary Adam Landa, a curatorial assistant and registrar of Wyeth's art working with Betsy Wyeth on a full catalogue raisonné. The figure sits on a fanciful chair made from animal bones, within a circle of antlers forming an animated abstract design in the surrounding snow. Wyeth has placed his initials on the side of her left boot, for two likely reasons: in this case, a signature in the snow at the corner would have been too blatant, and it no doubt seemed natural to associate himself with a subject he knew well.

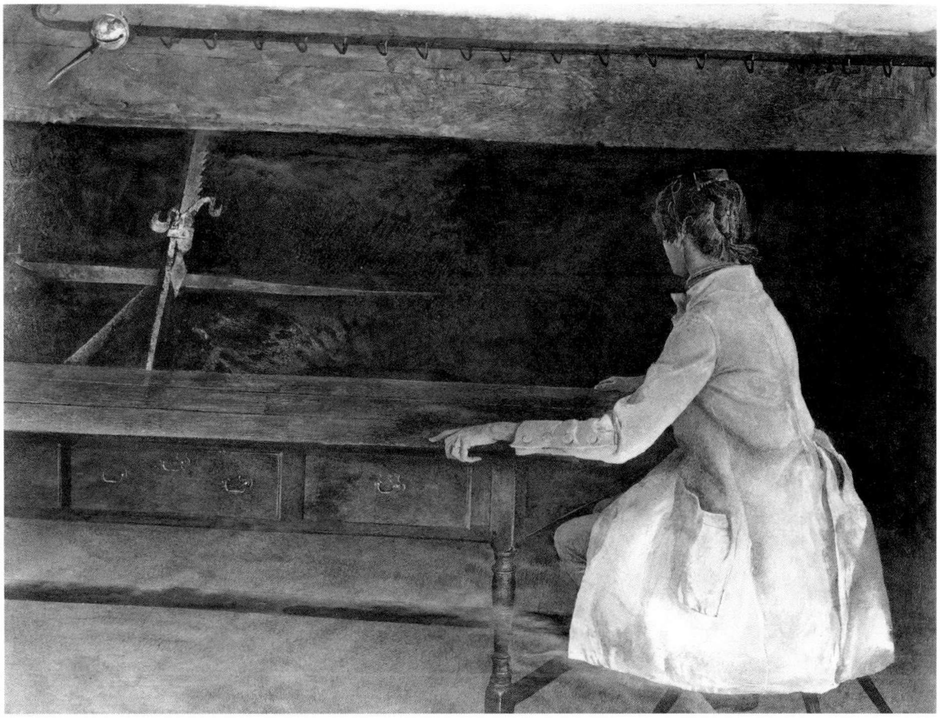

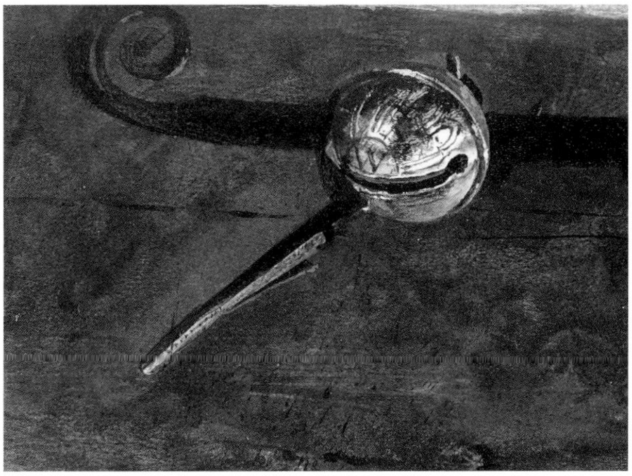

Fig. 148. Andrew Wyeth, *French Twist*, 1967. Drybrush on paper, 22 ½ x 28 ½ in. (57.2 x 72.4 cm). Collection of Andrew and Betsy Wyeth

Fig. 149. Andrew Wyeth, *French Twist* (detail of fig. 148), 1967

In another familiar setting, painted twice at a distance of more than thirty years, Wyeth put his signature on an antique bell his wife found in a shop and hung over the great hearth in the Mill. In *French Twist*, 1967 (figs. 148 and 149), he painted Betsy seated at a table before the fireplace, with the bell — possibly off a door or a sleigh — hanging diagonally above. Bearing his "W," it joins his presence to hers at the center of their domestic life. Moved

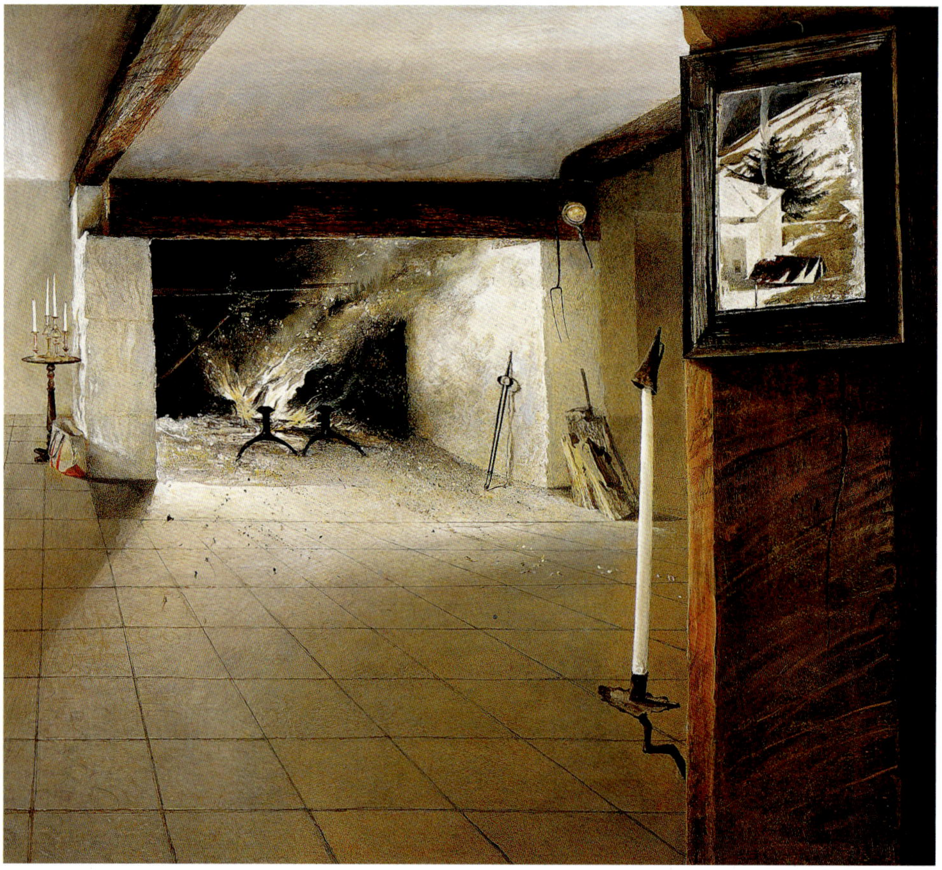

Fig. 150. Andrew Wyeth, *Sparks*, 2001. Tempera on panel, 44 x 47¾ in. (111.8 x 121.3 cm). Private collection

to the other end of the large wooden beam, it reappears in *Sparks*, 2001 (fig. 150), now in a more abstracted and telescoped space. In lieu of any human figures, the blazing fire gives light and warmth to the scene, over which the polished bell (and the artist's presence) presides like some all-seeing eye. This is the artist at home.

As American art moves into the twenty-first century, and electronic imaging becomes more commonplace, it is possible that the artist's hand will become less personal. But as long as the art and practice of painting continue, there will be artists who delight in transcribing picture spaces from reality as well as the imagination. And in an age of online transactions, paintings may be one of the few places left where individuals will impress their signatures, and artists will find refuge and meaning within their created spaces.

NOTES

CHAPTER 1. EUROPEAN PRECEDENTS

1. See the sensitive interpretation of this in Gabriel Josipovici, *Touch* (New Haven, 1996), 24–27.
2. For closer discussion of these images, see Victor I. Stoichita, *The Self-Aware Image: An Insight into Early Modern Meta-Painting* (New York, 1997), 205.
3. A little over a century later Annibale Carracci continued this model when he painted his *Self-Portrait on Easel*, ca. 1604 (Hermitage, Saint Petersburg), a scene of the studio corner with a standing easel on which rests the artist's palette and the canvas with his self-portrait. See Stoichita, *Self-Aware Image*, 207, 215.
4. See Stoichita, *Self-Aware Image*, 202–3.
5. See Sybille Ebert-Schifferer, *Still-Life, a History* (New York, 1999), 33–34; and Pierre Skira, *Still Life: A History* (Geneva, 1989), 50–51.
6. Louisa C. Matthew, "The Painter's Presence: Signatures in Venetian Renaissance Pictures," *Art Bulletin* 80, 4 (December 1998), 616–48.
7. Matthew, "Painter's Presence," 616, 620, 627, 633, 640–41.
8. Matthew, "Painter's Presence," 617, 620, 627.
9. Matthew, "Painter's Presence," 617, 620.
10. See Matthew, "Painter's Presence," 633.
11. On these two works, see Matthew, "Painter's Presence," 634–37.
12. Matthew, "Painter's Presence," 622.
13. See Matthew, "Painter's Presence," 639.
14. Matthew, "Painter's Presence," 642.
15. See Ebert-Schifferer, *Still-Life*, 76–80; and Stoichita, *Self-Aware Image*, 30–33. Other examples in the Spanish tradition, with signatures on a tablecloth or niche sill, are Lubin Baugin, *Jug, Wine Glass and Wafer Biscuits*, ca. 1650s (Musée du Louvre, Paris), and Juan van der Hamen y León, *Still Life with Sweets and Pottery*, 1627 (National Gallery of Art, Washington, D.C.). See Skira, *Still Life*, 36, 62.
16. On both the Murillo and the Poussin, see Stoichita, *Self-Aware Image*, 207–12.

17. Alan Chong, "Contained under the Name of Still Life: The Associations of Still Life Painting," in Alan Chong and Wouter Kloek, *Still-Life Paintings from the Netherlands, 1550–1720* (exhibition catalogue, Rijksmuseum, Amsterdam, 1999), 30.
18. For a fuller accounting of these works, see Stoichita, *Self-Aware Image*, 136–39, 228–29, 235–37.
19. On the Porcellis and the Gumpp, see Stoichita, *Self-Aware Image*, 41–43, 245–47.
20. A typical example is Bosschaert's *Flowers in a Vase*, early seventeenth century (Mauritshuis, The Hague).
21. See Chong and Kloek, *Still-Life Paintings*, 182–83.
22. Pun not intended, though savored.
23. Chong and Kloek, *Still-Life Paintings*, 103, 128–30.
24. For example, see Skira, *Still Life*, 78; and Chong and Kloek, *Still-Life Paintings*, 172, 267–69, and 275–78.
25. For a full explication of this work, see Chong and Kloek, *Still-Life Paintings*, 61–66, 221–27. A well-known related work, *Towell, Brush, and Letter Bag on a Door*, 1655 (Gemäldegalerie der Akademie der bildenden Kunste, Vienna), partially reveals the same gold medal and chain seen in his rack picture, part of his spectacles, and a receipt bearing his name and the date.
26. For illustration and discussion of these works, see Chong and Kloek, *Still-Life Paintings*, 62–63, 231–33.
27. The vanitas examples are in a Swiss private collection and in Boston, Copenhagen, Munich, and Dijon. See Stoichita, *Self-Aware Image*, 270–75.
28. These are illustrated and discussed in Christopher Brown et al., *Rembrandt: The Master and His Workshop*, 2 vols. (New Haven, 1991), 1:142–43, 176–77, 218–19.
29. Brown et al., *Rembrandt*, 1:230–32. See also Jakob Rosenberg, *Rembrandt: Life and Work* (Greenwich, Conn., 1964), 95–99.
30. See Brown et al., *Rembrandt*, 262–66, 272–74. One other religious painting, *Saint Matthew and the Angel*, 1661 (Musée du Louvre, Paris), reveals a close personal involvement in the figure of the young angel, who rests his hand on Matthew's shoulder and whispers in his ear. The face is almost certainly that of Rembrandt's son, Titus, who died shortly before he did. The artist's signature is on the wall at right center deep within the picture space, close literally and emotionally to the figure of the apostle.
31. For good color illustrations and discussion, see Arthur K. Wheelock, Jr., ed., *Johannes Vermeer* (exhibition catalogue, National Gallery of Art, Washington, D.C., 1995); Arthur K. Wheelock, Jr., *Vermeer and the Art of Painting* (New Haven, 1995); and Edward Snow, *A Study of Vermeer* (rev. ed., Berkeley, 1994).
32. Characteristic of the dozen or more so signed are *Duck Hanging by One Leg, Pâté, Bowl and Jar of Olives*, 1764 (Museum of Fine Arts, Springfield, Mass.), signed

on the table edge; *The Buffet*, 1728 (Musée du Louvre, Paris), signed at the base of the table supporting the still life; and *Tufted Lapwing, Gray Partridge, Snipe and Seville Orange*, 1732 (Musée de la Chartreuse, Douai), signed in the center of a curving stone step. See Pierre Rosenberg et al., *Chardin* (exhibition catalogue, Royal Academy of Arts, London, and the Metropolitan Museum of Art, New York, 2000), 138–39, 182–83, 300–301.

CHAPTER 2.
AMERICAN HISTORY, STILL LIFE, AND LANDSCAPE

1. For a full discussion of the subject and Copley's several versions, see Ellen G. Miles, *American Paintings of the Eighteenth Century* (National Gallery of Art, Washington, D.C., 1995), 54–71; and John Caldwell and Oswaldo Rodrigue Roque, *American Paintings in The Metropolitan Museum of Art* (New York, 1994), 1:99–104.
2. For example, see Albert Boime, *The Art of Exclusion: Representing Blacks in the Nineteenth Century* (Washington, D.C., 1990); and Guy C. McElroy, *Facing History: The Black Image in American Art, 1719–1940* (exhibition catalogue, Corcoran Gallery of Art, Washington, D.C., 1990).
3. For discussion and illustrations of some of these aspects, see Ellen G. Miles, *John Singleton Copley's "Watson and the Shark"* (exhibition brochure, National Gallery of Art, Washington, D.C., 1992); and Caldwell and Rodrigue Roque, *American Paintings*, 99–100.
4. Both the first version in Washington, D.C., and the second in Boston are signed identically inside the stern of the boat.
5. This work receives attention in all of the Peale literature, but two discussions especially are worth citing. See Lillian B. Miller, "Charles Willson Peale as History Painter," in Lillian B. Miller and David C. Ward, eds. *New Perspectives on Charles Willson Peale* (Pittsburgh, 1991), 145–65; and Laura Rigal, *The American Manufactory: Art, Labor, and the World of Things in the Early Republic* (Princeton, 1991), 91–113.
6. See Nicolai Cikovsky, Jr., et al., *Raphaelle Peale Still Lifes* (exhibition catalogue, National Gallery of Art, Washington, D.C., 1988). The most probing and provocative recent examination of Peale is Alexander Nemerov, *The Body of Raphaelle Peale: Still Life and Selfhood, 1812–1824* (Berkeley, 2000).
7. *Apples & Fox Grapes*, 1815 (Pennsylvania Academy of the Fine Arts, Philadelphia).
8. For its 1997 *Peale Family* exhibition, the Philadelphia Museum of Art marketed in its sales shop a baseball cap with the emblem of Raphaelle's curling orange peel.
9. I am indebted to Jonathan Steinberg at Princeton University for first suggesting this insight and to the illuminating analyses of Alexander Nemerov's writing on Peale.

10. For a full discussion of this work, see Elwood C. Parry III, *The Art of Thomas Cole: Ambition and Imagination* (Newark, Del., 1988), 244–48.
11. Matthew Baigell, *Thomas Cole* (New York, 1981), 54.
12. Asher B. Durand, letter to *The Crayon*, quoted in John W. McCoubrey, ed., *American Art, 1700–1960: Sources and Documents* (Englewood Cliffs, N.J., 1965), 110.
13. John Ruskin, *The Elements of Drawing: Three Letters to Beginners* (New York, 1857), 50, 131.
14. Good examples are *The Cordilleras: Sunrise*, 1854 (Alexander Gallery, New York), and *View of Cotopaxi*, 1857 (Art Institute of Chicago).

CHAPTER 3. GENRE AND LATER STILL-LIFE PAINTING

1. See, for example, *Courtship*, or *Winding Up*, 1836 (Nelson-Atkins Museum of Art, Kansas City, Mo.). Others in this category include *The Sportsman's Last Visit*, 1835 (Museums at Stony Brook, N.Y.); *The Long Story*, 1837 (Corcoran Gallery of Art, Washington, D.C.); and *Catching the Tune*, 1866–67 (Museums at Stony Brook). For a discussion of veiled political meanings, see Elizabeth Johns, *American Genre Painting: The Politics of Everyday Life* (New Haven, 1991).
2. See the discussion of this painting in Deborah J. Johnson et al., *William Sidney Mount, Painter of American Life* (exhibition catalogue, American Federation of Arts, New York, 1998), 49.
3. Stuart P. Feld, "In the Midst of 'High Vintage,'" *Metropolitan Museum of Art Bulletin* 25, 8 (April 1967), 292–307.
4. Johnson et al., *Mount*, 53–55.
5. See Johnson et al., *Mount*, 51–53.
6. For a listing of his works, their inscriptions, and types, see Judith Hansen O'Toole, *Severin Roesen* (Cranbury, N.J., 1992), 114–36.
7. See Gertrude Grace Sill, *John Haberle: Master of Illusion* (exhibition catalogue, Museum of Fine Arts, Springfield, Mass., 1985), 3, 6, 29. By the mid-1890s, Haberle's style and imagery had shifted to more conventional depictions of bowls of flowers set on tabletops, executed in a softer, more painterly manner in keeping with the rising impressionist taste in American painting at the end of the century.
8. Sill, *John Haberle*, 52.
9. Sill, *John Haberle*, 52.
10. One clipping reads: "of work of the kind yet . . . it is done entirely with a brush. . . . John Haberle the Counter . . . / (Special to the World) New Haven, Conn., Dec. 12 — . . . / ceives the eye into the belief that the . . ." The second says, "A Counterfeit / A Remarkable Painting of a Ten Dollar bill / sil . . . ited States' Bill / A . . . would humbug Barnum." Sill, *John Haberle*, 49. Another level of trickery is evident in the fact that the clipping is doubly bogus, since it was never printed in the first place. I am indebted to Sill for

much of my discussion of Haberle.

11. See Sill, *John Haberle,* 50.
12. See Sill, *John Haberle,* 16, 29, 36, 46, 53.
13. Sill, *John Haberle,* 42.
14. Major examples that come to mind are *Portrait of Benjamin Howard Rand,* 1874 (Thomas Jefferson University, Philadelphia), with its microscope and papers on the desk; *Portrait of Dr. Samuel Gross,* 1875 (Thomas Jefferson University), with its medical instruments on the foreground table; *William Rush Carving the Allegorical Figure of the Schuylkill,* 1877 (Brooklyn Museum, New York), with the pile of clothing on the chair at center; *The Chess Players,* 1876 (Metropolitan Museum of Art, New York), with its game-board and glasses on adjacent tables; and *Baby at Play,* 1876 (National Gallery of Art, Washington, D.C.), with its scattered toys across the garden terrace.
15. Typical examples include *A Wooden Basket of Catawba Grapes,* 1876 (Frye Art Museum, Seattle), *Still Life with Ginger Jar,* 876 (Manney Collection, New York), *The Banker's Table,* 1877 (Metropolitan Museum of Art, New York), *Secretary's Table,* 1879 (Santa Barbara Museum of Art, Calif.), *Still Life with Letter to Dennis Gale,* 1879 (private collection), and *Still Life with Letter to Thomas B. Clarke,* 1879 (Addison Gallery of American Art, Phillips Academy, Andover, Mass.). These are all illustrated in color in Doreen Bolger, Marc Simpson, and John Wilmerding, eds., *William M. Harnett* (exhibition catalogue, Metropolitan Museum of Art, New York, 1992), plates 1, 2, 6, 13, 15, 32.
16. See Doreen Bolger, "The Patrons of the Artist: Emblems of Commerce and Culture," in Bolger, Simpson, and Wilmerding, *Harnett,* 73–85.
17. See Bolger, Simpson, and Wilmerding, *Harnett,* 38, 79.
18. Doreen Bolger has thoroughly decoded the references of the imagery depicted in Bolger, Simpson, and Wilmerding, *Harnett,* 82. See also Bolger, "'Cards and Letter from His Friends': Mr. Hulings' Rack Picture by William Michael Harnett," *American Art Journal* 22, 2 (1990), 5–32.
19. See John Wilmerding, *Important Information Inside: The Art of John F. Peto and the Idea of Still-Life Painting in Nineteenth-Century America* (exhibition catalogue, National Gallery of Art, Washington, D.C., 1983), 186–204.
20. See Jennifer Hardin, "The Late Years," in Bolger, Simpson, and Wilmerding, *Harnett,* 185–92.

CHAPTER 4. IMPRESSIONISM AND REALISM

1. Lisa N. Peters, *James McNeill Whistler* (New York, 1996), 4.
2. One of his earliest Japanese subjects was *Purple and Rose: The Lange Leizen of the Six Marks,* 1864 (Philadelphia Museum of Art), which shows a seated woman in Japanese dress holding a piece

of porcelain ware in her lap; another piece, with bold blue markings on its lid, rests nearby on the floor. For a summary of Whistler's variant butterfly signatures from 1873 to 1898, see Andrew McLaren Young et al., *The Paintings of James McNeill Whistler*, 2 vols. (New Haven, 1980), 1:xvii–xviii.

3. See the informative discussion in Jonathan Weinberg, *Ambition and Love in Modern American Art* (New Haven, 2001), 3–28.
4. See the perceptive discussion of this work in Martin Berger, *Man Made: Thomas Eakins and the Construction of Gilded Age Manhood* (Berkeley, 2000), 70–84.
5. This is analyzed fully in Norma Lifton, "Representing History: From Public Event to Private Meaning," *Art Journal* (Winter 1984), 345–51.
6. See Michael Fried, *Realism, Writing, Disfiguration: On Thomas Eakins and Stephen Crane* (Chicago, 1987), 35; and Amy Werbel, "Eakins's Early Years," in *Thomas Eakins, American Realist* (exhibition catalogue, Philadelphia Museum of Art, 2001), 1–11.
7. Kathleen Foster, "Portraits of Thinkers and Teachers," in *Thomas Eakins*, 307–15.
8. See Berger, *Man Made*, 57–58.
9. Berger, *Man Made*, 67.
10. Related examples include *Professor William Smith Forbes*, 1905 (Thomas Jefferson University, Philadelphia), and *Professor Leslie W. Miller*, 1901 (Philadelphia Museum of Art).
11. See the eloquent chapter on this group of portraits in Sylvan Schendler, *Eakins* (Boston, 1967), 197–215. I am also indebted to "The Clerical Portraits of Thomas Eakins" by Brian T. Allen (December 12, 1991), a graduate student at the time at Yale University under Professor Jules D. Prown.
12. Lloyd Goodrich, *Thomas Eakins*, 2 vols. (Cambridge, Mass., 1982), 2:191.
13. Quoted in Nicolai Cikovsky and Frank Kelly, *Winslow Homer* (exhibition catalogue, National Gallery of Art, Washington, D.C., 1996), 14; and see Lloyd Goodrich, *Winslow Homer* (New York, 1945), 1.
14. Among the more pertinent are Jules D. Prown, "Winslow Homer in His Art," *Smithsonian Studies in American Art* 1, 1 (Spring 1987), 31–45; Henry Adams, "Mortal Themes: Winslow Homer," *Art in America* 2 (February 1983), 113–26; Christopher Reed, "The Artist and the Other: The Work of Winslow Homer," *Yale University Art Gallery Bulletin* (Spring 1989), 69–79; Marilyn S. Kushner et al., *Winslow Homer: Illustrating America* (exhibition catalogue, Brooklyn Museum of Art, 2000); and Nicolai Cikovsky, Jr., "Winslow Homer's *School Time:* 'A Picture Thoroughly National,'" in John Wilmerding, ed., *Essays in Honor of Paul Mellon, Collector and Benefactor* (Washington, D.C., 1986), 47–69.
15. Homer's various signatures are illustrated, along with those of other major American artists,

in Peter Hastings Falk, *Signatures and Monograms of American Artists from the Colonial Period to the Mid Twentieth Century* (New York, 1988).

16. Other examples are *Campaign Sketches: A Pass Time: Calvary Rest*, 1863; *On the Beach — Two Are Company, Three Are None* (*Harper's Weekly*, August 17, 1872); and *The Nooning* (*Harper's Weekly*, August 16, 1873). All these are catalogued and illustrated in Philip C. Beam, *Winslow Homer's Magazine Engravings* (New York, 1979).
17. See also *Campaign Sketches: The Coffee Call*, 1863, where the initials appear cut into the side of a barrel; *Campaign Sketches: The Letter for Home*, 1863, where the "H" follows the lines of the floor planks; and *Spring Farm Work — Grafting* (*Harper's Weekly*, April 30, 1870), where the initials look cut into the tree trunk.
18. See *Skating on Jamaica Pond, near Boston* (*Ballou's Pictorial*, January 29, 1859), *Coasting Out of Doors* (*Ballou's Pictorial*, November 28, 1857), and *Christmas Belles* (*Harper's Weekly*, January 2, 1869). Yet another easy spot to place his name was on a foreground rock in a landscape, presumably indicating he was imaginatively there, like Lane, Church, and Durand earlier in their works. This Homer did in *The Summit of Mount Washington* (*Harper's Weekly*, July 10, 1869) and *August in the Country — The Sea-Shore* (*Harper's Weekly*, August 27, 1859).
19. See Cikovsky, "Winslow Homer's *School Time*," 47–69.
20. For example, *On the Hill*, 1878 (collection of Mr. and Mrs. Allistair Bradley Martin), *Harrowing*, 1879 (private collection), and *The New Novel*, 1877 (Museum of Fine Arts, Springfield, Mass.). The practice continues in later works, such as *Burnt Mountain*, 1892 (Fine Arts Museums of San Francisco), where his name angles down the mountainside, and *A Wall, Nassau*, 1898 (Metropolitan Museum of Art, New York), where it sits on the side of the whitewashed wall.
21. Henry Adams, "Mortal Themes: Winslow Homer," *Art in America* 2 (February 1983), 113–26.
22. Thomas B. Hess, "Come Back to the Raft Ag'in, Winslow Homer, Honey," *New York Magazine* (June 11, 1973), 75–76.
23. Hess, "Come Back to the Raft Ag'in," 75–76.
24. Cikovsky and Kelly, *Winslow Homer*, 14.

CHAPTER 5.
MODERNISM

1. See Robin Jaffee Frank, *Charles Demuth: Poster Portraits, 1923–1929* (exhibition catalogue, Yale University Art Gallery, New Haven, 1994), 15–22.
2. Quoted in Frank, *Charles Demuth*, 73. See her full discussion of the work, 73–82; and the comprehensive analysis in Wanda Corn, *The Great American Thing: Modern Art and National Identity*,

1915–1935 (Berkeley, 1999), chapter 4.

3. I am indebted to Professor John Davis of Smith College for calling my attention to his observations on this picture. See his entry on *Rolling Power* in John Davis and Jaroslaw Leshko, *The Smith College Museum of Art: European and American Paintings, 1760–1960* (New York, 2000), 220. See also his entry on the picture in Linda Muehlig, ed., *Masterworks of American Painting and Sculpture from the Smith College Museum of Art* (New York, 1999), 180–83.
4. Quoted in Michael Crichton, *Jasper Johns* (rev. ed., New York, 1994), 41.
5. See Kenneth E. Silver, "Modes of Disclosure: The Construction of Gay Identity and the Rise of Pop Art," in Russell Ferguson, ed., *Hand-Painted Pop: American Art in Transition, 1955–62* (exhibition catalogue, Museum of Contemporary Art, Los Angeles, 1992), 179–203.
6. See the discussion in Crichton, *Jasper Johns*, 50–51.
7. *Souvenir* is in the collection of the artist; *Souvenir 2* is in the collection of Mr. and Mrs. Victor W. Ganz. Johns began sketches for the work while on a trip to Hawaii and Japan; hence this was nominally a souvenir of his travels. Crichton, *Jasper Johns*, 49.
8. See Crichton, *Jasper Johns*, 65, 97.
9. The series is analyzed fully in Susan Elizabeth Ryan, *Robert Indiana: Figures of Speech* (New Haven, 2000), 229–33.
10. See John Perreault in Louis K. Meisel, *Richard Estes: The Complete Paintings, 1966–1985* (New York, 1986), 1.
11. For some thoughtful commentary on Estes's reflections, see Matthew Baigell, "Reflections on/of Richard Estes," in *Artist and Identity in Twentieth-Century America* (New York, 2001), 202–12.
12. In conversation with the author, August 2000.
13. See the commentary on the oil and print versions in John Arthur, *Richard Estes: Paintings and Prints* (San Francisco, 1993), 108–9, 124–25.
14. Thomas Hoving, *Andrew Wyeth: Autobiography* (exhibition catalogue, Nelson-Atkins Museum of Art, Kansas City, Mo., 1995), 32–33.
15. Hoving, *Andrew Wyeth*, 78.
16. See Richard Meryman, *Andrew Wyeth: A Secret Life* (New York, 1996).
17. A full accounting of the series, its history, and aftermath is given in Meryman, *Andrew Wyeth*, 328–90. See also John Wilmerding, *Andrew Wyeth: The Helga Pictures* (New York, 1987).
18. See Meryman, *Andrew Wyeth*, 351.
19. Quoted in Hoving, *Andrew Wyeth*, 151.

ACKNOWLEDGMENTS

THANKS to Susan Lehre for assistance in preparing the manuscript and to the Publications Fund, Department of Art and Archaeology, Princeton University, for funding support.

Thanks also to Patricia Fidler and her associates at Yale University Press — John Long, photo editor, and Mary Pasti, assistant managing editor — for their efficient and sensitive contributions to the production of this book. Special appreciation goes to Alexandra Bonfante-Warren for editing the manuscript and to Susan Marsh for her effective and sympathetic design of the book.

INDEX

Page numbers in **boldface** refer to illustrations.

PHOTO CREDITS

© Addison Gallery of American Art, Phillips Academy, Andover, Mass. All rights reserved (figs. 81, 106); Photo by Michael Agee (fig. 134); © 2003 Bildarchiv Preußischer Kulturbesitz, Berlin. Photo by Jörg P. Anders (fig. 8); Photo by E. Irving Blomstrann (fig. 56); © The Cleveland Museum of Art, 2002 (figs. 18, 64, 65); © Collection of the New-York Historical Society (figs. 34, 41); Photo © 1979 The Detroit Institute of Arts (fig. 96); Photo © 1988 The Detroit Institute of Arts (fig. 71); © Erich Lessing / Art Resource, N.Y. (figs. 2, 6, 7, 12); © Richard Estes (figs. 141, 142, 143); From P. H. Falk, *Dictionary of Signatures and Monograms of American Artists: From the Colonial Period to the Mid-Twentieth Century*, Madison, Conn.: Sound View Press, 1988 (fig. 111); © Glasgow Museums (fig. 97); © President and Fellows of Harvard College. Photo by Katya Kallsen (fig. 98); Herzog Anton Ulrich Museum, Braunschweig, Germany. Photo by Bernd-Peter Keiser (fig. 26); © Jasper Johns / Licensed by VAGA, New York, N.Y. (figs. 137, 138, 139); Photo courtesy of Kennedy Galleries, Inc., New York (fig. 93); Photo by Melville McLean (figs. 114, 118, 119, 121, 122); All rights reserved. The Metropolitan Museum of Art (figs. 54, 55, 61). Photo © 1979 The Metropolitan Museum of Art (fig. 60); Photo © 1985 The Metropolitan Museum of Art. Photo by Geoffrey Clements (fig. 45); Photo © 1986 The Metropolitan Museum of Art (fig. 135); Photo © 1992 The Metropolitan Museum of Art (fig. 51); Photo © 1993 The Metropolitan Museum of Art (fig. 59); Photo © 1994 The Metropolitan Museum of Art (figs. 100, 101); Photo © 1995 The Metropolitan Museum of Art (fig. 42); © 2003 Morgan Art Foundation Limited / Artists Rights Society (ARS), New York (fig. 140); Photo © 2003 Museum Associates / LACMA (fig. 91); © 2003 Museum of Fine Arts, Boston (figs. 32, 33, 46, 52, 53, 58, 68, 69, 70, 72); © The National Gallery, London (fig. 1); Photo © 2002 Board of Trustees, National Gallery of Art, Washington, D.C. (figs. 79, 83, 88, 125, 128); Image © 2003 Board of Trustees, National Gallery of Art, Washington, D.C. (fig. 74); National Gallery of Scotland. Photo by Antonia Reeve (fig. 23); © Réunion des Musées Nationaux / Art Resource, N.Y. Photo by R. G. Ojeda (fig. 28); © Rijksmuseum-Stichting Amsterdam (fig. 22); © Scala / Art Resource, N.Y. (figs. 3, 5, 9, 14); Photo courtesy of Sotheby's, Inc. © 2003 (figs. 47, 48); Photo by Lee Stalsworth (fig. 105); Photo courtesy of USC Fisher Gallery, Los Angeles (fig. 16); Photo by Robert Wedemeyer (fig. 110); © Andrew Wyeth (figs. 144, 145, 146, 147, 148, 149, 150); From A. M. Young, M. MacDonald, and R. Spencer, with Hamish Miles, *The Paintings of James McNeill Whistler*, New Haven: Published for the Paul Mellon Centre for Studies in British Art by Yale University Press, 1980 (fig. 95).

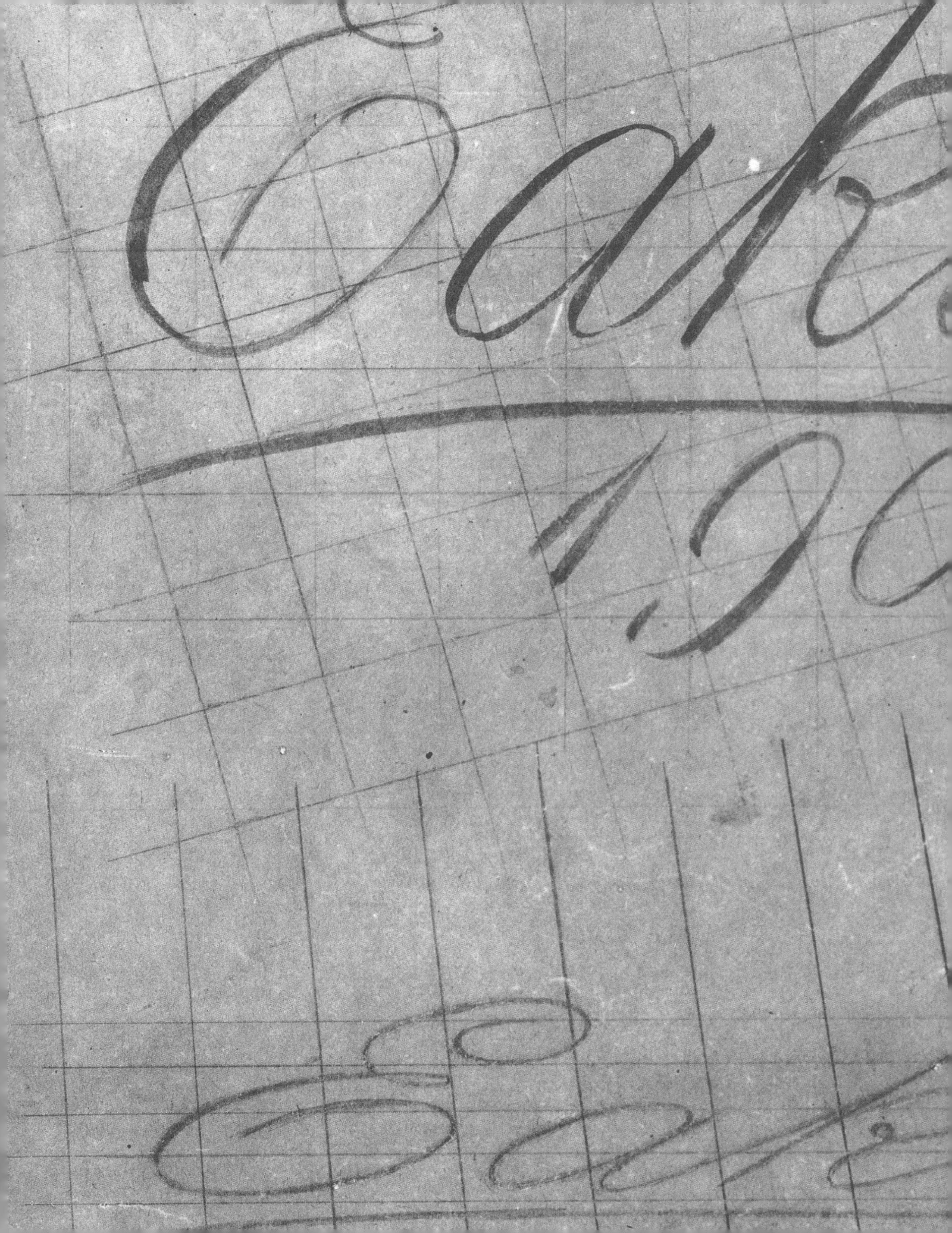